Exeter's University

Tracing the development of the University of Exeter over the six decades since it was granted its royal charter in 1955, this book tells the history of the institution and its community. Jeremy Black draws on a wide range of resources, from archival material to the personal recollections of staff and students. He records and analyses the story of the university as it engaged with the need to expand and evolve while responding to constant financial and political pressures. The book includes interviews with leading university figures, contributions from former students, and a postscript looking to the future. It charts the University of Exeter's changing place in the world of higher education.

Jeremy Black is a leading scholar in the field of British history and the author of more than one hundred books. He has held the Established Chair in history at the University of Exeter since 1996.

Exeter's University: A History brings to a wider audience an updated version of the story first published by Jeremy Black in *The City on the Hill* (University of Exeter, 2015).

from the author's Preface …

"In 2013–14, I wrote *The City on the Hill: A Life of the University of Exeter*, which was published in 2015 as part of the university's Diamond Jubilee. That extensively illustrated and very heavy book is a worthy memorial. This is a different book: it draws on some additional research, while the opportunity to rewrite the study, and bring it up to date has proved welcome. The work has been greatly eased by the great friendship and wonderful co-operation I have encountered. Staff and students, past and present, have given much time, to pass on information and opinion, to answer questions, and to read and comment on drafts."

Exeter's University
A History

Jeremy Black

for David Morgan-Owen and Robin Swinburne

First published in 2019 by
University of Exeter Press
Reed Hall, Streatham Drive
Exeter, EX4 4QR, UK
www.exeterpress.co.uk

© 2019 Jeremy Black

The right of Jeremy Black to be identified as author of this work
has been asserted by him in accordance with the
Copyright, Designs and Patents Act 1988.

British Library Cataloguing in Publication Data
A catalogue record for this book is available
from the British Library.

Hardback ISBN 978 1 905816 06 4
Paperback ISBN 978 0 85989 443 2

Cover image: Painting of buildings on the Streatham Campus
© Lowe. Photograph courtesy of the University of Exeter
The publishers have made all reasonable efforts to identify
and contact the copyright holder of the image.

Typeset in Goudy
by Forewords, Oxford

CONTENTS

The Chancellors and Vice-Chancellors	vii
Abbreviations	ix
Preface	xi
Chapter One — Introduction	1
Chapter Two — The 1950s: The New University	5
Chapter Three — Into the 1960s: Major Expansion	22
Chapter Four — The Later 1960s: Social Change	40
Chapter Five — The Early 1970s: The Brakes Go On	65
Chapter Six — The Later 1970s: A Divided University	92
Chapter Seven — The Early 1980s: Crisis for an Old Order	123
Chapter Eight — The Late 1980s: Difficult Years, Again	140
Chapter Nine — The Early 1990s: Change Starting	175
Chapter Ten — The Later 1990s	197
Chapter Eleven — The Early 2000s: Restructuring	233
Chapter Twelve — The Later 2000s to the Present: The Big Bang	263
Chapter Thirteen — Into the Future	307
Chapter Fourteen — Conclusions	316
Notes	321
Index	343

THE CHANCELLORS

Mary, Dowager-Duchess of Devonshire	1955–1972
Viscount Amory of Tiverton	1972–1981
Sir Rex Richards	1982–1998
Lord Alexander of Weedon	1998–2005
Baroness Floella Benjamin	2006–2016
Lord Myners of Truro	2016–Present

THE VICE-CHANCELLORS

Sir James Cook	1954–1966
Sir John Llewellyn	1966–1972
Professor Harry Kay	1973–1984
Sir David Harrison	1984–1994
Sir Geoffrey Holland	1994–2002
Professor Sir Steve Smith	2002–Present

ABBREVIATIONS

ADC	Academic Development Committee
APC	Academic Policy Committee
ASA	Academic Staff Association
AUT	Association of University Teachers
COSGOD	Composition of Senate and Governance of Departments
CUC	Combined Universities in Cornwall
CVCP	Committee of Vice-Chancellors and Principals of the Universities of the United Kingdom
DES	Department of Education and Science
DVC	Deputy Vice-Chancellor
EAUT	Exeter Association of University Teachers
EGM	Extraordinary General Meeting
fte	full-time equivalent
HEFCE	Higher Education Funding Council for England
IMF	International Monetary Fund
LEA	Local Education Authority
NSS	National Student Survey
NUS	National Union of Students
PMS	Peninsula Medical School
PRC	Planning and Resources Committee
PVC	Pro Vice-Chancellor
QAA	Quality Assurance Agency
RAE	Research Assessment Exercise
REF	Research Excellence Framework
RLA	Readers and Lecturers Association, initially Association of Readers and Lecturers
SHiPSS	School of Historical, Political and Sociological Studies
STEM	Science, Technology, Engineering, Mathematics

TES	Times Education Supplement
THES	Times Higher Education Supplement
UFC	Universities Funding Council
UGC	University Grants Committee
UUK	Universities UK
VC	Vice-Chancellor
VCEG	Vice-Chancellor's Executive Group

Board of Senate was the body established to meet before Senate and deal with all unreserved business.

1981/2 indicates the university year 1981/2, i.e. from the autumn of 1981 to the end of the summer of 1982.

In pre-decimal currency £1 = 20 shillings (sh) = 240 pennies (d). Therefore 1 shilling equalled 5 new pence.

Votes are given as pro – anti – abstentions. If there are only two figures they are for pro and anti.

PREFACE

A COMMUNITY AS WELL AS AN INSTITUTION, a university has a history that is of its own, with committee calling to committee from hillocks of power while staff and students toil in the valleys (well sometimes). A university, as community and institution, experience and aspiration, is also a reflection, willing or unwilling, of wider social and political currents. This element does not tend to receive due attention in university histories, which focus on the internal history and generally treat outside intervention as a malign case and cause of fiscal pressure. That leads to the somewhat disassociated character of these university histories; but that is not the goal or the method here. Instead, the relationship between the University of Exeter and the wider world is an integral part of the story, not an episodic add-on. With longstanding interests in Africa and the Arab world, the university has never been parochial.

In 2013–14, I wrote *The City on the Hill: A Life of the University of Exeter*, which was published in 2015 as part of the university's Diamond Jubilee. That extensively illustrated and very heavy book is a worthy memorial. This is a different book: it draws on some additional research, while the opportunity to rewrite the study, and bring it up to date, has proved welcome. The work has been greatly eased by the great friendship and wonderful co-operation I have encountered. Staff and students, past and present, have given much time, to pass on information and opinion, to answer questions, and to read and comment on drafts. Without this help, the study would have been much lessened. It has proved a particularly opportune moment to undertake research, as there are still staff, both academic and administrative, from the 1950s, for example Ken Schofield and Reg Erskine respectively, able to offer me shrewd judgements. They have also provided the sense of an institution whose culture at times can appear as those of earlier centuries, as opposed to that of only sixty years ago.

I have benefited from the friendly help provided by the staff in Research Commons and from the loan of personal and other papers and material, notably by Martin Biddle, David Catchpole, Kenneth Coe, John Noel Dillon, Mike Duffy, Nick Eastwood, Jeannie Forbes, Bob Higham, Richard Hitchcock, Geoffrey Holland, Roger Kain, Janice Kay, Stephen Lea, Ian Powell, William Richardson, Brian Ridge, Ken Schofield, Russell Seal, Malcolm Shaw, Michele Shoebridge, Mike Weaver, Stephen Wilks and Peter Wiseman. I would like to thank James Hutchinson for facilitating access to the Guild [Student Union] records. For this version, I have been helped by comments from David Allen, Simon Baker, Jonathan Barry, David Batty, Barrie Behenna, Bruce Coleman, Malcolm Cook, Kate Davison, Melody Dougan, Mike Duffy, Christine Faunch, Simon Holme, Rob Johnson, Janice Kay, Jacqui Marshall, David Morgan-Owen, Malyn Newitt, Tim Niblock, Ryan Patterson, Philip Payton, Steve Smith, Adrian Stones, Robin Swinburne, Nick Talbot, Andrew Thorpe, Christopher Thorpe, Richard Toye, Oliver Warman, Stephen Wilks, Peter Wiseman, Michael Wykes and George Yagi. It is a great pleasure to dedicate this book to two former students, now friends, and, in doing so, to recognise the satisfaction of staying in touch with so many former students.

Unless otherwise indicated, footnotes refer to documents in the university archives, although, as an instance of the range of other material available there exist totally unfair, but brilliantly dubbed, sections of the 2004 film *Downfall*. 'Exeter University Hitler Rant' relates to the disruption to student life caused by building projects, while 'Exeter University Hitler Downfall Parody' discusses student admissions.[1] Sources need interpreting. A blast from the past occurs in the minutes of the meeting of Works Committee on 8 October 1965:

> It was agreed that permission be given to members of staff wishing to shoot over the estate with either shot gun or .22 rifle for the purpose of keeping down vermin, provided that this took place in the early morning and was covered by third party insurance.

This was an echo of the university's background in an agricultural

PREFACE

county and with a staff many of whom had fought in 'the war'. However, before assuming that 1960s' Exeter echoed to the sounds of staff shoots, with students risking life and limb accordingly, an historian knows the need to read many, many series, so note the qualification in Council minutes a month later: 'The Council resolved that permission to shoot on the estate be given only to the two members of staff at present doing so and that only shotguns be used.' Again, contemporary sources should be amplified by means of interviews and vice versa, part of the multiplication of perspectives that helps confirm reports and opinions. David Trotter recalls:

> going shooting with my father [the first Professor of Spanish] on the University estate ... in pursuit of rabbits and pigeons, but also as part of a campaign to eliminate the grey squirrel population as a preliminary to the reintroduction of red squirrels. This was undertaken in conjunction with the then head of Biology. ... The campaign in any case failed dismally, for the simple and obvious reason that grey squirrels repopulated the estate from the nearby Stoke Woods. Nevertheless, it is an interesting indication of changing times that it could be thought acceptable for a professor and his eight-year-old son to prowl the University estate ... my function was ... a sort of human gun-dog.[2]

By the 2000s, rabbits were a selling point for the university, the sight of them on Open Day encouraging applications.[3]

This is a work of history by an historian, one designed to introduce readers to historical method, as well as to the history of the university. As such the book is deliberately reflective: it will not surprise readers to know that my favourite novelist is Henry Fielding, my favourite historian Edward Gibbon. The interplay of method and sources is a key matter for the historian, but handling very complex and heterogeneous sources, and turning them into a clear and coherent story, is a task that has to be framed in terms of the problems set by the individual goals of a particular work. Here there are the difficulties of a study that is at once institutional and about a community; one that relates to circumstances and events in which observers and participants are still alive, with all the problems, notably of recovered memory and taking offence, that poses;

and one where there is no relevant secondary literature covering the last three decades.⁴

Linked to these factors, there are strongly contested interpretations about the history of the university, and, notably, competing narratives about decline and revival, with vociferously voiced, but clashing, opinions about causes, course and consequences. There are also contradictory requests for more attention to be devoted to particular issues and achievements. Add to the mix a limit on the space available for the text, and of time for the author, and you have an indication of the problems involved as far as method was concerned.

Sources are also a major issue. They are particularly lacking at the departmental level: organizational restructuring and physical moves combined with pressures on space, have led to the destruction of most relevant material at that level, as well as by individuals.⁵ Moreover, few departments have much of a sense of their own history, at least in so far as moving beyond the opinion or sentiment of long-serving members is concerned.

There are also the standard problems with institutional sources: they are fit for purpose, and thus drawn up in accordance with the needs of the institution, and not the voyeuristic concerns of historians anxious to establish why, how, who, and to consider alternatives. The university archives give only a glimpse of the politics and contests of the past; and this glimpse became far less apparent as structures and practices were streamlined, notably by Ian Powell, who became Registrar in the autumn of 1989. Increasingly, records were stripped down to the essentials of decisions taken. From Powell, there was a stricter style of minute-writing. 'All the poetry is gone' complained George Duller, the President of the union branch. Staff who were prone to be suspicious were inclined to see this change as a step designed to erode the independence of Senate and to limit its potential for oversight; but this change occurred across the entire range of committees and in other universities, and was administrative rather than political in direction.⁶

Under David Allen, Powell's successor, the creation of a 'flatter' administrative structure, as part of his 'Dual Assurance' structure and thesis of governance, similarly affected the extent and nature of the sources. There were fewer committees to generate documentation, although a mass of information was put on the web, notably that generated by Dual

PREFACE

Assurance processes. As an aspect of the greater transparency in governance from the 2000s, this material set out the actions the university was taking.

The governmental structure of the university increasingly focused from the 1990s on administration without the attendant politics that had played such a key role in the 1970s and 1980s. Critics complained that only those who were 'on message' were consulted in a more tightly controlled management structure. This was not in fact the case. David Harrison and Geoffrey Holland, Vice-Chancellors (VCs) from 1984 to 1994 and 1994 to 2002, respectively, were very willing to talk to staff and were far more approachable than either James Cook (1954–66[7]), 'Grim Jim', who was particularly remote, aloof, austere and dour to most members of staff, especially junior ones, or the easier, but still remote and rather unsociable, 'Black Jack' Llewellyn (1966–72). Harry Kay (1973–84) and, far more, Harrison both entertained a lot at Redcot, the VC's residence. Interviewees sometimes complain that Harrison and Holland did not listen, by which they mean agree, but then VCs are not there simply to say yes to the academics. Under Steve Smith, who held the post from 2002, there were frequent public consultations with staff.

For an historian, the archives provide fewer indications from the start of the 1990s of the politics of both institution and community. To confront this problem, I have had to rely on material supplied either in the shape of interviews or of memoranda. This has proved enormously helpful, but also poses the problems of imprecision of memory, and the uncertainties we all encounter in seeking to distinguish our impressions at a specific moment from the later perceptions that are affected by the varied consequences of the passing of time.[8] Interviewees, wittingly or otherwise, may have their own agendas, and certainly their accounts, views and assumptions do not always agree. Memory can be diamond clear, disconcertingly so, but that clarity can be misleading, and demonstrably so when you bring together differing views of the same meeting; let alone the calendar and the minutes.

There are also the problems posed by being provided with material that is difficult to confirm or even evaluate, for example on Masonic influence in the 1990s, as well as items that are potentially libellous. Some (albeit not much) information has come with the 'you can't use this' label, and far more with 'don't quote me' or 'nervous of being quoted though': rogue staff of the 1970s are the subject of many, but not all, of these items. More seriously, there is the problem posed by the variable willingness to co-operate. Alongside the invigorating enthusiasm of many, very many, to revisit the past, to reflect on their experience and assumptions, and to give advice, has come the unwillingness of a few to provide requested information. That several of these latter individuals have done very well from the university underlines my disappointment. Lacunae here partly reflect such an unwillingness to respond. History, of course, is a mediation of sources.

Let us turn to the positives. I never thought reading Council[9] or Senate minutes, or Faculty[10] papers, or the mass of information created by a university, would be riveting, and, given the extraordinary amount of work involved as a result of the scale of the sources, I will not use the term fun, but, throughout, I have found this fascinating. It has taught me far more than I knew or understood when I served on Council, Senate and related committees, notably Finance. To me, possibly the most instructive is that I also taught, eventually as Professor, at the University of Durham from 1980 to 1995. Aside from the issues posed by Durham's undoubted ability to confront similar problems to those then facing Exeter, both more successfully and more rapidly, there is also the extent to which qualitative judgements such as those I offer are more successfully proposed by those who have comparable experience of other institutions. Many long-term members of Exeter's staff lacked that perspective.

These qualitative judgements vary greatly and unexpectedly. Whereas Brian Ward-Perkins, teaching on a one-year post before moving on to Oxford, recalls 'the then rather relaxed, pre-Thatcherite work-load (with at least one colleague who only came in one day a week) ... this pleasant and long-dead world hardly', Jim Sharpe, who went on to teach at York, remembers 'the cloudscapes and the blue skies'.[11]

Some will be offended by what I write. The process of writing on the recent past can have this consequence. At every stage, my comments represent my evaluation, as a trained historian, based on the information available. As such, it is historical fair comment. I trust that those who are offended will have the maturity to accept that there are always multiple narratives of the past, and we rarely do as well in those of others as we do in our own, nor are we as central and decisive in their accounts.

PREFACE

History is not an unbroken mirror reflecting our views, but a fractured glass swinging in the wind, with pieces missing or opaque and a general pattern that is difficult to distinguish, and impossible to do so to general satisfaction.

While much of this book is an account of difficulties and differences, and necessarily so in light of the strong archival steer, I have been struck throughout by the consistent determination of the institution and its staff of all ranks to help students fulfil their potential and the extent to which students respond to the many challenges and complexities of university life: '[F]atigue as my course got more intense, I lost the desire to go out three or four evenings a week.'[12] That is the nature of education: it is the bond, the trust, between the generations. Ultimately, the university has met that trust and fulfilled its bond.

CHAPTER ONE

INTRODUCTION

> In the last half century it has actually been several universities, as it has changed with government strategies, student and staff numbers, academic cultures and so on. Long-serving staff experience this sense of successive institutions, but students only experience the one with which they coincide. ... Despite the changes, good students are the consistent currency of university life.
> Bob Higham, an Exeter student who became a long-serving member of Archaeology[1]

THE WIDER SITUATION within which the university operated was not simply setting or context, but a central part of the dynamic of the institution and the flow of the community. As such, the history is one of multiple challenges and of several possible outcomes. The university has responded to demands and changes that are financial as well as economic, social as well as political, national as well as global. Its history repeatedly reflects a developing world and the altered circumstances this gives rise to. Thus, changing attitudes toward the 'rights' and living conditions of students are as much part of the story as the developing global engagement of post-Mao China, or the impact of the Internet on teaching. At the same time, although the whole UK higher-education system underwent major changes throughout the lifetime of the University of Exeter, each university also has a different story to tell, and this is Exeter's.

Particular pressures arose from the meagre founding endowment of the university and of its predecessor, the University College of the South West; and grave financial difficulties have been a central part of its history. The university archives reveal the repeated might-have-beens of planned initiatives had there been money and the extent to which the search for funds has guided policy. The financial history of the university also indicates the significance of adroit leadership, notably in eventually moving beyond responding to circumstances and, instead, shaping them and creating a highly effective strategy.

This wider context helps provide not only a dynamic element in planning but also in the politics of the institution. A reluctance to embrace the possibilities of change has sometimes characterized the attitudes of those university politicians, both staff and students, who are critical of developments and of 'management'; but the reality of higher education, of Britain and of the world, over the last sixty years, has been one in which standing still has not been possible.

The politics of the institution will form part of the history, not least as they were integral to the course and chronology of institutional development. The character, content and context of these politics changed greatly, with notable differences between the 1950s and 1970s, and between the early 1980s and the late 2000s. Many staff and students did not take part in university politics, but those who did adopted markedly contradictory positions on developments. Moreover, these contradictions are still very apparent today, both in the content and tone of interviews. At times, there is a humorous dimension to the divergent opinions, and I was reminded of the multiple views deployed to comic effect by Tobias Smollett in his brilliant but bitty novel *The Expedition of Humphry Clinker* (1771). Given its rich and fascinating cast of characters and range of episodes, it is not surprising that comedy plays a role in the university history. As Michael Rush (Politics) observed in the marking meeting mentioned in chapter 6: 'I vividly recall this meeting – put it in a David Lodge or Malcolm Bradbury novel and its veracity would at worst be doubted, at best thought exaggerated.'[2]

University politics were linked to the governance, indeed governability, of the institution, and to the policy debates related to governance. This issue brings up a potent cast including the six VCs as well as others who were, or sought to be, involved in running the university. Moreover, alongside constant features, the cast as well as the agenda shift. Thus,

INTRODUCTION

the 'old guard', whom Barrie Behenna, a senior administrator, referred to as 'the problem',[3] a somewhat predictable refrain in all institutions, had a different meaning, composition and context in the 1990s to that in the 1970s.

Alongside that concern, we have teaching and research. Just as teaching focuses on helping students realize, develop and fulfil their potential, so the institutional context also fosters the research and teaching creativity of the staff. Teaching and research were greatly affected by national and university funding and policies, but also had autonomous characteristics, many of which arose from disciplinary developments and all the intellectual, institutional and personal dynamics involved.

Only so much can be covered in the space available, but readers need to know that many of the academics were also key figures in the development of their subjects, a point that current students sometimes note with surprise.[4] John Ashford in statistics and operational research, Desmond Corner on unit trusts, Aileen Fox on the Roman archaeology of the South-West, Alex Haslam on social psychology, Margaret Hewitt on children in society, Mary John on children's rights, Dominik Lasok and John Bridge on European Law, Clive Lee on the artificial hip joint, David Rees on semigroup theory and commutative algebra, Bob Snowden on family planning, and, today, Neil Armstrong in sports science, Clive Ballard on dementia, Isabelle Baraffe on star formation, Ken Evans on auxetic materials (materials which expand under stress), Willie Hamilton on primary care diagnostics, Andrew Hattersley and Tim Frayling on diabetes, Jon Mill on epigenetics, Mark Jackson on medical history, Alex Pavic on engineering vibration, Gareth Stansfield on Kurdistan, and Andrew Watson in climate science were/are leading intellectuals and researchers; and this list can, and should, be greatly extended.

Whether in artificial hips (the Exeter Hip System is the most successful cemented hip joint in the world) or in family-planning studies, the analysis of unit trusts or the use of tithe records, Middle Eastern Studies or European Law, Exeter both repeatedly led and greatly outperformed its size and usually dire finances. At Exeter, research has always been centrally linked to teaching; and research-led teaching was, and is, a key element. Indeed, while the history of any individual university is in part a history of all universities, Exeter's distinctiveness owes much to the commitment and energy devoted to teaching. That has remained the case in the more research-conscious last two decades. Teaching also has seen major changes. The student population has expanded greatly. This is in line with national trends, but poses new requirements in terms of providing engaged and quality teaching to far greater numbers, not least, in light of challenging staff–student ratios, given the time involved in marking and feedback. Postgraduate teaching, another link to research, has become much more important than in the early days. This book seeks to give voice to the student experience, both of teaching and of university life as a whole.

CHAPTER TWO

THE 1950s: THE NEW UNIVERSITY

Charter. We're There!
Headline in the *South Westerner* [student newspaper],
29 October 1955

THE UNIVERSITY OF EXETER formally came into existence on 21 December 1955, when the founding Charter passed the Great Seal. The change of status for the University College of the South West reflected long-held institutional and regional aspirations. It was also located in a specific historical moment, one that gave the early university part of its character. The foundation of the university was an aspect of the 'New Elizabethan Age', the period, early in the reign of Elizabeth II, of optimistic hopes about a modernizing Britain building on the best of the past to help grasp the potential of the future. This was the Britain of atomic power stations, one governed by a Conservative party that was committed to maintaining much of the legacy of the 1945–51 Labour government, while also lessening central direction and giving full throttle to consumerism.[1]

Patriotism remained strong: the graduation ceremony held in Exeter on 8 October 1955 ended with the National Anthem. On the global scale, Churchill was Prime Minister when the year started. India had gained independence in 1947, but Britain was still a major imperial power. Empire was regarded not as anachronistic, but as a progressive force designed to develop colonies and to bring them to independence in a Commonwealth of Nations that Britain would lead.

The university drew on these aspirations in the role it developed as an institution of imperial and post-imperial education.[2] There were links with institutions, notably in Africa and the Middle East, and particular courses were developed accordingly. As a prime instance of its international links, the university, in the 1960s, offered a postgraduate Advanced Diploma in Public Administration, which was taken almost exclusively by overseas students, mostly from Commonwealth countries, particularly Nigeria. There were also various contractual links with several Nigerian universities involving members of staff teaching in Ibadan and Ife, and Alan Bartlett, the Academic Registrar from 1954 to 1975[3], took leave of absence in late 1961 to advise University College, Ibadan on developing an academic office. The university was also associated with the Diploma course in Government and Administration at the Nigerian College of Arts, Science and Technology. In 1963, the Liaison Committee was willing to offer leave of absence of up to three years for secondment to overseas universities. The committee supported twinning departments with equivalent departments in overseas universities, and mentioned Kwame Nkrumah University (Ghana), the University of the West Indies, and the University of Ibadan (as University College, Ibadan became in 1963).[4] Moreover, as other reflections of African interests, there was concern about the situation in South Africa as apartheid became more entrenched there. James Cook recommended the consideration for vacancies of academics dismissed for opposing apartheid.[5] In addition, Exeter was designated as the official UK repository of materials on Ghana.

Students from the empire and from former colonies could be found on the campus. So also with staff. In 1952, Sir Thomas Taylor moved from the University College of the West Indies to be Principal, only to die on holiday in 1953. James Cook, Regius Professor of Chemistry at Glasgow (1939–54), who became Principal of the University College in 1954, and then the first VC, serving until 1966, was particularly interested in Africa. In 1955, he was appointed by the Inter-University Council for Higher Education Overseas to be its representative on the Council of the new University College of Rhodesia and Nyasaland. Once retired, Cook went on to be VC of the University of East Africa.

THE 1950S: THE NEW UNIVERSITY

In part, with the empire, past and present, links carried forward earlier arrangements, such as the Diploma in English Studies for Egyptian students that was offered by the University College in the early 1950s. However, these sources of students were uncertain. Indeed, Senate heard on 2 February 1955 that 'the number of applicants from the colonies had fallen considerably'. The end, as a result of the Suez Crisis, of the course for Egyptian teachers of English hit hard in 1957/58.[6] The republican coup in Iraq in 1958 affected links there. The number of full-time overseas students following courses of at least one year fell from 14 per cent of the total number of students in 1956/57 to 7.7 per cent in 1960/61. Links with Nigeria largely ended with the 1966 coup and the subsequent Biafran War (1967–70). However, full-time overseas students were to remain a significant group until the rise in fees for them in the 1970s helped change the sources of this group, a process also linked to developments in the former empire and to Britain's entry in 1973 into the European Economic Community (now the European Union).

This imperial element was not an add-on to the university, but integral to its nature. The 'imperial' character of the university was subtle because it also related to Exeter's position within the British university world. 1950s Britain was a society and political culture in which the hierarchical assumptions were very much hardwired into the system. The Charter approved by the Queen at a meeting of the Privy Council on 28 October 1955 was delivered in person into the hands of the Chancellor on 8 May 1956 when the Queen also unveiled the foundation stone for the new Arts Building, later the Queen's Building.

That the first Chancellor, from 1955 to 1971, was Mary, Dowager Duchess of Devonshire (Mistress of the Robes to the Queen; 'my old Dutch' to the students[7]), was in line with a more general pattern. She succeeded her brother, Robert, Fifth Marquess of Salisbury, who had been President of the University College from 1945 to 1955 and who was Lord Privy Seal (1951–52), Lord President of the Council (1952–57) and Leader of the House of Lords (1951–57). In a similar fashion, the first Chancellor of Lancaster University was Princess Alexandra, while the first Pro-Chancellor was the Earl of Derby. Opened in 1960, Devonshire House was named after the Chancellor.

Such hierarchies were also seen among the academics. Many had been educated at Oxbridge and had a tendency to regard it as the acme of excellence and the setter of standards that Exeter should seek to emulate. Indeed, just as the university had a quasi-imperial position within the British empire, so Exeter was part of an Oxbridge empire; although Malyn Newitt, who had been teaching in Rhodesia, thought Exeter, when he arrived in 1966, had the feel of being a rural 'colony' of London. That the university college had taught for London degrees contributed to this impression.

'What did we do at Oxford?' was the question raised at Senate on several occasions.[8] Many academics spent part of their vacations doing research in Oxbridge and they shared in the less than vigorous engagement with hard work and new ideas that characterised much of Oxbridge, more particularly Oxford. In the life of the halls of residence, there were also elements of the Oxbridge model. Teaching was on an Oxbridge model, albeit with more lectures and fewer tutorials due to the different staffing.[9]

As a reminder of the need to avoid easy generalizations, a very different example of industry was set by Joseph Sykes, the son of a Yorkshire butcher, who took degrees from Leeds, was an active Methodist, and served as head of the department of Economics from 1926 to 1940 and 1945 to 1964 (Professor from 1947), and as DVC from 1958 to 1964. With a PhD (for which he worked while at Exeter) and several books to his credit, including on banking, public expenditure, local authority finance and the coal industry, the industrious and impressive Sykes was very different to many other academics, at Exeter and elsewhere.

Hierarchy was also present in terms of salaries. The move to university status was popular with staff who were now on a better salary scheme and pension. Professors dominated, with £1,350 pa in 1947, compared to £1,250 for the Registrar, £1,250 for the Academic Secretary, £500–750 for lecturers, and £350 for Assistant Lecturers. The junior lecturers remained very poorly paid, and therefore benefited from help with accommodation, which usually took the form of heavily subsidised flats in converted houses. Wealthier staff frequently owned flats in Oxford and London and spent the summer there, such that very little was then done in the university.

There was also a gender dimension. There were no female professors. Nevertheless, there were impressive female academics including Margaret Hewitt (1928–91), an LSE product who taught at Exeter from 1952 until

THE 1950S: THE NEW UNIVERSITY

she died, becoming a member of Council and head of Sociology, but never a Professor. In an age before women's studies became a major field, she focused on women and the family and published *Wives and Mothers in Victorian Industry* (1958) and (co-authored) *Children in English Society* (2 volumes, 1969–73).

There were gender distinctions at many levels. In 1947, cooks in the men's halls received £5, 5sh weekly, their counterparts in the women's halls up to £5. In comparison, the university's income for 1955/56 was £327,084, of which £241,903 came from the Treasury grant administered by the University Grants Committee (UGC), £19,300 from grants from local authorities, and £46,273 from fees.

In part, independence in the form of university status offered a resetting of hierarchies. Being dependent on London for degrees had proved humiliating and sometimes inconvenient, as well as a source of status. Thus, Standing Committee noted in June 1952 that London's External Registrar had decided that 'it would not be possible to arrange for the holding of practical examinations in Botany and Zoology at Exeter'. On 11 May 1955, considering minimum entry standards, Senate agreed to express doubts to the University of London about the promised removal of English Language from the list of compulsory subjects.

Even when Exeter became independent, the London External system continued to exert an influence on syllabuses and academic standards. Many academic staff, especially the older ones with service under Principal Keith Murray (1926–51), found it difficult to accept their new responsibilities, devising courses, conducting examining and deciding classes. The decision of what to do with failures proved painful and Faculty Boards, faced with unpleasant duties, and not having London to blame, could take many hours. More recent appointments helped overcome this problem. Cook warned against any sudden increase in Firsts and 2(1)s, and insisted that the London standard must be maintained.[10]

An important element in the early history of the university was provided by World War Two. The city itself still bore the scars of devastating German bombing. The main buildings of St Luke's, the Church of England diocesan teacher training college with which the university merged in 1978, had been gutted by the Luftwaffe raid of May 1942, and the 'restoration' completed in 1954 was in reality a patching-up operation.

Many of the university staff had served in the war, frequently with considerable distinction. They took over into civilian life much of the atmosphere of its military counterpart, while Murray was opposed to appointing conscientious objectors. In common with a general pattern for some time after both world wars, not just among professionals but among non-professionals also, military titles were sometimes used by certain academics: Colonel Garland ran German, Major Davies Geography, and so on: Arthur Davies was Professor of Geography from 1948 to 1971. Most staff, however, avoided the temptation. Roderick Ross, who became a Lecturer in Public Administration in 1949 and served as Secretary of the University from 1955 to 1975,[11] had spent six years in the army. Frank Barlow, Lecturer in History from 1946 until 1953 and Professor of History from 1953 to 1976, had served in the Intelligence Corps against Japan, eventually as a major. Alan Bartlett had been in Intelligence and in the RAF. Bartlett, Barlow and Fred Clayton (Classics) had all been in India at the same time. Clayton was a friend and colleague of Alan Turing at Bletchley Park. Bill Ravenhill (Geography) had been a Spitfire pilot and Keith Salter (English) in the Normandy landings. Tommy Revesz (Geography) survived a concentration camp, although he was not able to reach the West until the Hungarian rising of 1956.

The habit of command of wartime was also maintained, with junior staff and students addressed and treated accordingly. Henry Garland (German) proved a prime instance, ready to call in a junior colleague on the weekend to pin up anew a notice that had not been pinned up straight or to tell another who had brought a rug from home for his office to remove it on the grounds that lecturers were not allowed carpets. Garland also had a reputation for trying to restrict his colleagues from excelling at research by piling them with work.[12] Hearing the tramp of his approaching feet in the corridor terrified colleagues. Garland was a key figure under Cook, complementing the latter's austere character and serving as DVC in 1955–57 at a time when there was only one. Although Frank Barlow did not use his military title, he often referred to his war service. When discussing William II of England (r. 1087–1100), on whom he was an expert, Barlow argued that, as another military man, he could understand him, which was a travesty of their respective roles. Barlow was described as treating his colleague Bertram Wolffe as an NCO, which he had been in the war.[13]

THE 1950S: THE NEW UNIVERSITY

As a contrast to Garland and Barlow, David Rees, Professor of Pure Mathematics from 1958 to 1983, did not talk about his vital war work at Bletchley Park breaking the Luftwaffe Red Cipher which was used to communicate with ground troops. A very modest man, Rees became a Fellow of the Royal Society (FRS) in 1968. He gave his name to a number of algebraic formulations. Others on the science side had also been involved in war work, three of the chemists on the extraction of magnesia from sea-water for the Ministry of Supply.[14] Norman Rydon, who became Professor of Chemistry in 1957, worked at the Chemical Defence Experimental Station, Porton Down on agents for the decontamination of mustard gas. Keith Sykes, who had served in a naval anti-aircraft crew in World War One, worked in government in 1940-45, notably as Assistant Regional Controller for the Ministry of Labour and National Service in 1941-43.[15]

Many staff appointed in the 1960s had also been in the military. John Llewellyn, VC from 1966 to 1972, had served in the war, as had his successor, Harry Kay; while Barrie Behenna, later an important figure in the administration, was, when hired in 1962, an Education Officer in the RAF.

The military pattern persisted into the 1970s with individuals such as Duncan Mitchell, a wartime RAF officer and strong personality, who eventually served as Acting VC. Stephen Mennell, who arrived to teach Sociology in 1967, noted this aspect of Mitchell, as well as the fact he drove a Bentley (a point recalled by others), but also made comments that reveal the value of quoting at some length:

> Duncan proved to be one of the few politically Conservative professors of Sociology in Britain, but, as soon as he turned up, we actually got along very well with each other.[16] I look back on him with fondness. He had a military MBE and a military bearing. ... When I briefly took up riding a few years later, he gave me his pair of black riding boots. We joked that he had sawn them off the legs of a dead SS officer.
>
> Duncan did have broad interests. In particular, he was still interested in the long-term development of human society, which, under the influence of Sir Karl Popper among others, was already becoming unfashionable in British sociology (and history). Duncan

also adhered to the view that, besides sociologists *sensu stricto*, a department of sociology needed to have within it staff capable of teaching anthropology and social psychology – as we did, in contrast to the present day, when sociology seems to have become far more narrowly focused.[17]

Moreover, the military tone was sustained because National Service (conscription) lasted until the close of the 1950s. Thus, although the impact varied greatly,[18] new male staff had been in the military, as had some male students, while other male students went into the military upon graduation. Military service, furthermore, linked to the imperial theme, as the defence of imperial interests, in Malaya, Kenya, Egypt, Cyprus, Borneo and elsewhere, proved a prime function. As late as 1964, there were more British troops east of Suez than west of it.

The hierarchical practices of British society and academe were given an added twist in these circumstances. Expecting to be treated as officers, those of an ex-military background fancied that they had a natural authority. In practice, some were bullies. In several cases, although not that of Garland, who was a noted Schiller expert, their bullying concealed a serious problem, that of intellectual second-ratedness. In an academic community, there is an assumption that intelligence will be an attribute of position and a characteristic of activity. A failure to impress compromises respect, and bullying is a poor substitute.

The ex-military background was also seen with the support staff. In the 1960s, the porters were mostly ex-Navy and were run by a senior porter, Reynolds, as if he was a Chief Petty Officer. Congdon, the porter at the Queen's Building, was a very stolid ex-policeman, very reverent towards the academics, and with a *Dixon of Dock Green* manner. The porters, for example, later, Nobby Clark at the Queen's Building and John Nuttall at Devonshire House, were an important element in university life.[19]

More positively, military service may well have given students greater maturity, or, at least, self-control. Alex Copeland (1948–51), who had come directly from school, refers to 'the more mature, dedicated students who had first served in the Armed Forces'. Keith Meecham (1951–54) thought Mardon Hall 'not unlike the barracks I had recently left'. The return of servicemen also dealt with the 'man shortage' referred to by

Mary Rimington (History, 1944–48). Arriving as a student in 1963, Colin Fletcher found that many third years had done National Service: 'I think that this had given them a degree of maturity and broader perspective on life which many of us straight from school perhaps lacked – and I think we benefited from their views and experiences.'[20]

The 'man shortage' was not restricted to wartime but reflected the distinctiveness of the university's gender balance. The percentage of female students, 47 in 1955/56, was very high by national standards, making admission attractive to men, as many interviewees noted. Women and men could want for company as the personal notices in the *South Westerner* noted. On 27 May 1938, 'Passable Brunette (Lopes Hall) would like company of trustworthy man for evening walks once or twice weekly as escape from work', only for the following issue (3 June) to report:

> We regret to inform the authors of the flood of letters that we have received, requesting dates with the 'Passable Brunette' … that the lady in question considers none of the applicants to be suitable for her. All the applications, she says, were much too suggestive.

As a reminder that themes recur, an item headlined 'Wanted MEN' in the issue of 26 October 1955 reported:

> Three unattached ladies of a sociable turn of mind offer three desirable gentlemen the opportunity of enjoying a free – repeat – free – evening's entertainment. This marvellous, unbelievable, never-to-be-repeated offer includes entry to the Guild Ball and as many free drinks as you can carry while still remaining gentlemen.

A different aspect of the gender relationship was noted in the same issue under the heading 'The Pyjama Game', an account of the stealing and display of fresher 'ladies' night attire'. Such activity was an aspect of the raids on colleges and on college trophies that were frequently reported and that continued thereafter to be a prominent feature of hall life, notably in the 1960s. There were 'fairly regular raids' on the female halls from St Luke's which had a heavy focus on sport, notably the rugby that attracted many Welsh students.[21] James Smeall, the Principal from 1945 to 1972, was no intellectual, but a shrewd administrator who maintained strong relations with the cathedral and the city, serving as mayor in 1965/6. He chose Physical Education as the distinctive specialism he believed St Luke's needed in order to flourish and attract students.[22] In 2001, Ken Shaw recalled the manner of his promotion to Senior Lecturer in the late 1960s. Smeall took him to one side at the end of one of his regular black-tie dinners at the Principal's house: 'Shaw, I am thinking of having you promoted.' 'That's very kind of you, Sir.' 'Shaw, are you a communicant member of the Church of England?' 'No sir, I am a Nonconformist.' 'I thought as much and so have already arranged for the bishop to confirm you privately next Tuesday evening. I trust your wife won't mind.'[23]

Professors dominated the system in the university: Physics was Keith Conn, and so on. As was to be noted:

> Nominally it was the Faculty that had academic oversight of its constituent departments. In practice the University was a loose confederation of autonomous departments ruled by professorial heads who were appointed to hold office until retirement. Ruling their little fiefs, the old fashioned heads of department had every opportunity to exercise power in an arbitrary way and to develop the quirks of personality that often develop in those who are unaccountable. ... Faculty supervision was purely nominal. The heads of departments took it in turn to become Dean and refrained from interfering in the affairs of other heads.[24]

The first Senate meeting of the new university was held on 2 November 1955. A gathering of professors, of which there were eighteen, its business included the consideration of the Ceremonials Committee, an active body in the early years, which recommended that students should wear academic dress (gowns) at lectures, classes and tutorials, in Chapel and when visiting members of the academic staff officially, but not in the laboratories: 'Men on all occasion when academic dress is worn should wear a tie, women should wear a dress or a skirt.' The editorial in the *South Westerner* on 19 October 1955 suggested that 'certain features, evidence of a new age dawning, can be observed with satisfaction. The general relaxation of regulations in the Halls, the atmosphere of ease and freedom...'. However, the paper treated Senate's agreement to the new regulations on academic dress with the headline 'Mourning Becomes Exeter', adding that the female students seemed particularly bitter.[25]

In the context of the age of majority at 21, until lowered to 18 by the Labour government in 1969, the general theme, as expected certainly by the parents of female students, was one of control, reflected in the decision to allow the Guild (the Student Union) to sell alcohol at the Pavilion twice-weekly from 5 pm to 7 pm provided adequate arrangements for supervision were made.[26] There were no such concessions on the question of the entertainment of guests of the opposite sex in student rooms, an issue on which the Guild Council pressed from 1955 as they did not wish to be treated as 'adolescents'.[27] It was not until December 1958 that Senate agreed visiting hours of 7–10 pm on Wednesdays, Saturdays and Sundays, and 2–5 pm on Sundays, and then provided notice was given beforehand to the Warden. 'Serious misbehaviour' between men and women led to expulsion.[28] *South Westerner*, the weekly student newspaper, devoted much attention to the regulations. As Peter Whitfield, the *South Westerner*'s editor for some of the late 1950s, noted, the paper 'took a very politics-neutral stance'.[29] Sports grounds were not opened for Sunday play until 1970. Such formalities and restrictions were general to halls of residence across the university sector.

Cook, who had the stature to direct the new university and was able to command respect, told the Civic Dinner held to celebrate the Charter that it would be unwise to launch out into new faculties, and that the immediate duty lay in the consolidation of the present pattern.[30] Nevertheless, ideas about the university were debated by the senior staff in their consideration of plans for development. In 1956, the Quinquennial Developments Committee (the university body that matched the UGC's concern to plan on a five-year timespan) put its emphasis on a Chair in Geology, but turned down proposals for the establishment of independent departments of Sociology and Government. Outlining priorities to the UGC, Council, the governing body of the university, that July focused on an administrative building, stage two of the Students Union building, Chemistry provision, and a new men's hall.

These plans, all for development on the Streatham site to the north of the city, reflected the extent to which the university was still partly located in crowded and largely inadequate buildings around Gandy

Street in the city, the original focus of higher education in Exeter. In 1922, the year in which the Royal Albert Memorial College[31] became the University College of the South West of England, it had also acquired 120 acres of the Streatham estate. From what had once been part of this estate, an additional 17 acres was purchased in 1929 and another 21 in 1931. Land was then relatively cheap, but there was money for only two academic buildings to be begun before the war: the Washington Singer Laboratories completed in 1931 and the Roborough Library in 1940. Hatherly Laboratories, completed in 1952, followed after the war, by which time there were a number of halls on or near the Streatham estate.

Applications shot up once university status was achieved, the prospectus had to be reprinted twice, and the number of students rose: 454 students accepted offers of places for 1956, and 522 in 1957. However, because only about half of the 1,209 students in residence in December 1957 could be accommodated in halls, while 25–30 of those in lodgings were living beyond the City boundaries, Standing Committee decided on 16 December 1957 to accept only 500 new students in October 1958 (in fact the figure was to be 429), with the cut mostly occurring in the Arts. Stability in the shape of a total population of 1,300–1,400 students was established as a goal. In October 1959, there were 1,302 full-time students. In January 1958, the top four priorities outlined by the Works Committee were Chemistry laboratories, a hall, Physics laboratories, and another hall.

By then, the demand from government, and, therefore, the UGC, was for greater expansion in student numbers.[32] This led to pressure to move forward the building programme, pressure that could readily be met from the university's large campus. The Arts Building, on which work began in 1956, was opened in 1958: the Queen, who had laid the foundation stone, approved the name Queen's Building. The UGC approved the rephasing of building projects to be started, with Duryard I and II (halls) planned for 1960, Chemistry and a Lecture Room Block in 1961, Physics in 1962 and a hall in 1963.[33]

Meanwhile, new courses were proposed. The departments needed to construct degree syllabuses and courses, having previously had to follow the London ones. This was notably done in History with the 'Option' course which was a kind of preliminary Special Subject and was popular with students who disliked the bread-and-butter 'Outline' courses.

The syllabus invented the History practice of teaching courses every other year, which increased the choice for students and the variety for academics.

Appointments were also called for in new areas, such as Russian, Drama and the History of Art.[34] The Quinquennial Developments Committee agreed to consider, for the 1960s, an independent department of Psychology, and maybe, after 1967, Agriculture and Medicine.[35] Forty new posts in Science for 1962–67 were recommended.[36] The emphasis on expansion led to the expression of some concerns, but mostly about managing change. There was little doubt about the direction of travel. It is instructive to consider the case of Geology, which had gained its first full-time lecturer in 1947, a second following in 1950. The first custom-built Geology laboratories were in the Queen's Building, but they were too small, and there was a lack of storage space. In 1958/59, three more staff were appointed.[37]

For the student perspective, Peter Goodfellow (English, 1954–57), the first in his family to go to university, noted:

> [L]iving at Crossmead[38] was so cosy. All my meals were provided in the dining hut. ... I had a named laundry bag and all dirty clothes were left once a week at the bottom of the back stairs and returned days later, clean. The only cooking I learned to do was to make a cup of tea or coffee.

As Secretary of the Hall Committee, Goodfellow lived in for all three years. He regularly went to Cin Soc (Cinema Society), often attended Meth (Methodists) Soc 'squash', was an avid weekend birdwatcher, went to the pub on a Saturday, and recalled his teachers, including the Chaucer specialist John Speirs, 'a hopeless lecturer but a kindly tutor', and 'Professor Horrox, with flowing white hair, and always dressed in black jacket, pinstripe trousers, white shirt and black bow tie ... his tutorials with 2 or 3 of us were always very interesting.' David Horrox, Professor from 1924 to 1961, was not alone in sartorial elegance; Hubert Britton, his counterpart as Professor of Chemistry from 1935 to 1957, was 'invariably dressed in a black jacket with grey pin striped trousers, and silver grey hair'.[39] Horrox made up in the audibility of his lectures for his lack of publications, creating problems for John Fox (French) who lectured on the other side of a partition in one of the Gandy Street huts. Finances were an issue for Goodfellow, who found it essential to have a holiday job. Goodfellow went on to be Head of the Faculty of English, Drama and Music at a Plymouth comprehensive: 'Exeter had served me well.' Among the other popular societies, the Music Society, in an age in which most people did not have access to high-quality music reproduction, provided the opportunity to listen to a selection of records.

Alongside other discoveries, intellectual opening up was a key experience for many. Colin Winter (Mathematics, PGCE, 1944–48), the first in his extended family to go to university, referred to 'the expansion of life into un-dreamt of regions intellectually and socially'.[40] Christine Smith (Classics, 1955–58) recalled the hospitality of the distinguished, but highly eccentric, Reader in Classics, W.F. Jackson Knight, a Great War veteran:[41] 'If we had worries or troubles we would repair to Caroline House [his home] where we were always welcomed by the phrase "Have a cheap sherry!". He would cut a rose from the garden for us.'[42] The highlight in being taught by Hugh Stubbs in Gandy Street 'was whether a mouse peeped out from the ancient fireplace'.[43] John Mundy (Physics, 1952–55) was impressed by the teaching in 'a sink or swim environment. The examinations were tough and many students dropped out or were kicked out but, if you were prepared to study, the faculty helped you.' He went on to be a distinguished physicist, including editing the *Journal of Applied Physics*. Pauline and John Mackintosh (Zoology, 1953–57) observe: 'Our finals year was 10 so we knew all the staff and they knew us individually, indeed some remained as permanent friends. We felt that we were treated as adults: your course programme was there – how you used it was in the most part your decision.'[44]

Margaret Eley (née Helman) focused on her pleasure in moving from digs in Whipton to 'a coveted place in Hall – Birks Grange'. Hers is not an account of invidious Wardens:

> [T]his gracious residence was home to just twenty young women, gently but firmly overseen by the Warden, Miss Lillian Button. … Living there was almost like being in a private hotel. Quiet women in green aprons were always around, cooking and cleaning to ensure that the domestic arrangements ran smoothly; all under the experienced eye of Miss Tilley, the house manager. Each week,

THE 1950S: THE NEW UNIVERSITY

> Sunday lunch and several evening dinners were formal meals, attended by Miss Button, when gowns had to be worn, together with suitable attire – a dress or suit. After which, everyone retired to the Common Room for coffee and polite conversations.

'Perhaps because there were comparatively so few of us, there was the urge to fully participate in inter-Hall activities', of which Eley recalls the spring choral competition and Rag floats. 'Too soon, it was all over', adding 'Birks Grange: demolished and rebuilt in 1960s' concrete as a large Birks Hall'. Eley taught maths for a quarter of a century and then became a financial analyst in Toronto.[45]

St German's House, an annex of Lopes, 'felt like country house living' to Melody Dougan (1955–58).[46] Recording that the Warden, Miss Ross, told her that she had been accepted as she 'came from a good school,' she added that, in the initial welcome speech, the Warden: 'stressed how important it was for us "to hold on to our most precious possession." In later years, the joke was "I went around clutching my handbag to me for ages after that."' The role of wardens and matrons was captured in the photograph taken inside Hope Hall showing both, alongside the student President, receiving guests for the Formal, an occasion of dancing, refreshments and fireworks that marked, as the *South Westerner* reported in 1955, 'a very good beginning to the social programme of the university'.

Margaret Williamson (History, Education, 1948–52) also enjoyed Birks and captured a lasting value of the experience: 'Being away from home gave me a chance to find "me" and make my own decisions.' As a reminder of variety, she also observed: '[T]he best contribution Exeter made to my life was to give me the opportunity to learn contract bridge.'[47] Not all felt badly-off. Peter Dare recalls of his postgraduate period (1955–58):

> My living allowance grant of £300 per annum enabled me to share comfortable self-catering accommodation with 2–3 other postgrads in 'digs' in a 3-storey house on Pennsylvania Road, just a ten minute walk from the labs and close to town facilities. It is surprising now to recall how well one could eat on this grant and still be able to visit nearby hostelries and cinemas, and to afford train fares home.

Pleasant evenings were spent in the *Black Horse* discussing research experiences and worldly affairs with fellow researchers.[48]

Pubs recurred in other accounts, Ian Gordon (1957–63) recalling 'Saturday evenings were spent in pubs in and around Exeter. The White Hart (South Street), The Black Horse (Longbrook Street), The Tally-Ho, Ide.'[49] Kenneth Minogue, who taught Politics in 1955/56, before going on to a distinguished career in the LSE, noted: 'Merrydown cider was the widespread drink of choice, and known daringly as "babymaker".'[50] John Balsom (General Science, 1958–61), a butcher's son from Southall who was a very active sportsman, recalls 'the Crescent City Stompers at the Guildhall every week', while Brian Smith (Economics and Public Administration, undergraduate and MA, 1956–61) noted that many students went to the 'Saturday night hop' in Washington Singer where they danced to records.[51] Films were an item in several students' reminiscences and were extensively reviewed in the *South Westerner*. The paper was well aware of student interest in the quality of these reviews.[52]

The university was also a religious community. An annual University Service was held in the cathedral at the beginning of the academic year, with those attending processing in an impressive display; while, on 8 December 1955, a Service of Thanksgiving for the granting of university status was held in the cathedral. The *South Westerner* devoted considerable attention to religious news and discussion, notably major sermons and the meetings of religious societies such as the popular Meth Soc, which gave a strong social life to Methodists. This was not to be a theme in *Exeposé*, *South Westerner*'s successor from 1987.

The pleasantness of life in Exeter, however, was matched for many by poverty. Moreover, there was not just the poorer living circumstances and standards of a far less affluent society than that of today, but also institutional poverty. This was a hangover from the University College of the South West when Exeter was very much the poor country cousin of the big civic universities. The grant established when the College was founded in 1922, and was placed on the universities' grants list, was particularly small: this was the period of post-war retrenchment and the 'Geddes Axe' on public expenditure. With only a minor addition, this grant was to be the level of UGC grant for the new university. While the UGC continued to base its grants on historic funding, as it largely did until the 1980s, this was an immense handicap to a university without large endowments or alternative sources of funding. Indeed, given this funding, it is surprising what was achieved.

Under the naturally and necessarily parsimonious Cook, a meticulous custodian, who put the university finances on a sound basis and who once claimed that he was the only VC who had returned money to the UGC, the university coped by economising on staff. It employed fewer staff and administrators in proportion to student numbers than the average. Alongside what were then (not now) comparatively high staff–student ratios, the university was also very sparing in its promotions. These were not made to a comparative standard of merit over the years, but according to the limited funds available; which changed little over the years as the university also operated historic funding internally. Staff were consistently underpaid by national standards.

Exeter also had the smallest university library in the country and spent the least on its library in 1960/61: £25,450 compared to £31,090 for Leicester and £39,151 for Southampton, the closest in expenditure. Cook did not welcome pressure on the issue, and sought to block the circulation of a paper making the comparisons.[53] Ross pointed out that, although the amount spent was low, the percentage of total expenditure was also relevant: in 1961/62, the average for all universities was 3.8%; for Exeter it was 4.0%.[54] Moreover, in terms of expenditure per student, the 1961/62 figures showed Exeter as low, but not out of line.[55] Nevertheless, that still meant that there was not an adequate basis for research.

The financial origins of the university were also seriously to affect its subsequent development, notably the expansion in the 1960s. When the university sought to do anything new it always did it by halves. As a result, the disciplinary portfolio expanded, but with inadequate funding, ensuring that the university developed as one of many small departments, anxiously fighting over turf and funds.

CHAPTER THREE

INTO THE 1960s: MAJOR EXPANSION

I visited Professor Clayton and the [Classics] staff when they had transferred to the new building. They could hardly believe that they had NEW chairs to sit on.
Christine Smith[1]

By this time, the University was quite clearly that and not a subsidiary of anywhere else. It had, nonetheless, an air of newness and slight surprise that it had made it. Particularly among students it gained the affection that belonging to a genuine community engenders. … There was also a slight sense that everything physical, with the possible exception of the newly built Duryard Halls, was held together with string and sealing wax and by devoted staff – who could be joined occasionally by the Vice-Chancellor sometimes to be discovered from time to time deep in a Hall discussing laundry costs or curtain fabrics.
Richard Langhorne, Tutor in History, 1963/64[2]

THE UNIVERSITY WAS small at the beginning of the decade. On 18 October 1960, there were 1,430 full-time students in residence, 817 men and 613 women, with 527 in the Arts Faculty, 455 in Science, 267 in Social Studies, 134 Education, and 47 in Law. Nevertheless, growth was on the agenda. On 8 January 1960, Sir Keith Murray, the Chairman of the UGC, wrote to James Cook and other

VCs that the number of sixth formers was increasing more rapidly than had been anticipated in 1957 and that there was a 'national need' for expansion in both the 1960s and the 1970s. He sought indications of the university's building requirements. At this stage, external requirements were important but less dirigiste than they were to become.

A special meeting of the Senate, held on 29 January 1960, considered this letter, as well as one from Cook on the 25 January and the minutes of the Quinquennial Development Committee.[3] Concerned about both student numbers and grants, Cook outlined an expansion in range, into 'the field of technology', as he felt that expansion in pure science would be of limited value. Cook also outlined 'disturbing implications', in the shape of a radical alteration in 'the character of the University', and of attempting to plan for conditions in the 1970s 'of which we can have no knowledge'. In place of the current plan for 2,000 students by the mid-1960s, Senate agreed on a target of 3,000 to be reached during the 1970s, provided that new faculties and departments were established, as well as more residential accommodation built. This was an attempt to deliver critical mass. As there were then 4,245 applications for entry in October 1960, 1,000 more than a year earlier,[4] these numbers appeared viable: the final number of applications was 4,765. Aside from establishing a Faculty of Applied Sciences, there was interest in founding courses in Agriculture, Medicine, Architecture, Fine Art, Librarianship, Transport, and Administration, as well as a Sports Hall, a Mathematics building, a Great Hall for ceremonial occasion and examinations, and the expansion of the (Newman) lecture theatre block for the new Chemistry and Physics buildings. As the UGC wanted most of the expansion to be in Science and Technology, Cook was not keen on Schools of Architecture and Fine Art.[5] The Quinquennial Development Committee added a recommendation for a department of Economic and Social History.[6]

However, there were anxieties relating to the prospect and process of expansion. The Faculty of Science was dissatisfied with the slow building programme,[7] but, more seriously, thought a doubling of student numbers in size per decade an unrealistic goal. There were also concerns about the need to devise accelerated means of handling building projects, as well as about the lack of endowment or UGC money threatening the development of the 'appropriate research interests which are the life-blood of a university'. Rejecting expansion in its own subjects, the Faculty of

Science, instead, had called for the establishment of a Faculty of Applied Science. Meanwhile, Arts was concerned about the staff–student ratio, then 1:9.5 in the university as a whole.[8]

Money was a key issue across the university. The Guild Council complained to Senate in the spring of 1960 that a lack of money meant clubs could not visit other universities, while there was no margin of funds available for problems. The costs that would result in this respect from the expansion in student numbers were underlined.[9]

In line with the views of the Faculty of Science, a university delegation to the UGC on 17 March 1960 pressed the case for a range of Applied Sciences, including Applied Biology, Chemical Engineering, and Industrial Dynamics (an imaginative choice), as well as Architecture. The UGC gave a favourable response for Applied Sciences, but not for Architecture, Mining, Agriculture and Medicine.[10] The green light was also given to plan for more than 3,000 students.

Meanwhile, as a reminder that universities operate on several agendas simultaneously, the Executive Committee, on 4 March 1960, approved the enrolling of the university as a member of the North-East (Exeter) Rabbit Clearance Society, while also refusing permission for the local hunt to operate over university property, and threatening legal action against the hunt in the event of further trespass. The extent to which the halls still relied on estate-grown vegetables, a policy greatly developed during the war, helped make rabbits an issue.

The early 1960s saw major changes in the university sector as a self-conscious part of a deliberate modernisation of British society. Seven green-field, plate-glass universities were opened, beginning with Sussex in 1961 and ending with Kent and Warwick in 1965. The new universities also offered new initiatives in teaching and organisation. Their interdisciplinary curricula appeared exciting, and most of their new staff were young. Bold architectural schemes responded to the cult of the new. Sussex proved an important model, and was frequently contrasted with Exeter by staff who had been to both.[11]

Moreover, meeting in 1961–63, the Committee on Higher Education chaired by Lord Robbins recommended a marked increase in the number of students. The thesis of the Robbins Report, which was presented to Parliament by Harold Macmillan, the Prime Minister, in October 1963, was that every child with the potential for higher education should

INTO THE 1960S: MAJOR EXPANSION

receive it, if not at state expense, then with significant state subsidy. The Report represented more than a response to the baby boom that had followed World War Two. There was also an attempt to provide subjects and teaching linked to economic needs. Industrial problems and a more general sense of a lack of competitiveness created pressure for action as with other aspects of the policy of the Macmillan government (1957–63), notably economic planning and the attempt to join the European Economic Community, the basis of the European Union. The Robbins Report pressed the need to strengthen links between universities and industry in order to ensure that research was done.

For Exeter, which with its large campus was well placed to grow rapidly, Robbins meant even greater expansion: to 3,000 students by 1967/68, instead of, as already planned, 1972/73[12], although in January 1964 this was scaled down to 2,900 by 1967/68.[13] In November 1964, the university's Academic Development Committee (ADC) proposed an expansion to 4,000 students by 1971/72.[14]

Senate had established the ADC to make recommendations about expansion. New faculty totals were rapidly agreed, as well as an amended building programme to provide the requisite facilities. In October 1964, there were 2,178 full-time students in the university, compared to 1,877 for 1963, with the rises in Arts and Social Studies being from 677 to 798 and 345 to 404, compared to 636 to 691 for Science. The quota for Science was then increased to 300 per annum, and for Applied Science to 20, but Norman Rydon (Chemistry) stated that this increase could only be achieved by reducing entrance requirements. After the new Chemistry building was inaugurated in December 1965, however, it was argued that this was responsible for an improvement in the student entry:[15] most of the teaching wing had already come into use in October 1965.

More helpfully, Rydon pointed out the need for planning as a continuous process and not one reinstituted towards the approach of each new quinquennium. The struggle to develop and control planning, and to ensure implementation, was to characterise the following four decades. Senate tried to make expansion dependent on maintaining the staff–student ratio, but, both then and repeatedly thereafter, expansion was not to be on the terms of the universities.[16]

Senate and its committees remained dominated by the professors, but they did so as an extension of their departmental role, or, rather, rule.

The dynamics of this varied, with the secretary proving a key adjunct of professorial power, as in History:

> Far and away the most significant person in the department was Mrs Hawgood – no difficulty about remembering *her* name – the departmental secretary. She was a striking figure of modernity: slightly tinted spectacle frames and bright red lipstick and a will of iron – not of the 'I have been here a long time and am a fixture' kind, but more the 'you do as I say or I will leave and then Professor Barlow will hate you for ever' kind. Everything that has ever been said about the age of all-powerful professors applied in Exeter – Barlow, Clayton and Rydon exemplified it. Departmental meetings were a new idea and approached with nervousness for fear of annoying Barlow and, at the end of each one, someone proposed a vote of thanks to him for permitting a meeting to be held.[17]

On a visit in October 1960, the UGC was unsympathetic to a plea from the Readers' and Lecturers' Association for greater participation in the university's governance. The respective influence of the professors was important to the internal politics of Exeter. Richard Hitchcock suggests that, although Norman Rydon (Chemistry) and Clifford Parker (Law) were very powerful (he could have added Keith Conn in Physics), the main strength was with Arts' professors: Frank Barlow, Henry Garland, Moelwyn Merchant (English), Robert Niklaus (French), and Roy Porter (Theology).[18] Some professors lacked their clout. The general field for professors in the 1950s and 1960s was weak, in large part because the choice was restricted by the few appointments made in the 1920s–40s. Appointed in 1948, Fred Clayton (Classics) was brilliant, but lacked the focus and discipline to publish anything of significance, and presided over a poorly performing department.[19] He was a compulsive and interminable talker who could never make up his mind. Politics was less hierarchical than most departments, with its departmental meetings 'more like a traditional Cabinet'.[20]

Arriving to teach German in 1964, Bill Hanson recalls that Exeter was more conservative than Manchester where he had been, but that new staff were very free in all sorts of ways once they accepted that the Head was in charge, and, in particular, were encouraged to write across the

INTO THE 1960S: MAJOR EXPANSION

field. Moreover, Garland's role allowed Hanson to find a niche, notably in Admissions and in the Fine Arts Committee. Stephen Mennell recalls being told about Barlow by the latter's colleague Peter Morris, probably in 1968/69: 'Historians become like the periods they study, and Frank's period is the feudal kingdom of England.'[21] Yet, Barlow was a major scholar, one of the most distinguished members of the Faculty, as well, perhaps surprisingly, as an innovator in some respects. Martin Biddle's lectureship in the department in Medieval Archaeology was the first in Britain. Moreover, as Hanson and others make clear, such rule could produce comfortable conditions. At any rate, the practice summed up for Politics, 'he [Victor Wiseman] left one to oneself',[22] led to very different teaching styles. Wiseman was an active publisher and general editor.

Despite the generally hierarchical and autocratic nature of departmental governance, the university offered staff a friendly, collegiate community, one that was demanding only in ways they anticipated. Numbers (of staff and students) were small, and it was easy for staff to get to know their own students, as well as staff in other departments and in the administration. Lunch daily in Knightley, then the Staff Club, was common, and staff mixed there across ranks and departments. Moreover, academic staff mixed with administrative staff, albeit the latter only above a certain rank.[23] They were on the same terms of appointment as academics.

The university was sociable. Within departments, staff acted as personal tutors and it was common for personal tutees to be entertained in their tutor's home. Now the culture is less paternalist on the part of staff and more independent on that of students. In addition to regular formal dinners involving staff, halls of residence put on a range of events such as balls and garden parties. Students not resident in a hall were members of the somewhat hypothetical Bradninch Hall. This had a member of staff as Warden, an instance of the significance of the *in loco parentis* principle which reflected the then age of majority still being 21. The Hall also had a coffee bar, laundrette and lounges in the increasingly dilapidated Gandy Street building, now the Phoenix Arts Centre. The annual Bradninch Ball and the Guild Ball were major events, the latter attended by the then Chancellor. Staff Club parties, usually including a 'revue', were very popular. The Readers and Lecturers Association held annual 'soirées'.

The university building programme meanwhile was developing on the Streatham campus, with much troublesome red mud on the site as a result. Squelching along was a frequent experience. Northcote House and Devonshire House with its adjoining refectory were officially opened in December 1960, while, earlier that year, their architect Sir William Holford (later Lord), the planning consultant until 1977, was asked to include a theatre, an art gallery and a swimming pool in his plans. A Chemical Engineering building, a Biology building, and extensions to Chemistry and Physics were all marked in for 1966–68. The movement of the administration from Gandy Street in the city centre to the Streatham campus represented an important shift in the centre of activity. Holford also revised the previous, somewhat rigid, 1931 plan for the campus by E. Vincent Harris so that the university accommodated its development to the lie of the land.[24]

The development of the university as a community was a key theme, with emphasis placed on the experience for students of living in hall. This was also seen as an aspect of staff life, and that aspect was regarded as significant in strengthening the student experience. On 25 October 1960, the Halls Committee resolved that 'every facility should be provided and encouragement given to academic staff to take up residence in Hall'.

At the same time, there was an awareness that this experience would not be unchanging. On 30 June 1960, Senate agreed to a Guild request that the hours for entertaining guests of the opposite sex in private rooms in halls should be extended to 11 pm on Saturdays and added 5–7 pm on Sundays, while turning down extensions to 10.45 pm on Wednesdays and Sundays. The issue rumbled on. In 1961, the Guild Council applied to extend hall hours by half an hour, and this was done on Wednesdays and Fridays.[25] More radically, the wardens produced a report in 1960 supporting mixed halls, a development it was argued that would civilise the men:

> The men and women would live separately in their own units, but they would join together in a natural easy manner at meals and in the joint Common Room by right and not by invitation only, nor as intruders. The natural, easy mixing of the sexes would tend to abolish the too rigid pairing-up of men and women observed in the university at the present time. ... A Hall where both men and

women met naturally together would reflect better the present state of society ... students would probably work harder in this type of Hall, because they would see each other frequently at meal-times and at other regular intervals making it less necessary to waste time seeking out the other sex.

At the same time, social change was not considered outwith the context of institutional developments, in this case the prospect of large-scale expansion. The wardens suggested that 'the mixing of the sexes would break up too large a unit of one sex which would tend to upset the balance of the older Halls. This unit of roughly 700 students in Duryard and Birks Grange is bound to develop as almost a separate entity, which is desirable in some ways. ... The unit should therefore reflect the balance of the sexes in the University as a whole.'[26] The pre-war halls, notably Mardon, completed in 1933, were relatively small and were built in what Murray had referred to as a 'country-house style'.

The post-war situation was less spacious and more crowded, with the funds and norms provided by the UGC. Students were housed in single rooms each with a wash basin; but the proportional provision of common rooms was very different as a result of the much larger number of students, with each new hall housing about 150 students and several sharing a dining room. Halls were built in the grounds of Duryard House (purchased in 1946), Hetherington and Murray opening in 1963, while Jessie Montgomery followed in 1964 and nearby Moberly in 1966. In the grounds of the demolished Birks Grange, acquired in 1946, Brendon, Haldon and Raddon halls were opened in 1965–66. David Bates, who arrived as an undergraduate in 1963, noted: 'With their tiny rooms and the shared showers and bathrooms, they now seem hopelessly inadequate by the standards expected nowadays', but added: 'That a significant proportion of the student population that had previously lived in digs were now living on single sites must have made a huge difference to the University's dynamic.'[27] Alex Longhurst, a student who was to return in 1987 as Professor of Spanish, recalled:

> I arrived in Exeter for the start of the 1962/3 academic year and my most enduring memory is of the impact the beautifully lush campus made upon me, all the more so no doubt since I came from

the near-barren Rock of Gibraltar. I was housed in Reed Hall (in what was to be its last year as an undergraduate hall), and the tall redwoods and variety of flowering bushes all around made the place look Edenic. But it was not only Reed Hall gardens that stood out; the whole campus was a botanical park, a good deal greener – and of course much less cluttered – than it is today. Right at the top, beyond Northcote House, were the playing fields, which commanded spectacular views to the Exe estuary. At the bottom of the hill, where the Prince of Wales Road bends sharply, was Streatham Farm, which housed not only the Estate workshops and their machinery but also the departments of Russian and Spanish.

On a less positive note, I recall with some horror the quality of the food – or rather the lack of quality – dished out in the halls of residence and the refectory in Devonshire House. By contrast with the campus, there was nothing green about that. It was all spud and roly-poly pudding. It was the biggest difference I noticed when I returned in 1987: the gastronomic scene was now almost of gourmet quality by comparison, with umpteen eateries and healthy menus to choose from.

The other big change was in regulations. In the 1960s there were rules segregating the sexes in halls. Curfew was at 10 pm, and if you were caught with a guest of the opposite sex after this time expulsion from hall was the inevitable consequence (except apparently in Crossmead Hall, where the warden, the psychologist Richard Lynn, had progressive ideas of his own). Gown-wearing in lectures was in principle compulsory and some members of staff enforced the rule uncompromisingly. I was kicked out of class for not wearing it. A girl was kicked out for wearing the gown with trousers: she left the lecture-room, and returned immediately with her gown still on but minus her trousers! Dress code was strict for formal dinners: dark suit with tie of sober colour for male students and full dress of a subdued shade for women.

Academically I am inclined to believe that Exeter in the 1960s was more demanding than twenty years later. I doubt whether staff worked harder then (quite a few were chronic non-publishers), but they certainly made the students work, and the students took it seriously. Working in the Hall library after dinner

INTO THE 1960S: MAJOR EXPANSION

was de rigueur and pub crawls were limited to Saturday evenings. Syllabuses were pretty comprehensive and you could not expect to get away with 'sampling'. ... I think the foundations for the thriving academic community Exeter was to become, able to look competitor institutions straight in the eye, were laid in the 1960s.

Social life revolved around two locations. Devonshire House on the Streatham Campus was the major one, with the overcrowded coffee bar downstairs and the refectory and lounge upstairs. There was of course the Ram [Ramshackle Bar] at the end of a long corridor that featured all the club and society notice boards. So popular was this watering hole that it soon had to be extended, doubling its size. Devonshire House quickly became too small and Cornwall House [completed in 1971] was already on the drawing board by the time I left. The other social centre was in Gandy Street, where one went for lectures in Law and in Psychology. The coffee bar there was a very lively place. ... But though student life was lively, all in all Exeter was a genteel rather than rumbustious place. If not altogether unnoticed, 1968 went by in relative peace. After seven years in Exeter studying, writing my PhD, and doing part-time teaching, it was a huge cultural shock to arrive in Liverpool in the summer of 69 for my first full-time job.[28]

The general tone of the university still struck some as that of a large public school. Half-day teaching on Wednesdays and Saturdays reflected this pattern. The university took seriously its responsibilities *in loco parentis*, a situation that also reflected wider social norms. The practice of control was widespread in university life. For example, because the Guild Annual General Meeting in 1961 ended at 12.30 am, and not at the stipulated 11 pm, 'a serious breach of discipline', the Guild Council were each fined £5 and Devonshire House was closed for a day. The Guild officers cooperated by appearing before Senate on 15 March to apologise.

The situation was somewhat different in late 1964 when a demonstration was mounted in protest at Cook having responded to Rugby Club antics (a frequent occurrence) by closing the Ram. Peter Dewey remembers some hundreds of students, including him, marching to Northcote House, and forming 'up in orderly ranks, to await the appearance of the VC. He duly emerged, looking grave, and wearing his robes of office, and was presented with a petition by the Students' Union reps. Then we all went home, and shortly afterwards the Ram was reopened.'[29]

More generally, students were fined if they did not observe regulations on keeping term. Exeats were required and limited. In late 1961, unanimous support from Guild representatives for the allowing of smoking in Devonshire House was rejected. Senate rejected the 'Yard of Ale' drinking contest planned as part of the 1962 Rag.[30] That October, three (male) students were fined £2 each for being found in the grounds of Lopes (a female hall) shortly before midnight.

There was growing pressure for change. Made more important by its Chairman, Garland, the Working Party on Halls of Residence that reported in March 1962[31], noting the demand for more student accommodation, added:

> [T]he climate of opinion, among students and in the community at large, on the restrictions and responsibilities of living together in an academic community are being discussed more critically than in the past: students expect to have more of the freedom accorded to their contemporaries who are earning their living outside.

Wishing to retain a system of halls, rather than to turn to university hostels or flats, and thus to offer more than a relationship of landlord to tenant, the committee appreciated that this goal meant change in the halls, namely more independence for students. A study-bedroom for each student was seen as necessary, as was an end to compulsory formal meals, and the provision of keys. At the same time, looking towards Oxbridge colleges, or, at least, to a degree of staff oversight, there was a strong call for resident academics in a 1:40 ratio. A paternalism that was open to change was offered by the Working Party, a paternalism that was subsequently to be blown away in the wind of social transformation, but one that provided an engagement with development, reform and the student experience that was not always to be associated with the austere controls of the Cook years and his own dour personality. The Working Party also noted the social realities: 'For the majority of students coming into residence this will be the first time they have a room of their own and we are in favour of giving them an opportunity for self-expression' – in other words, decoration.

The report was considered by Senate on 5 December 1962: it agreed that all first years and half of the second and half of the third years should be in halls, as well as accepting the 1:40 ratio. However, a reduction in the attendance at formal meals was rejected. As signs of liberalism, permission for the installation of two more cigarette machines in Devonshire House was given in January 1963. This might seem ironic given Cook's important and continuing research on the relationship between cancer and, first, coal tar and, then, smoking. He had his own laboratory in the university and, as he noted in 1958: 'The machine which smokes six cigarettes simultaneously and collects and concentrates the smoke is always a focal point of interest for visitors to the University.'[32] Cook, who was knighted in 1963, personally favoured Havana cigars and the smell of a Havana coming from a room in Northcote House was sufficient to lead to the belief that Cook must be there.[33]

In February 1963, Senate endorsed the Wardens' recommendations to extend the visiting hours; these were now to be from the end of the evening meal until 10 pm on Monday to Friday, the same until 11 pm on Saturday, and from 2 pm to 10 pm on Sundays. Numbers of students, the costs of running halls, and the pressure for more liberal regulations combined to lead the Joint Committee on Residence on 4 December 1963 to recommend building a block of flats, albeit only for final-year students and postgraduates, while the expense of waitress service led to permission for Duryard to experiment with a general reliance on self-service. At the meeting of the Joint Committee on Residence on 18 February 1964, it was suggested that at Duryard 'formal meals might occasionally be arranged which would be attended by members of both sexes'. Richard Langhorne recalls:

> [T]he women's halls, particularly one called Thomas, were run by dragonesses, who liked to guard the social niceties of their charges and were much concerned with 'how to behave at dinner' as well as not entertaining gentlemen in their rooms. One more distant men's Hall [Crossmead] had a liberal minded Sociologist as Warden

[Richard Lynn] who had to resign after it was discovered that the loos had become blocked by used contraceptives.

Smoking remained an issue, with permission being given within Devonshire House, while, in an instructive guide to the liberalism and 'cool' of the period, a Guild AGM in 1964 expressed the 'unanimous view' that smoking was 'a matter to be left to students individually'.[34] Smoking was certainly part of staff life, and appears in Peter Dewey's account of being taught in 1964/65 in what in effect was a combined Social Studies first year: a student in Economic History, he went on to become an academic. Teaching styles and method were individual and distinctive:

> [T]he head of the department of Government [was] H. Victor Wiseman. His lecturing style was impressive. A short, solid man, looking a bit like Napoleon Buonaparte, begowned for his lectures, he usually entered at speed, puffing his pipe, and spoke rapidly. ... The impression was of a stock of enormous and important knowledge, imparted to us as equals. Quite intoxicating. ... The only other Politics lecturer who equalled him in student popularity was Dr Dowse, who impressed in what was really a rather showy way, dressed in expensive leather jackets and used slang to titillate the oh-so conventionally middle class audience. ... Derek Crabtree was dry and precise, but oddly impressive also. He sported a beautiful meerschaum pipe, which he smoked incessantly.[35]

Colin Fletcher, an Economics student from 1963 to 1966, commented on the friendliness of the student community, adding:

> The new Duryard Halls of Residence were very comfortable, the food good and plentiful. ... The arrival of the women was coupled with a sharper watchful eye on the part of certain hall wardens! In those days, one of the characteristics (and apparent appeal of Exeter as a University to potential students) was the approximately equal number of male and female students, and some claimed that this reduced the level of student activism compared with certain other universities. I remember that during my time at Exeter, the event that seemed to cause the most noticeable student

activism, including a mass demonstration outside Northcote House, was the closure of the Ram Bar following a particularly rumbustious Saturday evening ... something to do with a much celebrated rugby match victory by the University RAMS.

There also seemed to be a strong spirit of attachment to one's own hall of residence although this may in part have been an excuse for raids to capture another hall's mascot or xmas tree with the associated excuse to act in a rather juvenile fashion and use the hall's fire hoses for a bit of fun. There were occasions when the staircases in Hetherington and Murray were more akin to waterfalls than stairways.

Another feature of Exeter was the city's many pubs. It was not unknown for a 21st birthday celebration to involve a visit to 21 different pubs in the same evening. While this could naturally lead to a certain amount of noise on the way home (which led to one hall warden famously requesting that students should keep the noise down 'as there were local residents who went to bed early and had children'), perhaps what was noticeable then was that evenings of alcoholic celebration either on campus or in town always seemed to be good humoured, noisy perhaps but devoid of violence on the part of students and local youth.

And then there was academic study and learning! We economists had an easy life with relatively few hours of formal lectures and tutorials, particularly in the second and third years, in contrast to the scientists who spent many hours in the labs on practical work. It was certainly a contrast with life at school. The focus on self study and essays did, I think, teach us a lot of useful skills in terms of thinking around issues, finding information, deciding what was relevant, marshalling arguments, thinking for ourselves. The work rate was not all that it perhaps should have been (although the social life was excellent), and as the degree outcome in those days hinged entirely on the results of the summer exams, panic inevitably set in as the annual exams approached; suddenly the library was very full and the coffee bar rather empty! The amount of work and revision to be got through in a short time probably also helped to develop time management skills!'[36]

Fletcher's Economics contemporary Eric Pillinger was also attracted by the gender balance: 'unique at the time. Lots of us met our wives there', remembered 'playing in a rock group … many hours playing 3 card brag … lounging on Dawlish beach in the summer', and reflected '90% of my tutors and lecturers were very good. I could have learned a lot more from them if I had worked a bit harder!'[37] Many other students commented on their time on the beach at Dawlish. In recent years, Exmouth has become the beach of choice.

The appeal of the university site was also a factor. Dick Ellis, who came to Exeter as a physics lab technician in 1964, was delighted by the contrast between 'the beautiful Washington Singer and all the grounds' and Sheffield, which 'had a dual carriageway through it' and where many of the experiments could only be conducted at night due to vibration from the buses'.[38] The South-West was also a source of attraction. Dougan has 'lovely memories of wonderful walks' with the Walking Group. Arriving as a postgraduate mathematician in 1964, Ken Read remembers 'particularly the Out of Doors Society, which introduced me to the delights of hiking the moors and coasts of Devon and (occasionally) Cornwall, and to the less attractive experience of wet feet (we weren't called the bog-sloggers for nothing)' and 'the Heretics Society, a bastion of free speech in which you were welcome to articulate any creed provided you were prepared to defend it'.

Academic development, meanwhile, was pressed ahead in response to additional student numbers. Interviewed in April 1964 for a post in Politics, Michael Rush discovered that two were to be definitely filled that day. There were four new appointments in Politics in 1964, and 'the staff expanded ahead of the students', which greatly helped in the planning of courses.[39] The pace of expansion increased. Over and above the posts allowed for in the Quinquennial Estimates, there was a recommendation from the ADC on 5 May 1964 for ten additional posts in 1965/66, and another 25 additional posts in 1966/67. This was a period in which academic planning was handled at the university level, if it was handled at all, through the Standing Committee of Senate, along with a heap of ephemera. Expansion was largely demand-led, and the departments that shouted loudest tended to get the additional funding they wanted.

Although there were to be 'stops' as well as 'starts' in the 1960s, there

INTO THE 1960S: MAJOR EXPANSION

was far less competition for scant resources than there was to be from the mid-1970s. The relative ease in staff appointments, with academics appointed young and competition often limited, was to ensure, in some cases, long-term problems in establishing and maintaining quality. This was notably so for those academics who had been appointed without having to demonstrate much research activity or stamina other than carrying out some postgraduate work. The contrast with the major expansion in the late 2000s and early 2010s is readily apparent.

Although, on a visit in October 1960, the UGC warned against the proliferation of small departments, expansion permitted a greater range of teaching, including in minority areas. For example, Russian began at Exeter in 1960 with the appointment of David Richards, from Oxford via the Royal Navy. As an example of the then scale of what would later become one of the leading departments in the university, Psychology had first made its appearance as part of a departmental title in 1952 when its separate status was recognised in the then title of the department of Education and Psychology. Within this overarching department, which was broad enough to embrace A.M. Cummings as the sole university 'Lecturer in Gardening', (two) separate Psychology lecturers were listed from 1955. Psychology became an independent department for 1962/63 with just two posts, one of which, the Professor, Leslie Reid, was only appointed later that academic year.

Alongside money for new staff, however, there was a continuing squeeze on capital grants, in part reflecting the UGC's commitment to the new universities.[40] To cover the period from January 1965 to March 1966, the UGC only granted Exeter £780,000 for major building works.[41] In 1964, there were difficult negotiations, with both UGC and the contractors, over the Physics Building, in the design of which, by Sir Basil Spence, aesthetic values had prevailed. As Spence was also the architect for the Chemistry and Newman Buildings, he was an important figure in the visual character of the built university. On the Physics Building, attention focused on the very slender reinforced steel concrete columns that formed the external structural frame of the building. However, because Spence did not go for sufficiently wide concrete columns, the concrete was too thin and the steel inside rusted. This led to an expensive protective procedure, initially every two years. Moreover, the building was highly fuel-inefficient.[42]

The UGC approach to the university's expansion plans created issues, including for the practicality of Exeter's paternalism which depended on providing more halls. There was also no money for a Social Studies building, temporary or, preferably permanent, or for a Medical School.[43] Cook and some members of Council felt that UGC grants were inadequate for the expansion called for by government.[44] This problem was to recur throughout the history of the university. The university considered whether it would be possible to borrow,[45] but in the 1960s this was not the option that it was to be in the 2000s and 2010s.

Although there was no money for a Medical School, in 1962 the first steps were taken in what, four decades later, would become the Peninsula School of Medicine. These early days began with a small grant of £30,000 annually for five years from the Nuffield Provincial Hospitals Trust to create the Postgraduate Medical Institute. The first Director, David Mattingly, a part-time member of the consultant staff of the hospital and a part-time member of the university, was to deliver each year three 10-week courses for the induction of foreign-qualified doctors into British medical practice, and thus into the NHS. Operating with great energy on a new horizon and showing an entrepreneurialism and vision not seen with most of the departmental heads of the period, Mattingly was soon arranging short in-service courses for practising doctors, both in general practice and in hospital medicine.[46] That, in turn, led to an initiative by a then partner in the Denmark Road General Practice, Denis Pereira Gray, for the novel idea of a training course for GPs. His pioneering of education in General Practice led him eventually to be President of the Royal College of General Practitioners.

Developments in Medicine looked to the future. In contrast, there was already an established regional presence, as well as professional training offered in Law, notably through extra-mural activities. The department of Law was established in 1923 in response to an initiative by the Law Society to improve the education of solicitors. Lectures for articled clerks were put on in both Exeter and Plymouth, and the Exeter (originally London External) law degree was recognised as a route into the profession. By the 1960s, although the majority of students were reading for the law degree, lectures were still being provided for articled clerks. At that time, the majority of the academic staff were professionally oriented and saw themselves as producing recruits for the profession, rather than as providing a university education through the law. The emphasis was on teaching, which ranged from the scholarly to the anecdotal. In 1960, of the academics in Law, only Dominik Lasok was engaged in serious research and publication.

Extra-mural provision had expanded after World War Two, with ten full-time tutors by the mid-1950s, as well as occasional lecturing by other members of the university staff. Aside from the resident tutors in Devon and Cornwall who put on courses, some residential, there was also a tutor who organised courses and lectures for armed forces establishments in the two counties, an important task. Extra-mural lecturing provided staff with a wider experience of teaching and the region and also a source of a modest additional income. This activity provided a wider 'social capital' for the university and to the region.

While noting limited student radicalism and a 'small, comfortable, and cosy place', David Bates found the university 'a lively and stimulating one that nurtured many careers, lives and interests'. He commented on both social and academic life:

> Much social life took place in the relatively new Devonshire House. Coffee there after lectures was common. Saturday night hops were great social events, not only because they encouraged mingling among students, but because they also attracted young people from the town. Groups (as we then called them) with great futures performed there. ... The old Ram bar was also a significant social centre for many, myself included. These places and the Halls contributed greatly to encouraging social intercourse across all parts of the student body. ... Teaching could be said to have been by example. ... As an undergraduate, one did feel part of an academic community'.

Bates pressed on to refer to the development of a staff-postgraduate student seminar: 'I have a strong memory of giving a paper to it ... that tried to explore definitions of feudalism. ... The necessity to explore and explain Marc Bloch's *La Société Féodale* to a group of historians was a life-shaping experience. For all the conservatism and caution of 1960s Exeter, this one event typified how it could work beneficially and embrace change.[47]

CHAPTER FOUR

THE LATER 1960s: SOCIAL CHANGE

I DO NOT WISH to disappoint readers, but lectures on the 'Balance of Payments' do not commonly attract an avid audience of about 1,400 students, nor lead to organised chanting, contrary appeals for free speech, minor scuffling and press coverage. The Great Hall on 23 October 1968 saw a different outcome, with Enoch Powell (who had given his speech critical of mass immigration that April) abandoning the meeting after about fifteen minutes. The Assistant Secretary, who was present, estimated that the chanting was by a group of about 70–80, and that 'sustained applause from the great majority of those present' had greeted the appeals for free speech; and he questioned the accuracy of press reports about the throwing of objects and other violence. James Jones (Theology, 1967–70) recalled: '[I]t was standing room only. … The following day the press was full of lurid stories. It was my first introduction to the disparity between press reports and the real event.'[1]

The 1960s was becoming increasingly contentious in the university. The tendency to divide university history by the reigns of individual VCs is a tempting one, not least as they are the key figures. In the case of the 1960s, such a division appears sensible as Cook retired and was replaced by F.J. (Frederick) Llewellyn in 1966, and a different tone and content can be seen with university policy. Cook became VC of the federal University of East Africa, then Chairman of the Academic Planning Board at the University of Ulster, and finally retired to Budleigh Salterton.

THE LATER 1960S: SOCIAL CHANGE

At the same time, a focus on VCs risks downplaying a more significant change, that in society as a whole, a change that greatly affected the university sector. A number of interviewees observed that the 1960s only affected Exeter in the 1970s, but there were already significant changes in the late 1960s. The social life of students provided a key instance. When Joseph Sykes retired as DVC in 1964, his wife, Phyllis, 'was appointed as the first warden of the new mixed-sex Duryard complex. This was quite an eye-opener for a lady ... who had high moral values.'[2] The sexual liberation seen in society as a whole was also the case in Exeter where the attempt at moral policing represented by restrictions on guests staying in students' rooms was put under considerable pressure. At Cook's last Senate, on 28 June 1966, a student was fined £20 and sent down for the rest of term for having a 'local girl' in his room overnight. As an instance of the culture of the period, both Cook and Bartlett were consulted about the episode, while the moderate punishment (term was nearly over) was linked to the student writing to express his regret.

As far as student politics were concerned, guests (i.e. for many, sex) was the prime issue and it was one that took up a large amount of time and effort. Repeated demands for change were met with considerable hesitation, but Llewellyn proved more accommodating than Cook. As an instance of the more general process of liberalism, possibly highly relevant to this accommodation, 'Black Jack', as he was known, was also fond of women in the city, although there were no scandals. The serious alcoholism that was ultimately to mar his subsequent job, as Director General of the British Council (1972–80), was not yet apparent.[3] As a reminder of other links, Norman Rydon (Chemistry) earlier in his career had worked on oestrogens, helping to lay the foundations for the development of the contraceptive pill.

The wardens, who were a powerful group in the university, largely proved a conservative force. The female wardens were stricter than their male counterparts, in part possibly because the university had very few married women on its staff, and those did not want to be wardens. Possibly the spinsters who were recruited were more querulous about discipline, especially where relations with men were concerned, than married women would have been. Bates remembers Joyce Youings, a historian who was subsequently the first female Professor in the university, 'driving male students off the Thomas tennis-courts for wearing what she judged to be shorts that were too short'. Youngs was very firm on her charges. At the same time, Bates observed that many wardens 'treated students much more as responsible adults than their official conduct suggests. There was variation of course.'[4]

However, the strong wish by many students for a degree of social liberalism represented a rejection of the established pattern of control by wardens. Alongside students ignoring regulations on visitors, came others keen to live out. Partly as a result, the attempt to run aspects of Exeter as a sub-Oxbridge, with halls as pseudo-colleges, no longer seemed viable. A sense of change among the students toward a less disciplined body was captured by Cook when he spoke at the Joint Committee on Residence on 17 January 1966. Ian Gordon noted a difference between his period as a Psychology student in the late 1950s and his return as a lecturer in the late 1960s. In the former:

> Wardens ... particularly women wardens, thought nothing of bursting into bedrooms to see whether any sexual activity was taking place. In my undergraduate years one student's academic career was ruined when he was expelled after being found 'partially dressed' with his female companion.[5] I returned ... to find that the place had changed. Students were richer, were free to enjoy sex, and exerted a greater influence on university policy: a minor social revolution seemed to be in progress.[6]

The students wanted to have guests in at all hours, the polite fiction for staying the night and having sex. The university did not want them to sleep over, and its polite fiction was that it did not want overnight occupancy by anyone other than the student of a particular room. Keith Conn came up with a brilliant compromise: guests should leave 'by the early hours of the morning'. After that, 'sleepovers' were effectively legitimised as long as they were not too blatant and continuous.

New social arrangements, and their impact on institutional practices were seen across the range of student activity. From the autumn term of 1966, snack lunches were offered as an alternative at the Refectory, and by mid-October comprised about 200 out of 750 lunches. It was also agreed to permit the sale of hot snacks in the car park after dances, a sale already taking place unofficially.[7] Meanwhile, the dress code had

THE LATER 1960S: SOCIAL CHANGE

changed from shirt, tie and sports jacket for males to jeans and sweaters, noted David Meredith (Economic History, 1967–73) when he arrived.

Meredith was encouraged to apply by the high female to male ratio: '[T]hese ratios were a frequent topic of conversation amongst sixth-formers at my (all-male) school.'[8] Student life scarcely offered solace for feminists: the Rag Day in 1967 included a 'slave market' and 'ladies physical exercises'. Brian Langdon-Pratt (Economics, 1963–66), who found 'the weekly "hops" the best place to meet the opposite sex', recalled:

> one memorable 'pyjama party' when baby-doll pyjamas were all the rage. ... There were good gigs as well – Cleo Laine and Johnny Dankworth, the Scaffold, to name just two and there was a good Folk Club in the town which many students attended. Other lasting memories are the summer balls. ... These took place on the last Friday of term and after, as dawn was breaking, the tradition was to head for the coast to Dawlish Warren for breakfast of hot coffee and a bacon roll from a sea-front kiosk. Then a short sleep before the Crossmead Garden Party on the Saturday afternoon followed by a party again until the early hours. Our parents could never understand why we were so tired when we went home on the Monday.[9]

Brian met his future wife Pam at a weekly 'hop': a large number of students were to marry each other. Reading English (1964–67), Pam 'thought that her teaching was excellent under the leadership of the Reverend Professor Moelwyn Merchant, who was a gifted lecturer on Shakespeare'. She went on to teach.

Merchant was described by Mick Gidley, a junior colleague, as 'a robber baron of a professor ... often thoroughly unscrupulous in getting what he wanted. At what was to be the last departmental meeting under his chairmanship ... he even threatened to withdraw his resignation from the university if we wouldn't all agree to a reorganisation he planned to impose on his successor.' However, yet again as a reminder of the need to quote at length, Gidley added that:

> Moelwyn was a visionary teacher who fostered creativity: he instituted at Exeter, way ahead of any other UK university, the

opportunity for students to submit creative work as part of their degree assessment, and he brought to the campus numerous writers, musicians and visual artists, many of them personal friends. ... He himself was a poet, a proficient sculptor, a librettist ... he liked students.

Merchant, who found Llewellyn sympathetic, argued that English should be a centre of creativity within the university, and that drama, fine art and music could be related to the central critical and historical concerns of the subject.[10]

Indeed, on 2 November 1967, the Northcott Theatre opened with a production of *The Merchant of Venice*, starring Tony Church, its first Artistic Director. That night, Barbara Hepworth unveiled one of her sculptures in the foyer. The 433-seat theatre reflected the initiative of a local businessman George Northcott (who had tried unsuccessfully to save the Theatre Royal, demolished in 1962 to make way for an office block), a gift from the Calouste Gulbenkian Foundation, and land from the university. The theatre's repertory company proved particularly dynamic and innovative in the 1970s and 1980s. Members included Celia Imrie, Geraldine James, Lesley Joseph, Robert Lindsay, John Nettles, Bob Peck, Brian Protheroe and Imelda Staunton. Nicholas Hytner was one of the directors. After refurbishment in 2007, the theatre was able to seat 464.

Liberalism rather than radicalism was the order of the day, but there were pressures for political action on the part of some students. At the same time, at Exeter there was considerable institutional conservatism. In November 1967, Senate had voted 17–15 against student membership of the new Fine Art and Music Committee, while, on 22 May 1968, 'very strong reservations were expressed by several members' about proposals for Faculty Staff–Student committees. However, student activism elsewhere encouraged support in Exeter for channels of communication to express students' views. Llewellyn backed this policy and told Senate on 25 June 1968 'that although strong measures might be needed to counteract violence, the best weapons were those which would mobilise student opinion in defence of good order in the University'.

Leslie Robinson, who was Guild President in 1968/69, does not see Exeter then 'as a hotbed of militancy'. The events he regarded as of significance were 'the abandonment of the concept of university being "in loco

THE LATER 1960S: SOCIAL CHANGE

parentis" to its students, the establishment of departmental staff/student committees', and the events surrounding Powell's visit 'which "spooked" the University authorities of the time'. James Barber, who taught Politics in 1967–69, suggests that the composition of the student body 'meant that we avoided many of the student problems of the 1960s'. The Powell visit led to many debates about freedom of speech in his classes.[11]

There was also a degree of intellectual openness. The topics set for the Ballard Essay Prize Competition were 'Computers and the Arts; the "New Wave"; Picasso; and Censorship'. New staff appointments reflected this openness. On 13 March 1968, Senate recommended chairs in Political Theory, Social Administration, and Economic and Social Statistics. On 22 May, Senate agreed to change the name of the department of Government to the department of Politics.

With staff, the agenda of dispute changed. In March 1966, Senate, the meetings of which Aileen Fox found 'incredibly tedious', had 'a lively debate' on the use of university buildings for religious observances, with the battleground looking back to the clericalism and anti-clericalism of the past. As a linked matter, the status of Duryard Lea, which was purchased by the Catholic Church to provide a chapel, a centre for Catholic students, and a residence for a Catholic chaplain, became a long-standing issue.[12] The late 1960s, in contrast, saw the beginning of an attempt to transform the governance of the university by limiting the powers of the professorial heads of department. This pressure was not immediately successful, but it is important to note this 1960s' anticipation of the more sustained campaign for change in the 1970s.

This pressure for change impacted on a relatively conservative institution. The culture is captured well by Malyn Newitt, who arrived in 1966, teaching History until 1998:

> The prevailing philosophy was one that saw a University as a community of individual scholars. 'Collegiality' was a word often used and deeply felt by some people. ... 'Collegiality' meant in practice that scholars got on with their own work, showed a polite but not intrusive interest in the work of their colleagues and passed over in silence those whose personal or academic qualities were found to be wanting. It was a world in which nobody was ill-mannered enough to inquire

directly what you were doing, what your future plans were, what conferences you were attending or why no students ever signed up for your courses. Once you had acquired tenure [generally after three years], there were few external pressures. Curiously this did not prevent breakdowns and alcoholism taking hold, or many staff lapsing into a non-productive and academically inert existence ... there was no effective academic supervision of courses, degree programmes, standards of teaching, or research productivity, while the system of tenure meant that no one could be sacked ... no questions were asked of those who published nothing. Teaching was never discussed and the assumption was that a scholar would automatically be a good teacher.[13]

Newitt exactly captures the research culture, although that did not prevent many staff from taking an active role in significant research projects. For example, in Politics, Michael Rush and Malcolm Shaw were among those producing important work on legislative committees. Similarly, there was much committed teaching. Nevertheless, Roderick Ross, the University Secretary, reported that when a UGC party toured Exeter on 22 November 1968 to gain first-hand knowledge of the actual use of teaching facilities, 'the teaching accommodation gave the appearance of being rather under-used'. They had chosen a Friday afternoon. As a result, the UGC concluded that the university was over-provided with lecture theatres, and rejected proposals to fund more.[14] The consequences of this decision lasted for many years.

To return to the start of the period, it was not a happy meeting when Cook led a delegation to see the UGC on 29 January 1965. Cook pointed to an 'abrupt drop' in the level of capital grants for Exeter, from £750,000 each year in 1963 and 1964, to £50,000 in total for the two following years, and claimed that this drop had created 'alarm and despondency' among an academic staff unsure about what they had done to incur the UGC's displeasure. Pointing out that the university had increased its numbers by 500 students in order to meet the goals for the expansion outlined by Robbins, Cook argued that this had only been done by transferring Social Studies to prefabricated accommodation, an undesirable step as Streatham Court, completed in 1967 to UGC specifications, proved poorly insulated and flimsy. Rush recalls: '[I]t was stuffy in

Lecture Room A, so I asked students to open windows, at which point one fell out, fortunately outwards.'[15]

In addition, Cook claimed at the meeting that, unless new student accommodation was built, it would not be possible to use new teaching facilities in Science. A more general gloss was offered at the meeting by Rydon, a head of department who was also a significant academic, who

> pointed out that Exeter occupied a difficult position between the old and the new universities, still being only some two-thirds of the way along our growth curve. As a result of the uneven expansion, the university was at present unbalanced, and would need further expansion in order to restore the balance.[16]

A focus on building up the new universities was held responsible for the UGC's response to Exeter. As a consequence, although the trend in numbers at Exeter was upwards, only modest goals for expansion were suggested. ADC decided on 4 March 1965 to propose 2,920 undergraduates for 1967/68 and 3,670 for 1971/72, but the UGC did not prove accommodating. It agreed to 2,500 students for 1967/68, and its likely reluctance in accepting a 'very much higher figure' by 1971/72 was seen by Cook as posing 'very difficult questions' for the university. Council resolved to use every effort to persuade the UGC to accept about 3,800 students by 1971/72.[17] In fact, 2,742 students were registered in October 1966, while, by January 1968, there were 14,763 applications for entry (5,625 in Arts, 3,615 in Social Studies, and 3,314 in Sciences) in the following university year; an increase of 269 on the previous year. In February 1968, Senate agreed to 3,365 students for 1971/72, as well as 33 new academic staff at lecturer or equivalent rank.

A sense of frustration with the UGC had played an important role in the appointment of Llewellyn as Cook's successor. Like Cook and his predecessor, Sir Thomas Taylor, Llewellyn had a background in Chemistry, having taken a DSc at Birmingham, been a Lecturer at Birkbeck, and Professor at Auckland University College; although he was not an 'outstanding chemist' as Cook had been.[18] More significantly, Llewellyn had served as VC of the University of Canterbury (1955–61), before becoming Chairman of New Zealand's UGC as well as of its Broadcasting Commission.

As a reminder of the range of individuals appointed who were subsequently to be important in the university's history, the same Senate at which Llewellyn's appointment, which took effect in 1966, was announced (17 March 1965) saw the appointment of Michael Havinden, who was to be a key figure in Economic History, of Malyn Newitt, an old-Wykehamist who became first a radical and later a DVC, and of Peter Quartermaine, later head of the Readers and Lecturers Association. Slightly less pregnant with the future, Senate also agreed the affiliation of the Tiddly-winks Club to the Guild. The Transcendental Meditation Society was to follow on 25 November 1968.

Llewellyn was described by Anne Mayes as a 'bruiser' on Senate – 'not someone you would want to meet on a dark night. A fairly hard man who certainly did not suffer fools gladly.' She also thought him an effective chairman of Senate, more so than his two successors. John Stirling (University Librarian, 1972–94) recalls Llewellyn as 'certainly master in his own case', able to get business through Senate if he agreed and to block it if he didn't. A pragmatic figure, there was also a drive and dynamism associated with Llewellyn, an ability to make things work, and a willingness to engage with change not seen under the more conservative Cook. To Barrie Behenna, who became his PA, Llewellyn, a breath of fresh air, was a leader who saw the need to move away from dominance by the professorial big barons, a term much used at the time.[19]

In many senses, the university continued with its business as if the outer world was of limited relevance, but there were also signs of pressure. For example, the determination of the Finance Committee to limit the deficit on the Refectory in a period of rising inflation led to upward pressure on prices there. In place of the activism that would have followed a decade later, the Guild requested a special meeting of the Joint Committee of Management of the Refectory and Devonshire House, held on 17 June 1965, which respectfully listened to an address by Cook, before agreeing a compromise under which prices rose by half what the manager had requested. The following year, the issue was complicated by government price controls, which deferred the increase in the price of a coffee from 6d [2½ new pence] to 7d, with Devonshire House experiencing a shortfall, while the Guild was hit by wage increases and Selective Employment Tax.[20] The pressures of the outside world were readily apparent to Senate on 26 May 1965 when it considered a letter from Sir John Wolfenden, the Chairman of the UGC, disclosing that the UGC felt obliged to develop techniques of comparative analysis of university costs. Two days earlier, Council had strengthened its understanding of the outside world by electing Derick, First Viscount Amory, former Treasurer of the University College of the South West (1936–43) and a Conservative Chancellor of the Exchequer (1958–60), to be Chairman of Council and Pro-Chancellor Designate; he went on to be Pro-Chancellor and Chairman of the Council from 1966 until 1972, when he became Chancellor.

Meanwhile, the number of students rose. Whereas 2,157 full-time students came into residence in October 1964, the number for 1965 was 2,394. The pressure of numbers was upwards. In October 1968, of the 3,079 students (undergraduate and postgraduate), new admissions were 1,327. However, these rises helped create a sense of crisis in accommodation. The UGC had been told in January 1965 that 'with the difficulty of lodgings in Exeter there was simply no room for manoeuvre'. On 9 June 1965, the Joint Committee on Residence, thought it 'reasonably satisfactory' that two out of every three freshers could be offered a place that October, but also concluded that the difficult situation in Exeter meant that 'lodgings should be sought in inland towns and hamlets such as Crediton'.

The indications were of continuing demand on places and, therefore, accommodation. In the autumn of 1965, Exeter received 5 per cent of the national candidates for Arts, 4.5 per cent for Social Studies, and 3.7 per cent for Pure Science; percentages that were more than its appropriate share.[21] Overcrowding certainly happened in halls, but the wardens at the time thought that the university Buildings Officer wanted as many students in halls as possible in order to boost revenues and not because there was an accommodation shortage. The sharing of rooms increased while the extra spaces made were often of poor quality. On 8 December 1965, 'Senate expressed concern at the increase in the number of 3-bedded rooms in Hope and Lopes and expressed the view that the extra rooms converted to provide places for 3 beds in these halls recently should revert to 2-bedded rooms in 1966/7.' Nevertheless, a week earlier, the Joint Committee on Residence had recommended 'by a narrow majority', that twelve rooms in Moberly originally designated as single should be furnished as double rooms. Arriving in October 1967, David

Meredith was fully aware of 'an accommodation crisis', with all the first years he knew in digs, and the shock of sharing distant and uncomfortable accommodation with a complete stranger: '[O]verall it was a rather isolating experience.' In contrast, Duryard for his second year proved 'full of red brickwork and light' with 'small but adequate' rooms. The third year he thought typical: renting a house with friends.[22]

Pressure on rooms was linked to questions of control and behaviour. The university proved reluctant to accept the implications of students being adults. A cautious tone emerged from the Senate discussion on 15 March 1967 of the 11 February meeting of the Joint Committee on Residence:

> After discussion Senate decided that the Lodgings Officer should have discretion to allow first and second year students under the age of 21 years to occupy a house, flat, bedsitting room etc where meals and service are not provided, in special circumstances (eg in the case of married students) and that heads of departments should be consulted before students were allowed to move into a flat.

There were also the problems of managing growth. On 24 November 1965, Standing Committee authorised forty-one new posts for October 1966, eighteen of them in the Arts. Whereas Geography had had four academic staff in 1947 and seven in 1963, by 1971 there were thirteen, including the second Chair which had been created in 1969. Chemistry had five appointments in 1964, three in 1965, and three in 1966. The number of academic staff in Chemistry rose from seven in 1957 to twenty-two in 1978.

However, although understandable, not least in the light of the crises of the 1970s–1990s, the subsequent sense that the 1960s were all about expansion is in part misguided. Instead, there was a stop–start quality to the period alongside the growth. For example, the UGC was not encouraging at the start of 1966: not much of an increase in student numbers was anticipated between 1967/68 and 1973/74 and, in light of the greater number of universities, there was an emphasis on the need to focus on existing activities rather than embrace new ones. Visiting the university in January 1966, the UGC drove home this message, while also suggesting an improvement in communications with students.[23] At the same time, building on the campus underlined expansion and contributed to a sense of continual growth. Thus, the Sports Hall was opened in 1967.

The role of the UGC underlined the nature of the university's dependence on government, but that was also driven home by the policies, financial and otherwise, of the Labour government. Thus, in 1967, Senate only accepted 'with great reluctance' the 'unilateral action' by government that meant that fees for overseas students were increased from October.[24] There was also concern about the implications of the government's wages standstill for salaries. At the same time, there was pressure for change from within the university. Thus, in 1967, there was discussion of the discontinuation of closed scholarships, those for students from particular schools.

The sterling crisis of July 1966 reflected the degree to which Harold Wilson, who had won a triumph with the general election on 31 March 1966, was unable to master the economy. The Treasury used the opportunity to press the case of deflation, and the attempt by the department of Economic Affairs under George Brown to eclipse the Treasury failed. The National Plan, an optimistic blueprint for growth, produced by Economic Affairs, was ditched. The deflation of 1966 and the accompanying wage-freeze only bought time before the devaluation of sterling in November 1967, but the squeeze on government expenditure affected the universities. Llewellyn told Council on 19 December 1966 that the likely low rise in the recurrent (government annual) grant meant a need 'to review the proposed rate of student growth and the scheme proposed for the diversification of academic studies'.

The impact of government financial problems was also seen in the building programme, although buildings already approved were completed: the Physics Tower, the Mathematics–Geology Building (the Laver Building), the Northcott Theatre, the Sports Hall and the flimsy Streatham Court in 1967, and the Applied Science Building in 1968. After that, in contrast, no new buildings were completed until Cornwall House and Lafrowda Flats I, both in 1971, followed by Amory in 1974, the last academic building built under UGC rules. At least there was the idea in 1967 of seeking local finance for 'a block adjacent to Devonshire House where various commercial services could be provided'.[25]

On 20 December 1966, Wolfenden advised against new departments in Exeter, which led Llewellyn in January 1967 to recommend deferring the Postgraduate Medical School and Biochemistry until the government grant for 1968/69 was known. He also pressed for Chairs to be appointed in areas where teaching was heavy, and for cutting back Applied Science as it had insufficient students. Yet again in 1967, the failure to fill admission quotas in Science and Applied Science, a recurrent problem, was matched by exceeding quotas in Arts, Social Studies, Law and Education. This outcome, a relatively frequent one, encouraged pressure for growth in Social Sciences, to overcome the fact that its earlier expansion had started late.[26] The Committee of Deans recommended on 5 December 1967 that Science have a total undergraduate population of 788 by 1971/72 and Applied Science 61. Arriving to teach Sociology in 1967, Stephen Mennell found the university

> above all very small … I remember thinking, on first visiting the then-new Library … that it felt more like the library at my grammar school than the UL in Cambridge or the Widener at Harvard, where I had been accustomed to working. Besides being tiny, Exeter felt remote and old-fashioned. I was sent, during my first week, to talk about my pension arrangements with an official in Northcote House who rejoiced in the Dickensian title of Chief Clerk. In Sociology, there were only three telephones: one for the Professor, one for the head of the social work section, and one – for no very obvious reason – in the office of John Hughes, barely senior to me, where we had to queue to use it. The university switchboard closed down at lunchtime. There was nothing resembling a modern photocopier, just a wet-dry contraption,[27] which involved making a sandwich of your text between two types of negative paper, which was then run through a sort of mangle into a bath of developing fluid. One then pegged out the result on a washing line, to dry slowly. The department of Sociology had only just moved out of Queen's Building into Streatham Court, a prefab but a very comfortable one … known to some as 'The Dump', because it had been built on what has previously been a landfill site at the head of the Streatham Valley. Its defining feature, though, was that the rooms – square, spacious and well suited to tutorial groups – were all the same size.[28]

THE LATER 1960S: SOCIAL CHANGE

A different impression emerges from Sue Jackson, who was appointed aged seventeen as a secretary in Economics in 1965 at £445 per annum:

> There was a Senior Common Room in Streatham Court for the use of academics. When secretaries campaigned to be able to use it, it was decided by Dr Frank Oliver who was in charge of the SCR Committee that they could do so from 10.00 to 10.30 when they would have to vacate it so that academics could have sole use. In those days, secretaries were not really regarded as members of staff. Indeed, such was Professor Victor Wiseman's (Politics) belief in this regard that no secretaries were ever included in departmental photos up to the time of his death in November 1969. ... There was no such thing as maternity leave – you resigned your job and looked for another one when ready to resume working'.[29]

The lack of university independence troubled some lay members of university bodies,[30] but the need for government money led to an acceptance of government control, however indirect, over university finances and policy, a pattern that was normal in British universities.[31] The estimated recurrent income for Exeter for 1967/68 (i.e. excluding research grants) was as follows:

	£
Exchequer grant	1,510,000
Fees	197,000
Local Authorities[32]	19,550
Endowments	5,000
Miscellaneous (interest etc)	5,000
	1,736,550[33]

ADC asked Llewellyn to press the UGC to increase the recurrent grant so as to develop Applied Science, Biological Science and the Postgraduate Medical Institute,[34] but, although Llewellyn thought a figure of 5,000 students in 1980 a reasonable basis for planning, on a site which the Works Committee assessed had an eventual capacity of 9,000–10,000,[35] the short term was such that he saw expansion only in Applied Science,[36] the building for which was opened by the Duke of

Edinburgh on 21 March 1968. The university was therefore unable both to develop Applied Science, which had originally been planned with UGC approval, and to use the Washington Singer Laboratories as had been intended by creating a department of Biochemistry.[37] Ironically, as a result of developments in the 2000s–2010s, a department of Biochemistry is in effect what exists today.

Exeter in the 1960s was no Sussex, and personal and academic conservatism were certainly at play. Kenneth Strongman remembers a member of 'the Law department referring to "a new group, something to do with insects I believe", meaning The Beatles'.[38] A discussion in Senate on 24 May 1967 about more inter-faculty courses, to include Applied Science subjects, led the rigid Frank Barlow, an over-mighty professorial Head of the old school, highly distinguished scholar and accomplished ballroom dancer,[39] to complain 'that there was a danger of sacrificing high standards, symbolised by the emphasis on single honour schools in the University, in order to achieve numbers'.

On 14 June 1967, Standing Committee was distinctly unenthusiastic when asked to include 'merit and special responsibility' in promotions and salary reviews alongside age and experience, criteria with which they were familiar and happy. 'Such cases would be few in number and exceptional in character' it was decided, a position that remained the case for several years. The promotion 'queue' was managed with considerable rigidity. Regardless of merit, there was the practice of promotion only when academics had reached the top of the lecturers' scale. Wiseman (Politics) tried to get one individual promoted from Assistant Lecturer to Lecturer a year early, saying that he feared he might lose him to another university, only to be told that Exeter placed a great premium on loyalty to the university.[40]

Nino Pelopida (1964–67) recalls St Luke's as far from free and easy, with a rigid dress code and meals very much controlled: 'No one was allowed to leave until High Table said grace.'[41] Teacher education in England experienced a massive increase during the 1960s, which allowed St Luke's significantly to increase student numbers and to build. The College admitted women students from 1963 and female staff from 1964. The Robbins Report recommended that colleges of education should be fully absorbed into the world of higher education. This involved local partnerships becoming more formal. Each university Senate had to

THE LATER 1960S: SOCIAL CHANGE

decide on what basis (or whether) to recognise and validate the certificate programmes being followed by school leavers. The usual decision was to rename this course the BEd. Some universities awarded this to College students with honours, while others designated it as an ordinary or pass degree. At Exeter, the university recognised the St Luke's course as an 'ordinary' BEd in 1966, the stance of the majority of English universities at the time; after which, agreed improvements saw it awarded with honours from 1969.

A form of social snobbery was present in Llewellyn's otherwise prescient memorandum of September 1967 on long-term planning which included the comment about planned student residences: 'As one member of the administrative staff remarked "we would be building council houses amongst stately homes".' Llewellyn understood that UGC policy meant that institutions that lacked Oxbridge wealth would have to change the nature of student accommodation. Considering a situation in which 1,750 students were in halls, 25 in university flats, and 1,225 in digs, with the potential for about 1,600 in digs, new accommodation for 1,625 would be required if the student body rose to 5,000. As the UGC had 'virtually stopped financing Halls of Residence of the traditional type', it would be necessary, Llewellyn argued, to turn to flats that the university financed by loans. As a result of inserting these flats in the grounds of Hope and Lopes, the latter would become more like Birks and Duryard. Cornwall House, which was completed in 1971, would be required in order to provide a refectory and common rooms.

In the event, Lafrowda, a house in St Germans Road, was acquired in 1965, its grounds being used for blocks of flats completed in 1971, 1975 and 1976. There was a range of concerns about this development, including fears that the buildings would be claustrophobic and overly institutional, as well as about the viability of the project at the interest rates on offer.[42] Llewellyn pointed out to Council on 8 July 1968 that the self-catering flats would necessitate a 'complete reappraisal' of the regulations governing student residences. Lafrowda was to have an academic warden, but he was only a counsellor for people who wanted help. By 1968, indeed, there was an atmosphere of change. On 6 June 1968, the Joint Committee on Residences recommended that guests be allowed from 1 pm to 11 pm. On 11 July, Standing Committee resolved that all departments were to be urged to establish staff–student committees. In

1969, considerable time was devoted to considering the response to those found in possession of drugs, an issue faced with more sensitivity than in the past.

At the same time, there was a marked contrast to other universities. Arriving in Exeter in January 1969 from a post at Hull, Jeremy Noakes welcomed the better weather and spent his first year feeling as if he was on holiday. Noakes no longer found himself in a

> revolutionary situation. ... My first formal engagement was the History Society dinner, where to my surprise, the students all turned up in dinner jackets and the women in long dresses. I remember walking past the rows of student cars parked, while I went for the bus. ... The University had the reputation as a 'green welly' university where the public school intake stuck together and rather asserted themselves.[43] There was some justification for this reputation, although this tended to be concentrated in particular departments, notably law.

As a reminder of the need to consult a variety of sources, Jenny McEwan (née Bennett, Law, 1970–73) had a different experience: 'Many of my friends in Law were like me – old style grammar school children of single parent families. ... We thought ourselves more proletarian than students reading English or Sociology.' She was to become Professor of Law in Exeter. Statistically, the percentage of students with parents with professional or managerial jobs rose from under 20 per cent in the late 1950s to 42 per cent in 1968.[44] Sue Odell, who arrived in 1966 to study French and German, recalls that Exeter was the

> sort of university that middle-class parents from the South East liked to send their daughters to! When my friend and I came for interview, our mothers came down on the train with us. ... High grades needed for entry and high standards were expected. We worked very hard, especially in Year 1. There was a huge literature reading list and good spoken French was essential. Teaching methods varied, from seemingly elderly lecturers who read from their notes, to Roger Pensom who sang part of the *Chanson de Roland* to us![45] It was very formal – students were addressed as 'Mr'

or 'Miss' plus surname. Exam results were read out by Professor Niklaus at end of year and this could be excruciating. ... I spent three years in Lopes, known as the girls' public school hall, just as Mardon was the boys' public school hall.[46] There were strict visiting hours and boyfriends used to hide in wardrobes when Miss Ross[47] prowled, or get out of the window. I wasn't from a public school but the Warden liked the letter I wrote and had also previously had our Head Girl as a student. ... We all used to have a University green and white scarf. ... The campus and city were lovely, and trips to the seaside were on the agenda after exams. ... There were summer balls, in Hall and University, and we dressed formally for such occasions. Rag Week was quite something and I remember attending a pyjama breakfast in Princesshay in aid of it. I was a member of the Gilbert and Sullivan Society and University Singers and other musical groups. The French department performed a play every year and I appeared in one. We had a Medieval/Renaissance afternoon one year in Queen's quadrangle as part of which I sang in a Chansons group and did some Renaissance dancing (organised by Keith Cameron). The Academic Registrar played the crumhorn![48]

James Jones also 'enjoyed the Gilbert and Sullivan Society greatly', and led off his reminiscences accordingly. He provided a testimony to an important strand in the university life, and notably in its early decades, one that it is easy to overlook, namely the role of Christian fellowship:

Although I was a member of the Anglican Fellowship[49] I was also a member of the Christian Union. In those days the two were the polar opposite of each other. I had been brought up an Anglican and its liturgy nourished my faith. However, I also had a profound spiritual experience after listening to a speaker at one of the Christian Union meetings. I remember hearing the Baptist Minister, Leith Samuel, speak about the encounter Nicodemus had with Jesus. The speaker talked about the experience of being born again. I remember going back to my room in Raddon House in Birks Halls and kneeling by my bed and saying to God that I was sure that I was Christian but I had never heard about such a thing of being born again. ... By being a member of AngFell and CU I hoped to show that not everyone in the CU was necessarily a bigot and that you could still have a living and evangelistic faith as a member of the Anglican Fellowship and the Church of England.[50]

Jones, who became Bishop of Liverpool in 1998, indicates not only the strength of the Christian theme, one also seen in the Lazenby Chaplaincy, in the survival of the Theology department and its Christian character, as well as in the role of successive Bishops of Exeter on Council.[51] The Lazenby Chaplaincy was a bequest established in 1954. It was a Church of England role, in association with, but not strictly part of, the university, because of the university's non-denominational status. John Thurmer, the Lazenby Chaplain from 1964 to 1973, had a remit to offer both Church of England and interdenominational services in the Chapel. This he did with a Sung Eucharist on Sundays at 10 am (style moderate High Church) followed by a coffee break in Devonshire House, and a University Sermon at 11.30, delivered by a wide range of preachers in a short devotional setting. The former attracted a congregation of usually over 100 but most left after coffee. Thurmer was also a part-time lecturer of Theology and in History. Thurmer's successor, Ken Moss, found that having a chapel and an established congregation ensured that it was possible to gather an 'identifiable community' in a manner not possible in most universities. The same was true for the Catholic Chaplaincy.[52]

Jones's activities also reflected the variety of university life, which, he felt, 'had all the feel of a cosmopolitan village' with 'a strong sense of belonging' and 'the feel of being a unity in itself'. He was active in the Chapel choir and was involved in the Debating Society and in Dramsoc. Jones offered another instructive reflection, 'the older I get the more I appreciate those student days'.[53] Katharine Weale (English and French, 1965–68) shared this commitment to Christianity (she was Chairman of the Anglican Fellowship) and an interest in music, notably chamber music. She also noted an aspect of the gender dynamics of student society:

> In those days the Summer Ball was the social highlight, but the convention was that a girl waited to be asked by a boy, and that didn't happen to me until my third year. I was glad for my own

THE LATER 1960S: SOCIAL CHANGE

daughters that, by the time they went to university, they could simply go in groups of friends.[54]

University life meant new experiences. Christopher French (Economics and Economic History, 1965–68, and postgraduate 1968–72) noted:

> Most of the students came from the grammar schools created by the Education Act of 1944 and the one thing we had in common was the realisation that for the first time we were free to do what we wanted to – within reason, of course.

With his 'local authority grant, topped up by a parental contribution assessed by income', French had £50 per term as spending money which he found perfectly manageable as beer was about 1/6d (7½ new pence) per pint. He had his first experience of eating curry at The Taj Mahal, a restaurant very popular with students.[55]

Going to pubs remained a key element of socialising, not least because of limited opportunities for drinking in halls, other than pre-dinner. Pub culture was important. The Black Horse was the major student pub when Bob Higham arrived. It was a pub in a part of the town where many students lived, whereas now the major pub, the Imperial, is further from the town centre and in effect an extension of the campus. Ironically, the university had passed up the opportunity to purchase the former hotel. As a reminder of the finely grained nature of pub life, Higham added that the student Archaeology Society had its 'own' pub, the White Hart in South Street. The Arts postgraduates met every Friday evening at the Prospect Inn 'drinking large amounts of Guinness'.[56]

Departmental autonomy remained the order of the day, as throughout into the 1980s. This was an autonomy of autocrats. In her unsuccessful attempt to make Archaeology independent of History, Aileen Fox found Cook sympathetic 'but we both knew that he could not intervene to overrule the wishes of the head of a department', in this case the unsympathetic Barlow.[57] On 28 April 1965, the Board of the Faculty of Arts postponed a decision on the proposal for a separate department of Archaeology as concerns were raised about its viability. Barlow had allowed Economic History to secede, hoping to dominate it, and found he had ended up with the difficult Walter Minchinton. The Chair had allegedly been intended for W.G. Hoskins, a very distinguished local historian and a graduate of the university, but a libel case over his probably well-grounded suggestions about the City's attitude to planning permissions possibly led to a strong steer from the City against his appointment. If true, this story shows how far the university in the 1960s still felt itself part of a civic establishment. Minchinton was the third choice and demonstrated the age-old point that no appointment is better than a bad one. At any rate, Barlow was not going to lose Archaeology. As another instance of professorial power, there was a complaint in Senate on 6 November 1968 that non-professorial members of Botany and Zoology felt that they had not been sufficiently consulted about the conversion of the Washington Singer Laboratories.

Despite efforts, there was no coherent university plan, and each department submitted its own proposals for expansion. Occasionally, a new department would be created. The result was that the university grew as a collection of small academic units. Many departments were very small, only three or four staff. Russian became a separate department (no longer part of German), able to enrol Single Honours students when it gained its fourth member of staff. Small departments found it difficult to mount a proper degree programme, and some were even too small to contribute seriously to a Combined Honours degree. The range of teaching required therefore put pressure on research time. The situation was to be complicated by the proliferation of Centres, often completely detached from departments, and under no sort of control or supervision. These were little fiefdoms formed by anyone who could raise enough money for a letterhead and a notice on a door. Some were serious research centres, others more quixotic.

There was only scant control over, and coordination of, the departments. In practice, key decisions above the departmental level were made by the Standing Committee of Senate, a small body controlled by the VC and a few heads of department. Prior to the creation of the ADC, Standing Committee included vestigial planning in its pot-pourri of responsibilities. On 15 March 1969, this committee resolved not to change the Faculty system after a discussion in which one member presented Faculty Boards as unable to 'deal satisfactorily with matters of general University policy' while another 'considered that Faculty Boards at Exeter were weak and departments were often allowed to go their own way'. There were some attempts at coordination. In light, for example, of the UGC's view in 1968 of the under-utilisation of Exeter's lecture theatres, the Works Committee on 6 December recommended 'a unified time-table structure for the whole University, under which lecture theatres would be regarded as a University facility and not a departmental one'. Such an approach, however, came up against the pressure of departmental interests and power. Once the days of expansion were to end and the first 'cuts' in funding began, Exeter's profusion of small departments became a real problem, one that the university was ill-equipped to face up to. Prior to the 'cuts', however, there was scarcely a situation of plenty.

The close of the 1960s saw the corporatism and financial problems of the Labour government affect universities. The 1968 report of the National Board for Prices and Incomes (PIB) on the Pay of University Teachers worried both the CVCP and individual universities, including Exeter. The idea of merit awards by outside bodies was seen as invidious, and there was concern about the report encroaching on both the UGC and the universities.[58] A special meeting of Senate on 8 January 1969 expressed concern about the proposed concentration of research in a few universities, or university departments, designated by Research Councils. It was argued that this would benefit the larger universities and lead to the running down of research in other universities/departments, which would hit teaching there. Pressing for no shift in the teaching/research balance, Senate agreed that the PIB was the wrong body to consider questions of university policy. There was also opposition to proposals for toughening up probation and passing the Efficiency Bar, to discretionary payments for teaching, and to distinction awards to professors awarded by committees outside universities.

In late 1969, attention shifted to the Department of Education and Science (DES) demand for staff diaries linked to an enquiry into the use of academics' time. Again, this led to a Senate special meeting. Held on 29 November 1969, this meeting revealed reactions from outright anger and refusal to cooperate, to a reluctant consent. Barlow suggested that perhaps the time had come to make a stand against interference, but there was some support for the DES demand on the grounds that the government, as paymaster, was entitled to certain information and that staff presumably had nothing to hide. There was also the issue of confidentiality and, looking ahead to the 'List' controversy in 1977 under Kay, concern, if the scheme was introduced, about the existence of a list in Northcote House matching names and diary numbers.

In December 1969, there was another indication of scrutiny with a UGC letter about training in teaching. Senate, characteristically, felt that this could best be handled at the departmental level, where seniors could pass on their experience, and rejected the idea of formal courses of instruction.[59] Arriving in 1965, Havinden found that courses consisted of

> a one-hour lecture a week ... and three or four hourly seminar classes, each with about eight students in them. One student was supposed to read an essay followed by general discussion, but this proved rather boring, so I soon set the whole group a topic to be discussed. But this was only partly successful as some of the students would fail to do any background reading.[60]

The university continued to have international links, although political changes had sundered some with former colonies. However, the declaration of unilateral independence for Southern Rhodesia by a white supremacist group in 1965 was followed by the interests of the Politics department at the university there being taken up by Exeter: this led to a number of staff and students seeking refuge in Exeter, including Christopher Paterson who became the first sabbatical Guild officer. There were also links with Europe and the USA, although not on a major scale. Arriving to teach English in 1971, Peter Faulkner 'was impressed by the existence of the one-year *Testamur* course for overseas – mostly European – students, established ... in the spirit of post-war internationalism. It always ended with the performance of a Shakespeare play in the gardens of Reed Hall. There was also a Summer School for overseas students, in which I participated to a small degree.'[61] Faulkner's account of his department serves as an appropriate summary of the departmental level of the university at this stage:

> [T]he university was still run largely by the professoriate, with Moelwyn Merchant as Head of the English department. Staff

THE LATER 1960S: SOCIAL CHANGE

meetings took place in his room, emphasising his position, but in my memory discussion was fairly free – though decisions were largely his. My impression was that it was a good department, comparable to the one I had left in Durham; although the atmosphere was relaxed – the occasional game of billiards in the afternoon at the Staff Club – my colleagues were keen teachers, and we had good students – the popularity of the university meant that we could require high grades from applicants. There was a range of interesting Combined Honours courses, with Music, Philosophy and Fine Art (taught at the Exeter College of Art), while Drama and American Arts were taught in the department. There was little emphasis on research – the only person with an academic reputation was, I think, Maurice Evans – although people did pursue their own lines of scholarship. The general atmosphere was convivial.[62]

Eric Homberger, who had a temporary post teaching American literature in 1969–70, found 'the atmosphere in Exeter ... conservative, but somewhat lacking the disagreeable *amour proper* which seemed so characteristic of the English faculty at Cambridge' from which he had come.[63]

The general staff view was that Exeter was pleasant but, despite containing quite a few people of academic distinction, somewhat of an academic backwater, with meagre resources, but a strong spirit of collegiality. A serious intellectual enterprise, the university provided a fundamentally benign and industrious system. There was not a strong emphasis on publication. For example, David Horrox (English), who lectured once a week, claimed that too many books were written and did not purchase works of criticism for the Library; while Duncan Mitchell (Sociology) did not encourage grant applications, an attitude that on the part of some continued until the 1980s. In contrast, Victor Wiseman (Politics) argued that the university had to come to terms with a changing environment, notably the rise of the UGC and of the Social Sciences Research Council. While other professors talked of academic freedom, Wiseman emphasised that accountability for the expenditure of public money was coming and that government would have a view on how the money was spent.

The students, some of whom were Oxbridge rejects, were bright and articulate, and had a strong sporting reputation. Many worked quite hard. Relations with staff were good. Higham recalls: '[T]he worst sin which one could commit was not to attend one's essay tutorial: absence was not only a dereliction of academic duty but (perhaps more important) very discourteous to one's tutor.' Higham, who went on to teach at the university until 2003, contrasts 1968 when, he suggests, students were treated as adults, with a modern situation in which students are regarded as less mature and, as a result of 'the new industries of health and safety, data protection and so on', provided with more protection by the authorities.

At the staff level, there was, in the late 1960s, a 'pervasive complacency', which owed much to the relative ease in recruiting staff and students, and to the extent to which the city was small, comfortable and peaceful. Michael Duffy, who arrived to teach History in 1969, adds the key point that 'the stringent nature of Exeter's finances handicapped any thoughts to achieve much more. Exeter was Sleepy Hollow!'[64] A somewhat different perspective was provided the previous year by George Greenaway when he gave a 'Valedictory Address' at the end of nearly four decades of teaching. Although by then his scholarship was venerable, the hardworking Greenaway still had an ability to enthuse the students. Having commented briefly on the impact of the Depression in the 1930s, he added:

> Over the years I have observed the students becoming more mature, more adaptable, gayer and more light-hearted, their expectations and experience of life more sophisticated and expansive, their sartorial creations shabbier and more curtailed but their human interests, hopes and fears essentially the same. The pace of academic life both for staff and students has of course increased but the basic realities of our mutual relations remain unchanged.[65]

CHAPTER FIVE

THE EARLY 1970S: THE BRAKES GO ON

I met my future wife on the boat from Cape Town to Southampton. ... To help pay for myself I acted as an agent for someone in South Africa and bought for them a Porsche. At that time you could not buy luxury cars in South Africa, but I could and then bring one back. I had to run up some mileage so did from time to time drive it to campus. In those days not many people had cars on campus, most certainly not Porsches. I used to get notes inviting me to 'tea' or pubs etc to meet the scribe. I loyally turned these down until one day I noticed an attractive girl tucking it under the wiper and decided I would follow up. That night my future wife's roommate in London told her that her sister at Exeter University had met this fabulous guy from South Africa with a Porsche. My wife was on the next train down from Paddington and my social life was very clipped after that.
Robert Estcourt (Finance MA, 1972/73)

It was asked – in view of the anticipated 70 vacant places in Hall ... whether it were not possible to insist that all first-year students took up residence in Halls. It was agreed that, strictly speaking, the University could so direct its students, but it was thought that such direction would be both impracticable and impolitic, bearing in mind the present age of majority [18] and the current climate of social opinion.
Council, 18 December 1972.

MOST STUDENTS AT the time were unaware of the difficulties and uncertainties affecting the operation of the university in the 1970s. In reality, the optimism of the Swinging Sixties, the later 1960s, always an optimism in fact conditioned by concerns, notably about money, ran out in the more austere early 1970s. A series of blows hit the national and global economy, and Britain itself faced a crisis of governability by 1973–74, with the Heath government of 1970–74 unable to surmount successive shocks. This situation was also to engulf its Labour successor (1974–79), notably in 1974–76 and, with remorseless finality, 1978–79.

The universities were greatly affected by these successive and cumulative crises, not least because they lacked financial independence. There was a general restriction on public expenditure and a persistent sense of uncertainty over its future levels. The 1973–74 oil crisis ended the relative stability offered by quinquennial (five-year) funding. This situation was exacerbated by a marked build-up in inflationary pressures. These pressures made the level of governmental support for universities more urgent. Harry Kay, the new VC, told the Board of Senate on 31 October 1973 that it was impossible to make very detailed plans for expansion for more than a year ahead due to reliance on the level of supplementary grants given by government in order to counter the effects of inflation. Repeatedly, these were inadequate.[1]

The sense of crisis was driven home by a rise in industrial militancy. Whereas action by unions present on the campus attracted the more immediate attention, there was also a serious knock-on effect from labour disputes in the energy section. As a result of concerns about oil supplies and power cuts,[2] the very ability to keep the university lit and heated came into question, leading to a series of preparations and expedients, including staff starting work earlier in the day. The added cost of energy contributed to Exeter's financial crisis and to the specific financial problems of the halls,[3] problems that posed a challenge to the student experience of 'living in'. Moreover, a shortage of building materials delayed work on what was to be the Amory Building,[4] while the Biosciences building that was designed to go in next to Amory was not built. In the meanwhile, Robert Estcourt noted in 1972/73 the reliance on temporary accommodation: '[T]here were still demountables [prefabs] used as offices all over the campus and all our tutorials were in

THE EARLY 1970S: THE BRAKES GO ON

rooms in them. I do wonder whether students realise the luxury they live in these days. So, although the campus was already very attractive, it was a little more rudimentary.'[5]

At the levels of finance and viability, there were basic questions about the situation of the university in the short and medium terms, let alone the long term, questions that affected activity and attitudes across the entire range of the university. Crisis management entailed handling financial difficulties (usually arising from government policy) and balancing the books as best as possible, so that the university could remain a going concern. The university was coming from a position of very poor UGC funding, with little fat, few endowments, and hardly any significant local economy that could sustain and subsidise it, factors which should be considered when assessing policy and performance. In addition, the UGC and Council fiercely insisted that the university should balance its books and not run deficits. There was little scope for borrowing, except for ring-fenced income-generating projects such as the Lafrowda residences. Nor was there much scope for recruiting large numbers of high-fee-paying overseas students. Nor, before the legislation weakening tenure, was there a serious prospect of getting rid of staff except through early retirement or the actual closure of departments. By present standards, these were fundamental constraints on management.

In the 1970s, in place of the expansion, new buildings and hiring of the 1960s, came contraction, maintenance and staff losses, which came to play a major role on the agenda. Indeed, the issue of whether it would be possible to create a more viable staffing model without sacking staff assumed a totemic significance in the history of the university in the 1970s and 1980s that was only finally ended by the 2004/05 restructuring. In many respects, this situation proved a classic instance of the way in which issues that were short term and tactical swallowed up those that were long term and strategic. A disproportionate amount of management time and effort was to be spent on negotiating early retirements, and the resulting policy issues bulked large in the politics of the institution. Behind much of the rhetoric about democracy, accountability and collegiality, and much of the opposition to selectivity and management, there was a stark struggle about jobs. For universities, there is an intellectual and pedagogic need to ensure a continual transition, one in which new staff, mostly younger staff with new ideas, are brought in, but there can be a blank over this issue from those interviewed today.

Drawing on an 'us' and 'them' dichotomy, with 'them' being a conflation of Northcote House and the outside world, in the shape of government and the UGC, there is frequent reference to the strength of a staff culture in which work was combined with collegiality. Staff cricket in the shape in particular of the Erratics, the staff team established in 1934, plays a major role in accounts of the latter. Players included Frank Barlow (ninety-six games between 1947 and 1954), and David Walker, Professor of Economics. There was also a non-academics team called the Nomads. The Chemistry department fielded two teams, the Cooks (Physical Chemists) and the Bottle Washers (the Preparative Chemists), who combined as the Chemics.[6] In the interviews, in addition to an informed perception of academic activity, there is a nostalgia for youth, good fellowship, and a world in which there always seemed to be time and mutual understanding. Richard Hitchcock (Spanish) recalls:

> [A] marked atmosphere of collegiality in the Queen's Building. Colleagues from all departments would gather for coffee in the mornings, and many also for tea in the afternoons. Apart from members of the department of History who tended to converse mainly amongst themselves,[7] there was no sense of strictly departmental gatherings. Linguists, theologians, Classicists, and those from English mixed and chatted freely. The only segregation that was observed was between smokers and non-smokers. There may have been some gossip, but my firm recollection is of discussions relating to specific often academic topics. Colleagues were happy to be approached for their expertise. To some extent, senior professors, of French, Theology or English, for example, would hold court. We, the younger ones, got the impression that we were working towards a collective common goal. In this pursuit, the administration was there to help us in our endeavours.[8]

To Hitchcock, this harmony was 'brought to an abrupt close in 1977' due to the List affair (see p. 99) and the realisation that the administration, seeing the academics as different, was keeping information on them.[9] The value of the Common Room atmosphere was also recalled

THE EARLY 1970S: THE BRAKES GO ON

by Roger Cockrell who arrived to teach Russian in 1965 and records the gathering 'around the large central table over coffee time, during which there was a genuine interaction between different disciplines'.[10] This was a collegial, unmanaged interdisciplinarity, and one that worked. Common Room life also offered a safety valve.[11] In part, the collective culture was a response to bullying conduct by certain departmental heads, as well as being a way to ease the nature of hierarchy.

Meanwhile, there was a marked change of practice in the case of the Library. Although opened as recently as 1965, the Library was inadequate and was often cited as how not to design one. John Llewellyn, appointed VC in 1966, wanted a larger new library and, in order to have it planned properly, appointed John Stirling, a professional librarian with experience of running a university library, and had him serve as Librarian Designate in 1971/72, even though John Lloyd, University Librarian from 1946, remained in office until he retired in 1972. Given Lloyd's prominence in accounts of 'old Exeter', notably as captain of the Erratics (he kept the score books in the Library strong-room safe), it is instructive to note Stirling's comments that Lloyd, a former member of the English department with no professional training, was not only a gentleman and scholar, the theme in Brian Clapp's 1982 history,[12] rather than a librarian, but also far from a hard worker. Lloyd, who is reputed to have said that he thought the library had enough books and did not need any more, fitted a very long lunch into his 10 am–4 pm day, and spent much of the time on Friday afternoons, when he was supposedly in the Cathedral Library working on a history of the Cathedral, in Tinley's Tea Rooms,[13] a building which now houses Pizza Express.

There was also a tension between the money Lloyd wanted to spend on a new Library, and the roughly 60 per cent of this sum that the UGC was willing to finance, as well as between Lloyd's preference for privacy for readers and Stirling's advocacy of large open spaces. The latter matched professional commitment to a flexible space. In the event, the major use of automation in the new Library (opened in 1983) showed that Stirling's insistence on a flexible, modular design for the Library, and on the provision of trunking throughout for computer cabling, was fully justified. The Library therefore provided an early instance of the change and modernisation that was to be introduced more slowly in the more complex and politicised environment of the university as a whole. Stirling was also instrumental in setting up the system of Subject Librarians. They were visible (their offices were among the book stacks) and in general had close relations with academics and students, especially postgraduates. This effective system contributed to high student satisfaction scores for the Library in the mid-2000s,[14] but was then discarded.

Alongside collective culture, external pressures provided both context and constraints for the university. Financial issues were a problem for Exeter from the outset of the decade. On its visit of 3 February 1970, 'the UGC accepted that the University was under-financed', as it had been from its foundation when the very limited endowment of the University College was only modestly enhanced by the UGC. Addressing the specific issue of student residences in 1970, the UGC said that universities should not expect capital grants, but rather must seek loans on the open market. However, high interest rates reduced the viability of such a policy.[15] At this stage, it was clear that it would be difficult to fund the major expansion that was still anticipated. The UGC indicated that by 1976/77 there would be 310,000 students in UK universities and, by 1980, a capacity for 400,000 students. Exeter was offered a provisional target for 1976/77 of 3,100 in Arts-based courses and 1,700 in Science-based ones, a shift towards the Arts.

Arriving from Swansea in 1970 to be Professor of Social Administration, Robert Leaper found 'a rather cosy place of people who had connections with Oxbridge'. He thought Reed Hall a good staff club and was impressed by the positive relations between academics and administrators.[16] Some new staff were professors and had experience elsewhere of the hierarchical and deferential 1950s and early 1960s, as well as of its sub-Oxbridge ethos. However, many of the new staff, although not as militant as their counterparts in the LSE or Manchester, had an almost instinctual reaction against authority. The 1970s saw an upsurge in the attitudes and pressure usually associated with the 1960s. Student activism was present in Exeter, but so also was activism on the staff side.

The permanent control exercised by professorial heads of department proved the crucial issue; although it was but one of a series of interlinked topics, notably staff representation on Senate and, to a lesser extent, Council. The pressure was democratic in its thesis, but far more was involved. In part, there was a drive to give the staff power and to move authority from the executive, in the shape of Northcote House, to an overseeing legislature, in the shape of a strengthened Senate. In part, the drive reflected specific pressures at the departmental level, notably dissatisfaction with particular Heads, especially Walter Minchinton (Economic History). Other Heads, while not vicious, were arrogant and rigid. Arriving from Durham to be Professor and Head of German in 1972, Gar [Edgar] Yates

> did not get the impression of arriving at a university of much academic distinction, and the standard of students I first encountered ranged from very good to some weaker than I was used to. ... The powerful HoDs seemed to me, coming as I did from a much more democratically run Faculty in Durham, an anachronism: paternalistic and autocratic. Even encouragement of younger colleagues to get on with significant research was not universal.[17]

Arriving to teach Politics in 1971, Iain Hampsher-Monk recalls:

> Professorial Fiefdoms ... Clifford Parker, Professor of Law (and one unto himself) and G. Duncan Mitchell in Sociology (a man who had contrived to write a book entitled *A Hundred Years of Sociology* without more than a passing mention of Marx) both patriarchs of a pretty antediluvian stripe. ...[18] Under these men Exeter thought pretty highly of itself, and indeed managed to project this estimation on the kinds of informal rankings that predated the RAE [Research Assessment Exercise]. That ranking did not survive the advent of the first RAE.

With his LSE degree, his wide teaching experience and his publication of a number of books, the somewhat pompous Mitchell was in fact an academic of some note. Hampsher-Monk links professorial power to departmental autonomy and anachronistic practices. In the case of the History/Politics Combined Honours:

> [W]when the Politics representative presented their marks, as required by University regulations, in percentage terms, Professor

Barlow affected not to understand their meaning or relationship to degree classification, pointedly enquiring whether a 69 was 'really' an 'Alpha?–' or a 'Beta++'? In the end someone was assigned to stand next to him to 'translate'. There was no algorithm for deriving a degree classification – the marks were read out and someone was invited to 'propose' a class which was then debated. Class boundaries were vigorously defended. The default position for marginal cases was the lower category.

Barlow, who retired in 1976, reflected around then on the state of the universities and country. He argued that authority should always be challenged, but wrote critically about a middle-class élite whom, he claimed, had chosen to ape the working classes. Barlow also pressed for 'Fundamental Research' and 'Fearless Teaching'. While Barlow 'could barely conceal his impatience' with the Staff–Student Committee and the students on it, he was 'almost warm' to those involved in the History Society.[19] The exam questions during this period were certainly of a type. The paper on 'The Reign of George V' (not set by Barlow) included such joys as 'What weaknesses in the coal industry are shown in the Interim Report of the Coal Commission, 1919?'. Barlow's personal relations with Minchinton were so bad that the two departments shared little in common. However, there were also sociocultural and institutional-intellectual factors. Whereas Barlow was very much a Oxford product, and in a largely Oxbridge university, Minchinton, like most of Economic History, was non-Oxbridge. Indeed, the LSE played a key role in its background and ethos.

The situation in an individual department could change with a new Head. Politics was much happier under the very supportive, encouraging, social and hyperactive Wiseman (1963–69), a noted drinker who died in the Houses of Parliament while on a visit to attend a committee, than under Tony Birch (1970–77), a good academic who was not a people person.[20] Eddie Abel, as first Professor of Inorganic Chemistry, arriving from Bristol in 1972, found Exeter more hierarchical and the Head, Rydon, 'a terror' who ran the department 'overtightly'. At morning coffee in Chemistry, everyone was addressed by surnames, although gowns were not worn.[21]

Dissatisfaction over departmental heads was to fuel a debate over departmental governance. Much of this debate was to be conducted later in the decade, with the COSGOD (Composition of Senate and Government of Departments) proposals, accepted in 1979, being the key element; but the parameters were set in the early 1970s. So also with the contrast between the public narrative of the politics of the decade and the more complex inner reality. The public narrative, retold in many interviews, is of a struggle against an anachronistic system of authoritarian professors and their inappropriate governance. This account provides a way to link the earlier position in the university, as originally established, with a story of long-term pressure for more democratic governance. Moreover, present and past can be related in this account, however ahistorically. This account clearly meant, and still means, much to a group who variously saw themselves as reformers, modernisers and radicals. It was one of authority overthrown, the excitement of Paris, or, at least, the LSE, in the groves of Exeter.

As with most accounts, this one contained a degree of truth, while the very belief in it made it significant in the political culture of the institution and prepared the way for the very varied politics of subsequent decades. At the same time, this account failed to capture several key elements. First, there was no coherent, consistent and unchanging *ancien régime*, a situation that was more generally the case. Indeed, instead of the commonplace idea of a clash between a reforming radicalism and a rigid conservatism, the system proved more flexible; and, in practice, on the side of both radicals and conservatives.

In part, this flexibility was because the professoriate itself was changing greatly. As professors who were not heads of department were appointed (at first with great hesitation, but then more frequently, with many departments acquiring a second professor), so the automatic relationship between the two positions was broken. In addition, some professorial Heads clearly became fed up with running departments. The task was far greater than it had been in the early 1960s, in large part because departments had become larger, while the younger members of staff they now contained posed problems, not least as a result of their greater independence. Deference was a passing habit, not least because the experience of military service had been replaced by that of campus life in the 1960s and 1970s. The austere Henry Garland, who retired in 1972, would have noted a different university to that he had joined in

1947. His retirement was one of a large number in the 1970s, as staff went who could remember the University College and had served under VC James Cook in a senior capacity.

The character of the university at this period is recalled by David Gladstone, who arrived in 1973 as Lecturer in Social Administration in the department of Sociology:

> [T]here was still an 'old guard' hierarchical presence. ... Many had been in post for a considerable time and had shaped the ethos of the University. The ethos they shaped manifested itself in a number of ways:
>
> 1. The beginning of year University Service in the Cathedral with a procession from Gandy Street as a reminder of the University's origins.
> 2. Regular formal dinners with High Tables in Halls of Residence.
> 3. The University Ladies Club – the implication was that staff were male and ladies were wives who wore badges with their husband's designation and department.
> 4. Restriction on the Staff Club to academics and academic related staff above a certain grade. Initially the Staff Club was waitress service only.
> 5. Daily gatherings of coteries of academics in the Club on a regular basis and "long" lunches through from 12.30 to 2 pm.
>
> The influx of younger staff (often from non-Oxbridge backgrounds) from the mid-1960s meant a significant bifurcation in the University's tradition and ethos.[22]

In 1970, Senate, which was dominated by professors, opposed proposals to increase the representation of members elected by the Readers and Lecturers Association (RLA). However, alongside the wish of some professors to maintain the prerogatives of power, the recession of the 1970s made running a department and helping direct a university less attractive tasks. If the *ancien régime* was not totally rigid at the professorial level, the VC scarcely behaved like the austere Cook. Indeed, with his interest in national trends, Llewellyn was open to new ideas of governance. If the staff radicals encountered opposition, it was not to the idea

THE EARLY 1970S: THE BRAKES GO ON

of change, but to certain of the themes and ideas they proposed. Bruce Coleman noted a mixture of conservatism and innovation:

> Exeter struck me as small, provincial, inward-looking and often idiosyncratic ... here was a sense of limited horizons and even of self-satisfaction. ... The proposal under consideration in 1970/1 to increase student numbers from 3,750 to 4,100 was met with much doom-saying, though some heads of department fancied the prospect of extra staffing and it happened. The student body was even more conservative than the staff. ... Another aspect that struck me (particularly after Cambridge) was the [high] proportion of female students [a point noted by many contemporaries]. ... That Exeter was always seen as a good university for girls (safe environment etc) served it well over decades in which female participation in HE rose faster than male participation. Academically Exeter was quite interesting, even innovative. Though Single Honours degrees recruited the bulk of students, Exeter had the widest range in the country of Combined Honours programmes'.[23]

This number may have been a necessity due to the number of small departments. The range of Combined Honours programmes has been a very significant source of strength to Exeter. It culminated in the success of the Modular Degree, an initiative which began with the RLA-derived Teaching Select Committee in the late 1980s. The Interdepartmental Single Honours Degree, which was to be significant in the late 1970s and early 1980s, and the Combined Honours provision were both important, not least in mitigating some of the insularities and insecurities of small departments and compromising the power of departmental heads. These degrees, however, tended to get completely obscured in university planning and reporting mechanisms which were usually constructed as if only Single Honours subjects existed. There was a recurrent tendency, especially by DVCs lacking experience of running programmes, to assume that Combined Honours degrees were annoying minority activities which would ideally be swept aside to create 'simpler' structures, but they never got their way.

There were also scholarly achievements of note. In Geography, catchment studies developed. These had begun in the mid-1960s with Ken Gregory and Des Walling working on the headwaters of the Rivers Otter and Sid, before work in the late 1960s on the Rosebarn catchment, which documented the impact of building construction on runoff and settlement dynamics. In the early 1970s, attention shifted to the Exe basin. A catchment-wide monitoring network that at its peak included twenty measuring stations was established and remained in operation until 2010. During this period, thirty-five PhD theses were based on the basin, while many postdoctoral fellows were involved. The research resulted in many important advances relating to monitoring suspended sediment loads, sediment and solute dynamics, water temperature behaviour, sediment sources, and quality and floodplain sedimentation. Walling was to secure a £3.7 million extension to the Amory Building (which provided a purpose-built Geography department) from the Science Research Infrastructure Fund for Sediment Research Faculty that included a purpose-build radionuclide laboratory, other new laboratories and an experimental hall.

In the early 1970s, Law attained an intellectual and pedagogic eminence and impact that most Exeter departments lacked in these years. Whereas Clifford Parker, the permanent Head (and Dean), had resisted change and expansion and had a very limited view of legal education, development was pushed forward by new young staff and, in particular, the greater influence of Dominik Lasok, who gained the new chair. Subsequently, the move of Law to the Amory Building and the establishment of a third chair, for John Bridge, both in 1974, proved significant. Under Lasok's leadership, the LLB syllabus was broadened, and new LLB degrees, incorporating French or German law and study abroad, were introduced, as were innovative one-year LLM-themed courses. All of these initiatives put Exeter on the map as a pioneer in legal education. A recurring theme of these developments was the law of the European Community, and Exeter was the first English law school to make that a compulsory subject for the LLB. The publication of Lasok and Bridge's *Law and Institutions of the European Community*, which went to six revised editions between 1973 and 1993, was significant, as this was one of the earliest books on European Community law for English students. There was also important Exeter involvement in the establishment, in 1975, of the *European Law Review*, the leading English-language scholarly journal in the field. These changes brought a much larger staff and a very much larger and varied student body, including a flourish graduate research school, all from a wide range of countries. The links with the profession also adapted. From the beginning of the UK membership of the European Community in 1973, annual residential courses in European Community law for practising lawyers were held with considerable success.[24]

Another area of significant development was in statistics, under the leadership of John Ashford, who had become the university's first Professor of Statistics in 1967 and who was responsible for the department of Mathematical Statistics and Operational Research (MSOR) formed in 1974. Building up teaching and research in statistics, and expanding statistics to embrace Operational Research, Ashford was quick to see and exploit the potential of computers to analyse large sets of data, and actively developed national and international research collaboration, mainly in medical statistics and epidemiology. Providing a prime example of research-led teaching, MSOR was one of the first UK departments to incorporate Operational Research into the undergraduate curriculum, which contributed greatly to a high employment rate for the department's graduates.

The cutting-edge had a range of manifestations. Studying contemporary American performance art as a postgraduate under Mike Weaver, the founder of the sub-department of American and Commonwealth Arts and of the university's Audio-Visual Library, David Mayor recalls

> performing a piece by George Brecht called *Two Durations* at a Fluxconcert in the Students' Union which entailed drinking a bottle of red wine and eating a green salad. After that (rather drunk!) I performed another piece by Korean artist Nam June Paik, using my (long) hair to paint an ever-unrolling roll of newsprint that snaked its way through the building and out of the door ... I don't remember what happened after that.[25]

Weaver made important innovative advances in the teaching of film.[26]

Meanwhile, at the student level, there was a measure of radicalism, but that is far from the complete story of these years. Visiting hours remained a key issue. A Working Party of the Joint Committee on Residence Hall Visiting Hours that met in early 1970 concluded, in a concession to changing mores, that 'Visiting hours cannot, and should not, be a means of controlling the sexual behaviour of students', but presented the regulations as a way to prevent nuisance and noise, and to provide security. The first meeting, held on 14 January 1970, revealed a certain conservatism as well as capturing the extent to which a number of social contexts were necessarily at play:

> Some members thought that the existence of visiting hours was interpreted by the general public, including prospective students and their parents, as a sign of good order and of restraint in sexual behaviour. Abolition of visiting hours might tend to give the University an aura of disorderliness which would discourage prospective students and be an embarrassment to Exeter graduates. Most members agreed that since the University was maintained by public funds, it must have some regard for public opinion. Other members of the Working Party thought, however, that the impression which the University made on the general public had no connection with the existence or otherwise of visiting hours.

The discussion included an acceptance that 'early hours of the morning', the compromise advanced by Keith Conn, was capable of various interpretation. Some wardens continued into the 1970s to define *in loco parentis* very firmly. 'Maternal morality' was the position frequently adopted toward the female students, notably at Lopes and at Thomas. In contrast, the women wardens in Birks and Duryard had to adopt a *laissez-faire* attitude, because they were on a mixed campus and could not control what happened.

Pressure for change was increased by a series of Extraordinary General Meetings (EGMs) of the Guild, heady gatherings. That of over 400 members held on 18 February 1970 agreed to pay any fines imposed under the regulations and thus to try to negate their impact. A concerned Viscount Amory, the Chair of Council, warned that 'the long period of good relations' with the student body was at risk.[27] Indeed, under pressure from radical students, the Guild conducted a referendum on whether to take 'direct action': 329 voted for, 586 against, 116 voting papers were spoilt, and a further 214 had been lost when a ballot box had been removed and subsequently destroyed – it was allegedly thrown into the river. An EGM of over 800 students overwhelmingly rejected the proposed rules requiring guests to leave by the early hours and denying them access before 11 am. The Guild Executive then resigned because the Working Party Report it had negotiated had been rejected, and because the Executive's action in reporting the theft of the ballot box had not been supported by the EGM. The Executive also objected strongly to the pressure from militant elements whom they claimed were unrepresentative of the student body as a whole, an approach that was frequently to be taken by the university authorities, and notably during the sit-ins later in the decade.

The governability of the Guild was at issue as, subsequently, that of the university was to be. The relationship between executive and legislature was to be a vexed topic in each case, one compounded for the Guild by the annual change in its Executive. Moreover, the Guild Executive was generally a collection of individuals, with different affiliations; it lacked coherence. Questions of accountability and mandates can be found in the rhetoric, politics and governance of both university and Guild. Levels of maturity, notably understanding and acceptance of consequences, were not as apparent as might have been anticipated.

The student militants themselves had elected four representatives to convey to Senate their objections to the Working Party Report. On 11 March 1970, Senate agreed to the recommendations of the Working Party and, in an invitation to be more liberal, 'that the regulations should be operated with understanding and such flexibility as the circumstances of individual Halls made possible'.

On the ground, the situation was moving. An Appeals Committee on 22 November 1971 heard the case of a first-year Theology student at Raddon Hall in which the Warden 'found a girl' in the bed of a student, who was fined only 'a nominal sum of £1'. The appeal was dismissed. Drugs were also an area of change. On 25 February 1970, Standing Committee agreed to a Guild request to change the rules requiring an automatic suspension of a student convicted of a drug offence prior to their case being considered by the Disciplinary Board. Double jeopardy, punishing students already considered by the legal system, was a much-contested issue, one that drugs had brought to the fore in the

1960s. This issue meant that the actual right of the university to police its students was not at the centre of attention, but it was to be a topic that increased tension.

Student representation in university governance developed, at a modest level, when Senate, on 11 February 1970, agreed on a twenty-six-strong University Committee, a new body, including thirteen students. The Guild, however, refused to participate in the Committee, which it correctly saw as a stop-gap, and, instead, sought representation on Council in order to play a role in financial policy and that over new buildings. The latter was of great consequence as there was room for debate over whether to focus on student residences or on departmental buildings. Amory, who chaired the second meeting of the Working Party to consider representation, however, felt the students lacked 'real conviction' and argued that representation would be affected by a lack of continuity by individual members, who could not be treated as delegates.

The Guild EGMs of 18, 20 and 23 February and 3 March 1970, and the AGM of 4 March 1970, had built up a head of steam over a range of issues including Library weekend opening, student records, and university teaching standards. The concessions offered in March reduced the tension. Weekend opening was agreed, and Llewellyn provided an assurance that there were no secret files. On 11 March, Senate rejected the Guild's recommendations over ensuring teaching standards,[28] while, that June, the Joint Committee on Residence rejected the request to discontinue the wearing of gowns at formal meals. In October 1971, however, the more accommodating Standing Committee agreed, in response to a new request, to recommend that each hall should make its own rules for formal meals, and that otherwise gowns should only be worn at Degree Congregations.

Far more radical in the 1960s and 1970s than it was to be in the 2000s, the Guild, nevertheless, continued into the 1970/71 academic year to refuse to attend the new University Committee, in protest at students' exclusion from decision-making bodies.[29] On 24 November 1970, about 100 students presented at Northcote House the Guild's demands for 50 per cent representation on Senate and on the Joint Selection Committee for the office of VC, and 33⅓ per cent on Council, after which they dispersed quietly. Presenting these proposals as amounting to control, Senate formally rejected them in February 1971, but went on, in March, to accept participation in the deliberations and decisions of Senate and its committees, while being uncertain whether students would be mandated representatives of the Guild or independent. Council accepted the same principle.[30]

The extent of student participation was contentious. Senate finally agreed in May 1971 that six students would serve on a new Board of Senate, which would meet before Senate and deal with all unreserved business. Senate would then confirm the decisions taken without further discussion. The Guild, however, reiterated that autumn that 50 per cent remained its ultimate objective and that it wanted the new system reviewed after a year.[31] An EGM on 28 February 1972 voted 251–217–9 to reaffirm the commitment to 50 per cent and to renegotiate accordingly, leading to the resignation of the Guild President, Robert Francis. Senate on 8 March 1972 unanimously agreed that this demand was unacceptable in light of the detailed negotiations held for several years that had resulted in the terms already offered. Francis was re-elected, but the Guild Council only accepted Senate's offer as a step to its ultimate goal of 50 per cent representation.

As a background theme, there was also pressure from the staff for change in the governance of the university. As a result, it was agreed that, as of October 1970, the number of RLA members on Senate would increase to eighteen, and that they would be in a 1:2 ratio with professorial members. October also saw the first meeting of the Joint Consultative Committee of Council and the Exeter Association of University Teachers (EAUT), with four members from each side.

While governance was at issue, there were growing financial concerns. The UGC had included a Social Studies/Law/Geography building (ultimately the Amory Building) in its 1972 building programme, but the UGC warned that development funds thereafter would be very limited, which was seen as affecting plans for Arts' expansion.[32] Moreover, inflation and rising wage costs were problems in the early 1970s, notably with the technicians, while the long backdating of pay awards was regarded as a challenge to budgeting.[33]

Meanwhile, fiscal problems were building up another source of tension, with the rise of student grants below the rate of inflation causing problems for students over rents and, thus, for the university. If rents only rose at the rate of student grants, then there would be insufficient revenue for the university, and the viability of catering services and of the Hall system would be called into question.[34] As the basic pay for full-time female cleaners was increased only to 36 pence per hour (82.5 per cent of the male rate) in the winter of 1971–72, there were also serious issues of social and gender equity.

There were continuing tensions over visiting hours. The Guild complained about the interpretation of the regulations offered by the wardens, some of whom, indeed, took a restrictive view. The shift in tone from meetings in the Cook years was readily apparent. For example, in the discussion in December 1971 of the report of the Joint Committee on Residence, the Guild President complained:

> It had been understood that these rules were designed solely to prevent anti-social behaviour in the Halls, and not to enforce a code of morals. Some students who had been disciplined recently had suffered psychological stress as a consequence.

Llewellyn pressed the need to avoid multi-occupancy and squatting, while Mitchell, the DVC, 'pointed out that what had been asked for was the abolition of the rules'.[35]

Expansion was leading to consideration of the parameters posed by the Estate, which was itself hit hard in 1973 by Dutch elm disease. In discussing a Draft Development Report designed to ensure that planning would no longer be on the basis of 'too few and too late', Llewellyn argued that the Estate could be developed to accommodate a student population of 10,000. A meeting with the UGC chair on 19 January 1972 to consider the university proposals led to an agreement for a total of 6,500 students for the next phase of expansion after 1976/77, for a new Library for this number (subsequently reduced to 5,200) to be begun, hopefully, in 1975/76, and for a new building for Biological Sciences depending, however, on close scrutiny of the costs.

Cars proved part of the equation in discussing the possibilities of expansion. There was consideration of whether multi-storey parking or parking in a filled-in Hoopern Valley on the other (south) side of Prince of Wales Road to the academic buildings was required, and about how to control vehicle access. The 1971 Development Report, prepared by William Holford and Partners, the architects responsible for much of

THE EARLY 1970S: THE BRAKES GO ON

the university, in collaboration with the Building and Estate Officer, proposed such a partial filling in, with access through an underpass under the Prince of Wales Road from the Stocker Road control-point.[36] On 1 November 1972, Senate agreed to fill in part of the valley for car parks, but, in the face of vigorous public protest including from students, the application was withdrawn a month later. Instead, it was decided to limit student parking and to introduce restrictions for staff parking.[37]

Financial issues caused by increments, promotions and appointments for academic staff, and pay awards for support staff, as well as by higher heating and lighting costs, combined to make the job difficult,[38] and it was not surprising that Llewellyn resigned in order to become Director-General of the British Council from 1 October 1972. However, this step created a suspicion that he had regarded Exeter as a springboard from New Zealand back into Britain. A lack of commitment, real or apparent, from the VC was a particular problem for Exeter, given the small size of its management cadre; and concern over this issue was to recur. Llewellyn, who was referred to as 'camping' in Exeter,[39] appeared to find the Exeter job boring.

Senate sought a role in the developing situation, significantly, as it had not done in 1966. On 8 March 1972, it resolved that it did not want a replacement rushed through. Instead, a special meeting was held on 18 March to discuss the type of candidate required, and the views were communicated to Council, the body responsible for appointing a VC. The criticism of Llewellyn was scarcely coded: '[T]he hope was expressed by many members that a Vice-Chancellor would be found with a keen interest in and possibly willing to participate in the academic work of the University.' These remarks reflected the attitude of senior professors who felt that he had been disrespectful towards them.

Harry Kay, the eventual choice, Professor of Psychology at Sheffield from 1960, and PVC there (1967–71), was seen as a real academic who was known in Exeter as an External Examiner in Psychology. His appointment reflected the staff desire for a more sociable, communicative style.[40]

Mitchell, who had wanted to succeed Llewellyn, took over as Acting VC from 1 October 1972 to 1 April 1973, when Kay began his term. Mitchell found that problems soon escalated. The Hall fee for 1972/73, which had been fixed after negotiations with the Guild Executive, was now disavowed by its successor. At a Guild General Meeting held on 6 October 1972, and attended by about 1,000 students, a motion was passed calling on students to pay their termly fee to the 'Student Tenants' Association' which were instructed to pass on to the university only the sum thought appropriate in light of the grant. By the end of October, about 1,110 students had paid the university the money due, 400 had paid the Association, from which the university had refused to accept any payments, and 250 had paid neither. The Guild had also pulled out of Disciplinary Committees and reiterated its demand for the 50 per cent representation. Mitchell, supported by senior staff, argued that a 'small but vociferous and politically active number of students were endeavouring to manipulate the Guild', and that most students did not share their views. The Guild's views were rejected and a campaign of persuasion by the university was called for.[41]

A Guild General Meeting, on 13 November 1972, voted 289–208 to accept Senate's offer of six places for student representatives on the Board of Senate, but tension continued. On 29 November, the Joint Committee on Residence rejected a Guild General Meeting request to abolish the visiting hours regulations; while, supported by a demonstration in the Northcote House car park, a petition of 1,241 Guild members was presented to Mitchell demanding that the university publicly withdraw all threats of eviction and deregistration and, instead, submit a joint demand to the DES for a grant increase. The Guild President also handed over a letter complaining that the university had sided with the government over the grants issue. Despite this, letters were sent on 5 December to the 37 students who had not yet paid any of their term fees, informing them that they would not be readmitted to Hall next term, while the 136 who had part-paid were informed that they would be readmitted only on the understanding that they would pay off their arrears.

On 7 February 1973, Senate turned down a renewed student proposal to be on all university committees. It decided, instead, to wait a year to see the impact of membership of the Board of the Senate (a new institution which had first met that day), and then to consider specific cases for individual committees.[42] At least, Senate ceased to take the responsibility for approving societies seeking affiliation to the Guild.

However, alongside tension, it is worth noting the view of the visiting UGC delegation that met students on 1 May 1974: '[T]he students

THE EARLY 1970S: THE BRAKES GO ON

appeared to be more constructive and less destructive than elsewhere. Moreover, they seemed to have a concern with academic matters.' To Estcourt, accustomed to the sit-ins, marches, and tear gassing of Cape Town University, 'there seemed very little student agitation. Frankly Exeter seemed very tame.'[43] Jenny McEwan, later Professor of Law, offers a different perspective:

> Duryard Hall, Jessie Montgomery House, single sex. No posters allowed on wall, so room = white box for whole year. Very fierce housekeeper. Duryard had a common refectory for all Houses, where most nights Cornish pasties and chips were an option. The lawyers [taught in Gandy Street] couldn't come back for lunch so were given a packed lunch, usually last night's cold pasties. There was one television, in the central block, for the Hall. On *Monty Python* nights it was packed. Afterwards the men would all go for chips because dinner was so early (around 5.00 pm so staff did not work late). During my third year was the 3-day week, when different sections of Exeter would have power cuts, so everyone worked out geographically in which hall the TV would be working and would go there to watch *Monty Python*. ... Many of our days began with 9.00 am lectures meaning a brisk walk from Duryard in the 1st year. ... We got it down to 17 and a half minutes. Usually this involved getting soaked in the rain – couldn't afford buses. We all wore jeans and plimsolls for this reason (pre-trainers). We were rarely bothered to go up to main campus during the day ... and were amazed, if we did, by the glamour of the students there. They tended to wear floaty Indian dresses (female) and tie-dye T-shirts (male), which did not feature in Gandy Street at all. ... There were only 60 students per year in Law, and so we knew each other and the staff knew us pretty well.

The social life of Steve Potter (Zoology, 1974–77) revolved around hall, friendships, and the orchestra. He pioneered the gay version of Nightline, and noted of his later success in business: 'Exeter was the viral agent of an inclination to see team, community, corporation, industry, nation, culture, planet and individuals as living laboratories of processes and ideas.'[44] For Mark Overton (Economic History and Geography,

1969–72) one of the features of being a student was the 'groups that came to Exeter to play. They were simply some of the best in the world at that time (Pink Floyd, Who, Cream etc) in an era before stadium concerts became the norm. The Great Hall is far too small to host equivalent bands today.' The groups were mentioned by many interviewees, and remained a feature. Thus, Jools Holland performed at the 1993 Freshers' Ball.[45] Jim Miles (History, 1969–72) noted different cultural influences, capturing an element that has been significant throughout the university's history:

> As someone who spent his career working in the Arts and Leisure industry, the influence of the University on this career choice was profound. This was not just because of the student Music, Experimental Arts and similar student societies that can be found in every university although these were obviously a factor; it was also because of the availability of high quality professional music and drama immediately on campus. The Bournemouth Symphony Orchestra and Bournemouth Sinfonietta were regular visitors to the Great Hall. There were also regular professional chamber and instrumental music concerts in the Hall. Perhaps even more important was the presence of the Northcott Theatre on campus ... Jane Howell [Artistic Director], direct from the much more radical Royal Court Theatre in London. ... The Devon county audience looked on in some confusion at this change in production style and content, but were eventually won over by Howell's professionalism and commitment. The leading actors in the rep. company were John Nettles, succeeded by Roy Marsden and standards at the Theatre were extremely high.[46]

The need in university planning to think of the wider national dimension was pressed home when the UGC delegation, led by the UGC Chairman, Sir Frederick Dainton, visited Exeter on 1 May 1974. He emphasised to Council the severe financial constraints arising from the White Paper on public expenditure to 1977/78, and due also to the range of needs across the sector. Dainton stressed that the UGC had only one-fifth of the capital sum required to meet these needs, and this situation affected the response to Exeter's building requests. Dainton also pointed out the potentially deleterious consequences for Exeter's academic structure of university policy, both in the shape of a projected merger with the teacher training college at St Luke's, an issue that raised concern on the Board of Senate of 22 May 1974, and in maintaining 'small departmental activities'. He specifically mentioned Russian and Arabic.[47] Referring to 'small units', Dainton added:

> The professorial staff had argued for the presentation of some features of Exeter University of which they were proud, but it must be recognised that such preservation will limit the options available to the University in terms of its academic development policy. The UGC cannot 'short-change' students in other universities in order to support both broad development and the retention of everything which it is desired to retain.

Despite this, the ADC on 5 June 1974 agreed on the establishment of an independent department of Russian from October.[48] A department of Mathematical Statistics and Operational Research was also established in 1974, while the university's ICL system 4/50 computer, acquired in 1968, was replaced by the ICL 4/72, a more powerful model.

Government pressure and action was a rising problem and one that affected a range of activities. Thus, the loan financing of Lafrowda II was threatened by the possibility that rent costs might be frozen under the Counter-Inflation Act. The Rent Freeze Order was to be followed by the issue of Rent Tribunal protection. In the event, the Wolfson Foundation provided a grant of £27,000 towards these flats,[49] which were thus built, increasing the self-catering accommodation available in the university and reducing the role of halls.

The overall situation in Britain was far from propitious for the university. The collapse of the long post-war boom had triggered a combination of rapid inflation and rising unemployment. An economy, state and society that had been muddling through for decades, operating far below the level of effectiveness of other countries, but, nevertheless, at least, avoiding crisis and breakdown, slid into chaos. The election on 28 February 1974 led to Wilson returning to power, albeit without a Commons' majority. Wilson then compounded Heath's inability to control wages by positive measures that in fact let them rip. In 1974, he repealed the Conservatives' Industrial Relations Act and legal sanctions on pay bargaining, and announced, in its place, a 'social contract' with the TUC; but that could not contain a massive wage explosion that began with buying off the miners. Other unions sought to follow the lead. Industrial earnings, which had increased by an average of nearly 14 per cent yearly in 1971–73, went up by 19 per cent in 1974 and by 23 per cent in 1975. As prices also rose fast, there was pressure for further wage increases. The university academics found their pay not matching inflation, but the university faced inflationary pressures from the union representing the non-academic staff and also from suppliers. Wilson was unwilling to take on union leaders who refused to accept wage restraint, and was unable to move the economy from recession. As controls were placed on prices and dividends, company profits collapsed, there was a massive fall on the stock market, and there was no incentive to invest. As a result of this economic mismanagement, even illiteracy, 1974–76 was the closest that Britain has come to the fall of capitalism.

Meanwhile, Mitchell's period in office had seen a strengthening of the policy-making system, as Senate agreed on 6 December 1972 to the creation of an Academic Development Committee as a committee of Senate that was intended to advise it, a major step as that role had previously been the preserve of the VC. There had been such a committee between 1963 and 1967, its remit including a development plan for the years up to 1972. In part, this was an academic gesture against the autocracy that Llewellyn had typified. Mitchell really developed the input from academic staff in academic planning.[50] On its visit in May 1974, the UGC was to praise the establishment of the ADC, which had moved rapidly to try to accumulate the information necessary for policymaking. The ADC agreed in January 1973 that a survey of all the academic work of the university should be undertaken and, in February, discussed computer facilities. The background was of a willingness on the part of UGC officials to consider additional expansion, including a new building for Biological Sciences and a new lecture theatre block.[51]

At the same time, there were signs of problems with what would later be termed the brand. Applications for all faculties, bar Law, for entry in 1973 were down, with an average fall of 4.63 per cent compared to a national average fall of 0.06 per cent.[52] This led Mitchell to express concern about the feasibility of Exeter achieving the UGC target of

THE EARLY 1970S: THE BRAKES GO ON

4,792 full-time equivalent (fte) students in 1976/77. He also feared that such a target could only be attained by a major deterioration in the staff–student ratio.[53] The UGC proposal for 6,500 by 1981/82 was accepted by Senate on 30 May 1973, but was linked to the provision of sufficient buildings and recurrent grants. The UGC, however, gave little encouragement on the latter head.[54]

The problem of planning for student numbers led to a marked increase in tension between Arts and Sciences,[55] a factor that was to be significant to the governance and politics of the 1970s. Scientists warned Senate of the danger of Exeter becoming a Liberal Arts institution, an argument employed, then and on other occasions, to justify disproportionate expenditure on the Science side. Another linked, but also different, issue was that of the relationship between large and small departments, and, in particular, whether the former could be expected to accept a worsening of their staff–student ratio to enable the smaller departments to have the level of staffing they required to offer a reasonable teaching programme. The issues bound up in terms such as expected, required and reasonable were again politically significant, in terms of the politics of the institution.

Student numbers also raised the question of accommodation. As Kay pointed out, there were difficulties in providing more loan-financed flats at rates students could afford. There seemed scant prospect of the UGC providing the contribution necessary for new buildings, and, instead, a need to rely on a return to private lodgings. A survey of students indicated that most were not in favour of lodgings, while there were also fewer of the traditional landladies and, on their part, a lack of enthusiasm to have student lodgers with the kind of freedom they now expected.[56]

A tension within the university over values was readily apparent in the Board of Senate on 27 February 1974 which rejected a proposal from the Joint Committee on Residence for the conversion of Thomas Hall into self-catering flats. Kay had pointed out that small halls were expensive and affected by rapidly rising costs, while the Guild's representatives had emphasised the popularity of self-catering flats; but the Board voted 26–23–9 against the conversion. Kay then pointed out that Thomas Hall's deficit would probably have to be borne out of general funds, not hall fees. The economic viability of Thomas Hall was never established.

In early 1974, as a sense of national crisis mounted, the emphasis in Exeter switched to cutting projections for student and staff numbers and to anticipating a deficit.[57] There were major consequences at the disciplinary level. It was decided to leave the Chair of English vacant and not to expand the department to a school, as had been anticipated.[58]

Inflationary pressures affected the university. Wage agreements increased Exeter's anticipated deficit for 1974/75 and threatened to exhaust in one year all the reserves built up for the quinquennium. As a result, in October 1974, the month in which Wilson won a small overall majority in a new general election, Standing Committee agreed to a recommendation from Kay for a moratorium on appointments and replacements. He did not support consideration of redundancies, on the ground that they could not help in the short term.[59]

In response to the UGC requiring a reduction in planned student numbers for 1975/76–1976/77, the Working Party report on a merger with St Luke's College was delayed, while it became clear that the student expansion that did occur would not be supported by additional staff. The Arts Faculty Board had unanimously declared that taking more students was conditional on more staff. In response, Kay drew attention to marked variations in staff–student ratios between departments. The basing of resources on historic funding was going to be increasingly divisive as the general fiscal environment deteriorated.

There was a wider politics, including class, gender and nationality. Most of the staff were still male. In Geography, there were no women on the academic staff until the 1990s: '[M]y HoD Bill Ravenhill [1971–83] was quite open about not appointing them as they had babies etc.'[60] Anne Mayes, Lecturer in Economics, recalls: 'You could have a few weeks of Maternity Leave if and only if you did all your teaching and examining. When I was expecting my second child I was asked, "Isn't it time you became a full-time Mum?"' Tim Niblock recalls two members of Council worrying about appointing a woman as a professor on the basis of what would she do with her child.[61] There was also some sexual harassment of female staff. Avril Henry, later Professor of English, then a Lecturer, recalled being chased round the room by the libidinous Moelwyn Merchant. This clergyman professor also directed his attentions to some female students. The role of individuals and of the culture of specific departments or sub-departments was significant. Thus, in

Archaeology, where, initially, the staff were all or mostly female, 'it was hard to tell if we were held back because we were Archaeology, or predominantly female, or very junior. But we were not held back much, although it sometimes felt so.'[62]

The changes in Psychology are more generally indicative. At the time of its move from Gandy Street to Washington Singer in 1971, all of the academic staff were male and all had British degrees. The skewed gender bias in Psychology was notable given that its undergraduate classes at the time were dominated by female students; an undergraduate balance that has remained unchanged over the years since then. In contrast, in 2012, at the time of the 50th anniversary of the establishment of the department, over half of the academic staff were female, including representation at the most senior level. Several of the staff had non-British degrees. A similar transition occurred elsewhere in the university and contributed to a major transformation in staff culture.

CHAPTER SIX

THE LATER 1970s: A DIVIDED UNIVERSITY

Our activities can only be appraised against the background of a society in a state of fluidity, in which values are being reassessed, and in which governments, by the limits of resources, are more and more going to be forced to choose between alternatives and often conflicting objects of expenditure. ... We must choose our priorities and to govern is to choose.
Viscount Amory, Chancellor, inauguration of the Amory Building, 14 April 1975[1]

It was a period of transition from a life that I found dull, constraining and unfulfilling back in Essex. It opened up a whole new world for me – Devon itself, people, my husband. I never returned to Essex.
Yasmin Thierry (Social Administration and Social Policy, 1973–76)[2]

THE PROBLEMS OF the early 1970s were driven home later in the decade, and it is easy to appreciate how an awareness of difficulties led to a sense of crisis. At the same time, there was some improvement and development. In particular, the financial situation eased, in large part because a more viable staffing level was established. In addition, the merger with St Luke's, the college of education, agreed by the Board of Senate on 8 January 1975 by 46–18–3,[3] and by Council on 7 July 1975, led to a major strengthening of the university's role in

THE LATER 1970S: A DIVIDED UNIVERSITY

Education, a role in which it was to become nationally significant. In 1979/80, 15 per cent of the students were in Education, compared to the previous percentage of seven: total student numbers also increased, from 4,367 in 1977/78 to 5,103 in 1979/80.

The emphasis, in considering the university in the late 1970s, on crisis or recovery, or, less dramatically, failure or progress, was, in part, in keeping with the general situation in the country. The economic crisis was accompanied by a fiscal one. At a time of high inflation, industrial earnings went up by 23 per cent in 1975 and unions sought not to 'fall behind'. Strikes affected the university, with ASTMS (Association of Scientific, Technical and Managerial Staffs) members in the Computer Unit called out in pursuit of a national wage claim in June 1975, although service continued. Wage increases posed a major problem for the university, where wages had become the most significant element in hall costs.[4] The Guild was also hit by a steeply rising wage bill, which led to pressure from it for increased funds as well as criticism from the university of a lack of economies on the part of the Guild.[5] Labour legislation, notably the Trade Union and Labour Relations Act (1974) and the Employment Protection Bill (1975), became of concern to the university management.[6] In June 1975, the TUC agreed to a voluntary agreement on wage restraint that the Wilson government accepted. This agreement, which held firm until 1978, was to effect a significant reduction in the rate of inflation, which eventually fell to below 10 per cent in 1978. Nevertheless, labour relations remained difficult.

More seriously, the corporatism and control represented by Labour's pact with the trade unions drained the incentive and independence out of society and threatened the long-term viability of the economy. In 1975, the Industry Act established the National Enterprise Board, while the government took the majority of the shares in the newly consolidated car manufacturer, British Leyland. The British National Oil Corporation was created in 1975, and British Aerospace and British Shipbuilders in 1977. Moreover, the government confronted lower economic growth than hitherto, as well as high inflation, and deficits both in the balance of payments and in spending. In April 1976, Denis Healey, the Chancellor of the Exchequer, introduced heavy spending cuts. That September, a sterling crisis forced the government to turn for a loan to the International Monetary Fund (IMF). The IMF demanded cuts in government spending and, after a political battle within the Cabinet, these were accepted.

Universities were part of the corporatist world, albeit a part that was increasingly miserable. Tenure protected the jobs of the staff, but a lack of money in the sector ensured that real salaries fell and that these jobs were generally seen in somewhat defensive terms. Poorly endowed and not able to draw on the resources of a dynamic regional economy, a problem that continued into the twenty-first century, Exeter found itself, as before, dependent on a government it could not influence. Thus, in January 1975, when Exeter was affected by both a UGC supplementary grant for 1974/75 that only covered half the inflation rate, as well as a national reduction of planned student numbers for 1976/77, Exeter's projected undergraduate figure was cut to 3,500, although it was raised to 3,600 the following month.[7] Indeed, although the first year that arrived in 1976 was the biggest hitherto, VC Harry Kay was still able to address the entire first year at one sitting.

The fiscal crisis was not only one of central government, but also affected local government. Founded at Redruth in 1972, the Institute of Cornish Studies was a joint venture of county council and university, but there was a crisis in support from the former from 1974. The Institute's first Director, Charles Thomas, a distinguished archaeologist, did not disguise his impatience with some of the county councillors, and this soured relations between the county council and the Institute until Thomas retired in 1991.[8]

Economic circumstances also hit both students and their parents. Grants were related to parental income, but many 'middle-class' parents were not helping their children. The grants themselves rose at less than the anticipated rate, which made hall fees a more difficult issue for students.[9] Council was troubled by one possible solution, that of encouraging students to attend their local universities,[10] a measure that would have hit Exeter hard as it drew many students from outside the southwest; a point that remains relevant. The Library was hit by the rising cost of books and journals, an issue that troubled key professors.[11]

Government policy on raising fees for overseas students hit Commonwealth links and led to a focus on Arab states, with fewer students, for example, from India.[12] Related to financial support from the Middle East, this focus encouraged the development of Arab and Islamic

THE LATER 1970S: A DIVIDED UNIVERSITY

studies. The United Arab Emirates provided £25,000 in the spring of 1975, while funds from Dubai were to be crucial to the completion of the new Library in 1983.

Standing Committee decided that the recurrent grant for 1975/76 fell short of minimum requirements and the ADC responded by putting the future of Classics on the table, as well as chairs in Russian and Archaeology, and developments in Biochemistry and Fine Art. Given these problems, the idea of expansion to 5,200–6,300 students (including St Luke's) by 1981/82, as suggested by the UGC, appeared fanciful; but the ADC decided on a figure of 5,600, which was to be met by equal growth in Arts and Sciences.

In February 1976, however, in line with a cut in the national target, Exeter's projected undergraduate numbers were reduced by 350 students. In the event, even including the merger with St Luke's in 1978, the rate of growth in student numbers in the 1970s was half that in 1955–70; the latter had averaged 8.5 per cent per year, and in 1970–77 the rate fell to 3.5 per cent.

Individual departments had their own trajectories and solutions. Classics had seen a marked fall in applications as a result of the decline of Latin and Greek at school, but was saved, by adding to the traditional language-based Classics, new degree programmes in Ancient History and Classical Studies. After the retirement of Clayton, and the interregnum of an Acting Head, Peter Wiseman, an Ancient Historian who argued the case for the inherent interdisciplinarity of Classics,[13] started as professor and head of department in 1977 and strengthened the department to which applications rose markedly. Conversely, the failure to appoint to chairs had serious consequences. In the case of Russian, it meant that the department started to stand still at the moment when other university Russian departments of comparable standing were moving ahead. The decision also meant that Russian did not have a powerful advocate on Senate.

A different university crisis was threatened in 1975 by the AUT decision to withhold examination results in order to promote a speedy announcement of the arbitration award on academic staff salaries. RLA and NUS support for this stance was not shared by Kay, but the Board of Senate on 21 May 1975 backed the decision. There was an emphasis on trying to maintain consensus among the staff, and notably at the departmental level, an emphasis that worked to the advantage of those pressing for the AUT position. This policy caused complaints on Council on 2 June.

Kay had a range of qualities. As so often, personality was linked to policy and politics. A sympathetic individual and very nice man, who described himself accurately as a 'good listener' and who liked to feel inclusive, Kay's major ability was in one-to-one conversation, and this ability helped in negotiating the large-scale programme of early retirements that his policies required. Kay prided himself on avoiding any need for compulsory redundancies, an issue that had caused much unease and discontent among the staff and had repeatedly been raised in Senate. As Kay, a natural conciliator who did not like people to disagree with him, wished to keep the political atmosphere calm, this goal became key to his strategy. A sense of the university as a community, with a consensus environment, served him as goal and method, ideology and excuse. In addition, this programme helped create parameters within which his successors, notably his immediate successor, David Harrison, operated or against which they had to respond.

This issue indicates the difficulty in distinguishing between Kay's character and his effectiveness in dealing with some highly problematic issues at a very testing time politically and financially. Kay's policy can be seen in terms of the general constraints within which universities operated, notably the consequences of tenure, but it had unfortunate results. As was pointed out at the time, there was the swallowing of strategy by tactics. Kay claimed that he would not allow the chance factor of the willingness of individual staff to take early retirement to take precedence over the viability of departments and the needs of teaching; but this claim proved misleading. However, Exeter was not the sole university in which preserving posts took priority over structural planning. In Exeter, the decision was 'an open-and-shut one',[14] in large part because the political situation within the university and its governance left little room for manoeuvre: Kay had been dealt a poor hand.

Yet, responding essentially to the possibilities offered by staff willing to retire was part of Kay's more general tendency not to face difficulties, rather than to shape the situation. With a leadership style that was not robust, Kay wished well, but, in a very difficult situation, could not deliver what he hoped. He showed these characteristics in relations with staff and students alike, and found it difficult to lead Senate: the VC chairs Senate. Wearing his heart on his sleeve, Kay was easily worried and upset by Senate, and found it difficult to defuse issues. Many of the Senate (and other) documents from the period convey an unsettling sense of weakness. With his somewhat diffident manner, Kay did not find it easy to win people round. He wanted to foster a corporate identity, that of a university not controlled by professorial 'barons', but was unable to follow through his ideas.

At the outset, there was a deliberate, and totally unnecessary, belittling of Kay when the senior professoriate decided that he should be denied the title of professor, even though he had held a chair at Sheffield. In consequence, he was always Dr Kay and became known as Professor again only when he was granted an emeritus chair on his retirement. The 'old guard' did not want a strong VC, and they were determined that Kay should not be one. Possibly the appointment of a friend, Kenneth Nash, as Academic Registrar and Secretary, and the compilation of the List(s) were Kay's response to that attitude; attempts to strengthen his own position. At Sheffield, he had had a reputation for loving 'intelligence' and for collecting information on all his serious rivals in the field of British psychology.

The policy issues Kay encountered owed much to the problems of the university sector (both funding and tenure), and, more generally, of the country, but Kay did not always play his hand well. This was not simply a consequence of his personality, but also owed much to the serious vulnerability arising from the affair of the List, the background of which stemmed from problems in relations with students as well as issues with staff.

Relations with students had been strained, with the rent strike in 1975 involving a serious lack of communications. The Guild proposal for students to withhold part of their rents was countered by Kay issuing a special newsletter setting out the costs of operating the halls. On Council, the view was expressed that an annual rent strike was now predictable.[15] In March 1975, an EGM of the Guild voted 234–231 to support the rent strike, but, that October, a motion for another strike was rejected. The vagaries of Guild politics, and notably the troubled relationship between the Executive and general meetings, was a matter for complaint on the Board of Senate on 26 May 1976. This relationship paralleled the limited ability of trade union executives to deliver agreements in the face of shop stewards and local branches that were ready to thwart them.

Disputes between students and university were not restricted to rent. Mixing student accommodation in halls and Lafrowda was a major issue in the spring of 1976.[16] Noreen Gladstone, who was Acting Warden for Jessie Montgomery House, reflects on the difficulties of the university trying 'to maintain a tradition on Oxbridge lines (e.g. formal dinners) ... in the late 1970s when student attitudes and demands were changing, as illustrated by new developments in student living at Lafrowda'.[17] A student sit-in at Northcote House, the university offices, in March 1977 led to an unexpected crisis. Tension had built up in February with Guild representatives at the meetings of Council (14 February) and the University Committee (22 February) demanding that the university refuse to implement government policy on cuts and fees. After a long period when, despite sustained inflation, fees had not risen, the government, from 1975, pressed universities to raise fees significantly. Whereas only 10.5 per cent of the university's income in 1967/68 was from fees, in 1979/80 the percentage was 22, income per student rising from £698 to £2,978, although the value of this increase to the university per student was removed by inflation. For home (British) students, fees were then largely paid by Local Education Authorities, not by students themselves.

On 1 March 1977, a Guild general meeting decided on the occupation of Northcote House. The attempt to do so in the afternoon had been blocked, but, that evening, the students occupied the south wing, including Kay's office. He was encouraged to leave by Nash and Reg Erskine and escorted by them from the building.[18] There is no evidence for the report that Kay fled as the students broke into his office.

The university initially anticipated only a short occupation, but, on 3 March there was a voting fiasco at a general meeting of the Guild held in the Northcote House car park, with one vote for stopping the occupation and the other for continuing. The majority of the Guild Executive were then opposed to continuing the occupation, but a general meeting held in the Great Hall on 4 March voted 888–731 to maintain the presence in Northcote House.

Seeking a conciliatory solution, and certainly not willing to adopt a robust approach or to stand up to the students, Kay resorted to hoping

THE LATER 1970S: A DIVIDED UNIVERSITY

that another meeting, to be held on 8 March, would end the occupation; but he promised a special meeting of Senate, held on 7 March, that otherwise 'decisive action must be taken'. A few members of Senate wanted teaching stopped until the occupation ended, but they were not given a lead by Kay. The majority opposed this approach as they viewed the student action as against the government, not the university, and did not want the university to be seen as supporting the government. The meeting agreed by 47 votes to 11 that, if the occupation did not end as a result of the meeting on the 8th, then Kay should obtain an injunction, and that the students should be given an opportunity to leave peacefully without police intervention. The vote on the 8th was for an end of the occupation on the 10th. Alongside criticism of Kay, it is appropriate to note praise for his 'very skilful diplomacy' from Martin Myhill (Economic History, 1975–78), while Mike Dobson (Combined Honours Arts, 1976–79) recalls: 'Most students joined in just to see what it was like in the VC's office, and stayed just a short while.'[19]

Already, at Senate on 7 March 1977, an issue that was to have longer resonance had been raised, namely the discovery on 1 March on Kay's desk of 'a list of staff under various headings, one of which seemed to have political implications'. The students claimed to have found the handwritten document on his desk, while the university alleged that the desk had been broken into. The document found its way to staff (at least one of whom appears to have taken a role in the break-in), and caused a furore.[20] There was an historical background. On 2 March 1970, at a time of sensitivity over student activism, Kay's predecessor, John Llewellyn had issued a statement, endorsed by Senate on 11 March, that: 'No secret files containing information about the political or religious opinions or affiliations of students and other members of the University are kept by the University of Exeter.'

Kay, who 'was simply overwhelmed',[21] gave a somewhat limp explanation to Senate on 12 March 1977, claiming that the information found had been designed to help him in planning lunchtime discussion groups and lectures involving bright and stimulating persons speaking at a fairly general level. Asked by Kay to suggest possible participants, with an indication of what might be expected, Barrie Behenna, the Secretary of Faculties, who had attended such lectures as a student at Bristol, drew up a list accordingly. He cannot recall the various descriptions that he reported, other than 'Awkward', and had no idea of staff politics apart from for those who made no secret of their affiliation.[22]

In Senate, Kay conceded that 'some of the expressions ... "politically left" was the clearest example – could give the impression, if read out of context, that the Vice-Chancellor was concerned to compile lists or maintain dossiers about the political affiliations and personal characteristics of academic staff', a charge he denied.

Kay pressed on to suggest that the intention in publishing the list had been to divide the university, which, Kay claimed, had been achieved to some extent. Certainly, there were opponents of Kay who jumped at the opportunity to cause trouble,[23] but his account was not credited.[24] Greeted with widespread incredulity and much derision, Kay's explanation of the document seriously weakened him. Those who were on 'The List' were upset as well as some of those not on it, such as Frank Oliver. The fuss made the national press.

Additional concern was raised about reports that there were other lists. Three other ones existed, apparently drawn up by the combative Nash, and certainly not by Behenna.[25] One was on the vices of particular professors, one on their financial position, and one a list of staff with Yorkshire connections from which Kay and Nash came. The first contained very perceptive pen-portraits, for example 'Unchristian' for Roy Porter (Theology). The existence of these lists was widely known or, at least, believed.[26] They reflected Kay's interest in the psychological drives of individuals and his wish for information that would enable him to forward his policies.[27]

The net effect of the List affair was political weakness for Kay. There was ridicule following the Senate explanation. More seriously, once the powerful professors knew or suspected that Kay was accumulating information about them, then a number became suspicious, if not unhelpful. This was doubly unfortunate. Kay needed political support to implement any system of planned retrenchment, and notably if it was to involve any restructuring.

Moreover, there were professors pursuing dubious policies and stances as departmental heads, notably Walter Minchinton, the founding Chair in the new department of Economic History in 1964. On my first visit to Exeter, I was a witness to his swearing at length in public in Reed Hall at Stephen Fisher, his successor as head of department. His colleagues were cowed individuals with blighted lives, and Clapp's history of the university reflects this tone.[28] Minchinton was regarded as a joke in the world of Economic History, a reliable topic for conference stories, but he left behind a group of people who were all damaged to various degrees by his bullying. Minchinton's bullying, or attempts to bully, extended well beyond his department, but they were easier to resist outside it. He was capable of bursting into tutorials and demanding the return of library books he wanted.[29] There was also a continuous process of a use of resources solely for his benefit, allegations of plagiarism, claims of trying to wreck the career of academics elsewhere working in 'his field', as well as an issue of sexual favouritism, although he was also well known as an active figure in the discipline and published as a scholar, albeit not work of particular distinction. Michael Havinden noted that when he became Sub-Dean of the Faculty and formed a close working relationship with the Dean, Minchinton became 'very jealous and difficult'. He sought total control of 'his' department and held compulsory weekly meetings, while doing very little teaching, although he was keen on field trips which students enjoyed,[30] and could be charming to students. At one point, Llewellyn had descended on the department, an extremely rare event under the first three VCs, and told Minchinton that if he did not reverse a consequence of this favouritism that day the police would be called. Minchinton backed down. Kay never managed even that rare feat. Long a colleague of Minchinton, Roger Burt recalls that:

> [Minchinton] was aggressive, self-important, hectoring and was generally an absolute pain to work for. But on good days he could be OK company and interesting to be with (though he NEVER bought a drink!). These days I would say that he had a serious mental disorder – bi-polar perhaps. The 'University' knew all of this full well but did absolutely nothing to protect/help us. I think that I went 20 years without promotion (WEM never pushed people up) and all the others in the department trod water … though given the state of the job market, we continued to get good applicants. … You learnt to be tough dealing with him. Some of my own worst characteristics of aggression and response were, I'm sure, shaped by those days. He is the only person that I ever had to physically throw out of my room, when he invaded it with students present. On one

or two occasions I had to hit him (though I made sure that there were no witnesses and it was a body blow – no visible bruises).[31]

Recalling an unsuccessful interview for a post, Richard Davenport-Hines thought Minchinton displayed 'a cruel brand of aggression' and was warned by a referee that Minchinton 'had made his department miserable'.[32] The doubtless unpleasant Minchinton attracted rumour, but he was also unacceptable not only to his junior staff but more widely within the university. When Minchinton was to become Dean of Social Studies, an office that went down the professoriate in seniority, although the holder was technically elected by the Faculty Board, there was a rebellion in the Faculty led by the formidable Margaret Hewitt. The Social Studies professors were told that if they nominated Minchinton as Dean at the Board, the non-professorial members would make an alternative nomination of a senior non-professorial member of the Faculty, Harry Burton (Economics). The professors surrendered, and Minchinton was passed over in favour of the next professor in seniority. The COSGOD proposals to remove power from standing (permanent) heads of department were initially designed to counter Minchinton.[33] Minchinton did not endear the university to the city authorities by claiming that he had evidence of corruption in planning matters.[34] In Minchinton's case, the law was involved after his retirement in a case relating to the purloining while he had been head of the Fine Arts Committee of a painting by Alfred Wallis, a Cornish Primitive Artist, that was university property, his refusal to return the painting in question, university security, police, an altercation, arrest, a fatal heart attack. The painting has never appeared since.

Roy Porter, a Canon of Chichester Cathedral, who always wore his dog collar and rose to be Dean of Arts, pushed the concept of being a 'character' far too far. He could also be difficult. Not short of self-assurance, he drank a lot, was very rude and unthinking, personally harassed younger male staff, and did not stop the harassment of male undergraduates in the department; he was also extremely and persistently unpleasant to many female students.[35] This unpleasantness led one parent to hire a private detective to report on Porter. 'Evil, evil' remarked another interviewee. Porter was also involved in a murky episode involving propositioning and assault, which led to a legal case in which past conduct on

Porter's part was revealed, and his evidence was regarded as tainted; but he was acquitted, largely, it was widely believed, because lies were told on his behalf. The *Express and Echo* reported the case in some detail. The case involved a charge of sexual assault brought on the testimony of a young university gardener who said that Porter had picked him up in town, taken him home, and made sexual advances. Claiming that he had been assaulted, the gardener beat Porter up, whereas Porter said that he had been jumped on as he opened his front door by the gardener, who he did not know, and was beaten up. The leading witness for the defence, Margaret Hewitt, testified she had been with Porter at his home that evening. The case did not do the university's reputation much good in the city.[36]

Although Porter, a good and rigorous scholar, was also noted as a stimulating teacher, while 'you had to earn his respect' in the words of Julie Arliss (Theology, 1980–83), he was overly ready to belittle. James Jones (Theology 1967–70) recalls Porter 'holding up one of my essays by the corner as if it were some dirty handkerchief and saying, "Mr Jones I trust you copied this out of some cheap American paperback"!. In goading his students he expected you to engage with him.'[37] Porter could be a snob, but he could also be very witty and sociable. Moreover, he was less aloof than Henry Garland, Norman Rydon and Frank Barlow, and, indeed, took character parts in the Overseas Students' Play. Porter also oversaw developments such as the introduction of a Postgraduate Diploma in Theology in 1975 and had the university sufficiently at heart to endow a lectureship with a bequest.

It is indicative of the opportunities provided by distance, but also of contrasting styles of discussion, that Porter was referred to in Clapp's 1982 history of the university as an Old Testament scholar, who held the chair 'with distinction'.[38] Porter was not alone. Arriving in 1987 to teach in History, Andrew Thorpe noted: '[O]ne less than savoury feature of coming into the Queens SCR as a young man was that one became the object of some unwelcome attention.'[39]

Kay should have dealt with these men, who were exceptions to the total professional dedication and standards that characterises most of the academics. There is a view that Cook would not have put up with such a situation. The oft-expressed opinion was that Kay was scared of difficult academics, and notably of Porter who is described as 'swanning around the place' as if he 'ruled the roost'.⁴⁰ Kay also failed to stand up to Muhammed Sha'ban, the head of the department of Arabic, who used to shout at him. Serious accusations of professional misconduct against Sha'ban were not investigated.⁴¹

A nice man, but not a leader,⁴² Kay seems to have preferred to keep 'the lid on things' and was particularly uncomfortable about any publicity relating to episodes involving sex. As an instance of a narrative I cannot corroborate, I have been told that he persuaded a student hit by a male student, with whom she was trying to end a relationship, so seriously that a cheekbone was broken, not to take the matter to the police. Kay allegedly promised to ensure redress, but none was secured, and the student was left very bitter.⁴³

Another area that Kay found difficult was university administration. He made the sensible decision to end, in 1975 the 'two-headed' system,⁴⁴ the divide between the posts of Secretary (Ross) and Academic Registrar (Bartlett), a divide from the foundation of the university, at once institutional and personal, between the academic side and business side of the university that had created repeated difficulties. Ross did not talk to Bartlett. The two men found it impossible to overcome the major differences in their personalities and did not trust each other. Bartlett, who had a more relaxed attitude than Ross, although he did not neglect his duties, occasionally spent some of his working day in Northcote House practising his recorder.⁴⁵ Ross was due to retire in 1975 and Bartlett a year later, but Bartlett, who had cancer of the throat, was eased out early. At a special meeting of Council on 14 October 1974, their posts were united with the new title of Academic Registrar and Secretary, its holder to be jointly responsible to Council and Senate. The recommendations of the Working Party had been accepted *nem con* at a special meeting of Senate on 4 October. The title was chosen 'to indicate the importance of the holder of the office being in sympathy with the educational aims of the academic staff'.⁴⁶

However, having made this important structural improvement, Kay found it very difficult to find an acceptable holder for the new post. Tom Owen, Registrar at Aberystwyth, accepted the post with effect from 1 October 1975. He had a very good reputation, was highly personable, and would have guided Kay in the way he thought best. However, Owen then pulled out, allegedly because he could not get his daughter into the local school of his choice[47] and Kay could not help him. Kay was left in a difficult situation. He had lost his Registrar and was disillusioned by the experience.

In the end, Kay retreated to personal friendship to fill the post, and this did not serve him particularly well. Kenneth Nash, a Deputy Under-Secretary in the Ministry of Defence and a friend of Kay's from schooldays, lacked the necessary experience in the sector, and this helped weaken the university administration at a time when financial considerations were underlining the need for central planning and related selectivity. Kay was widely regarded as under Nash's thumb, and graffiti in the staff lavatory in Reed Hall claimed 'KN Rules HK': there is disagreement as to whether there was a comma after 'rules'. Nash very much had the civil service manner. He was a strong, active, sharp-edged figure, but most of the university did not want such a Registrar, just as they did not want a strong VC. Nash, who did not appear to like academics, was very opposed to trade unions and immensely irritated by the activists in the AUT branch, and they, including the AUT, responded in kind. Tim Reuter, a member of History and head of the AUT branch, who helped to negotiate new terms and conditions of service with Nash, came to see him, however, as very bright and hard-working, and even fair-minded. Had Nash's health held up, he might have provided stronger leadership for the university but, equally, relations with the academic staff might have become far worse.[48]

Alongside criticism, it is appropriate to note praise for Kay for reasons other than his very pleasant personality. John Bridge found him forward-looking. The views of Gar Yates in his favour are also significant as he worked with Kay at senior policy levels as ADC Chair (1980–83) and on Council (1976–79, 1981–84). Yates thought him 'a man of remarkably wide knowledge ... clarity ... intellectual command ... approachability ... could be decisively firm on appointment committees ... Backroom secretiveness was never his way ... absolutely unpretentious ... interested in everything ... interdisciplinary grasp of subject expectations'.[49] Kay was also prescient about the problems posed by internal promotion to personal chairs. Robert Leaper, Professor of Social Administration, thought Kay a clever administrator and organiser able to keep the peace while leaving himself room for manoeuvre.[50] Kay certainly handled the problems of the university better in 1981–84 than he had done in 1977.

It was thought that he had recovered well from the loss of face associated with the List.[51]

More generally, arriving as Professor of History in 1977 from University College, London, Christopher Holdsworth discovered 'customs which reminded me of Cambridge and Oxford'. Dinner in halls showed him 'how comfortably wardens and tutors lived and how seriously some of them took their duties. ... I was left very much to my devices in my teaching duties ... the higher one went the more [committee] proceedings were often dominated by a few, who mostly disliked change.' He noted scant pressure for research. At a more junior level, Douglas Tallack, who taught American and Commonwealth Arts as a temporary lecturer for 1976/77, before eventually becoming a PVC at Nottingham and then Leicester, found Exeter very different from the more liberal Sussex:

> I stayed four or five nights as a tutor at Birks Hall and that was truly awful: a top table, even at breakfast; idiot boys setting off fire alarms and playing with hoses; and hall-formals. . . . the burst of enterprise that has come with Steve Smith . . . obviously what Exeter needed but so different from the curious mix of provincialism and self-importance that, even in a temporary post, was apparent to me.[52]

The recent lack of new blood in some departments troubled speakers in Council on 13 June 1977. It was to remain a serious issue until the early 1990s. There were, however, improvements under Kay, as well as efforts at improvement, both in comparison with the Llewellyn/Mitchell years and with regard to Kay's early years. Noting 'a wide variation in the extent of the research activity of individuals', a more active ADC, chaired from 1975 to 1977 by Keith Whinnom, a very able Professor of Spanish and a strong presence in the university, pressed the case for more research activity as well as for a more uniform system of faculty planning so as to make it easier to plan at the university level.[53] The ADC sought to take control of planning from departments and faculties.[54]

The ADC also argued that, as universities and knowledge were inherently dynamic, a steady-state university implied that innovation and expansion could only be achieved by equivalent contraction.[55] In April 1977, the ADC discussed 'The Steady-State University', a memorandum from its Chair, that argued that 'the present situation cannot be seen as transient'. Pointing to a forthcoming decline in the number of 18 year olds, Whinnom observed:

> [W]e may in any case wonder whether any governments will consider it expedient to restore to any degree the not ungenerous levels of finance which universities only recently enjoyed, particularly as no road to economic recovery is yet apparent. During its recent discussions about the desirability of introducing new courses, the ADC took the view that universities are essentially dynamic institutions, have continuously sought, and should always be seeking change or innovation to provide the stimulus whereby they fulfil their objectives. ... Innovation ... can be achieved in one area only by contraction in another.[56]

To improve planning, the ADC called for data, notably, in 1977, on departmental costs per student.[57] Data was also a theme in teaching and research. The following year, a department of Computer Science came into existence. In 1976, computerisation began in the Library, with the automation of book issues. The drive for information was to become a major goal of university policy, but one that it took a long time to bring to fruition. There was pressure to this end from Council which sought more information and more planning.[58] Indeed, the lack of detailed transparency in finances was a major limitation on the possibility of radical academic restructuring, a situation that lasted into the late 1990s. Academic decisions, including crucial judgements on which subjects should be supported by new appointments, or which might be cut back, were made by criteria that were not really quantifiable. At the same time, the danger, in planning developments, of responding to changeable student demands was readily apparent.[59] Tenure certainly ensured that provision in response to short-term demand flows would have long-term financial consequences in terms of commitments.

Although modest, research income rose under Kay. An awareness of its significance encouraged Kay to press for effort and to consider directed resource allocation that would be linked to seed-corn investment, one of his more prescient steps, although Exeter was scarcely unique in this policy. Kay's establishment of a research fund provided both a public encouragement to research and a tool for the centre to help influence developments.⁶⁰ Yates presents Kay putting in place a 'groundwork of transformation, including a climate of enhanced expectation in respect of the intellectual life of the university'.⁶¹ When Yates took over as Chair of the ADC in 1980, the brief outlined by Kay included nurturing a research culture, a theme he had been pressing for a while; but the ADC was weakened by the need to cope with the Thatcher cuts and also by Senate opposition.⁶²

The 'steady-state' principle was not to the fore with the student 'work-in' at the Library in November 1977. As Hewitt told the Board of Senate on 30 November: 'We had expected the student representatives on the Committee to suggest different internal priorities if they objected to the size of the Library budget', a recurrent issue with Guild complaints. This 'work-in', organised in the Library over the weekend of 25–27 November, contrasted with the generally good recent relations between university and Guild, but reflected a student view that the Library cuts were an aspect of a wider problem with government policy and that the issue provided an opportunity to associate the university with its stance and to secure publicity. A lunchtime Guild General Meeting on 25 November had passed a motion for a 'work-in' despite warnings of possible disciplinary action. The minutes of the General Meeting also indicate a concern with national and international issues, specifically the NUS constitution, disaffiliation, and Israel, as well as the question of representation, Simon Hicks, the Guild Events Coordinator, complaining: 'The Executive is not really in touch with most of the students here ... only an average 5% of the students here turn up to General Meetings.'⁶³

Nash wanted a vigorous response to the Library occupation, with the students 'booted out', but Kay proved more cautious. A move by the Guild Executive to end the 'work-in' was narrowly defeated on a vote on the Friday evening (the 25th), and up to about sixty students then 'worked-in' for at least part of the weekend. There was no damage and the staff were not obstructed, although overtime had to be paid. Kay complained about action taken on the basis of a poorly attended general meeting and a very small majority, while the President of the Guild argued that the 'work-in' had failed because the university had regarded it as an attack on itself rather than the government. He asked if the university would fight cuts in general.⁶⁴

THE LATER 1970S: A DIVIDED UNIVERSITY

A different type of student criticism was provided by the two men who dressed up as women in 1978 in protest at 'The Cattle Market', the Crossmead party held at the start of the autumn term. The range of student life was indicated by the seven societies affiliated to the Guild in 1977: Backgammon, Caledonian, Rock and Roll, Sealed Knot, Social Administration, Survival, and Solidarity with Chile. The student experience was certainly far from luxurious. Martin Myhill recalls:

> I spent my first year living in Duryard Halls in the midst of a potato shortage which meant powdered Smash potato with everything at meal times, followed by two self-catering years in the newly opened but rather spartan Lafrowda House ... at a time when Exeter's main city centre supermarket ('Walton's') ... targeted the lower end of the market. While each Lafrowda floor of twelve individual student rooms were single-sex, the shared kitchens became very cosmopolitan meeting places at all times of the day and night.[65]

Although shared rooms were unusual by this stage, the popularity of the halls was limited. Most second- and third-year students did not wish to live in. As a result, the capacity of university accommodation was generally adequate.

The dangerous situation of universities in the face of a less supportive government and society was one of the reasons given for the merger with St Luke's,[66] which took effect in October 1978. At the same time, there was concern in the university about funding implications and over a dilution of academic quality as a result of the merger. As a result, the Board of Senate in 1975 agreed the ADC recommendation that there could not be any general integration of St Luke's other than into the School of Education.[67] The discussions over the merger with St Luke's brought up many of the issues later to be seen in the 1990s over the Cornwall initiative. In 1976, there was reluctance to follow up the forthcoming merger with St Luke's by becoming involved with Rolle College in Exmouth,[68] which, instead, merged with Plymouth Polytechnic in 1988.

The background for the St Luke's merger was the inappropriately titled 1972 white paper *Education: A Frame-Work for Expansion*. This anticipated that training places in colleges of education and polytechnics would need to decline by between one-quarter and one-third in the coming decade. At St Luke's, the situation was confronted by the new Principal, the somewhat unlikely figure of John Dancy, who had been a modernising voice among the headmasters of public schools. The university, with 20 staff and about 200 students in its department of Education (at Thornlea), was less troubled by the outlined changes. The PGCE programme, like others at universities, was protected through funding by the UGC, as was the higher degree and research work at the Institute of Education (in Gandy Street). The 1978 merger was really a merger of the department and the Institute, as well as the university and St Luke's.[69] One option for St Luke's was independence: a close parallel in terms of historic origins is the path forged by what is now the University of Winchester. A merger of St Luke's with Rolle, then under Devon County Council, was a possibility, but the Governors of St Luke's were insistent upon a future that was not LEA controlled, and on the St Luke's site. One specific benefit of St Luke's coming under the UGC regime was the clearing away of the 1948 student hostel and the temporary buildings in which much teaching had taken place, and their replacement by a large new teaching building, Baring Court.[70] St Luke's became the larger part of the Faculty of Education, and that, in turn, was concentrated on the St Luke's site, with the former premises in Gandy Street abandoned. This was a key element in the last stage of the university's move from its original city-centre site. The premises in Gandy Street became a bookstore for the Library before being sold.

The government encouraged Exeter to accept the merger by promising that the university could make appointments and expand student numbers in other faculties to match the reduction in the number of permanent staff at St Luke's. The opportunity for this reduction was given by the extent to which St Luke's had been appointing temporary lecturers, who comprised a quarter of its staff at the time of the merger. These lost their jobs, but, due to the general economic climate, the university did not gain other posts as it had anticipated. Of St Luke's establishment of 106 staff and 1,160 teaching places, 56 and 500 survived. Dancy took one of the new professorships. The new School of Education had 85 staff and over 800 teaching places.[71] It was the largest such university school of its type in England: the University of London's Institute of Education was bigger, but was a monotechnic college within the London federation. At Exeter, a large new School was introduced into a university of small departments. Michael Brock, a distinguished Oxford academic, worked as the new School Director to plan the move to St Luke's, but returned to Oxford to head a college before the move occurred.

The university then appointed Ted Wragg as the School's Director, and he saw the move through. A lecturer at Exeter university during 1966–73 but not promoted, Wragg had left for Nottingham which awarded him a chair at the age of thirty-five, the youngest in the country at the time. Wragg occupied the Directorship for sixteen years until 1994 (and retired from Exeter in 2003), and was a prolific academic author and media columnist. As such, he was frequently the university's most prominent member of academic staff nationally throughout the 1980s and 1990s. In part, this was a matter of charisma, energy and contacts. Wragg's memorial service in the cathedral in 2006 (he died the previous year) and the e-memorial condolence book testified to the extent to which he was hugely respected. He inspired a large number of teachers, notably with his child-centred approach to teaching and his emphasis on professionalism, not managerialism. Wragg pressed for evidence-based policy and for the initial training of teachers as a central task for universities.[72] Wragg's letter on the back of the *Time Educational Supplement* every week was required reading for teachers. He was also active in coaching student football and, throughout his career at Exeter, also taught regularly in local primary and secondary schools. A firm advocate for best practice, Wragg was a vigorous opponent of prescriptive bureaucracy, educationalist jargon and political direction. Somewhat didactic, he spoke authoritatively in interviews. Wragg also played to the gallery mercilessly: he was frequently not a high-level commentator. It was easy constantly to satirise Keith Joseph, the Secretary of State for Education, as the 'mad monk', but also glib and superficial. The lasting value of Wragg's intellectual work, specifically his monographs, is unclear, and he lived to repent his earlier advocacy for middle schools, a system that had proved particularly destructive in terms of educational standards in the city of Exeter.[73]

The St Luke's merger raises the issue of opportunistic policymaking, as the university responded to unforeseen circumstances, rather than being in a position to determine its own future. In the short term, this policy worked with reference to the funding obtained as a result of Education's fte students, research grants and research ranking, with the worthwhile by-product of financial support for Theology coming from a newly created St Luke's College Foundation. The initial scale of success at Education was not sustained. However, there was a subsequent recovery in Education, in the 2000s and 2010s. Moreover, the space for expansion, notably for the Medical School, offered by St Luke's was a valuable result of the merger.

This is an account offered from the university perspective. It is also important to remember that there were accounts from that of St Luke's, providing a strong sense of its identity and mission, as well as the loss and disillusionment caused by the merger. The process by which the staff were interviewed for their jobs left much bitterness, and many who were not kept on suffered badly, not least as a result of the difficulty of finding new posts and due to the impact of inflation.[74] Thereafter, there were to be frequent complaints, by the surviving and then new staff and students, that St Luke's was neglected and excluded by the 'main site', and by students that not enough events were held there.[75]

Meanwhile, pressure for a new system and culture of governance rose to the fore among the staff in the late 1970s. A working party of professors and RLA members was established in 1977 in order to discuss both the Composition of Senate and the Government of Departments (COSGOD). The RLA was uncertain about how best to select heads of departments, and was concerned, indeed, that a 'shifting Headship' might lead to 'autocracy' on the part of the Administration.[76] COSGOD was designed to sweep away the oligarchs, and to make the VC, Deans, heads of department and the administration all accountable.

The COSGOD report, debated in Senate on 12 January 1979, proposed a different political culture as well as practice for the university. Worried about the situation becoming more open and fluid, Kay had not attempted to lead, but had followed a policy of strict non-intervention in the deliberations of the Committee.[77] He was somewhat disparaging about the conclusions. Having expressed surprise that the role of Council had not been adequately considered, Kay added that 'the Report was somewhat inward-looking, and that there were exaggerated expectations of the benefits likely to accrue from the changes proposed'. Nevertheless, the 'List' affair had left Kay much weakened.

THE LATER 1970S: A DIVIDED UNIVERSITY

Clifford Parker, the Chairman of the Working Party, had sought to strike a middle way between permanent professorial Headships and departmental democracy. Having conceded the principle of election of the Head, he had been clear that 'the departmental meeting would not be able to give orders to the Head or other members',[78] and now noted that: '[T]he Working Party had clung to the concept of a Head who would run a department, though assisted by the departmental meeting.' The Working Party did not intend to promote rapid changes of Headships. A similar view was taken by Yates, a member: 'Heads should not be slaves to the departmental meeting.'

The subsequent debate revealed a range of opinions, both on the position and role of professors and on the culture of the institution. Bill Tupman, another member, sought a re-creation of the sense of unity which, he claimed, had existed when the university was smaller. He stated that junior staff wanted more responsibility and 'a piece of the action', in the shape of a degree of consultation that recognised that the department was 'theirs' not 'x's'.

Given that only 3/5 of the RLA had returned the questionnaire about governance, and, of these, 2/3 favoured some change, it seems apparent that Tupman was speaking for a portion, rather than a generation. At the same time, there were, as the debate made clear, generational issues. A degree of immobility in the profession, and notably for those without an international reputation, ensured that some sought an opportunity to lead, while, as Reid pointed out, staff were, on average, older and more experienced than over the previous decade. They were also all poorer in terms of real incomes, with the major fall in real income since 1972 compounded by a (justified) sense of being cheated by the government in terms of the handling of pay awards.

There was concern about the impact of the COSGOD proposals on professorial academic leadership; the nature of the latter an issue still pertinent today. Holdsworth argued that academic leadership could not be given equally well under the proposed arrangements, whereas members of the Working Party suggested that being freed from administrative responsibilities would provide more opportunities for such leadership. There was also concern about whether the changes would lead to more power for the central management, as a source of the necessary continuity/experience. The issue of whether, and how best, the university would be able to act to reform departments 'going downhill' was raised, a prescient view in light of the developing issue of national standards, and one that the emphasis on 'departmental interests' did not address. As the university had, with Maurice Goldsmith, a distinguished political theorist on the staff, Senate was informed: 'The real issue was whether departments should be under a collegiate or monarchic form of government. At present most departments were run by consent[79] and the proposed changes would not alter this situation.'

On 24 February 1979, Senate voted by secret ballot. The ballot over the then current practice of appointing a head of department for unlimited tenure saw 44 votes for change and 23 for retention, with no abstentions or spoilt ballots, and that for the composition of Senate, 27 for change and 40 for retention. It was agreed, in secret ballots, that departmental heads should be elected by the departmental staff with the nomination submitted to a University Appointing Committee.

Council approved the changes on 16 July 1979, despite Professor Harry Edmunds, Head of the School of Engineering, speaking of opposition, to varying degrees, by the Faculties of Science and Applied Science on the basis of managerial requirements. This view is underrepresented in interviews, which provides an instructive insight on the presentation of collective memory. Appointed on the old system, as professor and head of the department of Chemical Engineering, in 1979, Robin Turner referred to himself as the 'last of the dinosaurs'. Turner also mentioned the difficulty of managing departments when times were hard, as well as a shift to electing professorial Heads when 'departments realised they were losing out on appointments committees if they didn't have a professor making their case'. At the same time, Turner noted of Edmunds that he did no research, had bizarre ideas about teaching, and usually came in at 10 am and left at 3 pm, a fellow-professor remarking: 'He didn't want to be late twice in the same day.'[80] The old Heads sometimes continued in office for many years. Abel, who became Head of Chemistry in 1978, did not resign until 1989, when the first Elected Head, Dr Roy Moodie, was a Reader. David Catchpole, who was appointed Professor of Theology in 1984, served as Head for twelve years, although the style in Theology was emphatically collegial, with a weekly lunchtime staff meeting.

Criticism of elected Heads was expressed by some who were not in the professoriate. Tony Kelly (French, 1966–92) argued that the introduction of elected Heads began a decline in effective leadership and brought much acrimony as a result of clashing egos.[81] Worried that staff would seek election for the wrong reasons, Kay did not pay those elected much more. More seriously, the number of relatively small departments in the university aggravated the problem of Headships in the longer term, and sometimes in the shorter, in that the number of 'suitable' and/or willing candidates available was inevitably limited. Moreover, the increasing emphasis on research with the arrival and growing importance of the RAE in the 1980s and 1990s changed the role and responsibilities of heads of department, and made the position more onerous.

Nevertheless, as a result of the COSGOD process, Harrison was, in 1984, to inherit, as VC, a fairly democratic and largely transparent organisation, one in which most of the staff felt involved. Decisions affecting the whole university had to be explained and justified. Senate began to monitor the academic performance of departments and faculties. The elective principle enabled the university to discover and make use of those with energy, ideas and talent in a way that had not been possible before. COSGOD also encouraged new ideas and entrepreneurial activity of all kinds.

While the COSGOD process dominated the attention of university politicians, there were concerns about the viability of particular disciplinary areas. Despite UGC support for an increase in the percentage of Science students,[82] a serious shortfall in Science's intake for 1978/79 led to a drive for more students, notably with the introduction of a new course in Medical Physics.[83] Anxiety about the sustainability of small departments developed, with the ADC worried about the viability of Russian, namely its ability to teach a broad syllabus and to attract sufficient students.[84]

The university was also faced by a lack of applications from the north, although the emphasis on entrants from nearby areas matched a national trend. Policy in Wales affected Exeter. In the 1970s, Exeter had a surprising number of students from South Wales, but then Welsh LEAs decided to press their students to go to universities in the Principality. The proportion of Welsh students in Exeter never recovered to the level of the 1970s. It was particularly significant for Exeter that its nearby areas included the south-east as well as the south-west, as the former had a high percentage of schoolchildren staying on for sixth-form courses.[85]

There was also only a relatively small industrial working class in the south, and that was a group underrepresented in university entry. The importance of the recruitment from the south-east was shown with the 'university train' from London at the beginning of each term. The Guild hired a train and sold the tickets. It regularly sold out and is remembered as a packed experience that was great fun.

At the university level, there was to be no shortage of applications for entry. The number had risen from 18,386 for entry in 1977 to 22,021 for entry in 1979, albeit for a university enhanced by St Luke's. The ratio of 13 applicants per place was maintained for the 1980 entry. High application rates helped explain the upward trend in exam results. In 1978, 33 per cent of students gained 2:1s, which was above the national average and compared to 27 per cent in 1959; the percentage of thirds or passes had fallen from 27 to 12. The marking was still far tougher than today: in 1978 only 5 per cent obtained firsts, while 51% gained 2:2s.

At the departmental level, applications for Accountancy (which became a degree subject in Exeter in 1974), Biology, English, French, Geography, History, Law, Mathematics, Psychology and Social Administration proved especially buoyant; but Chemistry, Classics, German, Music, Philosophy, Physics, Russian, Spanish and Theology less so. These contrasts, which were not simply those of Science and Arts, affected the situation in these faculties, as well as in the university as a whole. In the Arts, the weaker departments were smaller ones, but, in Science, Chemistry and Physics were big subjects. Their difficulties in recruitment repeatedly affected the prospect of Science expanding as much as the university and UGC had hoped.

Developments at the departmental level were significant The 1970s' expansion of Psychology largely emphasised cognition and animal behaviour, but towards the end of the decade, there was an expansion in Social Psychology, creating an area of specialism that has continued to the present. The appointment of Dick Eiser to a Chair in the field (the second Chair in the department) was followed by a number of junior appointments. There was also the establishment in 1976 of a professional training programme, initially an MSc, in Clinical Psychology. Until then, the department's postgraduate offerings had been restricted to research degrees. As a reminder that institutional politics were not only carried out at the university level, and that many decisions that were important in the short and long term were made at the departmental level, there were differences of opinion in Psychology as to whether there was demand for a training for professional practice, and indeed whether there was the need for specialised staff to teach Social Psychology. In the event, trainees for the MSc were paid salaries which, together with the costs of fees, were underwritten by regional NHS funding bodies. The trainees were largely taught by dedicated staff, and an essentially independent subsection of the department involved with outside bodies and external stakeholders, notably the NHS, offered a model for development very different to that of the standard department at this period.

This was even more the case for the Institute of Population Studies (IPS), the new shape from 1978 of what had been the Family Planning Research Unit, one of the most successful non-departmental centres in the university. Relocated to Hoopern House (which the university had acquired in 1962), the IPS focused on postgraduate training programmes, mostly to overseas students, with grants provided mainly by the World Health Organization. Alongside the research undertaken, the IPS's teaching, which included local training workshops in a number of developing countries, increased Exeter's global profile.

In the winter of 1978–79, while the country suffered from industrial turmoil, the Estate and Maintenance staff struggled in harsh weather to keep the roads open and heating oil available, achieving a really impressive result;[86] although Ken Moss, Lazenby Chaplain and Senior Lecturer in Chemistry, recalls: '[T]he University decided that the Chapel could do without heat and on one memorable Sunday morning the guest preacher … suggested a quick run round the Chapel half way through his sermon to get warm.'[87]

There was a degree of optimism by late 1978. Despite an uncertain financial outlook, the establishment (in response to earlier retirements) of new posts, both in order to improve the staff–student ratio and in order to recruit young staff was agreed.[88] In response to lay opinion on Council that the projections of a falling national student population should lead to wariness about investing in additional residential places, Kay argued that more accommodation would make it easier to bid for extra students.[89]

As a separate initiative that drew on outside support, a department of Arabic and Islamic Studies was established in 1978 followed, in 1979, by a Centre for Arab Gulf Studies allied to the department. The key figure was Sha'ban, who was appointed Senior Lecturer in Islamic Studies in Theology in 1971 and who headed the new department until 1986. Moreover, a Chair in Archaeology was created in 1979, the year in which the department changed its title from History to History and Archaeology.

However, the finances were getting worse even before the challenge that was to arise from the spending cuts planned by the new Conservative government, under Margaret Thatcher, which won the election held on 3 May 1979. Two days earlier, the visiting Chair of the UGC had agreed that the university was under-financed, but could promise no rapid change. In July 1979, the Treasurer noted that for the first time in the university's history there would certainly be a deficit at the end of a financial year. This was estimated at £166,765 as of 31 July.[90]

The announcement in the Budget on 12 June, as part of a cut of public expenditure by £4,000 million, that the recurrent grant to universities for 1979/80 would be reduced led to a marked deterioration in Exeter's finances. As Kay pointed out in the Board of Senate on 3 July, earlier reductions had led to an apparently stable, albeit lower, baseline. Now it was necessary to accept that staff–student ratios were not likely to be improved. In response, there was the suggestion that the university deliberately court bankruptcy in order to put pressure on the government, but Kay countered that he believed the government would let bankruptcy happen.[91]

As the government also delayed announcing what the UGC would be able to provide, there was the problem of flying blind financially. In the autumn, the UGC advised universities to plan for a 10 per cent cut and, by November 1979, Kay anticipated a deficit for 1979/80 of £466,000: the budgeted deficit of £116,000, plus an anticipated reduction of income of £300,000. This compared with former expectations of 'an additional £570,000 in the last two years of the quinquennium, on the strength of which additional academic posts had been authorised for 1979/80'. Whereas 77.9 per cent of Exeter's income came from the UGC in 1967/68, the proportion for 1979/80 was 66.2 per cent, a serious cut in recurrent funding. Moreover, a cut in capital funding ensured that the focus would be on maintaining buildings, rather than on building new ones. Alongside problems with income, costs continued to rise. For

THE LATER 1970S: A DIVIDED UNIVERSITY

example, fuel costs were rising steeply. The university did not benefit from the fall in tax rates. Lower tax rates released purchasing power, pushing up inflation, which rose to 18 per cent in 1980, driving up interest rates.

On Council: 'Mr [Murray] Laver commented that not only was the UGC grant insufficient but the information about the insufficiency was communicated too late: this was a prescription for bad management.'[92] David Walker, Professor of Economics, the Senior DVC, explained to Council

> that the planned 10 per cent reduction in the undergraduate entry in October 1980 was intended to stabilise student numbers and soften the impact of any further reduction which might be needed after 1980. It was unfortunate that only six months ago the UGC had sanctioned a planned growth of numbers. ... He warned that a reduction in the number of overseas students [as a result of rising fees] would lead to a loss of income which could not be recouped elsewhere.[93]

In accordance with the recommendation of Finance Committee on 5 November 1979, the Treasurer's Working Party was established, so as to be able to consider any serious developments in the financial situation that might occur between Committee meetings, notably to react quickly after grants were announced by the UGC. The following month, the ADC asked departments how they would cope with the forecast 10 per cent funding reduction, which led to few useful comments.

It was agreed by Council on 12 November 1979 that proposals for major economies that required consideration by Council would be routed through Senate, as was done with the 1976/77 search for cuts, but the crisis that began in 1979 saw the start of a shift toward greater decision-making by Council. There had already been signs of Council irritation with what its lay members saw as a failure to keep them sufficiently informed,[94] and complaints about the failure during the UGC visit on 1 May 1979 to discuss matters with Council.[95]

Council sought to make its political position clear. On 8 November, a lunchtime meeting of students and staff in the Great Hall addressed by Kay had encouraged the Guild to opt in favour of joint action with the university in opposing cuts in grants, rather than 'direct action' on its own. Four days later, at Council, concern was expressed that the university might be seen as siding with the government over increasing overseas students' fees, only to lead Kenneth Rowe, the Pro-Chancellor, a lay member of Council, who was in the Chair, to reply that the Council had no party political affiliation whatsoever, but that it would take all such action as constitutional means afforded to protect the university's interests. This approach was a rebuke to the practice and nature of politicking elsewhere in the university, notably by some members of Senate and by the Guild, and reflected an attempt by Council members to exert influence.

Council is frequently the element of university life that sinks from attention in the comments of former staff, and notably so for the 1950s–80s as attention, instead, shifts from authoritarian professors to the impact of COSGOD. Moreover, the views of individual members of Council as a whole do not always match present sensitivities, as on 12 December 1977 when one member, a local councillor, 'emphasised the annoyance felt by many well-wishers when students interfered with local activities such as the hunts; students should understand that they were in some sense guests of the local community'. Furthermore, on 13 February 1978, Council voted 'by a large majority' to keep Glaxo shares, a position supported by the Finance Committee and the Treasurer, in the face of pressure for disinvestment in companies operating in South Africa. Council endorsed the principle of the duty to invest wisely in order to secure the best yield.

As a body some of whom were representatives of other bodies, and many of whom were local worthies with their worthiness owing a little to longevity and connections, Council was not yet the powerhouse of ability, energy, and national and international connections that it was to become in the 2000s, notably under Geoffrey Pope (1999–2004), Ruth Hawker (acting Chair, 2004–05), Russell Seal (2005–12), and Sarah Turvill (2012–). However, there were able individuals on Council in the 1970s and 1980s, and they were to help press for a policy that did not focus on rejection of government policy but, instead, took the idea of a steady-state university toward that of selectivity. Much of the policy shift can be traced to powerful figures in the ADC, notably Walker,

THE LATER 1970S: A DIVIDED UNIVERSITY

Whinnom and Yates, but they were also members of Council, and attitudes there were significant.

The net effect was of a political reconfiguration. It had been assumed by Parker that existing departmental Heads would stay in office until they retired, and the COSGOD change would be implemented gradually, but many Heads chose to resign their administrative responsibilities and allow more junior colleagues to take over. Parker himself resigned as Head of Law in 1983, and Bridge succeeded him as the first elected Head of Law. Parker subsequently took early retirement under the scheme administered by Kay. The changes that followed COSGOD had a major effect on Senate, so that COSGOD proved a central element in a process of assertion by a group of staff on, and through, Senate. This assertiveness gave a character to the university in the Kay years, one that continued throughout the 1980s, but the resulting politics of democratisation and culture of collegiality was challenged from a number of directions. One such, ironically, was that of the growing assertiveness on the part of the students. In the spring of 1979, in the immediate aftermath of COSGOD, there were student demands for representation on the ADC, Standing Committee, and Research Fund Committee, and in planning the long-term future of the university. These demands led to staff opposition, drawing not only on 'traditional' assumptions about control and deference, but also on the position of individual staff. Thus, it was argued that students should not be able to determine individual research applications as they lacked the necessary expertise.[96]

Changes in the university system were more significant.[97] Staff and students, both reformers and radicals, who had pressed for, and secured, change, and who continued to do so, had done so essentially at the expense of other staff and the 'management' in a largely conservative institution that was part of a conservative, corporatist world. This institution had been capable of considerable development, and the reformers and radicals were an aspect of it, as was the COSGOD process. However, far more profound change and pressure for change was to come, from 1979, as the result of a Conservative government that sought to practise Gladstonian liberalism and to introduce (eventually) free market capitalism. The Thatcher government was never consistently 'Thatcherite', as the fate of the NHS showed, but it certainly brought change.[98] Constrained by the power of government and the financial system, as well as by their governance, culture and ideology, the universities were to seem particularly poor at responding to the new environment. In the case of Exeter, this was only partly true. Indeed, the establishment of a research fund was to be followed by pressure for selectivity, while university concern about the viability of small departments was to be followed by national intervention as far as certain subjects were concerned. There was already, therefore, an awareness of the need for change before change was forced on the university. Compared with what was to come in the 1990s and 2000s with the impact of economic liberalism and globalisation, this forcing was not as wide-ranging as it could have been. Nevertheless, a new government, combined with a recession, were to make the early 1980s very difficult for the university.

CHAPTER SEVEN

THE EARLY 1980s: CRISIS FOR AN OLD ORDER

Once we had recruited a staff Entertainments Manager we were able to widen the range of bands coming to Exeter and bring more acts, including comedians, to Cornwall House ... Lenny Henry, Billy Bragg, Thompson Twins and Depeche Mode spring to mind. ... The concerts in the Great Hall were very popular and I remember queues all in front of Devonshire House coffee bar going up the stairs to Top Corridor, where they were sold in those days. My particular favourites were the Kinks and Bob Marley and the Wailers.
Diane Boston, Guild Administrative Officer/Permanent Secretary/
General Manager, 1975–90

The whole concept of the university as we knew it was in danger.
Harry Kay, Finance Committee, 6 July 1981

FINANCE, GOVERNANCE AND Politics were to the fore in the early 1980s, but, in detailing the key developments, it is important to underline the centrality of teaching and research for the majority of academics. The focus is on these other matters because they were highly important to the university context for teaching and research, and also because neither of the latter changed significantly in this period. Nor were there particular developments in student life.

By the beginning of the 1980s, there had been a degree of stabilisation in the governance and finances of the university. To an extent, this was a matter of movement from the low base of the situation in the mid-1970s. Nevertheless, there had also been a measure of improvement, due in part to incremental changes that Harry Kay managed to introduce, and in part to the shifting of the generations as power moved from long-standing staff to younger appointments, some of whom were more mindful of the university's need to earn its position, indeed any position.

A sense of stabilisation and gradual improvement is certainly recorded in the memories of staff of the period. In this narrative, offered for example from an informed insider position by Gar Yates, the Chair of ADC from 1980 to 1983, this improvement was rudely interrupted by outside pressure in the shape of the public expenditure cuts that followed the election of the Conservative government of 1979. Thus, a hostile outside world threatened a benign situation of progress. Indeed, in response to a UGC letter of 30 December 1980, Kay told ADC on 13 January 1981 that the ability of Exeter in the past to survive financial crises was no longer a guide, as 'no form of supplementary grant can be expected this time'.

The economic recession of the early 1980s put further pressure on public finances and thus on the universities. Indeed, 'The Future Pattern of Resources for Universities', a UGC letter of 15 May 1981, was to warn of significant further cuts for the universities by 1983/84. The severe cuts that followed were unevenly distributed and shook up the university system. On 1 July 1981, Exeter was notified that its recurrent grant would fall from £10.77 million in 1981/82 to £9.69 million (at 1981/82 prices) in 1983/84, a fall greater than anticipated by ADC,[1] with home and European Community full-time students in the Arts cut from 3,290 in 1979/80 to 3,170 in 1983/84. Moreover, the UGC provided advice. The university was invited to consider ending Drama (which it did not do), but an increase of 30 students in the Physical Sciences was recommended.[2] In response to the cuts, Kay 'called for extreme action' in the Board of Senate on 13 July. In the longer term, the handling of the cuts to state funding were to pave the way for research selectivity.

The standard account is accurate, but incomplete. Irrespective of the

Thatcher government, the university would have faced serious difficulties anyway in the early 1980s due to the impact of the severe global recession of the period. The fundamental problems facing Exeter arose not from a malign government, but from the combination of this recession and the dependence of all British universities on public, i.e. government, support. There was simply too little money coming in from other sources, and that issue had not been fundamentally addressed, by government or the university sector, in the 1970s. The low historic funding base, very modest reserves and lack of endowment income made this situation particularly serious for Exeter.

An added twist was to be given to this crisis for the universities by the poor relations that built up between the Thatcher government and much of the sector; and these relations repeatedly attracted the attention of staff and students who criticised government policy. Their criticisms were to expand to include a critique of universities that were held to cooperate with the government. Anger and suspicion conditioned the attitudes of many of the staff toward university policy thereafter and proved a wearing aspect of university society.

The root problem in the early 1980s rested in the consequences of the dependence of the universities on a government that was committed to cutting public expenditure and that was to pursue this policy irrespective of a serious economic downturn. 'The lady's not for turning' meant serious problems for the universities.

If that was the macro situation, there was also a micro situation that was of particular note in the early 1980s. Kay and his successors were to struggle to define policy in the face both of cuts in expenditure and, even more seriously, of uncertainty over future real levels of funding, notably due to high and continuing inflation which rose to 18 per cent in 1980. Kay repeatedly warned that it was unclear whether the inflation in costs, notably pay awards, would be funded by government. There was a lack of understanding of the government's intentions and of the university's likely real incomes.[3] An attempt, in response, to increase the fees for overseas students was heavily defeated in Senate.[4]

The death in office on 31 March 1981 of Kenneth Nash from a brain tumour after a painful illness contributed to a sense of the situation as being out of control, not least because, although inexperienced by background in university matters, Nash had been the key figure under Kay.

Malcolm Hislop, his successor, did not match Nash's degree of grip. 'Chernenko after Andropov' was the reflection of some of the academics.[5] A nonentity, Hislop came from the Property Services Agency and never appeared to show much interest in academic matters, as opposed to the Estate and the buildings. He also found it difficult to handle a balance sheet, or, indeed, his own staff.[6] It is striking that the university, under Kay, came to appoint two consecutive Registrars who had no managerial experience of universities.

Despite the sense of crisis, however, there was in fact some improvement in governance in the early 1980s, notably in coordinating the work of ADC and Finance Committee.[7] From the beginning of the 1980s, cost control and cutting was the central theme, and across a broad range of activities; in large part because increases in revenue could not bridge the gap. The timetable may not seem the most significant of concerns, but it is an abiding issue, both of management and of control, and involves costs. The report by the Timetable Committee discussed by the Standing Committee of Senate on 23 January 1980, preferred lunchtime, to evening or Saturday morning, lectures because of the implications for heating and lighting; although, in turn, there were catering consequences from the former.[8]

However, financial issues threw up governmental tensions within the university. The UGC response to a university delegation on 5 February 1980 made it clear that the sole capital grant that was likely would be to fund the second stage of the Library, and that the university was expected to fund other developments from its current income. The delegation pointed out 'that staff/student ratios on the Arts side were not such as to offer much prospect of economies from which to support developments on the Science side'. The ratios were poor by the then national standard.[9] In early 1980, the ADC decided, against the view of the faculty of Science, to support Low Temperature Physics at the expense of Geophysics, and not to back the replacement of the Reader in Geophysics; only for the issue to be brought up on the Board of Senate on 5 March 1980.[10] That meeting also considered the election of Deans in the context of clashing committees:

> The Vice Chancellor reminded the Board that the Standing Committee had recommended in the Michaelmas Term that no

THE EARLY 1980S: CRISIS FOR AN OLD ORDER

change in the present procedure be made, but this had not been accepted. The matter had been referred to the Faculty Boards and it was noted that four recommended no change whilst the remaining two were each putting forward a different proposal.

Kay made clear, at that meeting of the Board of Senate, his opposition to the 'growing complexity of the government of the University' and to 'the wrong way of tackling the problem', and feared that elections of Deans could be divisive; only for the Dean of Arts to emphasise the need to use elections to overcome '"them and us" feelings' and for the Board to vote, by a large majority, to ask Standing Committee to revisit the matter on the basis of allowing variations by faculty. The same Board considered the Report of the Working Party on Student Representation, issued on 19 February 1980, which recommended representation on university committees managing academic affairs and departmental staff meetings. Meeting opposition, this recommendation was given the verdict by procrastination of being referred to faculties and departments.[11] This verdict was one that was very common in the university during the 1970s and 1980s.

As staff costs for the poorly funded university were, at 70 per cent, the principal cause of expenditure, this situation led to pressure on the university to cut the number of academics: by natural wastage, by not filling vacancies, by encouraging early retirements, and by considering redundancies. Kay told the Board of Senate on 13 July 1980 that there would need to be a significant number of staff losses, and that his preference was for early retirements. This policy was supported by the Board, not least with mention of the 'internal harmony' of the university, despite the warning that avoiding redundancies might only buy time. The case for early retirement was argued in a 'Green Paper' prepared for the RLA by Bruce Coleman and Trevor Preist that worked out in some detail, using staff age-structures, how the necessary savings could be achieved. As older and senior staff were mainly affected, the cost savings were considerable. Kay was hesitant at first, but came around when the sole alternative, the closure of several departments, had been rejected. There was also the question of the structural viability of the university's plans: 'Doubts were expressed whether the University's policy of relatively strengthening Science and Engineering could be maintained, in view of the UGC's failure to provide the requisite funds.' ADC had recommended on 29 April 1980 planning for increased student numbers in Science and Applied Science, and restraint, therefore, on staff appointments in other areas. On 21 October 1980, ADC went on to recommend increasing Science students to 34 per cent of the student population by 1983/84, which would make Science the largest faculty. On 29 October, at the Board of Senate, the Dean of Science complained that the increase was not larger, only for Kay to observe that the university could not afford a larger increase.

The situation for the Library was more favourable. The UGC cuts of 1980/81 had reduced the number of grants for new building, but, with a generous gift of £750,000 from the ruler of Dubai, Shaikh Rashid bin Saeed, in July 1980,[12] the university was able to return to the negotiating table and was allowed to proceed with the building work. The new Library opened on 1 August 1983 (official opening by Princess Anne on 11 June 1984), and immediately proved very popular, in terms of turnstile counts.

The general financial situation, however, continued to deteriorate and Kay noted an absence of public support for universities.[13] Moreover, staff morale in Exeter was certainly affected by general insecurity. Kay proved effective in negotiating the necessary number of early retirements, a goal, largely financed by the government allocation of funds to subsidise such programmes, that he had to sustain over several years.[14] As a consequence, redundancies were avoided. However, aside from the more specific impact of retirements on the rising student–staff ratio, there was scant planning involved in the cuts, and the results unbalanced departments.[15] What were needed, at the very least, were new young staff, the establishment of a research culture, and the creation of structures able to enforce change, if not planning and implementing a more general restructuring.[16] The administration lacked such a drive, while departmental special interest pleas were deployed in response to the financial crisis; as well as a more general opposition to the government. Thus, in responding to ADC's proposal to cut Theology by a post, Roy Porter argued that 'actual cuts should be seen to be dictated from outside the University', only for Yates to point out that Theology had a favourable staff–student ratio.[17]

Special interests were also at issue in discussion over the composition of the Monitoring Committee and its role in overseeing student

THE EARLY 1980S: CRISIS FOR AN OLD ORDER

admissions: there was pressure to include faculty representatives, but also a feeling that a university view was required. Faculty representatives were not added. The tension between departmental/faculty views and a different university viewpoint was a mounting theme in the 1980s.

In the face of the threat to close down Theology in the early 1980s, when the senior staff members were on the point of retiring, the St Luke's College Foundation Trust set up and endowed the St Luke's Foundation Chair of Theological Studies in 1984, with David Catchpole as first holder. Already, the recasting of Exeter's rather old-fashioned Oxford-type Theology degree, with its emphasis on languages (Greek, Hebrew) but without Christian Ethics, into a degree in Theological Studies was being planned. Porter strongly disapproved of the introduction of the Theological Studies degree scheme, regarding it as an academic devaluation, notwithstanding the incontrovertible fact that the department would have perished without it. The shift of focus opened the degree up to students with wider interests, and from other departments, making languages optional while including options taught by staff from other departments: English, Classics, Philosophy and Sociology. There was a resulting decline in Exeter's previous appeal to High-Church Anglican students, some considering ordination. An all-male department gained female staff and a specialist in the Philosophy of Religion.[18]

The threat to Russian led to the creation of the School of Modern Languages, an attempt to rescue failing departments in the safety of a bigger unit. It had no formal status, but did have its own constitution and executive committee.

A new regime of government incentives distinguished between universities in the award of funds, while the quinquennial system gradually became more dirigiste, to use a word that gained increasing currency. State-run redistribution became the order of the day, awarding a new function to the UGC, with which Exeter's relations had long been poor, and thereafter, to its successor, the Universities Funding Council (UFC). Universities received resources under T (teaching), which was based on student numbers, and R and QR, which were both research-related. The T quota was far greater and the variations in funding under the early RAEs were quite modest in terms of the university's total income, but changes at the margins of resourcing always hit home. The RAEs offered the possibility of redistribution.

In the short term, there were also the 'New Blood' schemes under which money was provided to fund new lectureships in an exercise designed to strengthen Science research, but also to ensure that sufficient staffing was maintained to continue teaching levels. In 1983, Exeter only obtained two of the 230 'New Blood' posts, which increased its relative underfunding. Kay reflected that 'the University had always had the image of a teaching rather than a research university, and that despite the efforts over the last ten years it was proving very difficult to change that image',[19] a point to which he returned.

After a period in which applications had risen much more rapidly than for other universities, there were significant falls in applications for admissions in 1980, 1981 and 1982: by 3.2, 8.1 and 5.1 per cent respectively. The comparable percentages for all universities were +1.8 , −0.4 and +3.6 per cent. Exeter presented this as losing a weaker tail.[20] There was certainly a contrast between popular courses where it was becoming harder to get in and small departments which kept up numbers by offering lower grades.[21] From a peak of 22,000, applications had fallen to 17,230 by 1983, with concerns about the future of Exeter in the shape of the numbers of 18-year-olds in Britain. The trend gathered pace. In 1984, applications fell to 16,093, a 6.6 per cent fall, whereas the national trend was a 0.55 per cent increase, and the Admissions Officer was concerned that the quality was not as good as in the past.

Meanwhile, when Council considered the social equity of admissions and the possible need for 'positive action' in addition to A level grades, Kay raised the impact of competition for entry on 'the difficulty of allocating places fairly'. In Standing Committee, concerns about the extent of public-school entry and the role of grade increases in affecting social composition were expressed.[22] There was more sustained criticism from Guild members, with the complaint, on the staff–student committee known as the University Committee, on 14 February 1983, about exclusive groups from public schools and from the Guild President, that 'many self-confident students of this type did not seem to have the same academic commitment as their colleagues'. Staff members of the committee also expressed concern, worrying that this student self-confidence hindered teaching and affected the work ethos. There was criticism of this analysis at the Board of Senate on 23 February 1983, not least of creating a problem by attaching labels to groups, but Kay argued

THE EARLY 1980S: CRISIS FOR AN OLD ORDER

that there was a real problem, one experienced by staff and students alike.

The Guild paper on social mix produced in February claimed that students encountered problems due to 'the social, cultural and, apparently, academic predominance of an unassailable, unapproachable group, differentiated by manner, dress, diction, motivation and origin', a group described as the 'green wellies'. It was claimed that these students exercised verbal domination in seminars and tutorials, as well as dominating certain halls and societies, and affecting the outside reputation of the university. That June, there was concern about the increasing percentage of applications and admissions from public schools. For admissions, this had risen from 34.4 per cent in 1979 to 37.6 per cent in 1982, a trend that contrasted with a steady situation in the sector as a whole. As what was seen as a related issue in a kind of moral panic, there were claims, including by Kay, that drunkenness and misbehaviour were increasing.[23] He was referring to the students.

It was to take David Harrison to introduce a different dose of realism when he pointed out, in 1984, that 'it would be a slow process to change entrenched views of Exeter in the comprehensive schools; however, there were universities with a higher proportion of students from Independent schools than Exeter, and their situation attracted less attention. The University should talk less and do more'[24], a standard, and highly pertinent, refrain from Harrison in his early years.

In addition to the 'New Blood' schemes, another area of government support and UGC supervision came in the consolidation exercises of the 1980s. Subjects in which there appeared to be too much provision in the national level and/or too many small departments were rationalised with staff and, crucially, associated student numbers, being moved and the UGC meeting the costs, in Russian for example as a result of the Wooding Report of 1985. In contrast to its results in the 'New Blood' exercise, Exeter was to do very well out of the fully funded rationalisations, notably in the faculty of Arts, benefiting for example in Classics,[25] Russian and Spanish, although the added staff varied greatly in their academic contribution. Several of these 1980s newcomers took early retirement themselves in the 1990s, but the student numbers and the funding remained with Exeter.

The process serves as a reminder that the closure of departments which caused such a furore in Exeter in the early 2000s was, in part, an aspect of a long-term process which had at times been a national programme. The issues involved caused controversy in the 1980s, with UGC-backed pressure for departmental closures, for example of Drama. The Academic Structure Plan, Stage Two, was only approved by the Board of Senate in 1982 with considerable difficulty.[26] Malcolm Cook, who was appointed to teach French in 1978, recalled:

> I came to a department which was not a research department – teaching was important and was well done but not evaluated and research was done by some but not all colleagues. ... There was no concept of research leave and even a sense of pride that people could do research without leave. ... There were two schools, those who did (research) and those who didn't.[27]

A few brave souls were to resist the collective ethos, i.e. myth, and to suggest that Exeter was underperforming the sector and that there was a measure of responsibility for the bad news. One such was John Black in Economics, who was described by Desmond Corner as telling people what he thought they ought to hear, even in staff seminars.[28] Another was Robin Turner in Chemical Engineering, who told Council on 18 July 1983 that 'since the "New Blood" posts are primarily intended to promote research, it would seem that Exeter did not have a good reputation for research'.

When, in July 1984, Keith Whinnom, the senior DVC, thanked the departing Kay 'for the unifying effect of his practice of wide consultation on Senate business',[29] he was putting a gloss on a difficult situation. As Chair of ADC, Yates had warned the Board of Senate in November 1980 that 'there was a danger of stagnation, and the ADC was anxious to secure broad agreement on a measure of flexibility in academic appointments rather than to rely solely on retirements to provide economies'. In response to ADC's call for priorities,[30] however, Coleman, as Chair of the RLA, complained in December 1980 that it had caused 'concern to many staff' and expressed the fear that the long-term structure plan would lead to pressure for immediate economies.[31] Coleman was mandated for issues before Senate, and thus opposed in May 1981 the appointment of a mathematician as a Professor of Education on the

THE EARLY 1980S: CRISIS FOR AN OLD ORDER

grounds that 'with his strong research interests' he was not 'necessarily the best person to meet the School's teaching requirements'. The Education members on the RLA Committee had persuaded that body to oppose the proposal on various grounds because (supposedly) the School did not want the appointment.[32] Kay intervened to point out that the Board of Senate needed to trust the VC to carry out policy rather than intervening at every step over urgent staffing problems. Nevertheless, the RLA proposed that ADC's recommendation to appoint be rejected, only for Senate to defeat the motion 32–14.[33] On 4 November 1981, Yates called the bluff of the RLA by offering to resign if he lacked the confidence of the academic staff. Lay members of Council pressed the need to face the issue of redundancies.[34]

The issue recurred in 1982 when Malyn Newitt and Richard Seaford sought on Senate to block the appointment of a Professor of Pure Mathematics, preferring a junior replacement. This was in accordance with the pressure from the 'Caucus' for the appointment of young staff whenever there was a vacancy. Issues of policy, authority and the role of Senate came to the fore, with the motion defeated by 52–15 with 7 abstentions.

The same year, political volatility was apparent in Trevor Preist's election as the first non-professorial DVC. In the Senate secret ballot, he defeated David Walker of Economics, the most respected and one of the most powerful of the old heads of department, a popular figure who had already been a very successful DVC. Preist was put up with RLA backing yet did not expect to win; it was said that members of the 'old guard' professoriate voted against Walker because they were jealous of him and did not want him to have a second turn as DVC.[35] The same year saw Bruce Coleman elected as the first non-professorial Dean.

There was an undercurrent of genteel rebellion against the 'oldies', led by a radical group labelled the 'Caucus' which was active at faculty and Senate levels and was particularly strong in Social Studies. The Caucus proved particularly active against ADC proposals. Indeed, it was as if opposing ADC had succeeded COSGOD as the major cause for academic radicals. A key bond in the Caucus seems to have been AUT membership and Labour Party affiliation.

Kay endorsed the UGC's call for a positive response to the financial situation,[36] but, although he told Council that there were too many small departments,[37] he did not act accordingly. Similarly, he frequently complained about a lack of research income, but did not do enough about it. There was a change of tone after Harrison became VC, not least in the content and tone of Senate papers: Kay did not control Senate.

The response to social trends could also be contentious. The instructive discussion in the Board of Senate on 11 March 1981 about placing contraceptive machines in Halls saw the traditional Kay mindful of public views while the more radical staff sided with the Guild:

> Dr K Read[38] ... believed that the introduction of these machines would put unfair pressure on students to adopt certain modes of behaviour. Dr Oliver was opposed: contraceptives were already easily available to students and he did not believe that the proposal would do anything to reduce the number of unwanted pregnancies; students would do better to seek medical advice. Miss Trewavas, supported by Mr Laughton-Scott, said that in the Guild's view these machines would assist students to behave more responsibly; Mr Bennun[39] emphasised that there must be a limit to paternalism on the University's part; Mrs Chanceller felt that after the University's recent decision to sell beer and wine in its own shop it could not cavil at this less harmful measure. Mr Pisk said that if only one abortion was made unnecessary the proposal was justified; and Mr Davison thought that the objections to the machines for aesthetic reasons were groundless; they were no worse than chocolate vending machines. The Vice Chancellor mentioned that the sensational publicity given to this issue by the *South-Westerner* had resulted in a number of critical letters from the general public.

The Board approved the machines by 32–15 with 12 abstentions. Kay then regretted that the matter had been put forward as a separate issue and emphasised the importance of the Student Health Service and the Guild Counselling Service. On Council, on 23 March, Councillor Daw attacked the proposal as 'morally wrong' and as affecting the university's public image, but lost his motion 10–7: Coleman opposed him on the basis of limiting unwanted pregnancies. The earlier discussions at every meeting of the Board of Senate from 21 May 1980 about the university

THE EARLY 1980S: CRISIS FOR AN OLD ORDER

shop selling alcohol, with attacks on the grounds of social undesirability, had been settled in favour on 3 December 1980 of such sales by a vote of 32–21.

As another example of social policy, the university did little about academic staff having sexual relationships with students. In part this was a matter of the belief in freedom of individual choice among adults.[40] However, the vast majority of staff did not engage in inappropriate behaviour, while the 'culture' in this case was set more at departmental than at university level. Sex with students was allegedly more common in Psychology, English, French and Politics than in Science; and, even then, most academics in these departments did not have such relationships, which indicates that the terms norm and culture have to be used with care.

By 1983, there was a degree of easing in the financial situation. The UGC letter of 16 February 1983 revealed that the recurrent grant for 1983/84 would be £14.19 million, as opposed to the £13.62 million announced the previous May, an increase that modestly outperformed the sector average. There was insufficient to cover likely pay increases, but this was not cataclysmic. The sale of the Gandy Street property brought in capital, while the conversion of Crossmead from a hall into a conference centre produced income, as did the establishment of Exeter Enterprises to exploit consultancy work. As another indication of a lightening of the atmosphere, the Guild decided that the kind of demonstrations and occupations being organised elsewhere for the NUS 'Day of Action', called as a protest against government policy on Higher Education, would be inappropriate at Exeter.

Kay retired in 1984, a year early, to set an example of early retirement to others. His imminent retirement led to much discussion of what was required from a VC. Views ranged from not needing the post and leaving it unfilled for a period to save money, to rotating it among existing staff or relying on a triumvirate of wise men. It was agreed that effective leadership was required in order to obtain scarce funds, that the VC must command the respect of Senate, and that he should continue the current strategy for dealing with the cuts; in short no redundancies. Consultation with 'all interests' was called for, as was experience of more than one university and of a university of the same size as Exeter. It was assumed that the choice would not be for anyone 'associated with support for the contraction of the universities', in other words government policy.[41]

A slight financial easing, meanwhile, meant that new staff appointments could be considered alongside early retirements, although there was a reluctance to differentiate between departments on the grounds of quality and thus to increase the university's reputation and earnings.[42] There were warnings of a new start–stop sequence, but it was agreed in December 1983 that chairs should be filled in Theoretical Physics, Physical Chemistry and Engineering Science. As Kay pointed out, these chairs would not have been possible without the success of the early-retirement programme. The appointments in Science were made in order to improve research performance ahead of the first RAE. However, the chair in Social Policy and Administration was not filled when Robert Leaper retired in 1984, a decision in which funding issues were linked to tensions between departments.[43]

Indeed, 'stop' was more in evidence in 1984, as the UGC letter of 9 February revealed a cut for the recurrent grant for 1984/85 to less than had been announced in 1983. This was because the UGC had withheld the costs of early retirement for universities as a whole. At 2.3 per cent, Exeter's cut was less than it was for the sector as a whole (2.5 per cent), but it was a cut. Aside from problems for the funding of Science, this situation also put pressure on the staff–student ratio and made uncertainty over the budgetary implications of pay increases more serious.[44] The Library faced cuts in both staffing costs and book funds.

There was a degree of uncertainty in the politics and governance of the university in 1984. Aside from hostility to the end of tenure,[45] a hostility which scarcely matched the national public mood, there was the creation in Exeter of select committees for research, teaching and the region as recommended in 'Towards a Development Policy for Exeter', the report of the RLA/AUT working group. Designed to act as think-tanks for existing executive committees, these select committees were, in effect, an alternative to the ADC, but the Board of Senate of 14 March 1984 approved the idea in principle. The reports of the committees could be valuable, for example that on Combined Honours from that for Teaching, and they offered a forum for cross-faculty thinking and open debate on policy issues.

ADC, however, wondered whether there was a proper mechanism

THE EARLY 1980S: CRISIS FOR AN OLD ORDER

within the university able to fulfil the responsibility to formulate a research plan for the UGC. The possibility of the accurate surveying of teaching and research of highly specialist groups was questioned,[46] but there was a broader question, that of the very capability of the university at the end of the Kay era. Thus, the 1981 cuts were much debated. The ADC, the faculties and the departments were all invited to seek out 'pallid growths', a UGC phrase, but, despite losses due to early retirement, and 'compensated voluntary retirement' for younger academics, there was simply no mechanism for ruthless pruning. On the contrary, 'collegiality' prevailed. The difficulty of selection was also seen with the national relocation of academics as small departments were rationalised. Not all of those relocated to Exeter were a great gain in terms of cutting-edge research. As a separate issue, the university, like others, lacked an entrepreneurial character, although, in Exeter individual academic 'entrepreneurs' developed important initiatives.

From a Cambridge science background, David Harrison, Kay's successor, had the merit of already being a VC and at Keele, a university that had had to adapt to major cuts. Noted critics of the 'management' were argued down in Senate in a way that Kay had failed to attempt or achieve. Moreover, some of the wilder ideas about new governmental structures that had circulated in Kay's last years were successfully resisted. The idea that Senate's oversight of the administration ensured a continual right to revise was refuted. So also, eventually, was the extent to which Senate sought to encroach on the authority of Council, an issue about which Council had expressed anger on 19 March 1984.

Several of these developments lay ahead but it was already clear by late 1984 that the university had passed a nadir. As the next three chapters, however, will indicate, notably in the coverage of the terrible 1996 RAE results, that did not mean that serious problems had yet been adequately confronted, nor that the university was anywhere near the internationally well-rated institution it was to become from the late 2000s. Indeed, improvement was to prove a difficult process, and there was still to be a serious crisis of quality in the late 1990s.

Capability was linked to internal factors, notably structures, politics and culture, as well as external ones, notably financial support. Council lacked an understanding of research and of research culture, as well as of the national and international context of higher education. Paul

Webley (Psychology, 1980–2006), who arrived having spent a year as a temporary lecturer in Southampton and was to go on to be a DVC, found the university

> small, cosy, masculine, parochial, old-fashioned, complacent and amateur. In this it was probably not very different from most universities at the time, though it did seem a bit more traditional than Southampton and certainly had a more upper class intake of students ... I remember asking my head of department what I should do in tutorials and being told (not very helpfully) that it was entirely up to me. What I taught and whether I did any research or not, also seemed entirely up to me. The idea that a member of academic staff might be mentored or – heaven forbid – managed, was entirely alien. All the staff in the Psychology department were English – apart from one, who was Scottish. 2 or 3 of the students came from overseas, all from the Commonwealth countries. And students spent all their time in Exeter – apart from one week away on a field course on Lundy. ... All the academic staff were male. ... The old-fashioned nature of the place is nicely illustrated by the criteria for using the Staff Club (then, to put it mildly, a rather stuffy place). When my wife enrolled as an undergraduate student in Music (in 1988), the Staff Club committee had a discussion as to whether she could be an associate member (as undergraduates were strictly forbidden). It was decided, after a solemn discussion, that she could, as her status as a wife took precedence over her status as a student. ... The University changed very slowly in the 1980s, which is not surprising, as there was a policy of not appointing new staff if colleagues left (as a way of dealing with the financial problems facing the university) ... the lack of new blood meant a lack of change, as did the lack of change at the top of some departments ... this is one of the factors that precipitated the crisis of the 1990s: the University had become stuck in its ways and was living on a reputation that the development of league tables was beginning to undermine, and the successive versions of the RAE damaged considerably.[47]

The early RAEs were to put actual comparative measurements on Exeter's research performance, and were to expose the self-regard, even

THE EARLY 1980S: CRISIS FOR AN OLD ORDER

complacency, of the assumptions of some of the staff. The RAEs also offered a way out of Exeter's financial constraints; a way that, however, entailed management and leadership requirements. The RAEs were part of a process by which the UGC moved away from the historic funding, in which Exeter had done badly, into performance-related funding, a vital development for Exeter's subsequent improvement. Thus, external challenge offered significant possibilities, a repeated theme in the history of Exeter, and of universities in general.

However, although the RAE offered good possibilities for improved funding in the long term, it did not do so very much initially. The RAE judgements for R and QR were for some time modified by 'protected' funding. The only way to improve research performance dramatically was to appoint significant numbers of new staff, but Exeter did not have the money for that. There were also problems in holding on to some of the best staff, many of whom went elsewhere in pursuit of salaries, promotions, research facilities and teams that Exeter could not afford.[48] Several came back to Exeter when the finances had improved and they could be made better offers.

Given that Exeter had a continued ability to recruit good students, the university's position was better than its governance, politics and academic culture might suggest. At the same time, this ability to recruit ultimately rested on a perception of the university's quality as well as character. With the development of models and measures of relative capability, that perception was to be challenged in the 1980s and 1990s, but students at the time continued to enjoy the place. Adrian Stones (Music, 1983–86) 'enjoyed the town and made a point of going off campus as often as was reasonable ... there were enough restaurants and bars to give us places to go at the weekends'. He found the department 'extraordinarily friendly', adding: 'There was probably about the normal amount of inappropriate contact between students and staff and there was one sexual predator whose behaviour was curiously tolerated despite its being widely remarked upon.' Stones was a highly successful President of one of the university's major societies, the Gilbert and Sullivan Society.[49]

CHAPTER EIGHT

THE LATE 1980s: DIFFICULT YEARS, AGAIN

It was in the middle of the Thatcher winter and Exeter felt a frozen place – I had a temporary post since Brian Harley's job was not replaced with a permanent job, and I joined a group of talented and ambitious fixed term people, none of whom stayed on I think, but all of whom went on to interesting jobs elsewhere. My two years at Exeter were formative and exciting, and laid the basis for my career since. ... I also met individuals in other departments, often, whose work inspired me (Mick Gidley in American Studies for example). ... I did a ton of teaching and although it was backbreaking, it did put me in a good position in later posts. The students were generally high calibre but not really tested much, or so I thought as a young turk. I notice that the Exeter Geography department has radically changed and is now a very lively place.
Felix Driver (Geography, 1986–88)[1]

I had spent far too long in the coffee bar writing stories, and far too little time at lectures.
(Joanne) J.K. Rowling (1983–87)[2]

THE LATE 1980S: DIFFICULT YEARS, AGAIN

Harrison's heyday occurred in the late 1980s. By the early 1990s, there was a sense that his thoughts and ambitions were elsewhere. First, there was his focus on the CVCP, which he chaired during the difficult period of the response to the government's Bill to reform universities (passed in a watered-down form in 1992) and to the end of the binary divide between universities and polytechnics. Secondly, it was widely felt that he was anxious to return to Cambridge, where he had been a Fellow of Selwyn College before moving to Keele in 1979, and where he kept a house which he rented out. He did indeed return to Cambridge, as Master of Selwyn. The memory of Harrison's later years as VC were to colour subsequent recollection, but there were at least three stages to his VCship. The first stage, replacing Kay, consolidating power and establishing a new tone, moved into the second, which dominated the late 1980s.

These were years in which the challenge (the word of our days) of improving research standards was faced, and with some of the implications that this might entail for selectivity between departments confronted. Harrison's background, first as a Chemical Engineer[3] and secondly in Keele, lent itself to this goal and he had the skills of a very able administrator; but the task was clear anyway. Had Harrison not tried to lead, then the university would have continued in a downward spiral with a marked disconnect between its internal self-valuation and external criteria. 'A backwater when Kay finished', was the view of Eddie Abel, Professor of Inorganic Chemistry.[4] Harrison was appointed as a reaction to Kay.

Harrison's policies entailed seeking to benefit from RAE-linked funding, which was the key element in the process by which the university was expected to justify itself in the context of national academic standards, rather than its own market niche. The latter was well established as far as student intake was concerned. The university was considered to be small, human, and in a safe and attractive part of the country. It was much favoured by middle-class parents for their middle-class daughters, a preference reflected in the high female to male student ratio, and by 'public' (i.e. private) and grammar schools for pupils who could not get into Oxbridge. Indeed, Exeter was seen as providing a similar 'university experience', and prepared students for fitting into the social life of their peers/would-be peers when they arrived for work in

London. A cartoon showed parents commiserating when a child failed to get into Exeter and saying at least he had got into Exeter College, Oxford.

The similarity of the experience to that of Oxbridge owed something to the slightly sleepy sense of self-importance and self-confidence of much (but certainly not all) of the university, something to its organisational structure and ethos, and something to the students. Departments had almost a 'family' air, as collegiality extended to students as well as the staff. The secretaries were treated, and behaved, like equal colleagues and treated the students with great warmth. Student welfare was not articulated, but was the driving ethos of departments. While only some academics socialised with students, the student–staff ratio and the size of departments ensured that the students could be known as individuals. The quality of teaching was generally very high.

With regard to a minority of students, albeit a minority who made disproportionate noise and attracted disproportionate attention, Exeter was regarded and presented as one of the leading preparation centres for metropolitan 'Sloane Ranger' existence. Living in country cottages and driving in by car, the Sloane Rangers prepared for metropolitan life with dinner parties. Exeter, Sloane Square in the country, appeared to fit in well with the values outlined (and satirised) in Ann Barr and Peter York's *The Official Sloane Ranger Handbook* (1982), values that became more pronounced and chic with the attention surrounding Lady Diana Spencer, the personification of 'Sloane Rangerdom', who married Prince Charles in 1981 and who was discussed as a Sloane in *Exeposé*.[5] Benedict Kelly (1979–82) recalled 'a clique of students who lived in neighbouring cottages (some very run down) and who drove in to the campus for lectures ... there was definitely a rather unpleasant division of students who lived on campus/in the City and those who lived in the cottages; not much mixing'.[6] The Pimms Society and 'Coc Soc' (the Cocktails Society) were part of this world.

This ambience, this niche, had been the cause of disquiet for a while on the part of both the Guild and of some of the staff, but ceased to seem an option as Exeter acted under Harrison in order to preserve its claim to status as a rounded mainstream university that included the full range of Sciences as well as the teaching of postgraduates. As a result of this goal, there was a shift in mission and culture, so that the social interaction by

THE LATE 1980S: DIFFICULT YEARS, AGAIN

staff with students and with the local community both declined. The university did not opt to remain small, nor to become a type of Liberal Arts college. Neither was viable given the size of the Science side, although the long-term practicality of developing that side in the shape of the cross-subsidies required was not fully considered.

Meanwhile, alongside differences in background, there was the enduring point that university life gave students (and staff) an opportunity both to remake themselves and to form friendships that subsumed any pre-existing divides. This point was made eloquently by Sajid Javid (Economics and Politics, 1988–91), who, with his working-class background from a Bristol comprehensive and as the first member of his family to go to university, and a 'person of colour', found unfamiliar a world containing many students from independent schools, but also made masses of friends from that background as well as playing a key role in student politics. This first exposure to student politics took him towards becoming MP and, in 2018, Home Secretary.[7]

The specifics of finance, standards and politics in particular years interacted with longer-term trends, in causing the coming and going, waxing and waning of disciplines. Some of the decisions were the university's own, but others were shaped or forced by changes of policy by governments and other funding bodies, and by shifts in the larger economy. These changes were very difficult to predict. To have suggested in 1985 that Engineering would survive, while Chemistry disappeared, would have been surprising. So also were the subsequent problems of Education and Law, the flourishing of Arab and Islamic Studies, and Sports Science, and the establishment of a full Medical School.

The sense of unpredictability was enhanced in the 1980s by anxiety over the direction of government policy and by the financial situation. There was an emphasis on living within means, which meant keeping (i.e. reducing) academic expenditure within the university's capacity to manage it from current income. It would not have been acceptable to the UGC (nor to the university) to adopt the solution of the 2000s and 2010s when investment was financed by a borrowing serviced from future growth in earnings.

While that was not the policy of the Harrison years, there were greater efforts to find alternative sources of income. There was some progress in the recruitment of international students through an International

Office. Moreover, the merger with St Luke's had given Exeter one of the largest Education departments in the country, and this was supported in what was a first attempt to step away from doing things by halves. This department was to achieve research grants and RAE ratings that helped prop up university finances until the 1996 RAE. Moreover, continuing the pattern established by earlier entrepreneurs, individual academics were given their heads to see what grant income they could attract and were allowed to set up research centres based on results in attracting grants and postgraduate students. Applications to the research councils and charities increased enormously.

In part, accepting the shifting and porous nature of categories, the entrepreneurs were linked in a highly critical stance toward both the management and the radicals, seeing them as rooted in ideas and approaches that were reactionary and ill-fitted to the contemporary situation. These entrepreneurs, or 'extreme critics' to employ a description offered by Tim Niblock, favoured both removing staff not 'earning their keep' and encouraging academic–entrepreneurial schemes. This policy appeared too risky to the management and unacceptable to the radicals. Uninterested in the 'vacuous' conflicts in Senate 'between these two groups of fundamentally conservative backwoodsmen', the 'extreme critics' developed entrepreneurial undertakings that did not emanate from university initiatives. The Institute of Population Studies, the Middle East Politics Programme, the department of Arabic, the Centre for Arab Gulf Studies, and the Centre for Police Studies, were the key examples, although the last was headed by Bill Tupman, a radical.[8]

If Ted Wragg was the entrepreneur for Education, Muhammed Sha'ban did the same, from a far weaker background, for Arab and Islamic Studies, which became the most successful of the university's initiatives, not least because it stayed the course. Although a difficult individual, Sha'ban had the contacts and negotiating skills to attract substantial funding from the Gulf potentates. The Middle East component was further developed with the introduction of an MA in Middle East Politics in the Politics department. Although there were well-established Middle East area studies programmes at other universities, this was the first such MA in a European university. The initiative was carried forward by Niblock, who had transferred to Politics from the Centre for Arab Gulf Studies in 1982.

THE LATE 1980S: DIFFICULT YEARS, AGAIN

These developments were of wider significance for university and city, both of which had been somewhat insular. Most of the university staff had been of European, largely British, background, while the interests of staff in the Arts and Social Sciences tended not to move beyond the parameters of the Western world. Now, there was a steady stream of non-Western students, mainly but not exclusively Arab, attracted by the specialisations on the Middle East which were now on offer and by the international reputations of the key staff. The facilities of the city, too, began to reflect the gradual widening of the university's ethnic composition. Initially a house converted for mosque purposes, the mosque in York Road was opened, and the number of shops and restaurants catering for non-Europeans grew.

The main achievements of the programmes at this time were registered in international academic impact. The stream of students coming out of Exeter soon came to populate university departments around the country and around the world. This was a time when interest in the Middle East and Islam was growing, and new Middle East studies units were being established. It was also a time when the universities of the Middle East, especially in the Gulf, were growing and venturing more into the Social Sciences than before.

Intellectual quality played a key role. The approaches to Islam offered in the department of Arabic were uncluttered by the 'Orientalist' obfuscation so common elsewhere, while the Middle East Politics Programme also represented a distinctive approach, one focusing on contemporary realities and rooted in the wider perspectives of the Social Sciences (particularly political economy), rather than treating the Middle East as unintelligible to any wider logic or experience. The annual conferences of the Centre of Arab Gulf Studies constituted the main international gathering point for those with specialist interest in the Arab states of the Gulf, while the Middle East collection built up in the main Library and the documentation centre on the Arab states of the Gulf became important research resources. The Middle East librarian, Paul Auchterlonie, was critical to this development.

Harrison's call for selectivity by research quality entailed a political tussle in the university, not least because he sought to displace the status quo, that which had developed under Kay. Doing so was made more difficult by the political and cultural shifts of the 1960s and 1970s, notably the decline in the power of professors, the increase in the size of the teaching staff and its democratic aspirations. The young turks of the 1960s and 1970s had become a new orthodoxy, one that was sure that it represented the university.

There were also specific career issues at stake that made this group more difficult. The expectations about promotions held by staff in the 1970s could no longer be justified, as the 40 per cent rule limited the number on the grade of Senior Lecturer and above. This rule, which posed the serious issue of equity between the generations,[9] an issue of greater bite as the once-young acquired new commitments and expectations, accentuated concern about the creation of new chairs. The entire issue exacerbated the impact of the major fall in the value of salaries, allegedly by 22 per cent since 1974, due to increases below inflation.[10]

At the General Meeting of the Board of Senate, on 20 March 1985, held to discuss the reports submitted by the three select committees appointed in 1984, there was an unwillingness to accept the need for selectivity in expenditure. Instead, there was pressure for better rewards for good teaching, support by teaching assistants, more money for research, and a regional policy. This process was an aspect of the involvement of staff in university management and of the flow of ideas upwards. The COSGOD changes had put Exeter among the leaders of democratisation of university government, but there was a measure of scepticism about these views on the part of senior professors. Thus, on 20 March 1985, Robin Turner emphasised the need for more publications to increase profile, while Yates was sceptical about the value of research reports prepared by departments. There was a disciplinary dimension. Representation in Senate varied greatly by faculty, being lowest in percentage terms in Education, the distant faculty in St Luke's, and highest in Arts, notably History. The contrast was accentuated in the case of Senate activism. UGC pressure for a research review was greeted by the faculty of Arts with suspicion as likely to move resources to Science.[11]

Arguing that the number of universities and the resource issue meant that research selectivity had to be pursued, Harrison emphasised the need to pursue national and international excellence and reputation. He had his eyes on the outside world and on the way in which policy was developing nationally. Although willing to pay lip service to the regional

THE LATE 1980S: DIFFICULT YEARS, AGAIN

theme, Harrison clearly treated it as a lesser goal and certainly did not wish to preside over a cosy regional university. Indeed, Harrison led the sensitive to feel that he regarded talk of the region as a cover for mediocrity; which was a fair assessment of the research work of several of those involved. Instead, Harrison offered his constant refrain of the need to consider the views of those 'east of Taunton'.

Given the role of the UGC and the RAE subject panels in funding research and developments, this was a reasonable viewpoint. Harrison was a close friend of Peter Swinnerton-Dyer, the Chairman of the UGC. Under Harrison, Exeter had far more warning of what was coming from government and the UGC and, eventually, became more confident and decisive in its responses. Harrison was particularly well informed and involved in managing professorial appointments. He was very keen to get these appointments right, on the ground that the professors provided a basic structure. Harrison selected good external assessors, ran the appointment committees well, and listened carefully before making his decisions. Harrison's excellent national connections helped in this regard. A more critical view was that he turned to 'cronies' for advice, for example in History, and that this influenced appointments; but the process of seeking advice is rarely free from controversy.

Harrison was not alone in pressing the wider stage. The forceful Abel, eventually a DVC (1991–94), was prominent in the UGC and various national Science committees, and backed the 'east of Taunton' stance. He became President of the Royal Society of Chemistry and was an important backroom adviser to Harrison. 'East of Taunton' meant the nation as a whole, indeed, the world, and both were changing. The Northern/Midlands triangle of universities (Manchester/Leeds/Birmingham), the principal rival to the 'Golden Triangle' of Cambridge, Oxford and London, was in relative decline, in large part due to the long-term crisis of manufacturing and the more specific regional dynamics of Thatcherite economic and fiscal policies. As the relative economic prosperity of the South increased, notably in London and the Thames Valley, the Southern academic world had been changed by improved transportation and by population expansion from the South-East. The extension of the M5 from Bristol to just past Exeter, combined with the introduction of diesel-powered 125 rail services on the old GWR line in 1976, made Exeter appear less remote and ensured that an 'east of Taunton' policy seemed plausible. Earlier, Exeter had seemed isolated and provincial.

A national rather than regional commitment did not mean that there was no provision of professional education. Indeed, at the close of the 1980s/start of the 1990s, the university had one of the three largest teacher-training schools in the country as well as a large and well-rated School of Law which was developing postgraduate conversion courses with a new Centre for Legal Practice. There was an important and prestigious Social Work section within the department of Sociology, while Politics provided in-career courses in Public Administration for students from local authorities and from other countries. As a reminder of counterfactuals, it was far from obvious that these areas would wither later. For example, the Centre for Legal Practice was closed and moved to the University of the West of England in Bristol: it suffered from the limitations of the approach and its practitioners when faced with RAE demands. Moreover, teacher-training was to be confined to a reduced range of subjects in the PGCE.

In contrast, the eventual expansion of the School of Medicine and General Practice into the Peninsula Medical School (PMS) proved to be one of the few positive developments in professional training. Leadership and institutional support played key roles, but so also did the extent to which medical research has always been well funded, when other forms of training had little or no research support. There was also the possibility with Medicine, through synergies, of helping related areas in the Sciences, and thus dealing with the persistent issue of how to fund the Science side.

The logical conclusion of Harrison's 'east of Taunton' refrain, that regional tasks could be left to Plymouth while Exeter offered the South-West a national institution pursuing international excellence, was one that was not clearly established by the time he resigned in 1994, causing serious problems thereafter. This reflected a more general problem with the Harrison years, that of mixed messages and an incomplete policy. As with other VCs, Harrison of course faced serious political problems, not least the limitations on his authority and power and the extent to which there was strong pressure for consultation.[12] If he moved and manoeuvred far more adroitly than Kay, was far more in control, and was skilful in defusing Senate, not least by putting off issues, he still had to take note

THE LATE 1980S: DIFFICULT YEARS, AGAIN

not only of the power of Senate but also of the degree of opposition there to 'management'. Moreover, he faced a committee system described as 'ridiculously large and complicated' by Sue Odell, who took on much of the committee work of Reg Erskine when he retired as Deputy Registrar in 1986.[13]

Harrison, however, was to establish a Joint Committee of Council and Senate which rationalised this system as well as an initially informal VC's consultative group, the basis of the later VC's Advisory Group and then VCEG, which provided him with a reliable sounding board and source of advice. At the same time, Harrison had the skill, experience and personality to get his way through the thicket of committees. In particular, well informed at the national level as well as politically adroit and perceptive, Harrison could direct ADC better than Kay had done.

Harrison left Senate as it was and its members went on saying what they wanted. He did not like 'taking on' Senate, or at least the critical element within it, directly or personally, and tended to look to others to take the lead. That reflected a trait of personality but may have been accentuated by his experience at Keele where a radical reform plan advanced to deal with the 1981 cuts received a hostile response in Senate. Harrison was distrustful of Senate when he arrived in Exeter and had been briefed on the problems Kay had had with its radical elements.[14]

To an extent, Harrison lessened the impact of the opposition to 'management' by joining in much of the criticism of the government. He was active in presenting the staff case over the retention of tenure and salaries, the student case over grants, and the demands of the sector over funding. This stance, however, did not address the politics of the situation at the national level. In June 1983, Thatcher had been re-elected with 397 seats, gaining a substantially increased majority, and, although this was reduced in the June 1987 election, the number of seats (376) and majority (101) were still very large, and there was no need to hold another election until 1992. The critical arguments of the CVCP therefore fell on deaf ears and, indeed, helped maintain poor relations between government and the sector.

The government pressed ahead with its plans for greater accountability as an aspect of Higher Education contributing to economic regeneration. The 1985 Jarratt Report on Efficiency in Universities pressed for a structure that would make it easier to take decisions. One of the major recommendations was that the VC should be the chief executive of the university, which reflected the UGC stance in the early 1980s that VCs were in effect the chief executives of their institutions, and so could not duck responsibility for how they performed. Tentative steps in implementing the Jarratt Report were taken by some universities, but with differing degrees of enthusiasm.

In the meanwhile, the urbane Harrison had some room for manoeuvre, but did not use it with sufficient determination to alter the situation on the ground, i.e. at the departmental level. Although he did not solely spend his time in Northcote House and east of Taunton, and was a marked improvement on what had come before, Harrison was still in the tradition of somewhat distant VCs.

Staff comments are instructive. Harrison is praised for being an able administrator, a shrewd and effective delegator, for his skill as a chairman, moving the business on, and summing up very well, for being expeditious, for being a very hard worker, and for being pleasant: very polite, courteous, very kind and caring, approachable, a source of encouragement, able to treat staff as human beings, and someone who had learnt the skill of constructive and sympathetic listening. Harrison was strong enough to avoid the trap of seeking favour by promising the unbelievable. He held a series of lunches so that he could get to know staff while they could get to know each other. A manager of his office in the widest sense, Harrison held all the strings. He was very good at reading documents, and had his finger on the pulse, both nationally and in the university. In the latter, he was helped by his formidable and highly efficient secretary, Anne van Geyzel, who controlled access to Harrison. Harrison restored Vice-Chancellorial authority, helped by his ability to rely on a number of effective figures, including Bruce Coleman, Trevor Preist and Gar Yates.[15]

There are also frequent complaints that Harrison was distant, as well as suggestions that he wanted a quiet life and did not wish to rock the boat.[16] It is not of course the job of the VC to be the personal friend of the staff. More instructive is the application of a distinction offered by Philip Harvey, later Academic Secretary and Deputy Registrar, who commented that Steve Smith, VC from 2002, was highly unusual because he had a 'granulated' understanding of the situation, whereas most VCs only saw departments as a unit.[17] Harrison had visited the departments in his early years, a step Kay had not taken, but he did not subsequently use the information he obtained when it was necessary to implement the policy of selectivity he endorsed. This was significant because only such an effort could have counteracted the conservatism of anti-selective collegiality at the level of all-too-many departments. Moreover, an interventionist VC was necessary in order to counteract those departmental heads who were not up to the job, or unwilling to push selectivity, in part because they were insufficiently research-active.

The move to elected heads, Deans and DVCs was (and is) a controversial step. To critics, it was somehow responsible for the decline of the university. There were clearly specific problems. As Stephen Mennell, who was not convinced it was unambiguously a change for the better, pointed out, 'some of the elected, non-professorial heads, rather blatantly used their position to manoeuvre for vacant chairs'.[18] However, the disappearance of the old oligarchs was essential if the university was to change, and this change was achieved by the introduction of elected heads. On occasion, no satisfactory person could be found, but the new system also threw up able 'commoners' who would never have had the opportunity to show leadership under the previous system, for example Gareth Shaw in Politics (1980–85). One unexpected consequence was that many professors became extremely reluctant to put themselves forward to election and refused to adopt a leadership role on the new terms.

On 19 February 1985, ADC considered a memorandum by Harrison on research selectivity and a report from the Research Policy Select Committee, both of which were intended to increase awareness of UGC views on research. The UGC, indeed, was reflecting Treasury pressure for accountability and results from the substantial sums handed to universities under their block grants to support research. Top-slicing and research selectivity were put on the agenda for ADC to formulate the necessary policies. Allowing for the different tones of particular periods, Harrison's memorandum scarcely struck an urgent note: '[W]e need to have some regard to the pattern that is developing nationally and to consider what discrimination in the distribution of our funding for research is possible.'[19]

The Board of Senate 'warmly received' the report, while, although presented largely in terms of finances, Harrison pursued in effect another strand of research improvement by arguing that the continuation of the early retirement programme, under which about 100 staff had already retired in 1981–84, would be helpful, even though it would be now funded by the university as there was no more government help available.

Finances were certainly pressing, although the wider context was greatly improved as a result of the fall of inflation under Thatcher in 1982–83: by the mid-1980s there was both greater prosperity, more stable money and lower interest rates than a decade earlier. Nevertheless, although the UGC increased the recurrent grant by £525,000 to £15.31 million for 1985/86,[20] Derrick Sims, the Finance Officer, predicted that it would all be absorbed by inflation running above the grant provision, so that the 1984/85 deficit, which approached £300,000, would carry over into 1985/86, rising to a potential shortfall of about half a million by the end of 1985/86.[21] This situation led to caution in appointments,[22] and accentuated the problem of only obtaining one 'New Blood' post in 1985. Falling student applications were also of note. Whereas the national trend in 1985 was for 0.15 per cent more applications, the Exeter trend was very different: a fall of 8.07 per cent in 1985. Harrison presented this as the loss of a tail, but there were also attempts to encourage applications.[23]

Meanwhile, external pressure increased. 'Planning for the Late 1980s', a letter sent by the UGC, combined with the Secretary of State's warning of a 2 per cent cut in university expenditure per annum, represented a new series of cuts on top of those of 1981, serious as those were. Complaining of the university's 'long and acknowledged history of under-funding', ADC anticipated a cut of about £2.5 million by 1989/90. In response to the requirement to discuss with the UGC the means to adjust to lower levels of funding, ADC, after meetings on 16 July, 10 September and 1 October, formulated a revised Structure Plan, finally settled on 4 October 1985, which called for 'an even-handed application of the next round of cuts', in part because funding made it very difficult to move toward Science while there was a 'need to preserve those Arts-based activities on which the reputation of the University in great measure depends'. There was no emphasis on an entrepreneurial response. In a troubling sign of political breakdown, only one of the six faculties had responded to ADC, which itself pointed out that a negative approach was not 'a proper exercise of stewardship'. At the same time, ADC warned about 'academic and financial disaster' if the predicted situation occurred.

THE LATE 1980S: DIFFICULT YEARS, AGAIN

On 11 October 1985, Council and Senate had an unprecedented joint meeting which, as there were two student observers, was also the first Council meeting to include students. ADC's report was considered on the basis of the undesirable necessity of planning for 10 per cent cuts by 1989/90. Speakers agreed that cuts of this scale would require the restructuring of the academic organisation of the university. The alternative of ignoring the UGC target of 4,600 home students was thought overly grave: there would be a fee income of £500 p.a. per student but no more grant. The ADC proposals were agreed *nem con*. The Treasurer had made clear that there was no prospect of balanced budgets after 1985/86. Harrison slapped down the call from Tupman, who was recruiting foreign students for his Centre for Police Studies, for incentives for departments to take overseas students, by responding that such income was required in order to save jobs.

Another breath of reality had come from the report of the Working Party on the Provenance of Students, which, summarised for the meeting of the Committee of Deans on 6 November 1985, arrived at a conclusion still relevant today:

> Dr Witkin reported that their researches revealed that the university selectors were even-handed; in fact, applicants from the state sector had a better chance of an offer from the university than those from the Independent sector.

Departments felt that they were being fair if they made offers to the same proportion of applicants in each sector. However, because of the comprehensives' poorer take-up rate, the entry was unbalanced. Interviews with interviewers of the period support this conclusion. There were policies of attempting to secure balance in gender, type of school and geographical area, but the third proved more intractable. Attempts to recruit students from the North, for example from Halifax and Manchester, did not have a success that reflected the effort involved, although increasing applications from that part of the UK were noted in May 1988, a year in which the university's applications rose 16.2 per cent compared to a national trend of 4.3 per cent.[24] Peter Faulkner recalls of English, where he was Admissions Tutor for two spells:

> We were satisfied with the quality of the applicants, but some were concerned about the proportion of students from public schools ('Wellies'). We operated an interview system, and it was accepted in the department that lower grades might be required from state school applicants. We also agreed at one point to aim for a 15 per cent mature student intake, aimed mainly at local applicants.[25]

The practice in English of interviewing all applicants helped ensure that its offers of places were accepted, but also contributed to pressures on staff time, helping lead to a marked lack of focus on research.

The contentiousness of admissions in part reflected the divided nature of the academic community at that time, one that survives in the comments made by some of the interviewees. The meeting of the Committee of Deans held on 6 November 1985 recommended a more balanced entry (by type of school) 'by all possible means', only to divide on implementation; which, more generally, was true of the period. Colin Jones and Tupman pressed for enforcement of this policy, whereas Robert Leaper and Robin Turner opposed positive discrimination, while David Perrott, the Dean of Law, declared: 'He would only apply a crude policy of lower offers to comprehensive students and higher ones to those in independent schools in response to a direct order.'

The last was a key play in institutional politics as governance, worked in large part by persuading people to internalise goals without such orders, not least because it was difficult to generate the support to introduce and sustain a policy by these means. On 26 February 1986, the Board of Senate agreed that departmental admissions officers 'should seek by all proper means to secure a more balanced entry', an approach that continued the situation of effective autonomy.

The final report of the Working Party was presented to Standing Committee on 11 February 1987, a meeting that also faced Guild pressure for the university to clarify its policy on AIDS. Presenting an evidence-based report reliant on statistics, an approach very different to many of the contributions made on Senate, Bob Witkin (Sociology) showed that a third of Exeter's students came from the independent sector, which made up just under a quarter of applicants to all universities. The statistics also showed 'that a student from the maintained [state] sector stood a slightly higher chance of being admitted to the

THE LATE 1980S: DIFFICULT YEARS, AGAIN

university than one from an Independent school'. Witkin argued the need to establish links with newer institutions – 'sixth-form, tertiary and FE colleges' – which would alter the range of the state entry. Querying the link made between admissions and behaviour, Witkin then suggested 'that the altogether separate issue of the local cultural context at the University, and the strong feelings of students about what they saw as an unsatisfactory social mix, had more to do with the management of the social aspect of student life than with admissions policy'. He added that 'adverse publicity had been the greatest obstacle to those trying to improve the University's student intake situation'.

In light of the contention over admissions, it is worth noting the eventual destinations of alumni. The fifth (1994) edition of *Here We Are Now!*, the product of the Alumni Network, had 394 entries from Surrey, followed by Devon (350), and Hampshire (214); 2,591 (51.3 per cent) were from the South-East, and 940 (18.61 per cent) from the South-West, followed by 218 (4.32 per cent) from the West Midlands, and 155 (3.07 per cent) from the East Midlands. Of the 505 entries from abroad, 91 were from the USA, 58 from Australia, 46 from Canada, 37 from Germany, and 33 from France. The leading occupations were teaching (824), further and higher education (463), and law (337). 1,689 had married another Exeter graduate.

There were to be reiterated complaints about those typecast, fairly or unfairly, as Sloanes.[26] Despite this issue, most students had a pleasant, indeed very pleasant, time. The small scale of the university and its departments is cited in many recollections. Thus, James Garnett recalls:

> My overriding impression of the music department in Exeter [in 1986–89] is that it was small and friendly. I felt I knew the staff well, and I knew many of the students in the other year groups, including the postgraduates. This was partly because of the relatively small numbers, but also through department social events (the most memorable of which was the annual croquet competition) and involvement in the various University ensembles, to which many of the students contributed actively.[27]

There were also valuable teaching initiatives, such as the Modular Degree, which was to expand steadily over the years, becoming Flexible

Combined Honours. The evaluation of staff teaching was now on the agenda.[28]

The Board of Senate of 20 November 1985 revealed problems with policy and implementation. Harrison announced that, in order to balance the budget by 1989/90, about sixty academic-related staff would have to go, while there would be a 10 per cent cut across the board, except for heating, lighting and the Library, which would face 5 per cent cuts over the five-year period. As soon as the Board considered the Minutes of ADC, there was a bitter debate over whether to fill, as it suggested, chairs in Organic Chemistry and European Law. Arguing that they could not be afforded, Malyn Newitt anyway favoured junior over senior appointments, but Perrott claimed there was a threat to Law's academic credibility. Harrison pressed the case for 'progress' and 'momentum' over 'paralysis', and claimed that Chair advertisements by other universities were aimed at the UGC, which, indeed, was committed to the model of the research university, alongside a degree of concentration of research funds. The ADC minute was approved, but, as an instance of the febrile atmosphere, Harrison had to deny rumours of plans to abolish the faculty of Engineering. Indeed, in 1984–85 some thought Exeter should discontinue Engineering. Harrison was strongly opposed to that and, on becoming Chair of ADC in 1986, Coleman was told that the issue was no longer up for consideration.[29]

Meanwhile, there were cultural shifts and a generational change was at issue, one that marked a change in tone. Dominik Lasok (Law), Ivan Roots (History) and Ken Schofield (Chemistry), all professors significant as scholars, retired at the end of 1985/86. At Senate on 20 November 1985,

> Professor Turner drew attention to the customary notice, circulated with the agenda for the first regular meeting of the session, in which members of Senate are encouraged to wear academic gowns to meetings. He suggested, and Senate agreed, that, as this notice was largely disregarded, it should not be repeated. Members who wished to could, of course, continue to wear gowns.

There were moves to consider monitoring equal opportunities, though Council rejected the EAUT view that it was essential to do so by a Joint Working Party.[30] The EAUT pressed again on the matter in 1987.

THE LATE 1980S: DIFFICULT YEARS, AGAIN

The key issue remained resource allocation. Exeter's readily apparent requirement for a strategic planning body matched the emphasis in the Jarratt Report of 1985 on the need for each university to create a small lay/academic body responsible for planning, resources and accountability. The Board of Senate agreed on 26 February 1986 to Harrison's proposal for such a Council/Senate committee for 'University Planning: Resource Allocation and Accountability', to make recommendations to Council and Senate for medium- and long-term plans designed to further teaching and research, with particular reference to the allocation of resources. Acknowledging the role of institutional politics, Harrison referred to 'competing interests' in this allocation. Agreement by the Board of Senate was conditional on the new committee including four Senators elected by the entire academic staff. The Planning and Resources Committee began its work in October 1986.

In May 1986, the UGC revealed that Exeter's recurrent grant for 1986/87 would be £15,660,000, including £150,000 earmarked for capital expenditure. With an increase of 1.9 per cent over 1985/86, Exeter had done relatively well, coming ninth out of fifty-three institutions, but the inflation rate and a steep rise in the cost of local rates ensured that the anticipated deficit for the end of 1986/87 might be half a million pounds. The 5,135 fte students allocated for 1989/90 was more than expected, with the Social Sciences and Arts benefiting.

The introduction of a common funding base, rather than historic funding, had helped Exeter, but research ratings in the 1986 RAE posed an issue: there were concerns about the situation of Science, as Biological Sciences, Physics, Geology, Computer Science and Chemical Engineering had been rated below average, alongside Philosophy and Sociology (which had had no new appointments for eleven years). There was resistance in the university to the research ratings. On the Board of Senate, Newitt pressed that the university not be 'over-influenced by UGC ratings' and urged it 'to trust its own judgment', without explaining how this process would raise standards or revenue. Newly appointed as a Lecturer in French, David Trotter recalls

> being surprised at the sense of injustice when the first research assessment exercise results emerged, and Exeter (at least in French) emerged looking fairly average, which, frankly, it probably was.

There were at that time, for example, still quite a lot of people in academic posts who published virtually nothing, and who (or so it seemed to me) had little intention of publishing anything, and who in many cases did not hold higher degrees. Many, of course, were outstanding teachers, and they were generally highly intelligent and interesting people.

Trotter felt that Modern Languages required 'some renewal'.[31] He went on to become Professor at Aberystwyth.

There were constructive responses to the RAE results, but largely only after the event. In response to an evaluation of eight of its nine departments as average or below average, the faculty of Science's Planning Sub-Committee correctly noted on 25 June 1986 the national trend of rewarding big departments, and thus the importance of critical mass. Indeed, Exeter's history of small departments hit hardest in the Sciences, where prestige, money and, now, RAE scores, flowed to the large. The Science departments needed both staffing of all sorts and expensive buildings and equipment to operate most effectively. The Dean pressed the case for 'a more structured approach to research … selectively encouraging the more active research groups', seeking a higher national profile, and evaluating 'fully the concept of staff appraisal and encouragement'.

Faced by a small department, most of whose members were close to retirement, and that was rated below average, ADC pressed for the closure of Philosophy, a step opposed by the RLA, but eventually carried out as part of what was presented as the sector-wide rationalisation of small departments. The remaining staff member was to move to Nottingham.[32] This closure enabled the faculty of Arts to reach much of its quota for cuts, whereas in Social Studies it was more a question of equal misery. Philosophy was subsequently reintroduced as a subject in conjunction with Sociology.

Influential academics of the period included Paul Kline in Psychometrics and Maurice Goldsmith in Political Theory. A Hobbes expert who wrote a pioneering series of articles on Bernard Mandeville, culminating in a significant monograph *Private Vices, Public Benefits: Bernard Mandeville's Social and Political Thought* (1985), Goldsmith himself reflected the international strand in Exeter. Born in New York and educated at Columbia, he taught in New Zealand after Exeter. Politics was also the base for *History of Political Thought*, the leading journal in the field, which was founded by Ian Hampsher-Monk and Janet Coleman. Interdisciplinarity alongside innovation could be seen with some of the academics, for example Mark Blacksell. A geographer appointed in 1967, he served as Dean of Social Studies (1989–93), before moving to Plymouth in 1994. The founder of the sub-discipline of Geography and Law, Blacksell showed how development control decisions changed the rural landscape, and then carried out ESRC-funded research on the geography of legal access in rural Britain. An active publisher who collaborated in his research with university colleagues, Blacksell underlined the themes of research activity and excellence at Exeter alongside some of the more disheartening subject-matter and tone of part of this work.[33]

The RAE eventually had a cultural effect by encouraging a realisation that the effort, or lack of effort, of particular individuals would affect the reputation of an entire department. It also led to a growing focus on the career implications of a research reputation. Dobson recalls that the 'Queen's coffee room emptied out' in an 'end of collegiality' as academics put more of an effort into their research. The process was actually more gradual, and many did not make this effort, in part because of the emphasis on teaching but also due to other activities, such as administration. The common rooms did not start emptying until the early 1990s.[34]

More generally, Exeter and its academics were scarcely alone in finding it difficult to adapt to the RAE. This was a national problem: one of institutional and individual complacency in response to a ruthless system, and also of cultural conservatism owing much to professional norms in research, teaching and administration, as well as to personal convenience.

There were also to be developments in response to the new demands. In part, this was a matter of generational shifts. There was a broader process of change at St Luke's. Sean Lang, a PGCE student there in 1983/84, who became a lecturer in Humanities (1988–92), recalls an 'old guard' at St Luke's approaching retirement: 'The big new influence in 1988 was of people who were coming to a university department and had no connection with the old college; nor did they really want any.'[35] For the main campus, Peter Faulkner recalls a longer-term improvement in English:

Academic standards probably went up with the appointment to professorships of Gamini Salgado from Sri Lanka (whose memorable Inaugural Lecture told us that his grandfather in Sri Lanka had been illiterate) and Michael Wood from Columbia. The latter played a major role in the 80s in introducing Theory to a largely traditional department in a benign and uncontroversial way. Social changes like the development of feminism played a part in changing the atmosphere at the time, and I think usefully challenged any complacencies. Another important change was of course the development of computer provision.

The university had an active and enterprising Computer Unit under Howard Davies as Director. A South-West consortium was put together to increase computing power for the Scientists, while in the early 1980s, the university had established Project Pallas, the first purpose-designed computing facility for the Arts in British universities. It won notice and commendation from the UGC. Faulkner also noted a lack of commitment to research:

> We didn't tend to ask ourselves whether there was more we could contribute to the department by publishing. We assumed that good teaching was the primary requirement, and I think most people were committed to this and were quite good at it – we tended to feel satisfied after the final examiners' meetings![36]

In contrast, research and publishing was far more the case in some other departments, including Classics, Geography and History.

In interviews, staff from the period sometimes complain that the university was overly conservative in its expenditure, notably in not spending more of its reserves. Sims, in contrast, recalls 'a constant struggle to cope with the reduction in funding'.[37] Without cuts to limit the anticipated deficit to £600,000 by July 1987, the Treasurer predicted a deficit of £1,300,000, which would more than soak up the uncommitted reserves (£1,100,000), leaving no money for the early retirements necessary to bring down staffing levels and thus contain the deficit.[38] By the end of 1986, the potential deficit for 1986/87 was £863,000, while the reserves had fallen from £1.8 million in July 1985 to £1.2 million in

THE LATE 1980S: DIFFICULT YEARS, AGAIN

July 1986.[39] Significant borrowing, especially for academic purposes, was not allowed by the UGC. The UGC provisions for the years to 1989/90, revealed in a UGC letter of 10 February 1987, allowed for an increase in grant that did not match rising costs, notably in pay.[40] Harrison was very short of options throughout his time as VC.

The finances led Harrison again to emphasise the need for priorities, including more research, and a new Structure Plan from ADC.[41] The Planning and Resources Committee met for the first time on 30 October 1986, part of its task determining an overall academic budget that ADC could then decide how best to allocate. The new Committee was part of a process through which departments had explained to them the source of their resources. This process helped change the basis for disputes over funds and policy in a positive direction. As Exeter's national position in research income was low, there was consideration of how best to create incentives by means of adjusting departmental grants accordingly.[42] Attracting more overseas students was also seen as a resource priority,[43] although little was done to encourage it.

The ADC sought not only the containment of spending within strict limits by 1990, but also planning, in the shape of a University Structure plan, for a more distant horizon. Despite Wragg complaining about a cut in Education staffing, ADC's recommendation for staff cuts was accepted in the Board of Senate on 25 February 1987. A sense of volatility led to further disagreement on the Board of 27 May, as the proposal that admissions issues be tackled by removing quotas from high-demand subjects resulted in concerns over the implications for shifts in staffing. Science was receiving insufficient applications.[44] Cuts made departments uneasy about their relative position, as with Classics, Engineering and Education complaining that they were receiving too low a percentage of Library expenditure.[45]

The cuts ensured that the forecast for the deficit for 1987/88 was £250,735 (compared to £638,000 for 1986/87), but, to finance early retirements, maintenance expenditure had merely been deferred, which created a need for different economies for 1988/89. Inflation remained a threat and indeed rose to 10.9 per cent in September 1990. With a surprising degree of confidence, Harrison assured Council in July 1987 that *A Strategy for the Science Base*, the proposal, from the Advisory Board for the Research Council, for national consolidation of the Sciences, was one to which Exeter could respond. Underplaying the weakness of centres in a university still dominated by departments, he also argued that their development was in line with the interdisciplinary approach of outside funding bodies.[46] Departmental dominance, however, threatened Combined Honours, which Geography sought to withdraw from in order to focus on Single Honours.[47]

Concern over the Sciences was accentuated with the Oxburgh Report, the national Review of Earth Sciences, which led, with its emphasis on size, to the closure of Geology. The argument that the optimum size for a department was twenty academics found fault with the size of Exeter's Geology department (which then had eight academic staff); but, ironically, some of the large departments at the time lacked Exeter's success in admissions and teaching.[48] Exeter's Geologists remain convinced that the report was unfair. Moreover, the longer-term consequences were unfortunate. As Tony Brown, a member of the department, points out:

> In hindsight it [the closure] probably could have been resisted, and it should have been as it altered the balance between Plymouth, Camborne School of Mines and Exeter, and not in Exeter's favour. It [the department] could have been a growth pole and strengthened rather than weakened research and teaching partly by taking the university in a more 'environmental' direction earlier.[49]

Worried about the impact of the closure of Geology on the Arts/Science balance, the faculty of Science sought a university commitment to Science, and Harrison accordingly emphasised a determination to bid for extra resources for Chemistry and Physics, thus retaining the balance.

ADC's projected staff cuts for 1987/88 were reluctantly accepted by the Board of Senate.[50] However, early-retirement schemes were quite successful as most of those who went wanted to go. By 1990/91, the Library's staffing bill had been reduced by 30 per cent from the 1980 baseline. There was major improvement in winning outside grants,[51] and a willingness to consider new investment in 1988/89 in priority areas even at the cost of a greater deficit.[52] With the UGC pressing for a progress report on the implementation of research selectivity,[53] tensions, nevertheless, rose within the university over management. 'Statement on Development Policy', a RLA paper presented to the Board of Senate on

16 March 1988, was an aspect of a defence of consensus management and an attack on what was presented as ADC authoritarianism, a reference to ADC's Chairman, Coleman, and to Harrison behind him. Tupman and what remained of the fading Caucus were fierce enemies of ADC and of its policy of selectivity. The university's history was deployed, with Tupman, who presented the paper, claiming that the RLA members 'feared the return of the "philosopher kings" and the erosion of some of the COSGOD gains', by which they meant GOD (Governance of Departments) as COS (Composition of Senate) had not been accepted by Senate in 1979. Pressure for RLA participation in ADC led to the response that it was best if the RLA contributed in departments and that the ADC preferred small working parties, which indeed were needed in order to encourage initiatives. The AUT, however, wanted wide consultation on subject reviews.

None of this addressed the consequences of the UGC grant not keeping pace with inflation, equivalent to a loss of about five posts annually which meant that the university could not even keep to the 1990 Structure Plan. Indeed, five days later, the Treasurer underlined the acute need for economies when pointing to a £400,000 deficit for 1988/89.[54] Harrison pressed the need to reach near break-even by the time the UFC took over from the UGC in April 1989, or to have a good explanation for the deficit. He also pointed out that the switch of some of the UGC budget to the Research Councils underlined the importance of the latter. The degree to which two cultures were in opposition was indicated by the repeated complaints made on the Board of Senate on 25 May 1988 about the use of the language of management, complaints that clashed with Harrison's emphasis on the need for reliable data to guide policy. The latter was supported in Science and Engineering in particular, with one Engineer pointing out that the historical basis of recurrent grant allocations to departments was no longer justifiable.[55] This basis was used by ADC when dividing up the funds for expenditure.

A blunter call for change was delivered by Swinnerton-Dyer when he led the UGC visitation to the university on 15 November 1988. By stating that they had found the students and non-academic staff 'conspicuously' above expectation, there was a clear criticism of the academics and management, one underlined by reference to the need for the university to define what its mission would be in the 1990s. The academics were condemned for wanting to 'turn the clock back' and urged 'to give more emphasis to considering how to adjust to the requirements of a changed world'. Calls for more resources were robustly pushed aside by Swinnerton-Dyer, and some of the Exeter contingent complained about him. In truth, as some perceptive participants in the discussions pointed out, he was less critical of the university than the headline quotes suggested, indeed declared that 'Exeter was no problem'; and the UGC simply had no money to meet requests.[56] One of the problems with the visitation was that the RLA had managed to persuade Senate that it should have its own meeting with the visitors, thus gaining equal status with ADC. The complaints in the RLA meeting angered Swinnerton-Dyer whose uncomplimentary remarks were viewed as aimed mainly at the RLA team rather than university policy and leadership itself. He was anyway too close personally to Harrison to savage him.

The UGC delegation was told that the underfunding of the consequences of inflation was leading to the postponement of the university reaching break-even. Largely due to the failure to achieve the hoped-for savings in non-academic staff, the forecast deficits had been revised upwards in the summer of 1988: to £350,000 for 1987/88 and £500,000–£600,000 for 1988/89.[57] Indeed, despite a major rise in external research funding, from £2.2 million in 1986/87 to £5.1 million in 1987/88, the eventual deficit for 1987/88 was £404,593 and those projected for 1988/89 and 1989/90 were £357,000 and £500,000–£750,000. The deficits for the previous three years had wiped out the General Research Fund, and only about £1 million remained in uncommitted reserves. The risk of a sudden large building maintenance bill was pointed out by Peter Chalk, the Chairman of Council.[58]

The finances put the astonishing rise in undergraduate applications into the shade: in December 1988 they were 33 per cent above the previous year's level at that point, compared with a very small increase nationally. By April 1989, this had become 31.4 per cent, most clearly in Arts (the second highest increase nationally), against a national trend of 6.4 per cent. This rise in applications seems to have encouraged those in the Arts who did not wish to meet the expectations of change. An instructive clash occurred on the Board of Senate on 22 February 1989. Newitt, the Dean, expressed his opposition to a target for research income being set for Arts departments, to be told that there would be

THE LATE 1980S: DIFFICULT YEARS, AGAIN

targets. Preist, a former DVC, observed 'that times had moved on and that pressure to raise income from outside also applied to sectors of the University other than Science and Engineering'. A complaint from the EAUT about targets as an instance of performance indicators was also unavailing. The same Board saw moves to strengthen the position of ADC against criticism, over bids for new posts, over ADC no longer guaranteeing staffing up to Structure Plan levels, and over not seeking the approval of a head of department in changing the further particulars of a job.

A clash between 'the real needs of a department [French]' and ADC's concern about 'the shortage of resources' came to the surface in the Board of Senate on 24 May 1989. Some departments were still seeking to appoint staff to plug gaps in the teaching programme without much or any attention to research ability or potential. ADC wanted to change that and to gain an editing and amending power over job particulars. This sharp clash was indicative of the tensions between centralised direction and the old departmental autonomy.

The wider context was the RLA and EAUT pressure for 'strengthening the academic basis of the centre',[59] a drive for participation in ADC and for greater interest, which, in practice, meant consensus on behalf of a particular group as well as continued departmental independence that entailed a degree of ungovernability, or, at least, a reluctance to address financial exigencies. There was also tension in 1989 over the AUT threat, in pursuit of a pay claim, not to mark exams. Harrison pointed out that faculty boards had not made the necessary distinction between the actions of AUT members and the responsibilities of the Boards, and he emphasised the legal liabilities that would arise for the university and for those who went on strike.

Separately, there were issues with students. For some years in the late 1980s and early 1990s, the Guild was effectively controlled by a group of Socialist Workers Party students. Although a small group of some 25–40, they were enough to dominate Guild politics, and proved difficult for both the university and more moderate students. Many of the latter were driven out of Guild politics by their vehemence and extremism. In 1989, there was the question of the university's legal responsibilities in the face of errors in Poll Tax returns caused by students not registering. Student protest bubbled over on 6 March 1989 when Guild members occupied Harrison's office in protest against the government's student loan proposals. An order for repossession was obtained by the following morning, and the students peacefully left the building. Harrison did not take disciplinary action, but a bill for over £1,600 in costs was presented to the Guild whose representatives broadened their target to include alleged neglect by the university.[60]

Tensions with staff and students built up in the spring, to create an atmosphere of division not seen since the Kay years. With the Treasurer pointing to the risk of a deficit of £600,000 for 1989/90 Harrison worried about how a pay award could be funded; the EAUT maintained a strong opposition to any separate pay negotiations for Exeter; while Council was concerned about litigation if the exams were disrupted. The possibility of suspending staff responsible was mentioned.[61] Harrison drew attention to the Senate decision in 1975 that marking could occur, but with the marks withheld.[62] In the event, the AUT accepted a national settlement on 1 June, ending the dispute, but the context was now different. The corporatism reflected in the support by the Guild for the AUT 'action'[63] did not compromise the legal rights of individual students to exam results.

The crisis in governance affected plans for university expansion, with the Guild Executive rejecting the principle of loan finance by expressing its opposition to paying off the cost of new residences through rents. Previous Guild Executives had agreed to this policy, but had made clear that they could not bind their successors. Harrison commented on the implications of this stance for the repeated attempts by Executives to become a major player in university management. Pointing out that the Guild had put 'great pressure' on the university to build new residences, which it was clear would have to be financed by loans, he 'hoped that the Executive realised that it was saying that it was incapable of entering into any contract with the university which ran into the term of office of a new Executive'.[64]

The Guild argued that the resulting rents would only be affordable by rich students and the President declared that, if the UFC would not pay, the university should declare that it could not afford to expand. The university had already committed £600,000 on the project and the alternative was no extra student accommodation.[65] Harrison, who had a very good feel for relations with students – firmness combined with exemplary courtesy – took the view that the university had a responsibility to

THE LATE 1980S: DIFFICULT YEARS, AGAIN

provide accommodation for as many of its students as it could.[66] There were indeed serious pressures, with students living in kitchens and single rooms used as doubles that autumn.

As a reminder that the Guild played a number of political roles, it was responsible for the Tiananmen Memorial Sculpture secretly erected by night outside Devonshire House as a memorial to the students and others in the Democracy Movement suppressed by the Chinese army in Beijing in June 1989. The sculpture was later relocated to the lawn below Queen's Building.

Another source of tension in university governance in 1989 arose from the Wallace affair, although this proved an ephemeral *cause célèbre* rather than having any permanent impact. As a result of a complaint from a student about rape, Dr R.S.O. (Segun) Wallace, a Lecturer in Accountancy, was facing police action. He was dismissed following consideration of the episode by a Joint Committee of Senate and Council which had met on 18 January and 15 February 1989 and which had then made a unanimous recommendation to Council. An episode that involved issues and charges of sex, race/racism (both Wallace and the complainant were black) and black magic (sex allegedly as a cure for bad spirits) was now made combustible in terms of university politics by charges of abuse of power directed against both the administration and Council. The interests of the student concerned rather fell into the background while Senate was treated to expostulatory gems of conceit: 'Such action was what one might expect from a merchant bank, not a university. A university was a community of scholars and should not be looking to make the rules work against its staff.'[67] Council voted 16–8 at its meeting of 7 June not to discuss the issue of procedures raised by Newitt, the Chair stating that there was legal advice not to do so while the possibility of appeal by Wallace remained. The head of the RLA registered 'extreme disquiet'.

There was then a lengthy discussion at Senate on 3 July 1989, including criticism of the Chair of Council, in part on the grounds of a conflict of interest arising from the source of the legal advice. Chalk was the senior partner in Michelmore's, the university's lawyers, which (not Chalk personally) had advised the university on the case. Pointing to a genuine difficulty in reconciling the regulations about university procedure and the law, Registrar Malcolm Hislop, who had not handled the situation well, rejected the suggestion of a lack of good faith and offered to resign.[68] Meanwhile, the case had gone to the Crown Court where Wallace was acquitted. He did not return to his job, but the university had to pay damages.

At Senate on 3 July 1989, Witkin had said that 'lawyers' hands should be removed from administrative shoulders'. In practice, there was to be no such autonomy. The rewriting of the Condition of Service Manual produced under Kay was an unpopular step. An exercise led by Personnel, it was necessary at least in part because of changes in employment law. Similarly, changes were needed to statutes and other documents to reflect the abolition of tenure which was ended under the legislation of 1992. Handled through the established negotiating machinery with EAUT, the outcome was inevitable.

At one level, the Thatcher years had brought an increase in the oversight by central government of previously more autonomous agencies, including local government and universities; but there had also been an extension of individual rights and legal scrutiny at the expense of bodies that were accustomed to be self-governing, notably trade unions, but also universities. This process looked toward the emphasis, first at the national level in the Major years (1990–97), on the customer with the Citizens' Charter *et al*. In the case of universities, there were to be changes in student expectations and vocational aspirations, along with the greater governmental surveillance of universities in terms both of inputs and outcomes. This development not only changed the university as a university, but also as an institution that its staff and students experience on a daily basis.

The ability of the universities to respond varied, but this was even more the case for many of the staff. An ageing staff with relatively few new members is not generally the basis for an embrace of change, and this was especially the case because anger, fear and nostalgia all played a role in staff culture, as did an intellectual engagement with the problems posed by many of the ideas and practices now being pressed. Academics were well placed to draw attention to contradictions, ambiguities and biases present or latent in these policies. At the same time, there was on the part of many (but far from all) a determination to take this ability to an undesirable extent. Clashes were instructive, as in the 1989 review of Law, whose head questioned the suggestion of 'a more entrepreneurial approach', only

THE LATE 1980S: DIFFICULT YEARS, AGAIN

to earn the ADC rejoinder that 'had the department "played the system" more ruthlessly, it might have acquired additional staffing'.[69]

The 1989 RAE ratings were certainly instructive. Exeter showed itself capable of achieving excellence on the 5-point scale, gaining a 5 in Psychology, but there were also appalling results – 2s in Engineering and Politics – as well as all-too-many 3s, including Biological Sciences, English, French, History, Law and Physics. Classics, Chemistry and Education with 4s showed potential and helped greatly with the university's reputation and finances; but the overall results were well below where they should have been for a university with Exeter's public reputation and self-esteem. No one in the university had been properly in charge of the RAE returns or known how to present them most constructively, and for some departments, such as Politics, there had been a lacklustre and amateurish approach, alongside a hit-and-miss crudeness on the part of the RAE which did not match the more sophisticated character of later exercises.[70]

The results also reflected real problems with performance. Academic leadership, academics and the administration had all publicly failed. No one resigned or was dismissed. There was no coherent university process for judging research in Exeter prior to the 2001 RAE, the university did not know how to deliver research outcomes, and there was no coherent process of providing information and support to foster a culture of research grant-winning: the Research Office was really only an accounting process. In contrast, the development of management accounting from the 1990s played a role in creating a capacity for management that was to combine in the 2000s with the necessary leadership.

In the 1980s and 1990s, there was much criticism of the RAE process itself, John Inkson, Pro-VC in the 1990s, noting:

> The response of many departments to very poor results in the RAEs of 1989 and 1996 was to blame the exercise/reviewers and to dismiss that they had been judged lacking by their peers and needed to do something about it. The solution most often offered was to be given more resources to grow.[71]

In the end, the RAE was to introduce a sharper edge into university operations, and largely superseded the rather bland quinquennial visitations (and intervening subject visitations) directed by the UGC. By putting funding at issue in this way, the fortunes of departments and the careers of individual academics were put on the line; but only eventually so. Exeter did not move speedily.

Arguably, the 'centre' or 'management' lacked the political power and administrative oversight to implement policy. The administration as a whole was certainly not as well staffed as it was to become in the mid-1990s and, even more, 2000s. The systems in operation were dated and very basic, and consequently the services provided were of limited value to the recipients and were slow to be delivered because of the need for significant manual effort. The service was therefore very reactive, and certainly not proactive. There were, however, one or two key staff in the Finance Office at the close of the 1980s. Appointed in 1987, Adrian Davey, the only qualified management accountant in the Office and a much overworked figure, produced the budget reports for the departments. The university's year-end financial statements were produced (largely manually) by Assistant Finance Officer Ray Bird up to 1989, and then by his replacement, Keith Blanshard.

As the university had grown and the demands for more financial information and for quicker information had increased, investment was needed in systems and in staffing, in particular in management accounting so as to support and help the academic departments and aid planning. Inkson, who was to serve as DVC Academic Planning and Resources, noted deep-rooted structural problems:

> [T]here was no real planning mechanism, no unassigned resources available and a need to control or even reduce expenditure due to reductions in funding following poor overall performances in the RAEs. The forward assignment of departmental resources based upon the academic plans put forward by the departments was crude in the extreme. It was based on qualitative plans and forward assessments of student numbers with no reference to past performance or the national trends. Only a small number of departments, those who were deemed to be in deficit, were required to present more detailed information.[72]

The aspiration to improve standards and reform practices was not

THE LATE 1980S: DIFFICULT YEARS, AGAIN

therefore matched by an adequate managerial grasp, nor by a sufficient change in the culture of the institution and in the level of achievement of some of the academics. Limitations that were to contribute significantly to Exeter's 1996 RAE crisis remained in place, and that at a time when, as Harrison warned, other universities, such as Durham (which was better funded by the UGC and had significant reserves and endowments), were significantly raising their game.

Meanwhile, the pressure for change to take note of developing social norms and to clarify institutional norms accordingly was clear on the University Committee on 6 November 1989 when the Guild presented a paper on sexual harassment, pointing out that the university needed both a definition and a definite procedure. The paper emphasised the effect on the victim. In response:

> Dr Coleman was concerned about some of the examples of sexual harassment given in the definition. He thought that some bordered on normal behaviour of some people, and that unless the Guild sorted out what it meant it could blunt the whole effort.[73]

The same meeting heard from Ian Powell, Registrar and Secretary from 1 October: 'Mr Powell told the meeting that the University had to make up its mind what sort of institution it wants and aim for it.' Assistant Registrar at Salford from 1969, Powell had been Deputy Registrar (Academic) there from 1975 to 1988, before being seconded to the UGC in April 1988 as Assistant Secretary responsible for research policy and institutional planning and management. Effective in helping to sort out universities that were in difficulties, notably on the financial side, he had been Swinnerton-Dyer's right-hand man on the UGC,[74] where his absolutely clinical conduct had earned him the nickname 'ice man'. His Salford and UGC experiences gave Powell an excellent grasp of funding models.

Powell's unfamiliar tone contrasted with that of the weak and incompetent Hislop, who 'only seemed interested in buildings and porters and cleaners'.[75] Not the least of Harrison's wise steps in shaping the reform process was agreeing to appoint as strong and determined a figure as Powell. The new tone was driven home at the Board of Senate on 15 November 1989 when Powell declared that 'this was "make or break" year for Exeter and that, if it was deflected from the course set by Planning and Resources Committee, it would run great risks for the future, not least to the academic future of the University'.

The alternative prospectus offered in the university was that for working together, in accordance with its tradition of democratic involvement of staff, to determine how far the university should go along with government and UFC policy. The head of EAUT warned against creating despondency by shifting resources away from departments with a low research rating. This dispute played out in the debate on the 'Aims and Strategies' for 1991–95 document held in the Board of Senate on 6 December 1989. There was particular contention over whether the democratic structure of the university should be an aim, as the RLA wanted, with Harrison pointing out, in contrast, that Senate was subject to Council. Opposing selectivity, the idea that all staff should be able to pursue research was pushed by Newitt. This debate related to the manner in which the RAE would empower staff, whether staff as a whole or only the achievers, and, if the latter, how achievement was to be defined. Powell's subsequent verdict on the university at this juncture was highly critical:

> Viewed from the outside, Exeter had a Sleepy Hollow/God's Little Acre image. It lacked a strong identity and was vulnerable to increasing public and political demands for universities to be openly accountable for the use of public money. Exeter's position was worsened by its over-reliance on block grant from the UGC as a percentage of total income. Even allowing for its academic profile, Exeter was very poor at seeking and attracting research funding. Exeter had an unbalanced academic profile, undersized science departments, oversized School of Education and too many mediocre arts and social sciences departments. ... Management arrangements for academic departments were weak and a culture of refusing to be managed was pervasive in non-science areas (and even some science ones).

Powell was critical of 1980s 'management', which he felt had not taken the difficult decisions needed to lay the foundations for academic success, and of the academics, many of whom he claimed lacked sufficient self-discipline and did not challenge lax practices, ensuring that the university needed shaking up and reinvigorating.[76] Not the easiest of people to get on with, he expected and desired an argument on most things and worked on the basis that if someone really wanted something he would fight for it. While willing to be flexible, he was not prepared to bend the rules. A man of strong personality (he struck one close observer as shy) and great ability who was decisive and forceful, Powell, who was not noted for smiling, had little sympathy for those academics and administrators whom he thought were underperforming, and many thought no sympathy for any academics. He also worked extremely hard, was very professional and understood the university. Powell, who marked the beginning of 'management' in Exeter and indeed of the ascendancy of the university, represented a cultural change in administration: from the administrator as facilitator to the big academic barons, to the thrusting planner and dirigiste innovator focused on metrics, with scant time for the big barons, such as were left, and their ilk.[77] With the increasing unwieldiness of Senate, Powell was only too ready to move into a vacuum that in part he created.[78]

Powell was to be the key player at the local level of a national trend for universities to have a centrally directed leadership in which the senior academics played a more restricted part while the operation and planning of the university was transferred to senior members of the administration, overtly or covertly. The RAE accelerated that process, as the old generation of academics left the stage and the incomers had to concentrate on their research to keep their jobs, with little time or inclination to play politics. As in other institutions, the recruitment and retirement of staff, and their impact on the management of the university over time, was important in the way national policies were worked out at the local level.

The RAE was to play a transformative role prior to that which was to follow in the 2000s–2010s from the major growth in the number of students. Both developments led to major consequences for the organisation and governance of the university. Systems and practices that had appeared desirable at a time of limited scale, lower external scrutiny and a slower pace of qualitative change, now seemed less so; although not to all. The issues of scale, development and accountability led to pressures and requirements not only for a more effective central management but also for growth in the intermediate tier of administration. Intervention by faculties into departmental activities had 'tended to be light-touch', but there was now a move toward what would be the 'fuller control'[79] exercised from the late 1990s by schools and, subsequently, colleges.

There were structural as well as cultural problems in Exeter at the beginning of the 1990s. For example, only in part for financial reasons, although these were significant, the cuts of the 1980s had been achieved by early retirements. The hard decisions to reduce significantly the number of disciplines were not taken, and departments just became smaller. Salami slicing was a phrase often used. However, the university had begun to turn to other ways of funding itself, through grants, project funding and overseas recruitment. The long-term genteel decline seen, despite his efforts, under Kay was resisted by Harrison. The 1990s were to witness further efforts to transform and modernise the university.

CHAPTER NINE

THE EARLY 1990s: CHANGE STARTING

It was small enough to know well, far enough away not to be tempted to keep returning home and above all it was a very pleasant city to live in. The pubs were good, the Lukey Bop and the Lemmy the places to be seen and lunch was taken in the Ram.
Jon Cresswell (French and History, 1992–96)

Special gratuitous photo-cover! Blackcurrant jelly and people without many clothes on.
Exeposé, 30 November 1992 (a reference to the jelly-wrestling of the Indoor Sports Society)

IN JOHN LE CARRÉ's *The Secret Pilgrim* (1990), the retired George Smiley has 'some kind of sinecure at Exeter University'. Truly fiction. Le Carré, who received an honorary degree from Exeter in 1990, may have been thinking about the former ambassador Sir Anthony Parsons, who became Honorary Research Fellow in Arab Gulf Studies in 1982, of Glencairn Balfour-Paul, another former Political Agent and Ambassador who also became an Honorary Research Fellow in that department, or of Richard Clutterbuck, a retired Major-General who taught in Politics and was a counter-insurgency expert,[1] but there were no sinecures in the early 1990s.

At the beginning of 1990, hurricane-force winds hit the Estate hard, causing extensive damage to the trees. Adapting to government policy created greater difficulties. The Board of Senate on 21 February 1990 revealed a strong unwillingness to confront the political situation. The Guild President's proposal for the rejection of any scheme involving repayable student financial support apart from repayment through normal taxation was defeated by a large majority, but 'the Board reaffirmed its support for a fully-funded student grants scheme and its opposition to the Government's White Paper on Top-up Loans'. In the face of the demand for stronger participation at a senior level, the proposal of the Working Party on the Organisation of University Business for a Vice-Chancellor's Committee was approved, but ADC's minute on staffing was referred back in full by 29–28 with 7 abstentions, despite its chair stating that it was based on the Structure Plan and the need for a balanced budget. ADC was also criticised for secrecy.

Selectivity remained a contentious issue. The debate on the Institutional Plan at the Board of Senate on 14 March 1990 saw Harrison explain the Research Committee's inclination to give preference to departments that had made a credible RAE-linked submission, as well as discussing plans for a new system of research allocation and management. At the same time, the Chair of the Academic Staff Association introduced a paper prepared by the Association pressing for the inclusion in the Institutional Plan of wording about the university as a flexible and self-governing community where decisions were made democratically. This view enjoyed considerable support despite Council, not Senate, being, as Harrison pointed out both then and in December 1989, the university's governing body. Moreover, Senate voted 27–24 for a motion requiring ADC to reconsider two bids for posts it had rejected, despite the Chair of ADC explaining that it had acted in accordance with the Strategic Plan. Indeed, two days earlier, ADC had unanimously reaffirmed its earlier recommendations in the face of Senate complaints on 21 February.

Serious disputes over academic structures and institutional culture did not prevent agreement on a bid to the UFC for expansion by 1994–95. This bid represented a modest increase (by 250 students) above the number agreed by the university for 1992/93. Particular expansion was planned for Education: an undergraduate increase of 25.4 per cent between 1989/90 and 1994/5, compared to 7.3 per cent in Arts, 8.0 per cent in Social Studies, and 13.2 per cent in Science. The bid

THE EARLY 1990S: CHANGE STARTING

also emphasised selectivity in research allocation, as well as the system of regular Departmental Reviews established in 1990. Powell demonstrated commitment when he appointed a Research Officer.

Writing, in the June 1990 issue of *Staff Forum*, on 'The Challenge of the 1990s', Ian Powell pressed the need to grasp the opportunities posed by the rapid change he anticipated. Arguing that the university spent too much time on short-term issues and lacked an agreed long-term vision and a strategic framework for development, he claimed, correctly, that the Institutional Plan to 1994/95 was essentially a consolidation and rolling forward of the university as it then was and pressed the need to consider a prospectus for the 2000s. Powell warned that long-term aspirations required strategic plans which implied choices between options, including considering new ventures in preference to existing ones.

In the meanwhile, Powell focused on the finances, which were difficult, with a deficit of £250,000 budgeted for 1990/91, scant government provision for capital funding, and government pressure for efficiency gains.[2] This situation encouraged a reform of resource allocation. Moreover, the new Planning and Resources Committee proved a useful tool in teasing out significant issues requiring attention and in promoting an integrated approach to running the university. Chaired by Neville Bennett, the Chair of ADC, a Resource Allocation Working Party that reported on 5 November 1990 offered a damning indictment of the existing situation:

> At present, the UFC sent to the University a global sum of money, unallocated for the various sections of the University, Planning and Resources Committee decided the proportion to be allocated to the academic sector and Finance and General Purposes drew up a budget, incorporating accounts for individual departments. The criteria were not known; departments were allocated the previous year's budget plus or minus x per cent. Responses to bids for staffing were given by ADC, based on a policy of 'equal misery' deriving from the Structure Plan. There were built-in inequalities: SSRs, for example, ranged from 6:1 to 17:1.

As Bennett pointed out, the existing system lacked understood and agreed criteria, and suffered from almost total rigidity, a high degree of centralisation, and a lack of integration, which resulted in uncertainties for the departments. Instead, his new system offered an algorithm or formula to convert UFC and other funding streams into resources for departments, providing a systematic method for distribution. A safety net for losers was to be provided, but they were to be required to aim for a balanced budget.

At the Board of Senate on 5 December 1990, revised recommendations from the Working Party were agreed by 47–21 with 7 abstentions, Bennett reporting: '[T]he Working Party had concluded that a more explicit judgmental factor should be introduced through ADC, to consider the position of all departments, using the product of the model as a basis from which to proceed.' In the debate, there was general agreement about the need to move from the 'historical' method of resource allocation. Bennett's report was the spur for the creation of ICE (Income/Expenditure Exercise) which was developed by a working party and finalised by 1995. An earlier model, RAM (Resource Allocation Model), developed under the chairmanship of Bruce Coleman, was used prior to ICE, but did not prove popular because it was quite complicated to understand. RAM became more unpopular following the introduction of an additional column in the final summary allocation table which was entitled 'judgemental factor', the contents of which proved difficult to explain or justify to many. This factor was introduced by PRC at the suggestion of Mike Duffy when the university faced the prospect of 10 per cent cuts across the board. Instead of this, it was agreed that there should be different bands of cuts according to judgement of the health and future prospects of departments. APC opted for 5 and 15 per cent bands, and when this was accepted it was the first serious breach in the united power of the departments in the system.[3]

The serious effort to understand the costs and benefits of the different areas of the university provoked very great discussion of the relative cost bases of STEM (Science, Technology, Engineering, Mathematics) and non-STEM subjects and of cross-subsidisation. However, this data existed alongside other models (notably historic ones) and planning processes. Most of the attempts to meet the challenges of the 1990s and early 2000s found much of their difficulty in the fact that it was very hard to forge a consensus when there were competing models and centres of power without a VC and Registrar who would, and could, back any of them

THE EARLY 1990S: CHANGE STARTING

decisively. Prior to 2004, there was data, but it was not the basis for policy or rhetoric.

Harrison sought to inject a further note of reality into the discussion on the Board of Senate on 20 February 1991, in which there were assurances that there would be no redundancies as a result of the new allocation system. He pointed out that:

> [M]uch of what was contained in the Senate papers was predicated on a broadly steady course. This was in considerable contrast to the world outside the University which was entering the depths of a recession and where jobs were being lost. Many were well aware of the pressures affecting the Research Councils and of the effects of the Gulf War [with Iraq]. If, against this background, the University managed to maintain a steady course, it might be in quite a privileged position.

In turn, Harrison proved somewhat complacent in his response to *Higher Education – A New Framework*, the White Paper, published on 20 May 1991, that heralded the end of the binary divide between universities and polytechnics. With some condescension, an approach also remembered by former students and staff and seen in the hostile Senate response to congratulating Plymouth on its new university status, he declared that the government was 'dismissing a relationship between resources and quality'. Given the problems with student drunkenness and discipline discussed by the same Board of Senate, and the degree to which, as PRC pointed out, Exeter's research performance was 'not held in such high regard as its teaching', the quality was scarcely assured.[4] Harrison did not have good relations with John Bull, Plymouth's VC.

Since becoming Chairman of the CVCP, Harrison found himself increasingly committed to national Higher Educational policy and could spend four days a week in London.[5] The Bill to reform universities included controversial proposals to increase the accountability of student unions and to give government powers over curricula. Harrison played a major role in opposing these measures, notably by cooperating with Conservative peers led by Lord Bellof who disliked the powers the Bill gave to government. Eventually, the government backed down on the two controversial clauses, and the Bill was watered down.

A new committee structure to which Powell had greatly contributed came into place in the summer of 1991. ADC was replaced by an Academic Policy Committee (APC), with a Research Committee, from August, a sub-committee of the latter. APC and the departments were to discuss the creation of departmental plans running to 1994/95 that were intended to affect the budget, student numbers and resource trajectories, which were to be incorporated into a revised Institutional Plan that was to be submitted to Council in December 1991.[6]

This timetable was part of a more widespread change in the university's internal structure over a longer time period that helped begin a badly needed process of modernisation and reform. Standing Committee went, while high-powered committees were created to oversee teaching and research, each headed by a DVC. This was important to the process by which a distinct area of responsibility was allocated by each DVC. The establishment of a Teaching Committee, and of a Research Committee, was part of the move to replace the autonomy of departments (and to some extent of faculties) with central policymaking. Some departments, notably Classics, fought hard against both committees and against institutional standardisation.

Senate provided the location for policy debates that were not being offered anywhere else, but was an unwieldy setting for such debates and more so as it grew to a ridiculous size in the 1990s as every additional *ex-officio* professorial member (many of them quite unsure of their role) had to be matched by an increase in the RLA/ASA-elected quota. More positively, reading the minutes of Senate, as of other democratic processes, can give an impression of chaos, of forces pulling in different directions, of no one being in control; but this is the nature of the sources for such processes. There was discussion, debate and compromise, and these produced not just delay but also an adaptation and development coming from the reality of a society of scholars contributing to national and local communities and to international links in a variety of ways. Moreover, some of the radicals were really just looking to exercise their talents by doing something to help modernise and develop the university; their 'radicalism' was often born of frustration that there did not seem to be much interest in using their talents. A failure properly to talent-spot and encourage those who might appear difficult is always a problem for institutions.

THE EARLY 1990S: CHANGE STARTING

There was debate as how best to ensure research selectivity, a theme in the 1991/92–1994/95 Institutional Plan;[7] with John Inkson pressing the need 'to produce an environment in which quality research was seen as the norm'. The Green Paper 'on Exeter's International Research Standing in the Year 2000' proposed differing commitments to research, teaching and administration for individual members of staff, PRC commenting on 'the dichotomy between the duty and right of all academics to pursue research and the need for selectivity in the application of scarce resources to encourage excellence'.[8] The author of the Green Paper, Inkson, noted: 'This was the only Green Paper that was concerned with research and was only added after lobbying Harrison. The work we did on this highlighted the lack of priority given to improving the research base and the absence of some key areas of infrastructure.'[9]

Opposition to the government meanwhile played a role in excusing underperformance. On 1 July 1991, the Board of Senate agreed a resolution by George Duller, the retiring President of the EAUT, that argued that falling (real) academic salaries were so undermining morale that staff were working less. At the same time, Duller rejected local pay bargaining. With more pointed criticism of the university, Malyn Newitt sought machinery to ensure the accountability of the Registrar's Department, only for Harrison to emphasise that this was a matter for Council. The radicals' suspicion of Powell as an authoritarian was matched by his view that they were irresponsible. External agencies were certainly pressing for more supervision of the academics. In November 1991, the CVCP Academic Audit Unit, on a visit to Exeter, expressed concern about the university's assessment of teaching quality and course assessment. At the same time, it was pointed out that administrative and teaching demands were jeopardising the possibility of quality research.[10] The significance of the latter was clear in the UFC allocation of funds to universities for 1992/93, in which an increase in research funding was based on the 1989 RAE.

To help with funding, the student numbers planned for in the Institutional Plan by 1995/96 were revised up to 8,200 in November 1992. In December 1991, the assumption had been 7,200 by 1994/95. In taking greater numbers, contrasting with a markedly low increase in 1989–92, the second lowest percentage in the country, it was hoped that the university would widen access and balance its books. Concern about the academic implications was tackled by Harrison who pointed out that recent growth was modest compared to that in other universities, while there were infrastructural investments to cope with increasing numbers. Harrison acknowledged that expansion would put pressure on 'the preservation of teaching quality'. It was hoped to cut the deficit of £1.4 million to zero by the end of 1994/95 partly by this expansion, and partly by using the surplus in the Retirement Benefits Scheme.[11] This surplus was to be very important for Exeter's situation in the 1990s.

Finalised in November 1992, the Institutional Plan for 1992/93–1995/96 referred to an annual breakeven and a general reserve restored to £2.7 million by 1995/96 as well as proposing that additional resources should be used largely for supporting the existing academic staff, essentially in the current subject mix, rather than for new initiatives. There was also a willingness to borrow in order to fund expansion, but only on the security of residential building and its associated income streams, and not to invest in purely academic developments. Lafrowda was the model for Rowe House and James Owen Court, built in the early 1990s to match increased student numbers. On 13 December 1993, Council agreed to accept a loan facility of up to £6.5 million from the National Westminster Bank in order to finance provision of new residential accommodation on Sidwell Street.

Two months earlier, there was the Conker Finals Triumph: 'The night deteriorated into one of wine-imbibing, part-dart throwing and general wibble-wibble enjoyment!' Although there was the problem of 'The Mid Term Blues' across the range, staff could not respond by flocking home or boredom, as many students did. Political activism had declined, as seen with Guild General Meetings.[12] Instead, energy focused on socialising: 'The usual "tranquil" setting of Sprey – an annexe of Hope Hall, nestled in the trees was transformed into a drunken orgy of Romans last Saturday night, as the ever-so-predictable student toga party was under way.'[13] A key political issue that year, which led to a Guild Day of Action on 11 March 1993 in which the university supermarket was picketed, related to the university limiting mid-week Guild concerts at the Lemon Grove, the lounge in Cornwall House. Questions of noise and complaints from students in Lafrowda and from nearby residents interacted with the issue of control by the university.[14]

Another side to university life was revealed when Nightline moved

THE EARLY 1990S: CHANGE STARTING

its Exeter base onto the campus in 1993. Somewhat different concerns were shown that year when the postcards on display in the Porter's Lodge in Cornwall House led to complaints on the grounds of depiction of women. Domestic Services, freedom of expression and the *Daily Mail* were all brought in. In the event, the postcards were taken down.[15]

Expansion in student numbers and residences, and the strength of student applications, however, could not conceal a number of failures, which Harrison indeed acknowledged, not least because they affected external evaluation and funding. The 1992 RAE was officially presented as 'encouraging', but this was misleading. Eddie Abel, Chair of APC and Research Committee, was in charge of the process and read all the departmental returns. He recalls that Drama's information was only produced with great resentment, and that he had to help write the return. There had been significant improvements, notably Education (4 to 5), French (3 to 5), Engineering and Politics (2 to 4), and Physics (3 to 4); but, aside from falls (Psychology 5 to 4, Law 3 to 2), the major problem was of a failure to improve, either from 4 to 5 (Classics, Chemistry), or from 3 to 4 (Biological Sciences, History, English). Although the university presented its case well and held its position, it did not do as well as Powell had hoped. The size of Education ensured that the university's overall position at 14th was much better than many of the departmental returns suggested.

In addition, as other universities had been improving, a similar departmental result was, in relative terms, a failure. Moreover, the RAE did not have the positive financial consequences that had been anticipated when the recurrent grant for 1993/94 was announced. Because only 92 per cent of the eligible academic staff had been submitted, there had been a loss of about £750,000 in that figure, while the consequences of the end of the binary divide and the resultant need to spread research income across a large number of universities meant that Exeter had 'lost' about another £500,000.[16]

A separate problem was posed by the recent expansion of Education and its major significance in the RAE, in which all its staff had participated. Education had seen a major physical expansion, as well as one in resources: £5 million from the UGC, in addition to university investment, underpinned growth in Education's student numbers. The Institutional Plan for 1992/93–1995/96 projected an increase from 1,030 in 1988/89 to 1,497 by 1995/96. The expansion of Education, however, created an over-reliance on one faculty, one accentuated by the possibility of a shift in Initial Teaching Training toward school-based training.[17] Both of these factors were to come into play in the late 1990s. While universities elsewhere had to manage increasing government control over teacher training funding and content in ways similar to Exeter, the scale and prominence of the St Luke's operation made this an especially complex task for the university. From 1991, Wragg built back student numbers on the BEd and PGCE programmes. But in the context of the 1996 RAE the university authorities were to regard the associated staffing at St Luke's as an unacceptable dilution of research concentration, most of the faculty having been appointed to teach these programmes from frontline teaching posts in schools, rather than having been trained, first and foremost, as academic researchers.

Another form of university underperformance was in research grants and contracts. These had become far more important but were not always well managed by the university. In 1990/91, 9.7 per cent of total university income came from this source, thanks in part to the effective work of the European Union Funding Unit established in Northcote House by Harrison; but in similar universities the percentage was closer to 13 per cent.[18] The X-Ray Laboratory in Chemistry, designed to help assist research in crystallography and opened in 1995 as part of the university's fortieth-anniversary celebrations, was in part funded by a grant from the Biotechnology Directorate of the Science and Engineering Research Council.

The poor performance in grants and contracts may have been related to the balance of disciplines and to the 'Liberal Arts' tag, so that there was less Science than in the 'redbrick' universities and less of a culture of seeking grants. Many departments treated research grants as an add-on, while some of the most significant providers were in independent centres, notably the Institute of Population Studies, which were overly dependent on the initiative of a very few key staff, with scant university help toward long-term viability. The problem of succession was a key one with centres. That Institute was to be wound up in the late 1990s, and its significant balance transferred to the Peninsula Medical School (in an instance of the cross-subsidisation that was to become more contentious in the 2000s); but a lack of due administrative support was already apparent in the early 1990s.

THE EARLY 1990S: CHANGE STARTING

More generally, there was a mixture of reform initiatives with a degree of complacency, a mixture that did not divide administration from academics, but that characterised both. The pace of change was somewhat slow, but there was change. Classification was a key element. On 4 February 1993, with an eye to the 1996 RAE, Research Committee, under the chairmanship of John Bridge, considered a memorandum on staff who were not producing research, on how to identify them, and on what to do. Research was defined to include publications. In March, Research Committee adopted a policy to identify underproductive areas of research. Under this policy, departments were required to review individual research activity and, where necessary, give support and guidance to individuals who were underperforming. Support and guidance was also to be available through the Staff Development Unit. Where such an approach did not succeed or was inappropriate, then, with the full agreement of the individuals concerned, their contractual duties could be amended to exclude research so that they would not be submitted.

This prospect provoked a hostile reaction. The EAUT, led into battle by Jo Melling (Economic History), accused Research Committee of a witch-hunt and of asking colleagues to inform against each other so as to get rid of 'dead wood'.[19] The actual implementation of the policy was a matter for Heads of Department and the response from them was mixed, although some staff were, with their consent, moved on to non-research contracts. Had such contracts been available earlier, they might have helped change the culture a bit faster, a point that illustrates the limitations of the position of Heads.

The other major development had been the Departmental Reviews with their external assessors. The system of reviews, which extended to divisions of the Registrar's and Secretary's Department, was conceived and designed in 1990–91 by Powell with the support of Harrison. The main motivations were to start to sharpen research performance, to weed out underperformance, and to highlight the need for improved management at the departmental level. All departments were to be reviewed over a five-year period.[20] Many external assessors were distinguished and some, such as Basil Deane for Music, were also shrewd. They offered a qualitative source sadly absent for most of the university's earlier history. The documents prepared by departments are interesting, but so, even more, were the eventual reports. Most reviews, however, were not sufficiently driven home to change academic culture. The Politics review (1992) was very useful and had excellent outside assessors, but it was all 'very civilised' and 'pulled its punches'.[21] At the same time, this review pointed out considerable potential, and correctly so as Politics' RAE grade was to improve from 2 to 4.

The review on the School of English and American Studies, a report drawn up in September 1993 of a School that dramatically underperformed in RAE terms throughout the 1990s and was only improved in the 2000s, was made aware of a strong commitment to teaching, but was clear that the School had not achieved results commensurate with its potential, either in teaching or in research. There were also serious issues of good practice: 'Pressures from increased student numbers necessitated new codes of practice to ensure uniformity of treatment between students; the panel did not believe that there was uniformity.' Research quality, coherence and planning were all doubted, and School resistance to selectivity was noted.

Democratic governance was seen as a problem. Indeed, in March 1994, APC discussed why English had made two junior appointments even though the Review had pressed the need for a senior appointment in order to raise its research rating. APC decided that, in future, it would be necessary to take the recommendations of Review Panels into account. In 1993, APC had expressed grave concern at the tenor of Russian's response to the Review Panel.[22]

In light of teaching pressures, the 1992 review of Theology suggested that students' responsibility for their own learning should be fostered, while student-run seminars should be developed. There was also a need for a 'convergence of research interests to minimise possible effects of isolation'. There were interesting developments in the range of Theology courses reflecting new appointments. Ian Markham (1989–96) taught philosophy of religion and introduced the study of comparative religions. Jeremy Law (1994–2003) offered an inspiring and very popular module on Latin American Liberation Theology, while in 1993 Christopher Southgate introduced the study of science and religion.

In 1994, the review of Biological Sciences discerned overteaching, the need to strengthen the coherence and visibility of research groups, and some laboratories that were in 'unacceptable physical condition'. The review of Engineering in 1994 emphasised the need for a 5- to 10-year

THE EARLY 1990S: CHANGE STARTING

plan and a management team, and commented on the recent RAE improvement:

> The Panel believed the improvement in rating represented a shift in the culture of the School, but did not believe that this shift had yet been reached and been accepted by all staff. Departments could no longer view themselves ... as primarily teaching departments.

The Panel also pressed the need to appoint young staff with high research potential.

The kind of departmental self-sufficiency, about which Kay, and even more Harrison, had grumbled, persisted, and neither VC had really altered the situation. Moreover, although there were appointments from outside in the early 1990s, including scholars to established chairs who would eventually be significant academic leaders (for example Stephen Wilks, Politics), there were too few to change the culture. Upward drift was typical across the sector as a whole, with the combined percentage of senior lecturers, readers and professors rising, while that of lecturers fell.[23] In the case of Exeter and many other universities, promotions compounded an instinctive institutional conservatism, one expressed in long-established and often underachieving empires within big departments such as Physics, in distinct departmental identities, and in the use of Senate to limit pressures for change. Senate, with its democratic impulse, its post-Vietnam/anti-Thatcher positioning and its populist heroes, often seemed to besiege 'management' figures who were regarded as bogeymen, such as Bennett. It was also somewhat at odds with the politics of the students, many of whom were to the Right.

There was resistance to finding the space, financial, physical and political, for new people, new research and new ideas. Much of the dynamism of the university was in the centres, rather than the departments, for example the Centre for Energy and Environment established in 1979 which came to focus on energy use in buildings;[24] the Centre for Population Studies which the Queen visited on the university's fortieth anniversary; the Children's Health and Exercise Research Centre; and the Centre for Business Studies, which became the Business School. The Dictionary Research Centre organised international conferences. These were linked to other signs of dynamism including exchange programmes in staff and students that linked Exeter with the wider world, the Distinguished Visiting Professor programme, the opening of an art gallery in the Queen's Building, the energy of the University Press which published a large number of important works, and the establishment of close ties with regional colleges.

Wilks, who provided a new emphasis on research, recalled: 'In Politics there was strong resistance to a research/publications-led department and it was almost impossible to overturn the champions of old-fashioned tolerance. The elected Head principle didn't help and Harrison was complacent.' There was certainly tension in Politics, although, alongside the difference noted by Wilks, there was the argument that an overemphasis on publications might undermine the excellence of research supervision as part of a research community. In practice, the departure of four staff (accompanied by postgraduates) to other universities caused significant damage to the Middle East Politics Programme, and led the *Express and Echo* to offer the headline 'Brain Drain on Campus'. As Head of Politics in 1992–95, Wilks found it difficult to achieve the transformation he was aiming for.[25]

Trevor Preist was more positive than Wilks about the long-term change in governance, arguing, from his background in Physics, that thanks to 'the democratic structures that had evolved many were involved in the decision-making process and understood the need for change'.[26] Preist also felt that, always a scientist, Harrison was particularly interested in what was going on in the Sciences and that his expertise in Engineering was important to his success in the restructuring of the faculty of Engineering.

That the outside world did not share the assumptions of the culture of at least some Exeter academics was to be driven home in external teaching assessments[27] and, even more, the 1996 RAE. It was already apparent in the small number of applications for some senior posts,[28] although relatively low pay in Exeter was also a factor, as was the inability to offer meaningful resources to build up research teams and facilities.

When Harrison resigned in 1994 to return to Cambridge, the process of appointing his successor indicated much about the nature of Exeter at this point. Sir Rex Richards, the Chancellor, a distinguished Oxford chemist, and Peter Chalk, the Chair of Council, a local lawyer, turned down the suggestion from Abel, the Senior DVC, that the

THE EARLY 1990S: CHANGE STARTING

university employ headhunters as he was used to doing in his national roles. Opposed to the cost of the process, and probably to its novelty and unpredictability, Richards and Chalk preferred the idea of advertising for applications supplemented by writing to the great and the good. The resulting field was fairly small. The frontrunner, Michael Stirling, Brunel's VC, had attracted favourable comment through the CVCP. His appointment was regarded as highly likely, but he pulled out because the illness of an in-law led his wife to decide to stay put. Stirling's withdrawal left the post open for Sir Geoffrey Holland, the Permanent Secretary in the Department of Education. Holland was keen on the West Country where he lived, knew Harrison through the latter's role in the CVCP, had poor relations with John Patten, the Secretary of State, and wanted a new start.[29]

There is a tendency to break the 1990s with the change in VCs, but to do so puts the focus too much on their role or, at least, leads to a downplaying of continuities. Holland shared with Harrison a concern with the wider dimension, although, in each case, the focus was national rather than international. Harrison's political feel was essentially through the CVCP while Holland's emphasis was on government. Linking both was the managerial change led by Powell, a key player in the way no former administrator had been, although, in part by using his DVCs to counter Powell, Harrison kept him from the power he was to enjoy under Holland.[30] Alongside serious continuing problems, investments were made in staffing and in systems, and service provision became more professional, more accurate and more responsive in the mid-1990s. These developments made planning more viable, and planning was directed at change.

The mid-1990s were important in the area of Human Resources (HR). As so often, a change in personnel was significant, but so also was the wider drive in university policy as well as the national context. Under Jim Mathieson, the Personnel Officer who retired in April 1996, the role entailed few decision-making powers, and instead serviced twelve personnel-related committees responsible for even the most routine decisions. In February each year, the unwieldy fifteen-strong Academic Staff Committee (ASC) would meet to consider the award of additional increments (typically worth about £1,500 each) to members of the academic staff. ASC would then make a recommendation to Senate, which would, in turn, consider the recommendations before asking Council to endorse them. Senate and Council did not overturn ASC recommendations. The awards were only implemented in October, so that from the time a Head of Department began preparing a case to the point at which the recommendation was enacted took almost a year. A new Director (Stephen Cooper) who was one of the first to come from outside the Higher Education sector, a new HR strategy endorsed by Council, and a national lead with HEFCE launching a fund aimed at modernising HR, all led to change.[31]

As another important instance of change, teaching was placed on a more professional basis, partly as a response to outside reviews but also driven by internal concerns about the nature of the provision that Exeter was offering. Until the 1990s, the quality of teaching was accepted as being a given, with responsibility very much in the hands of the department. There was a light touch at faculty level where the focus was mainly on the approval of new and revised programmes. Exeter had always been seen as a good teaching university (it attracted bright students), and little further control was apparently needed. It therefore came as rather a shock to some when national-level auditing, introduced in the early 1990s obliged the university to establish a much more structured approach to the monitoring of its teaching quality, with the creation of a Teaching Committee, codes of practice and review procedures. Quality assurance meant that all teaching programmes had to be assessed and adjusted, and monitored on a regular basis. Departments had to be prepared for visits of external quality assessors.

Many academics were initially unhappy at the imposition of this additional level of bureaucracy, and the time and documentation required to sustain it. In addition there were substantial demands from the four or five yearly audits carried out by the CVCP Academic Audit Unit (which carried out an academic audit in November 1991, reporting in January 1992), the HEQC (Higher Education Quality Council, which carried out an academic quality audit in March 1997, reporting in August), and its successor, the QAA (Quality Assurance Agency), which first carried out an institutional audit of Exeter in November 2003, reporting in 2004. Nor were academics overjoyed at the prospect of the national subject-teaching quality assessments carried out by HEFCE in the 1990s. Systems for the regular review of teaching, a reorganisation of all modules

THE EARLY 1990S: CHANGE STARTING

and programmes on a basis of levels and credits, and procedures for the vetting of all new teaching proposals, were just some of the measures put in place. These were very radical for Exeter, and very unsettling for traditionalists. One idea behind this was to make university teaching more flexible and to facilitate part-time and mature student study and transfer between universities.

The university also reorganised its validation and accreditation arrangements with other institutions, with all externally taught Exeter awards being controlled by a Validation Board. Important measures were adopted to make Higher and Further Education more widely available in the community, in particular through modular programmes. The university bid successfully for a wide range of funded projects, which was an attempt to make the university address real social need.

Meanwhile, there were indications of change at the university level that looked toward the future and also reflected the culture and politics of the time. Thus, in 1992, the consensus view emerging in consultation 'was that the time had come for the University to adopt a single policy which would limit smoking to controlled areas. However, it was noted that any decision would need to reflect the awaited response from the Student Affairs Committee.'[32]

As another important cause of change, the merger with the Camborne School of Mines on 1 August 1993 was a major stage in the development of a presence in Cornwall, in part a case of the tail wagging the dog, although the university also had a role through the Institute of Cornish Studies and the work of the Extra-Mural Department.[33] Once with a great reputation, Camborne was facing major difficulties, as were the other British mining schools. These schools were facing the sort of small-subject review seen with Earth Sciences and other subjects in the 1980s and Camborne was in a difficult position as not being part of a university. The merger represented a rescue of Camborne as its finances were poor. In part, the merger was an aspect of regional competition with the new university in Plymouth that seemed increasingly successful in signing up local alliances; Exeter offered Camborne more scientific and social cachet than Plymouth. Critics suggested that Harrison's background in Engineering was in part responsible for the merger with Camborne (and indeed from preventing major cuts to Engineering), but the drive for expansion appears more significant. Camborne increased the size of the faculty of Engineering and also provided a home for the university's Earth Resources Centre. Peter Swinnerton-Dyer was a significant progenitor and supporter of the merger.[34]

The merger was not to be an easy or happy one. While frequently complaining about neglect, Camborne proved a financial black hole, with its finances less promising than had been suggested. The merger, which was on a different scale to the Institute of Cornish Studies, also helped encourage the move into Cornwall which sought to make sense of the Camborne commitment. The merger, indeed, was the catalyst that led to the 'Cornwall Initiative' and, eventually to the formation of the Combined Universities in Cornwall and the founding of the Cornwall Campus of the University of Exeter. In March 1994, APC decided to refer the report of the Working Party on the University of Exeter in Cornwall for wide consultation, both within the university and in Cornwall.[35] Harrison and Inkson were in favour of the Cornish initiative, while Abel was opposed, and remains convinced that the policy was mistaken.[36] As a lesser commitment, in 1991 the Plymouth-based College of St Mark and St John, predominantly a college of teacher education, entered into formal affiliation with the university.

Other changes also looked toward future trends. In recommending to Senate and Council the Institutional Plan for 1993/94–1996/97, Planning and Resources Committee on 3 November 1993 pressed 'the need for departments to adjust to worsening resources and deterioration of student/staff ratios through fundamental reappraisal of teaching and learning strategies, supported by the work of the Teaching Committee'. Departments were to be required to produce plans to cover staffing, recruitment and research. They were expected to fit into financial frameworks designed to keep the university solvent and to focus effort in areas that were likely to deliver results in terms of grants, student recruitment or innovation. There was also acknowledgement of the need for greater support for lay members of Council 'to enable them to make a better and more informed approach to their participation in the government of the University'.

The finances were improving due in part to more fee income. There was a surplus of £979,200 for 1992/93 and a forecast, by March 1994, for a surplus for 1993/94 of over £1.1 million. This permitted consideration of expansion, although there were fears that the high vacancy level in university accommodation, combined with the deficit in the halls' accounts arising from rents that were too low, would lead to a deficit (of £8.2 million by 2000) that would swallow the build-up of a reserve.

The rents themselves seemed too high to students trying to cope with a financial context far harsher than that in the 1970s. On 9 June 1993, there was a sit-in at the Accommodation Office in Northcote House until a grim-faced Harrison agreed to receive a petition from 850 students complaining about proposed rent increases which were to be passed later that afternoon by Council on a 16–9 vote. Harrison argued that students should address themselves to John Patten, although this approach ignored issues about the consequences of university policy on the financial situation in 1993, notably the merger with the Camborne School of Mines and, at the time of the 2000 complaints, the development of a Cornwall campus. However, relations with the Guild were better than in the late 1980s. It helped that, in 1992, the university had financed a major improvement and refurbishment of Devonshire House and Guild facilities, including the bars.

The general university situation put a premium on leadership and on the context for leadership. Neither was without problems, although both were more favourable than in the mid-1970s. Arguably, with all the benefits of hindsight, the central management did not respond adequately in 1992–94, when the financial position had eased. There was not sufficient investment in academic development far enough ahead to make a difference to the 1996 RAE. The policymaking team was stuck in a defensive mind-set after the repeated financial crises of the 1980s and was too cautious to spend money when opportunity offered. This was also the attitude of Council and of successive University Treasurers. The emphasis from Council and others in 1992–94 on restoring the depleted reserves was at the expense of more useful things that could have been done with such resources as were available.

This context is significant when considering Harrison's contribution. Views vary, as are only to be expected. DVC in 1984–87, Preist recorded that: 'Harrison made consistent and constant efforts to improve the research profile of the University through the internal structure, professorial appointments and the encouragement in the growth of postgraduates.' He remarked that because any Head of Department could speak directly to Harrison, they felt involved. To Derek Partridge, the unwilling Head of Computer Science, Harrison was 'personally accessible, approachable', hospitable, 'hard working and competent'. Powell thought Harrison 'a pretty good VC', but was troubled by the culture and its effect on management: '[T]here weren't many go-getters here frankly ... and it was also a time when university Councils had let their grip of things drift ... academics and university Senates ran things, which means they basically weren't run. They drifted. It became internal politics and squabbling ... the research income was pathetic.' A fair summary would be of Harrison as shrewdly cautious. He was often oracular and his DVCs had to learn to divine his views.[37]

The tensions that were to affect the transitions in the university in the 2000s and 2010s were readily apparent in the 1990s. The ethos and financial concern represented by Powell did not appeal to many of the academics. Newitt remains highly criticial.[38] The conflicted memories of these years bulk large in the interviews. In part, there are questions of the vision of the university, as well as issues of practicality, and, more specifically, of how far and how best to respond to a changing world.

With regard to Exeter, there is also the matter of competing interests. In simplistic terms, the Science side had requirements for development that were different from those of the Arts. Or, at least, the pressure for change seemed more urgent for Science. For the Arts, it still seemed possible, however mistakenly, to think largely in terms of teaching and of the individual variations (in staff, students and courses) involved, whereas, in Science, there was a need for research quality and mass to ensure grants and continued fitness for purpose. In some departments, the strength of a commitment to traditional teaching practices meant there was a degree of unwillingness to consider how best to teach far larger numbers of students. The declining unit of resource – money gained for each additional student – made this a significant issue.

It is important to remember other legacies of these years. One of the most impressive was the plan by Bob Alcock, Director of Buildings and Estates, for the Peter Chalk Centre, a conference, teaching and examination space officially opened in March 1994. Prior to this building, development had been largely related to the provision of buildings to serve particular subjects or subject groups, each one independent of the others, and with each one having its own seminar and lecture space. The only real deviation to this pattern had been the creation of the

THE EARLY 1990S: CHANGE STARTING

Newman Lecture Theatre complex in the 1960s which was created to provide science lecture space, largely for Physics and Chemistry. Yet, the student population on the Streatham campus rose from 3,400 in 1970/71 to 8,800 in 1995/96.

During the period of the intensification of the use of existing buildings which followed the completion of the Amory Building in 1974, several issues had arisen. The provision of seminar and lecture spaces within existing buildings became increasingly too small for group sizes that were rising. At the same time the pressure to provide dedicated space for postgraduate students was also growing. Moreover, there was a departmental culture that the seminar and lecture room in 'their' buildings belonged to 'them' and were not, despite centralised timetabling, a resource for the university as a whole.

The Peter Chalk Centre was a direct response to these three issues. It provided twelve seminar rooms that were designed to meet the changed level of demand, it allowed the conversion of poorly used seminar and lecture provision within existing buildings to meet the increased demand for dedicated postgraduate workspace. It was clearly a central facility that did not 'belong' to any department in particular. In that sense the Centre was groundbreaking for Exeter and was possibly the first physical evidence of the transfer of power from individual departments to the university.

An unusual feature of the building was the role of mobile partitions which could respond to demand for changing group sizes or be completely removed to allow large open flat spaces that could accommodate exams and large exhibitions for conferences and other commercial bookings outside term time. For example, the launch of the range of the new Ford Transit van in Exeter took place in the Centre. Also in 1994, there was an extension to the east end of the Amory Building to provide office and library space to accommodate the proposed new Legal Practice Centre.

The Peter Chalk Centre was also in a visually important position at the junction of the Queen's Drive and Stocker Road, and the curved front recognised the setting of the building within the landscape. This was the first building in the university to exemplify the design principle that 'what can be seen of the inside of the building from the outside' is as important as 'what can be seen of the outside from the inside'. This principle was subsequently included in the design briefs for the Arabic

Building, Xfi and the Forum in Exeter as well as the Environment and Sustainability Institute on the Penryn campus in Cornwall.[39]

Lacey Hickie Caley, the Exeter-based architects of the Peter Chalk Centre, went on to do much work for the university. Peter Lacey, the managing partner on the project, was to be the Chairman of the Buildings and Estate Committee, a member of Council, and the Lay Member with responsibility for Dual Assurance on matters concerning the Estate in the late 2000s. Looking out at the grounds, and to both the cathedral and the sea, the Centre fits in ably with the 1960s' buildings, contributing to the extent to which the university is not merely a jumble of structures.

The university by 1994 was in a better state than it had been in 1984. The RAE trend was apparently upward and there had been marked improvements in the managerial structure. On the other hand, the administration of the early 1990s bears considerable responsibility for the parlous 1996 RAE return that was to colour the Holland years. Throughout, there was continuity. The university remained small enough for much of its middle-rank academic staff to know a good sample of academics and, more importantly, most senior management. It was also large enough to provide stimulation and most facilities (just). Moreover, the semi-rural campus continued to provide an element of tranquillity.[40]

Interviewed for this history, Harrison presented himself as handing over a university in good condition, well run and fit for purpose; whereas Holland described a university in a 'dire' situation, one not well run, a university that was like one a hundred years earlier, and where 'student life was at 30 mph'.[41] This contrast, which only in part reflected the differing viewpoints of the academic and the civil servant, clearly has significance for the wider assessment of the two VCs and of the two halves of the decade.

CHAPTER TEN

THE LATER 1990s

The 1996 RAE was in part the result of the old Exeter and the inability of Holland and Powell to turn it around fast enough: it is worth bearing this in mind because for all his faults I think Holland did at least see Exeter needed to change, he just had the wrong (or incomplete) recipe.

Andrew Thorpe

How did we conduct a social life without mobile phones?
Robin Swinburne (1997–2001)

THE 1996 RAE RESULTS dominated the later 1990s in Exeter because they created a sense of failure. Politically, this sense helped drive forward Holland's agenda for improvement, although much of this agenda was somewhat tangential to the problems accurately depicted in the results of the RAE. This formulation captures the contextualisation of policy in the politics of the institution, but there were other political contexts that were also significant. Within universities, the change, under the Major government (1990–97), toward greater power for University Councils, and toward University Councils that were not numerically dominated by academics, increased the possibilities of new initiatives. Moreover, this change enhanced the power of VCs as those who were adept politically were generally able to affect greatly the composition of Council. The transition was encouraged in Exeter by Powell as part of an 'undisguised agenda to re-empower Council to circumvent the obstruction of some elements of Senate'.[1]

The relationship between the VC and the Chair of Council became an even more crucial one in the politics of the institution. As a consequence, although academics tended to think of the late 1990s in Exeter in terms of a Holland–Powell duopoly, Geoffrey Pope, the business-like and hugely conscientious Chair of Council from 1999 until his death in October 2004, was a crucial figure. A former civil servant, Pope had an understated and gentlemanly manner, which contributed to a tendency to underrate his significance. 'Attention to detail'[2] was an important figure of his oversight.

At the national level, there was a series of initiatives in the late 1990s involving Higher and Further Education aimed at addressing the country's economic problems in the shape of skill shortages, notably the Dearing Report (1997), which, basing itself on the argument that educational standards were not absolute, but relative to circumstances, argued that, to be competitive, a 'learning society' had to be one in which Higher Education was not an elitist achievement but a general aspiration. Holland had been a member of Dearing's National Committee of Enquiry, one of only two VCs on it.

There was also the continuing legacy of the Thatcher years and the positioning, by Tony Blair, of the Labour Party he led to power in 1997 in terms of a 'New Britain', allegedly at once description and prospectus. Albeit coming from different directions, there was a landscape of change that institutions needed to read. The financial context was being transformed. In 1989–97, there was a 36 per cent fall in the unit of resource provided by the government per student as well as a significant capital backlog in new construction and maintenance. As a result, irrespective of the already contentious issue of research selectivity, there was the need to consider how to ensure greater income. Under Harrison, there was no real effective plan to deal with the fall in the unit of resource, but that situation was unsustainable, as was the overdependence on the block grant and historic funding.

These changes, this pressure for change, this vocabulary for change, provided opportunities for the politically adroit to mould local circumstances and frame local developments. Ironically, some of those who, as young radicals, had sought to do so in the 1960s, were now outmanoeuvred and, indeed, presented as the defenders of an anachronistic, even failing, system. There were other cases involving a

THE LATER 1990S

cooperation stemming from a shared commitment to reform. In some cases, there was possibly a 'your enemy is my enemy' syndrome: if 'traditional elements' criticised Holland, then he could not be bad. Thus, Malyn Newitt, a former young radical and founder member of the Caucus,[3] served as a DVC from 1995 to 1998. He was subsequently to reflect: 'It took him [Holland] some time to understand how universities worked (perhaps he never really did). … Those who wanted Exeter to be a research-led university never saw Holland as "one of us". … He gave Powell a lot of rope while he tried to use his national connections to deliver pet projects.'[4] Holland himself argued that there was a pent-up demand for change. Naming Gar Yates, Eddie Abel and Charles Desforges, Holland discerned the 'brightest sparks' as wanting change and 'straining at the leash'.[5]

The 1996 RAE was to play fully into pressure for change. In part, like RAE results for all universities, there were very difficult technical issues affecting the score, notably who and what was submitted as the return. The choices made by those who were responsible for the return have since been repeatedly criticised. Surprisingly, the blame was not more widely diffused across the management structure. At any rate, the results provided an opportunity to give new direction and energy to the reform policies that Holland had sought to push from April 1994, when he arrived. Holland saw a vocational focus as a solution to the financial woes of the time, although, like everyone else at this stage, he had no real answer to the problem posed by an absence of critical mass in the Sciences. This posed a major problem in the 1992 and 1996 RAEs as the potential numbers of Science staff that could be returned (let alone the percentage judged good enough to return) was too low, not least to provide the leverage necessary to get good scores. In the 2000s, the adoption of the Science Strategy addressed these problems.

Senate had considered Holland's strategy plans in 1994/95, notably his discussion document 'Towards a Medium and Longer Term Strategy',[6] but without the urgency Holland considered appropriate. In part, this response reflected reluctance to accept the full range of initiatives he was pressing, in part reluctance with the particular strategy, and in part a measure of opposition toward him from a portion of the staff. There were complaints on Senate about the direction and costs of Holland's initiatives, about the lack of a sufficient emphasis on research provision, as well as concerning an apparent absence of commitment to staff interests in the shape of salaries, equal opportunities and collegiality.[7]

APC had its own views, some of which matched Holland's, while others looked in a different direction. APC argued on 30 November 1994 that 'reliance on public funds looks increasingly uncertain and dangerous', that 'growing in size ... should be a means to an end', and not an ambition in itself, and that, 'given its importance in funding and in staff activity, research might be expected to be given a higher profile in the paper'. Indeed, APC pressed for research facilitators in every department.

It would be too easy to link Holland's policies to 'New Labour', and, as a senior civil servant, Holland had briefed Blair when he was Leader of the Opposition, but in fact Holland's agenda was very much in place before Blair came to power. Instead, there were initiatives that reflected Holland's personal convictions and the values, policies and idioms he had embraced and advanced during his period at Employment (eventually as Permanent Secretary, 1988–92) and, more briefly, Education (Permanent Secretary, 1992–94). Holland argued that the existing situation could not be maintained. He informed Senate on 1 March 1995 that there would be a cut in recurrent funding in real terms in the university sector for the next three years. Holland also located his policies in a wider socioeconomic context, pointing out that the CVCP had told the Secretary of State that it was committed to vocationally relevant skills in Higher Education and wished to play a part in the development of a framework for higher vocational qualifications. Holland had made his name as Director of the Manpower Services Commission from 1982 to 1988.

Committed to the idea of a university as a public service institution, and keen to use this to address the financial situation, Holland was very interested and animated when it came to education, training and 'learning'. This interest was mainly economic and closely linked to goals and means such as regional development and national competitiveness. These goals explained Holland's commitment to 'Cornwall', as well as the regional centre at Yeovil, where courses were run in conjunction with the University of Bournemouth, and his instinct to preserve, enlarge and refashion extra-mural work as the Department of Lifelong Learning, and to place it at St Luke's. Holland told a gathering of St Luke's staff that the School of Education was 'the jewel in Exeter's crown'. It was no accident that Keith Atkinson, the Head of the Camborne School of Mines, became Chair of the APC and a DVC; this was part of a broader vision. Other appointments under Holland reflected interests in a broad academic strategy, including William Richardson (Education) and Jonathan Gosling (Business Studies), as well as an attempt to raise the game for the administration by modernising it (Philip Harvey: Academic Secretary; Stephen Cooper: Personnel). The regional theme was scarcely new in Exeter's history. Indeed, there had been strong interest in the 1920s in the idea of a federal university of Exeter and Plymouth. However, Principal Murray and the UGC had cut short the developing connection in the 1930s.[8]

Holland's ambitious ideas were unwelcome to most of the academics, not least because they were out of keeping with the established practices of the university. These ideas represented the intrusion of a different world. They were made more troubling because Holland intended to drive policy, which increased criticism of him, if not hostility toward him. In addition, many of the academics felt that Holland lacked a real interest in research[9] or a consistency in policy implementation, and there was criticism that he failed to use Redcot (the VC's residence) sufficiently for entertaining or to stay there at weekends.

Holland's commitment to the idea that the university tender, against Plymouth, for nursing education in the region and create a School of Nursing, drove home the vocational, as well as the regional, dimension, as did his concern for medical professional development and his interest in a training course for barristers. The grafting of Radiotherapy onto Physics was part of this strategy, although, in practice, it proved a distraction with Radiotherapy's weak research base matched by weak entry grades.

Holland's arrival intensified the already lively and long-standing debate about what kind of university Exeter should aspire to be. There was a strong body of opinion that thought Exeter should be research driven and aim to be accepted as one of the major British research universities. All effort should be focused on achieving this. Although there was a failure to give adequate recognition to the postgraduate dimension, high-quality teaching was part of this profile, alongside selective research;

'the old notions of scholarship and inspired teaching', in the words of Alasdair Paterson, who became Librarian in 1994.[10] In the political and funding climate that was to develop in the 2000s, expansion in regional and professional work was to be seen as a cul-de-sac for Exeter, a point made by Steve Smith when he became VC. The extent to which this was already the case in the 1990s was a matter of controversy then.

There was another vision; that proposed by Holland, who was very good at advancing ideas. This vision did not deny the importance of a strong research base, but saw Exeter as essentially a regional university leading the provision of Higher Education in the South-West. His wife was a major figure behind the creation of Tate St Ives, and perhaps his ideas complemented hers. Holland's goal meant more emphasis on outreach, on part-time provision, on validation and accreditation, and outsourcing teaching to local colleges from Yeovil westwards, and on the idea of a Faculty of Academic Partnerships. A major innovation was to offer a modular programme of professional education at Masters level. A unit was created to apply for funding for a wide variety of local projects in professional development. In practice, although this educational vision was broad and exciting, it lacked coherence.

A strong local profile was also part of the agenda. Claiming that Harrison had failed to cultivate the city, its Council and interests, Holland set out to do so, establishing the 'Vision Partnership' to consider strategic issues. Highly active in this sphere, Holland proved very good at smoothing the city's sensitivities, won planning permission for developments, and helped lay the basis for the move of the Met Office to Exeter. As instances of what was also an important entrepreneurial development, and which looked toward his idea of a 'University for Industry', the Exeter Business Forum was developed under Holland, as were Exeter Enterprises and its spin-off companies.

This activity was linked to the prominence of Domestic Services (residential and catering), which, under Derek Phillips, was one of the most entrepreneurial parts of the university. The halls were transformed from self-running enterprises (housekeepers bought their own food) into a unitary operation under the control of Domestic Services which already ran the central refectories, and then added the Staff Club. Extremely centralised management took power from the wardens, who were to be replaced by Resident Tutors and Senior Resident Tutors. Affected by the

University's drive to charge more costs to support services, and from the difficulty of raising charges to students, Domestic Services had moved into supplementary sources of income. This took a number of directions. Increased vacation income was realised from both conference and holiday accommodation, and Exeter became one of the most successful UK universities for conferences. This provided a financial basis for an increase in residential provision with an extensive building programme that included the construction of the first purpose-built en-suite student study bedrooms in the UK. Holland noted that the specifications of the bedrooms reflected not only the requirements for conferences but also pressure from parents for better accommodation.[11]

In catering, apart from hosting a number of local professional organisations, Domestic Services began to provide an extensive off-campus catering operation, including the professional rugby and football clubs and the racecourse. Many wedding receptions were held at Crossmead or Reed Hall. This expansion in services allowed Domestic Services, which had a very large turnover, to operate without subsidy, a situation achieved in very few universities. The profits from services, which included a burger van managed in a cash-only way, helped ensure that student rents could be subsidised. In 1999/2000, £15.7 million of the university's income of £85.6 million came from residences and catering, while £14.6 million of the £83.4 million expenditure was spent in this area. The student experience of Domestic Services, however, was far less positive, and this was responsible for a serious deterioration in Guild relations with the university in 2000.

The clash of cultures between the differing goals for the institution dominated all debates and never led to a meeting of minds:

> I recall Stephen Wilks standing up in Senate with the University's Annual Report in his hand and asking Holland if he realised that the word 'research' was not in it anywhere – it was all Cornwall, engagement with the region, 'thickening our relations with Somerset' (an actual phrase I saw in documents more than once at that time), etc.[12]

As the university was to have to restructure financially, it was important to be clear about priorities, and these were never clear. Newitt refers to this in his evaluation of these years alongside his argument that this was not a period of decline, but, instead, an exciting time when Exeter began to expand its horizons and displayed a hitherto unexpected ability to innovate and to 'think outside the box'.[13]

However, there were also less successful features. The need to confront a willingness to tolerate highly variable staff performance was not really faced, and the culture of insularity and long service that was common to the university system, but particularly strong in Devon, remained a problem. Holland awakened some entrepreneurship, but directed this along lines that were not to be best suited, in the emerging political climate, to Exeter's need to find a distinctive excellence. Engagement with many of the staff was limited, while declining real incomes did little for staff morale, and led to a day's strike in November 1996.

The emphasis on change was seen in the 1995 document *A Strategy for the Next Decade*, which announced plans for an administrative transformation. As with other strategies for change advanced in the 1990s, this had a corporatist dimension, albeit not one that was identical with those of earlier decades. This corporatism reflected a degree of public–private partnership, but the emphasis was still very much that of, and on, the public sector. The possibilities of an alternative in which governmental funds and requirements played a much smaller role appeared remote. Exeter, however, like other universities, was to face the problems of public services in a period of increasing turmoil. The cuts of earlier decades were to be succeeded by an era of transformation.[14] In teaching terms, this was an era in which the inconstant, sometimes indifferent, nature of a public service could not last. In managerial terms, the adjustments to non-governmental opportunities, as well as to changing governmental policies, were to pose serious problems.

Presented as a key opportunity, the Cornwall project rapidly gathered weight and momentum under Holland, but at the same time raised reasonable concern on the main site over the question of any diversion of funds. On 1 March 1995, Holland stressed to Senate 'that any expenditure connected with the development would have to be *new* money. There would be no transfer of funding from any existing department.' However, Senate was informed, on 27 November 1996, that £135,000 had been committed as a seedcorn investment for the Cornwall initiative. Holland saw Camborne, as well as a large and growing youth population

THE LATER 1990S

in Cornwall, as presenting major opportunities. He complained that much of the main site did not care about Camborne.

This was part of a wider divide. To Holland, education as a whole had to contribute centrally to regional and national regeneration through skills and innovation, but some universities were 'lost in the world of academia'.[15] Holland's plan was for a quick feasibility study followed with the establishment of a funding project, hopefully with the support of Falmouth School of Arts and of Cornwall County Council, which was very keen to see Camborne's future guaranteed within a bigger framework. The feasibility study produced by John Inkson suggested demand and support to go forward. It became clear very quickly that the best hope of funding was the Millennium Fund and an application was put together once the site, Trereife in Penzance, and campus design were finalised. The initial campus choice came about, in part, from a day's coach outing for Council members to Cornwall, visiting four possible sites (near Falmouth, Newquay, Penzance and Redruth), three of them based on country houses and their estates. The resulting plan was for the construction of a campus costing £59 million and with space for 1,600 students. The university was assured by HEFCE that, if the capital was forthcoming, the necessary funded student numbers would follow, a key step.

The Millennium Fund, however, proved unhelpful, while the project encountered a high level of local objections as well as local support. There was an outbreak of parochial infighting between Cornwall's districts once the choice was known. Cornwall's districts wanted a new university development, but not necessarily in a competing district's backyard. In addition, aside from rival local educational institutions, there was also opposition from Cornish nationalists to an Exeter-directed project. There was also a very strong local competitor for funds in the Eden Project. In the end, the application was rejected in 1996, on the basis that it did not fit the parameters of the Millennium Fund, at the point when a large part of the Fund itself was diverted to the London Dome.[16]

Prior to the announcement of the RAE results on 19 December 1996, there was already growing pressure for change at Exeter. As so often, finances were an issue. Compared to the recent crises, Exeter was in relatively reasonable financial health, but, like other universities, was heavily dependent on government funding. This took the form of the RAE, of teaching income and of external Research Council income. However, the second was effectively frozen and the third was low.

The impact of the financial situation was accentuated by inflationary pressures within the sector, both for salary increases and for promotions. On 22 May 1996, Holland pointed to a deteriorating position when he told Senate that, in order to obtain a break-even budget, a cut of £532,000 in addition to what was already planned would be required. He added that there were 'no immediate plans for compulsory redundancies among staff in 1996/7. Departments would, however, need to deliver their business plans, particularly so far as income generation was concerned.' Indeed, despite serious problems with acquiring clear data, business plans were to become central to university decision-making, a process developed by Philip Harvey as Academic Secretary from 1997.

APC, working with Powell and with the Director of Finance, Keith Blanshard, had introduced a structured planning system covering all departments. This system covered all areas of income and expenditure with the exception of space charging (for which there was no data) and began to judge the ambitions of departments in the light of past performance and future prospects. Proper departmental financially based planning was seen by APC as an initial solution to the academic planning problem. Highly unpopular, this system highlighted a number of anomalies and set the scene for evidence-based planning in the light of future changes in RAE results and student income trends. The system came into its own as part of the major APC review that followed the 1996 RAE.

The 1996 RAE increased the pressure for action. It was a serious failure of activity and organisation. As the RAE approached, members of Research Committee were each allocated departments, the submissions of which they monitored, reviewed and fine-tuned prior to approval and submission, including decisions about whom not to submit. By introducing this element of objectivity to departmental submissions, it was hoped to maximise the research rating, but departments were not uniformly cooperative in this exercise, some members of Research Committee were given a hard time, it was only possible to work with what departments produced, and the Committee itself did not seem to understand all the rules of the RAE process, let alone its nuances. In some departments, too many academics were submitted.[17]

THE LATER 1990S

Against the background of a genuine attempt to improve Exeter's research rating whilst maintaining collegiality, the outcome of the RAE was particularly disappointing. Overall the university suffered the biggest fall of any: on the *THES* league tables Exeter was rated 47th, a fall from 14th. Some departments went up from the 1992 results, including Classics, History and Law, while others went down, including Education, Engineering and French, but too many failed to reach 4 (national excellence in virtually all sub-areas) on the scale, notably Biological Sciences, Engineering, English, Law and Archaeology. Moreover, the upward trend across the country since the 1992 RAE results[18] was such that, as in the previous cycle, standing still, as Politics did at a 4, now represented a failure. The same was true of gaining a 4, which did not send a positive message, and notably for postgraduates. Only five subjects gained a 5: Applied Mathematics, Economics, Accountancy, Classics and Hospital-Based Clinical Subjects. The loss of Education's 5 was particularly grave as it was the largest Department in the university and a major cost-centre. French's loss of its 5 was also serious as it was the largest language department. Of the research active staff, the graphics in the *THES* for 20 December 1996 presented 8 per cent of the 'research active staff' as 5, 54 per cent as 4, 25 per cent as 3A, 11 per cent as 3B, and 2 per cent as 2.

Education went from 5 to 4C (C meaning only 60–79 per cent of staff returned in the research submission). Cynics attributed this to Wragg no longer chairing the Education Panel, as he had done in 1992. Given that research has established a linkage between Panel membership and grades, the cynics probably had a point. More seriously, there were long-standing problems with Education. As Neil Armstrong pointed out, 'the ethos was very much that of a Teacher Training College rather than a university ... research was a very low priority'.[19] Relatively few staff from the old St Luke's had survived into the 1990s. The problem was that nearly all the newcomers recruited in a surge in 1988–92 during the vast expansion of the School had little or no research experience or vision. Wragg had been happy with that – 'his' (*sic*) staff were primarily to train teachers, not to do research – but it caught up with him and the School in the 1996 RAE.

Powell recalled the result of the 1996 RAE as 'the rest of the world saying you're not actually very good'.[20] Holland had been warned by Stephen Lea and Wilks that the results might be bad, and he found them a shock. Initially seemingly uncertain what to do,[21] Holland wrote to staff on 4 February 1997, arguing that, in light of the results, as well as the financial cuts, a focusing of resources had become necessary. On 5 March, he told Senate that the overall performance 'had been disappointing ... about a grade lower on average than other comparable universities'. The percentage of staff not returned had been higher, at 19 per cent, than in most 'old' universities': Bristol 14 per cent, Durham 12 per cent. Holland argued that the RAE demonstrated the need to consider 'the size and range of the academic units within the university' in order 'to produce a substantial number of financially-secure academic units, all of which were capable of achieving a grade 5 by the year 2000, or at the latest 2004'. In the 1996 RAE, Exeter had submitted more units of assessment than any other university of its size. The old fault of too many departments persisted.

Determined to show that he was not simply responding to the RAE[22] or a budgetary cut, Holland correctly claimed that this action had been foreseen in the 1995 document *A Strategy for the Next Decade*. The suggestion in Senate, by Roger Burt, that, on the analogy of a failing football team, the manager should go, was ignored. The census dates of the 1996 RAE indicated that much of the period covered by it in fact predated Holland's VCship, although there were elements of serious management failure in the handling of the submissions.

There were immediate political consequences from the RAE. It was the death knell of the old departmentalism. The crisis created by the RAE results ensured that Heads of Department could no longer thwart Holland. On 18 March 1997, Senate agreed to a Schools-based structure, Holland stating that the criteria should be quantitative and academic. A week later, he wrote: '[T]he status quo, in my view, is not an option ... in a University where if the School of Education sneezes the rest of us catch a serious cold and where some of the very small and least successful departments are no longer separately viable, something has to be done.'[23]

Meanwhile, financial exigencies were driving home the pressure. Whereas the average increase in grant for institutions in 1997/98 was 2.8 per cent over 1996/97 figures, Exeter's grant had been reduced by 0.6 per cent. Transitional funding of £2 million was allocated to the university for three years as safety netting, to moderate what would otherwise have been a reduction of about £4 million in real terms, including £2.1 million due to the major fall in the research income that followed the RAE scores. Holland was given credit for obtaining this. Transitional funding, then a real barometer of risk at the national level, proved, by the standards of the late 2000s, a luxury that became a mere memory. Indeed, the contrast between this response to the 1996 RAE and the harsher situation for universities that did badly in the 2008 RAE helps underline why the Smith–Allen revolution in the university in the 2000s was prescient.

Alongside the RAE-related cuts following the 1996 exercise, there was the annual reduction (in real terms) in national funding to Higher Education institutions that the government was pursuing. In order to adjust to the lower levels of grant support from its main funding source, the university had to resort to the implementation of across-the-board cuts in its resource allocations to both the academic and non-academic sectors. Voluntary redundancy programmes affected staffing, but, as ever prior to 2004/05, there was only limited strategic planning in these losses. Funding pressures ensured that new capital developments and investment were limited.

For the APC review after the 1996 RAE, APC members plus co-opted senior academic staff, mostly previous DVCs, went into all departments to assess future prospects, and the changes required to achieve future success in terms of the RAE and student recruitment. This was an unprecedented exercise in terms of scope and effort. A report on every department was produced and discussed, and a plan, APC1, was produced. This plan was based on the view that, in the light of the financial constraints, there would need to be significant staff restructuring, with targeted early retirements funded by a central fund, in order to recruit new staff. The level to which this was required and the net savings required of each department varied. Major savings were expected from Science and Engineering, to reflect their relatively generous historical funding, while some other areas were considered too small and uncompetitive to be continued.

APC's approach failed to win the support of Senate, where there was a reluctance to accept any plan that involved staff changes and especially departmental closures. To critics, Senate was in effect a collection of vested interests, unfit for purpose as a decision-making body, and accustomed to blocking significant changes. Holland had been fully supportive of the changes at APC, but he avoided conflict and was unable or unwilling to give the necessary lead at Senate.[24] As a result, APC2 was written as a modification to APC1 and quickly adopted. It retained the analysis, but rolled the staff changes and cost savings for each department into a net financial cut. Although APC was to have oversight of key underperforming areas in order to try to bring the necessary changes about, the new plan moved the decisions more into the hands of the Heads of Departments. In the event, the early retirement fund was used extensively, ensuring that staff changes were implemented, but not generally in the targeted way envisaged. Except for a few departments, noticeably English and Arab and Islamic Studies, an opportunity for significant change was missed, and this was reflected in the extent to which, although the 2001 RAE registered gains, these were still disappointing.

On the positive side, APC1 and APC2 informed and enabled the Schooling process that followed. The ability of the existing structures to deliver results was questioned as part of an attempt to gain the initiative for the centre by reorganising the governance of the university. At Senate on 10 December 1996, introducing two reports from the Working Group on Management Structures, Holland emphasised the need for rapid decision-taking, for structures to achieve better use of academics' time, and for streamlining to allow leadership to flourish, especially among Deans, who, he argued, should be integrated into top management.

A bald indictment of the existing managerial system was offered by Stephen Lea, a major figure in the Holland years, when he discussed in Senate the second report from the Working Group on Management Structures, which he had helped to draw up: '[T]he university's current structures were incomprehensible and unconvincing to outsiders.' Indeed, when they were asked to create business plans, the Heads of School complained that the internal accounting procedures were incomprehensible. There were significant improvements in accounting procedures made in the late 1990s under Blanshard by Adrian Davey, the Management Accountant. This situation was further improved from 2005 when Allen brought in Jeremy Lindley from Birmingham as Director of Finance, and he implemented necessary changes, alongside Paul Webley as DVC.

As evidence of poor structures, Lea cited faculties consisting of only one or two departments which he claimed were incapable of delivering independent academic review. The sufferers, Lea claimed, were the students, although he produced no evidence for this indictment of Law and Education (single-department faculties): in each case the students were highly employable. Lea continued by stating that the posts of Head of Department, Dean, and DVC were difficult to fill, resulting in a lack of balance of representation and occasionally bad appointments, and that the link between the policy-forming centre and the departments, where most of the money was earned and spent, was indistinct, in part because Deans had no financial responsibility and could therefore be undermined by powerful departments which approached the university committees or VC direct.

Offering an historical perspective, Lea argued that 'the university's governance had been democratised in response to a previously oligarchic situation some twenty years ago; it was no longer appropriate to a changed world'. Instead, he pressed for what was often described as the Warwick method, because it had been developed at that successful university. Moreover, Harvey brought this model with him when he arrived from Warwick in 1997, succeeding Barrie Behenna as Academic Secretary, and he soon made a major impact with some senior figures.

In place of a focus on departments, Lea pressed, in Senate and elsewhere, for larger units in the shape of Schools comprised of similar disciplines. Lea argued that this new focus would permit difficult decision-making, in the shape of prioritising disciplines, and provide critical mass, adding 'such units should be members of the decision-taking bodies at university level, thus empowering both sides: departmental and central management'. The response at Senate was underwhelming. Most speakers offered 'strong support for maintaining the subject department as the prime unit of academic management' and suggested that creating Schools would prove a distraction. Holland proposed a fudge that responded to the mood, but also ensured that the eventual restructuring would take even longer and would, for a while, lead to the single-disciplinary units that Lea had deplored. Holland told Senate: 'There was overwhelming opposition to movement to a new structure by central prescription and change should be effected by cognate disciplines entering into voluntary associations with each other.' This fudging approach was responsible for some of the highly questionable units that were created, which is code for what one DVC referred to as 'nonsensical'. Linked to this, instead of forming twelve Schools, the original intention, eighteen were created initially.

There was no additional funding for Higher Education in the Labour manifesto, the party having won a landslide victory in the general election on 1 May 1997. The university still faced the loss of its transitional funding. Inkson, the perceptive Chair of APC, told Senate on 28 May that the university needed to cut £2.8 million per annum in the core academic sector, and that over a tenth of the staff would have to go. Holland said that compulsory redundancies would only be pursued in the last resort. The Senate debate was instructive, not least with the argument that the crisis was long standing, indeed 'had been developing since the 1989 RAE', which was an apt indictment of policies earlier in the decade.[25] There was general recognition of the need to tackle the serious financial position, but sometimes a lack of constructive suggestions by the critics of APC's remedy of selectivity. Much of the criticism was of process, notably a lack of proper consultation and access to documentation, as well as criticism of the RAE as a system and a calling into question of its results, but there was also informed questioning of the APC planning.[26]

On 7 July, Holland increased the pressure, telling Senate that Gordon Brown's abolition of tax credits for pension schemes was bad for the Universities Superannuation Scheme (USS) and that the 1996/97–2000/01 reduction in core recurrent income was of the order of 10 per cent. His stress on finance cut the ground from most critics: 'The emphasis must be on the incentive schemes now in place for international student recruitment and research grant overheads', a long-overdue policy. There was much criticism in that Senate of 'Future Academic Profile and Academic Management Structures', the previous month's report from APC which had spelled out the consequences of the strategy for research and teaching excellence, and financial security. Proposals included the abandonment of BA courses in Arts and Humanities that Education was to have launched for 1998/89, and the closure of American and Post-Colonial Studies as part of a concentration of the activities of the School of English. Law's research activity was criticised in the report,[27] and Chemistry was told to meet the cost of upgrading its infrastructure principally through generating the necessary income.

In practice, there was a lack of clarity over how best to create a plan able to deliver cuts and maintain outcome. Inkson informed Senate that student numbers and associated resources should be allocated to where it seemed to be in the best interests of the university as a whole; Powell warned that 'if realistic plans were not made and implemented … there was a risk of HEFCE withdrawing the transitional funding'; and Holland said that Council would need to be convinced that there was a clear strategy and appropriate timetable for achieving the necessary economies: 'Any lack of clarity from Senate would need to be corrected by Council.' In the face of amendments from the Academic Staff Association rejecting particular APC recommendations, only part of the report passed.

Nevertheless, the direction of change was very much as outlined by APC. A combination of APC's Implementation Groups, Research Committee, and Team 2000 drove forward this change. Powell, who became more powerful after the 1996 RAE, was in favour of taking funds from weaker units, rather than salami-slicing. Staff who were considered weak in research terms were encouraged to take early retirement, being offered eight added years of pension contributions. There was also a redundancy scheme for those not old enough to retire; those whose redundancy was approved were offered two years' salary. These changes, combined with the recruitment of professors, did make a significant difference in terms of perspectives and expectations.

Although Powell had perforce to devote more energy to controlling the finances than to future growth and the focus was therefore on stabilisation,[28] there was also the successful development of some interesting and innovative projects. For example, a unit was established to give Exeter a leading role in bidding for EU TEMPUS funding in the former Soviet Union. This unit worked with a range of Western European universities and colleges to set up IT and curriculum development projects in Russia, Uzbekistan, Ukraine and Mongolia. Powell encouraged the bidding for project money and established a unit for overseas recruitment. This activity drew on the development, from the late 1980s, of engagement within Europe across the university. From then, there had been much research collaboration with European universities, which was organised by the EC (European Community) Funding Unit. In addition, many students had gone to EU universities such as Rennes (the city's twin town) under the ERASMUS scheme.

The TEMPUS projects made the idea of closing Russian appear a reflection of contrasting priorities in different parts of the university. In the event, Russian was retained, albeit with reduced staff numbers. Its prominent role in the promotion and running of interdisciplinary courses, at both an undergraduate and postgraduate level, within Modern Languages helped preserve its position.[29]

A key international initiative occurred in Gulf Studies. In the mid-1990s, the Middle East-related operations in Exeter had gone through a period of reaction, in part due to the move of some key staff to other universities, notably, but not only, Ian Netton to Leeds and Tim Niblock to Durham, where they established or developed similar programmes to the ones they had run in Exeter; and in part due to obtaining a 3 in the RAE. For a time, it was a question, notably under the APC2 plan, whether Exeter would keep Arabic as an independent Department or subsume its courses into Modern Languages. At this critical stage, approached by Keith Atkinson, a DVC, who saw Arabic as a strategic asset, Sheikh Sultan Bin Mohammed Al-Qasimi, ruler of Sharjah from 1972, came forward with an offer of substantial funding to finance a new multidisciplinary institute for the study of the Arab and Islamic worlds. The Sheikh referred to the university as 'family', having earned his PhD at Exeter in 1985, his thesis being published as *The Myth of Arab Piracy in the Gulf* (London, 1986). The funding was both for a new building and for several new posts. The Department of Arabic and the Centre for Arab Gulf Studies were incorporated into the new Institute of Arab and Islamic Studies, which was established in 1999, with a returned Niblock as Director, to cover the Islamic world as a whole. This was to be a highly effective unit, covering a multidisciplinary area of studies. New Al-Qasimi chairs were established in Gulf Studies, Arabic, and Islamic Studies, as well as more junior posts.[30] The Sheikh was also a major benefactor in other respects, providing funding for the Postgraduate Centre and for the Forum.

In the late 1990s, there was a greater emphasis than hitherto on reducing dependence on government funding by promoting initiatives within both the academic and non-academic sectors that produced external income. This included the residences and catering activities which were targeted to increase income as a result of improved management action to improve occupancy levels. The suspension of employer's contributions to the University of Exeter Retirement Benefits Scheme (ERBS) brought a significant financial benefit, reducing the pressure for cuts. The later implications of this decision for non-academic pensions which would come to the fore in 2002 were still some way off.

Meanwhile, the university applied the outcomes of the Transparent Approach to Costing Exercise (TRAC) with a view to determining more realistic overhead rates, an improved approach to resource allocation, and a better basis for future investment decisions. Significant investment was made in student residences, funded from bank loans. Powell was to play an important role in ensuring that interest rates were kept low. A long-term financial model was developed to ensure that all student residence budgets and decisions on the setting of student rents took full account of the annual costs of borrowing and of internal targets for the elimination of approved negative carry-forward balances that were being temporarily funded from the university's overall general reserves. At the student level, this meant rent increases, although there was also an element of cross-subsidy for social purposes, with rents for basic rooms in Lafrowda and Rowancroft kept low by introducing very high rents in the en suites in Rowe House, Nash Grove, James Owen Court, St Germans and Clydesdale Rise.[31]

* * *

Rents were a key issue in student life. So also was sex, the varied aspects of which were covered by *Exeposé* in a detail that would have surprised readers of *South Westerner* in the 1950s. Public education was a key theme, as with discussion of the advantages and disadvantages of different types of contraception, on whether you can get AIDS from toilets, and on HIV and carbon monoxide poisoning as twin threats.[32] Technology in a different form was at issue in the new problem of e-mail sleaze and harassment.[33] Concern over the latter was also expressed in the 'reclaim the night' stance that reflected a degree of fear that did not accord with what in fact was a very low crime rate.[34] Food was a topic. 'Those vile ectoplasmic squares of "pizza" sold in the Ram' (which had been expanded in size in 1993) were a matter of complaint in *Exeposé* on 10 February 1997. The problems of not getting enough sleep were also mentioned.[35]

The major and costly development in Sport was largely funded by sponsorship and by the selling off of the university playing fields at Gras Lawn off Barrack Road, leased in 1903 and bought in 1912. Indeed, it is striking that in his interview Powell was proudest of and keenest to talk about the development in sport facilities, although his account was largely about his skill in arranging the sale of Gras Lawn for what was then the highest price per acre paid for building land in Exeter. That the City Council would permit development was part of the equation, indeed of the politics of the deal.

Exeter had always been a decent sporting university, and its standing and performance were enhanced by the takeover of St Luke's, which had a very strong sporting tradition. Rugby, hockey and cricket were the main beneficiaries. Exeter, however, had had rather limited facilities and funds to support its sporting ambitions. The catalyst for change was probably a mixture of the rebranding of polytechnics as universities and Powell's personal interest, one shown since his retirement in his prominent role in the development of the Exeter Chiefs (rugby club) on a major new site. Several new universities, notably Leeds Met, knowing they would remain limited academically, decided to invest heavily in sports facilities and sports scholarships in order to attract more students and to achieve success that would be noted elsewhere. They began to take on, and beat, many of the older universities, which were forced to decide whether they wanted to compete like-for-like or to concentrate on their academic reputation. In Exeter, the decision was effectively made by Powell, who set up a Sports Office in 1999 with a new Director of Sport. Previously, there had only been a Director of the Sports Hall, a more limited post with lower grading and responsibilities. This move was accompanied by a major programme of investment in facilities. The £4.2 million obtained by selling Gras Lawn was earmarked for new sporting developments. These included a new 23-acre sports site out towards Topsham, extensions and improvements to the Sports Hall (including extensive exercise suites), an Astroturf pitch for hockey, an indoor tennis centre (opened in 2004), and additional outdoor tennis courts. The university also established a programme of Sports Scholarships financed jointly by sponsors and from the student residences account. In terms of personal commitment, sport for Powell proved the equivalent of Cornwall for Holland. Very few of the academics were engaged with either commitment.

This investment set a pattern that has remained significant. The university came fifth out of 173 institutions in the British Universities and College Sport competition in 2012/13, a return to the standing it once had. Much of this result came from a plethora of minor sports which reflect the depth and breadth of sporting interest among the sort of students the university recruits, for example lacrosse.

At the same time, there have been significant achievements in the major sports, including cricket. Hockey and rugby have achieved outstanding results in recent years. In 2012/13, over 5,800 students joined one of the fifty Athletic Union sports clubs. At Exeter from 2005 until 2013, David Morgan-Owen later reflected:

> I invested the majority of my time pursuing various sports (particularly rugby) in both a playing and coaching capacity. Indeed, it was really only in the final years of my PhD that I took full advantage of the university as [a] seat of learning. This may seem a careless waste of one's time, but ... it actually reveals much about what is excellent about British universities and Exeter in particular: I learned far more about people and institutions from my practical experience of transforming the rugby league club from a fringe concern to a nationally competitive side who received significant support from the university ... than my mind would have been able to absorb from purely learned pursuits. The freedom to invest one's time in this fashion – as one sees fit – was a great gift and, through allowing it, Exeter did much to imbue a self-reliance and entrepreneurial spirit which has served me well.[36]

In contrast, Rob Johnson (1995–99) was disturbed by 'the arrival of post-modernism/post-colonialism as an all-pervading ideology amongst arts students ... coffee bar discussions were closed down by a series of slogans, mantras and accusations'.[37]

Whereas, in 1993, a Guild vote rejected, by 643–625, a student sporting charge (as the Athletics Union wanted), as opposed to pay-as-you-go,[38] sport is now publicised as a selling point and an investment in the enhancement of the student experience. Student satisfaction surveys indicate its impact, while the apparel favoured by many in the student body (the tracksuit look) implies that they are conscious of belonging to a 'sporting university' whatever the level of their individual participation. Sport is also being used deliberately as a means of integrating and retaining overseas students who come to Exeter.[39]

While significant, a focus on sport can lead to a failure to note the greater contribution to university life made by the range of student societies, which of course do not enjoy the expenditure lavished on sporting facilities. To take the experience of Matt Rendle, a student who arrived in 1995 (and returned to teach in 2010):

> Broader university life took some time to settle down. I did not particularly like the people I shared a floor with in halls – Birks Halls – primarily because we had different interests. I didn't like halls much – fixed meal times, not enough food (!), and noise throughout the day and night. With a couple of others from surrounding floors, I moved into Lafrowda for my second and third years which was close to campus, had the independence of self-catering, was cheap and had a good, multi-cultural atmosphere as this was where many of the foreign students lived. Most of my social life, however, revolved around societies, particularly the Expedition Society. … With Exsoc, there was a walking/camping trip most weekends, social events on Wednesday nights and, as I made friends, we tended to go out at other times too. The massive advantage of the societies was that it brought you into contact with people from across the university.

And Robin Swinburne in 1997/98: 'If I hadn't have met such good friends, I would have felt a bit cold inside due to the sparse décor and Gulag feeling of the Birks building.'[40]

* * *

Meanwhile, the range of external scrutiny and pressure continued to increase in the late 1990s. The HEQC Institutional Audit Report urged the university 'to strengthen the strategic role of Teaching Committee, to make examination conventions explicit and ensure their harmonisation across the university, to monitor the maintenance of academic standards, to clarify the relationship between teaching and research, and to avoid undue delay in quality assurance processes'. This report was stage-managed by Newitt in order to generate the recommendations he wanted.

THE LATER 1990S

The politics of change was driven home in the context of the reorientation, for some disorientation, created by the formation of Schools, as advocated by the Working Group on Management Structures, and by the new demands of finance, research and teaching. The novelty and managerial ideas linked to Schools were unpopular. These managerial ideas reflected the extent to which Schools were designed to replace not only departments which were seen as too many and too small, but also the existing faculties. The latter had proved weak and Deans found that they had responsibility, not power, notably financial power. By the end of 1997, the new Schools had been defined and their Heads elected. Student applications and admissions were buoyant,[41] with international student numbers increasing by 12 per cent. Exeter was 'fashionable' with the kind of students it was willing to accept.

In most cases, there was little actual change towards multidisciplinary Schools, and a situation developed in which a few large confederations were managed alongside smaller single-discipline units, which made aspects of management and data collection cumbersome. People could not agree on how to School. The decision to part with some academic areas was too painful to be made easily. All kinds of vested interests and faddish theories came into play, and the process reflected scant credit on the university. Over Schooling, the DVCs did not work well as a team, with Newitt and Inkson disagreeing bitterly, which was part of the more general case with the DVCs in the late 1990s. Departmental votes against Schooling were ignored, and departments found themselves physically moved into unfamiliar spaces and joined to unknown partners. Restructuring irritated a number of academics who felt that the departmental and disciplinary identity was the one that really counted;[42] while the new larger identities tended to make many academics feel more detached from everything that was going on. There were bitter complaints, for example from Peter Wiseman (Classics), who argued that there were no academic reasons for Schooling; he pressed Holland to accept that the rationale was solely managerial, and there were long debates in Senate on keeping the name of the Department of Classics.

A big motivation for Schooling was breaking up the Faculty of Arts, which had not only contained those that considered themselves to be some of the best departments in the University, but also housed a hotbed of criticism of Northcote House and successive VCs. For the management, getting History out of the equation (and out of Queen's Building), and into links with the Social Sciences (and Amory) was a great result. Newitt was very much in favour of the move which was opposed by much of History. Some Schools worked well. Modern Languages, which had been one for many years, provided some innovative link courses, although it was hit hard by the decision to remove languages from being a compulsory subject in the school curriculum.[43] Drama and Music were joined in a School but, as Paul Morgan (Music 1969–2007), noted: '[A]lthough some attempt was made to bring the two disciplines together, it was found that the style of teaching was very different and not much headway was made.'[44] Perhaps the most significant change for the future was that Business and Economics were separated from the old Social Studies Faculty (which they had long disliked) and allowed to shape their future as an independent School. A great deal followed from that decision in terms of the expansion of Business Studies in the 2000s.

Council rejected Senate criticisms of new structures, while the Joint Committee of Council and Senate on the Working Practices of the University revised the latter in a more dirigiste fashion. The reduction in the size of Senate was used to try to make it more accommodating, while the influence of professors was lessened. The proposal that professors should automatically sit on the Management Boards of Schools was rejected; in addition, the Established Chairs lost their position on Senate. Moreover, Holland eased the promotion process, creating more professors, although not to the extent seen under Smith.

Other significant changes included the creation of the two new undergraduate and postgraduate faculties, and the establishment of a senior management group. The former enabled the university to modernise its quality management in such a way that it passed through all the QAA challenges of the 2000s, and also to take a serious grip on postgraduate education. The latter created a viable forum for policy debate which engaged a reasonable range of people outside Senate, thereby in the long term dooming Senate to irrelevance unless it is reformed for a new purpose, which has not yet occurred. As a result, the modern management of the university really began in 1997/98, although it required the Smith–Allen partnership to harness the dynamism and efficiency of what was created then. In terms of educational delivery, the university

THE LATER 1990S

was more effective by the end of the 1990s than it had been when Holland became VC.

The Departmental Reviews begun under Harrison were stepped up and were chaired by Holland, who handled them effectively.[45] As earlier, the presence of senior external evaluators served to challenge the positive self-assessment by departments, very noticeably so with Law, Chemistry and Education. Heads were asked to explain these contrasts.

Law indeed had lost its way. Other universities had successfully challenged Exeter's pre-eminence in European legal studies, and the imagination and initiative which had produced that status did not survive to move the department into new areas of legal study. Andrew Tettenborn, who arrived from Cambridge as Bracton Professor, recorded:

> Law in 1996 gave the impression of being pretty laid-back in Exeter. Many members were long-term fixtures, rather like in some Oxbridge college about 1970. The place largely rested on its laurels. ... Until about 2000, when the RAE mentality kicked in big-time, not much was actually expected of anyone: it was a bonus if they did write, but no-one worried too much if they didn't.[46]

As the Review made clear, the department was claiming a reputation it no longer deserved. This reflected a poor record of research and publication, the loss of key staff and a failure to replace them, issues with leadership, and the establishment of the Centre for Legal Practice which proved to be costly and ultimately unsuccessful. In part, there was a clear case of decline, and therefore failure, at the departmental level, one shown in very low morale,[47] but this also reflected the serious weaknesses of structures, processes and leadership at the university level.

The Departmental Review process was useful in promoting change,[48] but, in addressing problems, only so much could be done at the departmental level. In the case of English, a department with significant tensions, including between the professors, it proved necessary for the university to intervene and gain an external 'steer' on policy.

Philip Harvey, the Academic Secretary, joined what he later described as a 'burning platform' in which the 1996 RAE exacerbated the falling block grant. Instructed to act as a new broom and to forge a proper academic strategy off the back of significant contraction, he both helped turn round important departments that became significant sources of strength, such as Arab and Islamic Studies, and encouraged, focused and equipped with data a more general consideration of enhancing the university's research. In both cases, Harvey sought to pursue a selective incentivisation of academic activity.[49] Seen as a possible successor to Powell, Harvey was to go on under Allen to be Deputy Registrar.

In November 1998 Harvey and Atkinson commissioned a review of the School of Education by Jim Campbell, Director of Warwick's Institute of Education, and David Galloway, his Durham counterpart. Delivered in January 1999, this report endorsed the view of APC that the School's Business Plan 'did not address substantive matters of strategic importance'. Poor leadership resting on a dysfunctional culture proved a key issue:

> There appears to us to be a lack of vision, particularly among senior staff, about how the School might develop in a changing and continually hostile climate. The fear, suspicion and animosity which, in many Universities, is directed towards Ofsted and TTA, at Exeter is directed towards the University's own senior management team. ... The management structure, with the Director and other professors merely *primus inter pares*, may have been sustainable in an earlier and more relaxed era. Today it generates 'mutual dyslexia': an inability to read the writing on the wall.

Criticising the elective system of management, the report called for a 'more directive leadership structure' and a more committed staff. The entire report provided not just a highly critical indictment of the ethos and practices of Education (one much resented within the School), but also, in effect, of the university as a whole. At the level of individual departments and academics, many cases of poor performance were ducked; although, conversely, as the Nine Factors Cultural Assessment survey of May 1998 indicated, the university's management did not command the confidence of a section of the academics. Moreover, the answer 'Do you have confidence in the way the University is run?' produced a result well below the national average.[50]

Given the aspiration for change and the direction of policy, it may be asked why the Holland years were subsequently treated as a

THE LATER 1990S

disappointment. Indeed, there are signs that some of the policies and trends associated with the Smith years, notably a weakening of Senate and a process of specialisation and resource allocation, were already present under Holland. Powell was to claim that, by 2001, 'the University was financially sounder and ready to start making significant advances academically'.[51] In 1999/2000 £10.8 million of the £85.6 million income came from research grants and contracts. By about 1998, in fact, there was a real head of steam among the more enterprising and ambitious academics that was taking the university forward once again on research, at the same time as the Teaching Quality Assessments were increasingly returning 'excellent' ratings. Taking this further, the RAE improvements of the 2000s can in part be traced to the late 1990s.

Alongside his concern with ensuring that the university lived within its means, the unpopular Powell was a key transition figure in Exeter's modernisation. 'Steadying the ship', he encouraged Holland in broadly the right direction, effected a power shift from professors to administrators, and modernised business planning, notably once Harvey had arrived from Warwick. A theme of improvement certainly came out at the time of the 2001 RAE. Newitt, by then at King's London, wrote congratulating Holland on 'an excellent RAE result … it has vindicated the tough decisions that you had to make'. Less positively, 'Holland, who was far more interested in Cornwall, got his way over that and Powell essentially ran the main site.'[52]

There were also important developments at the departmental level. For example, the formation of Astrophysics in 2000/01 was a completely new venture for Physics and, as such, a major risk based upon a successful plan to attain a 5 in the 2001 RAE, a result that put the small department alongside competitors such as Bristol, Manchester and UCL. Astrophysics quickly established itself as an international player in the area of star formation, developed rapidly and became a key element in the department. This change was an important element of Inkson moving Physics onto a sustainable footing, out of expensive specialties and into less expensive ones.

Sports Science under Armstrong was another area of development, with a Queen's Anniversary Prize awarded in 1998, a reflection of the major achievements of the Coronary Prevention in Children Research Group founded in 1985.[53] Seeing the writing on the wall for a large-scale

School of Education in Exeter, Armstrong moved Sport and Health Sciences out of the School into the Postgraduate Medical School. Like Astrophysics, there was to be significant continuity of development in this field.

However, there were also major discontinuities between the Holland and the Smith years. In part, these were matters of policy and in part of delivery, the two being closely linked. Holland's emphasis on the region, particularly, but not only, in the shape of Cornwall, sat oddly with the declared stress on strengthening the university's research and teaching, notably in light of the RAE. In part, this was an aspect of the degree to which Holland had to spread himself thin in order to meet a number of challenges. Critics claimed that he tried to do too much, and that this involved too many contradictory promises. There was the problem of coming 'from outside' into a difficult world where it was hard to achieve outcomes and, indeed, to understand how best to pursue them. Holland's frustration was readily apparent at his last Council meeting where he said that the staff were his biggest difficulty, an unwarranted view in light of the very hard work of the overwhelming majority, and one that was rebutted at the meeting. Indeed, in 1999, after a second academic had died of a heart attack in a meeting chaired by Holland, a 24-hour helpline was launched for overworked university employees and their families. Moreover, the Bett report in 1999 had amplified the observations in the Dearing Report about the serious national decline in academic salaries.

If more than one man was involved in the governance of the late 1990s, there was only so much attention and effort that was available. This was one of the principal charges against the Cornwall project, that it was an immense distraction of efforts. The second stage of the project, backed by HEFCE and the European Union, succeeded in launching the initiative as the Combined Universities in Cornwall (CUC). Large public meetings in Falmouth, Newquay, Truro and Penzance raised the profile of the university as a major would-be economic force in the South-West, and helped ensure government support.[54] The Government Office of the South-West used the work already done in the Millennium Fund bid as the flagship project for Cornwall's successful bid for EU Objective One funding.

The project was widened to include funding for Falmouth College of

Art (FCA) and the Further Education Colleges supported by Plymouth, but with the Exeter-proposed campus very much as the central component. The largest physical change in the project from Exeter's perspective was the move to the Tremough site that FCA had already purchased with a grant from HEFCE. It was not possible to put the campus at Redruth/Camborne because this location would not attract many students. Tremough was chosen because it was in the constituency of the sole Labour MP in Cornwall, an MP who was going to see jobs lost in the Camborne half of her constituency and therefore hoped to see them gained in the Falmouth half. With the Structure Funding assured, the project took off. HEFCE confirmed that the necessary student numbers would follow, with the proviso that they would stay in Cornwall and that no numbers could be transferred to the Exeter campus. The exercise was nearly derailed as a result of tremendous pressure from FCA, Cornwall College, and Cornwall County Council to move to a University of Cornwall. Exeter's threat to pull out of the project ensured that the CUC route was maintained. Problems were also posed by Falmouth's strong opposition to Exeter's requirement of a substantial long-term interest in the site before going ahead. After HEFCE made the logic clear to Falmouth, the university acquired the 50 per cent interest it required.[55]

CUC was a multi-institute project based around a concept of a 'Hub' and a 'Rim'. The 'Hub' was to be at Tremough and all the Further Education Colleges were to form the 'Rim'. Exeter, Falmouth and Plymouth were to be represented at the Hub and, apart from Falmouth, the emphasis at the Hub was to be on Sciences in Phase 1 as it was felt that this would most easily satisfy the requirement of supporting 'regeneration' in Cornwall. All partners recognised that Science and Engineering were difficult subjects to recruit to at the undergraduate level, but, for long-term sustainability, the Business Plan for CUC had to be based around these areas. Very quickly, Plymouth decided to withdraw from the 'Hub' and took on the role of validating courses at the 'Rim' Colleges.

From Exeter's perspective, obtaining EU funds by means of Cornwall, and also more student income by this means, helped the university to gain the finance and mass it otherwise lacked in a period when these could not be readily increased because of serious limits to both. Powell argued that that was an important policy and legacy:

The Cornwall Campus and the Peninsula Medical School were important developments – not just in themselves but also for the access they gave to new sources of finance and significant opportunities to improve existing subjects. The personal intervention of Geoffrey Holland was crucial in securing a public funding package to make the Cornwall Campus possible.[56]

David Blunkett, as Secretary of State for Education, a strong ally to Holland in getting money to start the Cornwall project, remarked:

> The truth is that Geoffrey was not only the driving force for the combined university but pivotal to achieving success! It was his tenacity, his networking and contacts, and his refusal to take no for an answer that achieved the goal! Mine was a bit part. I was able to oil the wheels and facilitate the process. I did so because I believed that it was essential that the peninsula had higher education provision which not only met the needs of those living in Cornwall but also the scattered communities and diverse needs of existing post 16 and higher education facilities. ... I knew that the investment would be critical to the wellbeing economically, socially and educationally of the region. ... The byzantine process of getting agreement for university status (and facilitating combined approaches to meeting need) makes speedy action difficult. Geoffrey needs every commendation for making not only the outcome possible but also the process as effective and immediate as it was.[57]

Yet, the Cornish campus proved a close-run thing.[58] Managing the search for funds, as well as the inveterate suspicions and bitter divisions of Cornish local politics, took up much time. Employing his Whitehall experience and skills, Holland was remorseless at pushing on the project despite a deep-seated reluctance to pursue that project at every level, notably among the academics. When Senate voted in favour in July 2001, no fewer than two of the three DVCs (Collier and Wilks) voted against,[59] a sign of a greatly divided managerial team. Student opinion was also hostile. With a derogatory caption attached to a photograph of Holland, *Exeposé* devoted its front page on 29 June 1997 to an attack on the project, which it presented as likely to dilute Exeter's standards and as 'a diversion away from the spiralling decline of the University', a clear response to the 1996 RAE. In contrast, the non-academic members of Council provided overwhelming support.[60]

Once established, Cornwall proved a financial problem. There was insufficient working capital, by about £3 million over its first five years, plus an underestimate of support cost. As a result, Cornwall was 'underfunded' by about £820,000 for 2003/04. Smith referred to this underfunding when discussing the financial context for the 2004/05 restructuring.[61] The burden of meeting Cornwall's inability to cover its costs pressed hard on the Exeter site and became a major unplanned cross-subsidy, such as those decried between the Exeter subjects in 2004/05. The suggestion that without the Cornwall campus, Chemistry could have been retained[62] is of course hypothetical. Without the campus, however, there would certainly have been the potential to improve staff–student ratios on the Exeter site.

There is also the question of whether the initiative fulfilled the goal of reviving a depressed area by extending local Higher Education to its population. Local recruitment in fact is modest, and the Cornwall campus relies, like that at Exeter, on national recruitment. At the same time, the local economy benefited considerably, while the university was to profit from the Cornwall presence as it allowed Exeter to lever additional fully funded undergraduate student places, for both the Cornwall and Streatham campuses, out of HEFCE in the early 2000s when these were in very short supply.

The Peninsula Medical School (PMS), established by Exeter and Plymouth in 2000, was the first new medical school for nearly thirty years. The School also involved significant expenditure, but was a major achievement for the university and the South-West, and one that proved a counter to a marked underprovision of medical investment in the region. Medical education provided an important opportunity to bid into national growth, with a competition for new medical schools set up by the Department of Health and HEFCE. For NHS reasons, going it alone without Plymouth was not a possibility, but a medical school with a decent financial and political settlement was seen as offering a transformative effect for the university, in particular the Sciences.[63] The first students were admitted in September 2002; the PMS led to the expansion of the medical footprint on St Luke's, a process linked to the continued reduction of Education.

The PMS proved a far more valuable addition to the university and considerable legacy from the Holland years than the earlier plan for a School of Nursing. Like Powell, Charles Desforges, the DVC in charge of the discussions, had been sceptical about the value of a large School in which research played no role. By making the university plans for Nursing include a research component, he left, probably deliberately, these plans more expensive than Plymouth's successful bid. This proved a wise approach. Powell supported Desforges's stance because of the threat to the research agenda and to the upmarket brand that had to be protected.[64]

From the perspective of national and international status, the original conception of both Cornwall and the PMS was only partially thought through. They both needed recasting for a research-led institution. Although each provided the opportunity for more home undergraduates, there were high transaction costs in bringing this about, and neither institution made the university more coherent.

While focusing on the regional and national dimensions, Holland appeared content to run the university through relatively strong DVCs, notably Desforges, Inkson, Newitt, Lea and Wilks, although there was nothing new in that as the 1980s had seen the rise of powerful DVCs and Chairs of ADC alongside the VC in order to meet the growing need for strong central management. However, under Holland, the centre was fragmented in a way it had not been under Harrison, with DVCs disagreeing with each other and with Holland and Powell, such that the first female DVC, Mary John, a distinguished figure in the area of children's rights, resigned.

Meanwhile, as another cause of tension, there was a preoccupation with staff assessed as non-RAE returnable, and they were targeted up to the 2001 RAE. Although it was denied, there were claims of a list of staff unlikely to be returnable, and of a drive to get them out. The ambience was different to the negotiated early retirements of the 1980s, as was the harsh tone of the surrounding discussion: was this a witch-hunt or were these people parasitic?

Team 2000, set up by Wilks, certainly acted as a catalyst for change and was a 'glimmer of hope'.[65] Wilks emphasised the need for benchmarking against comparable institutions. However, a lack of sufficient focus at the departmental level ensured that the 2001 RAE results still represented a disappointing result, even if an improvement on 1996. The university needed to make significantly more progress to improve its performance when compared with its peers in the 1994 Group – the coalition of smaller research-intensive universities founded in 1994 to defend these universities' interests following the creation of the Russell Group by their larger counterparts that year.

Linked to this, a sense of drift also developed toward the end of the 1990s. Although Council was informed via PRC, which contained its senior lay members, it did not ask searching enough questions about policy and implementation. Appointed to Council in 2000, Stuart Bosworth felt that it failed to focus on outcomes that December when debating a strategy paper presented by Holland, and that Holland accordingly was let down.[66]

More generally, there was an awareness on the part of the perceptive that reorganising academic structures, notably by creating Schools, was a means, not a result, and, moreover, a time-consuming means. As a PhD student, Katherine Astbury was conscious of the 'painful move to being a School of Modern Languages, with endless debates over how to harmonise essay length over all the departments'. It was (and not just in Exeter) difficult to homogenise the Modern Language departments because of the hugely different language skills students had in the various languages, and because of the disproportionate size of French. The length of these debates reflected the wish to make changes based on democratic decisions;[67] less favourably a tendency to procrastinate and complain. Other areas were able to move more rapidly to establish new structures and processes. However, the heavy loss made by the School of Business and Economics in 1999, and the pressure this put on the budget of other Schools did not encourage confidence.

More dramatically, on 20 March 2000, 600–700 students demonstrated in front of Northcote House against standards in university accommodation and specifically against Domestic Services. There were complaints about raised hall fees, the cancellation of formal meals at Birks, about the infrequency of cleaning, and about poor complaints procedures. *Exeposé* presented this as a wider challenge to a Domestic

Services that, it claimed, could not handle its own affairs but had taken on too many external commitments.[68]

As an indication of a sense of malaise among the staff, rumours circulated, rumours that still have a trace today. The single most surprising items submitted to me in researching this history and in seeking information via memoranda and interviews were letters from two former DVCs of these years claiming that a Masonic lodge directed the affairs of the university in this period. Of the four senior figures named, Holland was apparently a Mason, two others I have asked have denied that they were Masons, while contradictory reports surround the fourth. I have devoted some time to the issue, but cannot corroborate the report, which may in part have arisen because the university did occasionally hire out rooms in Northcote House to a lodge. Council proposed that being a Mason should be declared on the Register of Interests, but no one ever declared being a Mason.[69] The issue suggests the rumours that sometimes circulate among academics. Other enduring rumours were that there was a secret NATO communications bunker located somewhere on the campus, and that the builders had mistakenly built the Washington Singer building back to front. The issue of the Masonic lodge is also indicative both of the 'us' and 'them' attitude developed toward authority that was accentuated in the wake of Schooling and of the tensions within the management group itself.[70] These tensions were to play a role in the politics of the early 2000s.

During the 1990s, and particularly in the aftermath of the dire 1996 RAE, the anxiety about the university's status and future was to many staff increasingly focused on research issues. There was also a focus on teaching, one encouraged by increased national scrutiny of teaching in the 1990s, and by institutional changes accordingly. As a result, there was a tension over priorities. At the departmental level, personal rivalries, notably over promotion, were inscribed, often deeply, into this tension over priorities. This practice reflected the small size of departments, the longevity of most of the staff, and the limited amount of promotion.

Partly as a result, a change toward a greater emphasis on research was never going to be easy, nor without personal and policy contention. The 1996 RAE result pushed this forward, and the results in terms of accord or discord were different in each department as they played through with personal differences. A significant one was that of age. There was no exact correspondence, but younger staff tended to be more concerned about research and national status. The resulting divides were often shifting, and at the departmental level, there were alliances for particular issues. But, there was also a more structural element. The COSGOD generation now appeared, at least to critics, variously dated, defensive and complacent, and their answers no longer relevant to the intellectual, institutional and financial challenges of the late 1990s.

In turn, an emphasis on teaching, not research, was deployed against the call for change, this emphasis proposing the idea that there was an inherent clash in priorities. Thus, research could be suggested as somehow alien to the true purpose of a university. This interpretation proved somewhat self-serving, as it offered an explanation for a disinclination to focus on research or, at least, for a preference for research at a level set by the individual scholar, and not by the RAE. There could be a linked disdain for entrepreneurship. Arriving in 1996, Steve Rippon (Archaeology) 'soon realised that Exeter was an institution rather set in its ways – there was a strong degree of conservatism, and a lack of focus on supporting research excellence'.[71] In part, the former practice of criticism of the central authorities was directed against what was presented as a new order imposed in accordance with unwelcome external demands by a controlling new administrative culture that identified with Powell. His autocratic style, and his influence over strategy and finance, and over Holland, led to criticism.

There were also many staff who were disenchanted with this criticism of 'the management' and, in particular, with the failure to ensure high research standards and related research-led teaching. Under Holland, there was no decisive lead given to those who wanted a greater focus on research. Moreover, the regional drive was interpreted as providing fresh impetus for a teaching- and training-led university, while Schooling did not ensure a focus on research, notably with Law and Business. This situation was to change under Smith, with the priority on research made clear and promotions largely awarded or denied accordingly. Schooling eventually led to Colleges which, in essence, were the original faculties, with all the power to the Deans and none to the departments.

Possibly, there was relatively little that could have been done in response to the early RAEs until several waves of early retirements had created some scope for new appointments of younger and more research-orientated staff. It was only really after the 1996 RAE and, to a degree, after the arrival of Smith as VC in 2002, that that response could become a dominant theme in policy, rather than the earlier theme of always trying to balance the books.

Outsiders and arrivals, such as myself in 1996, can fail to appreciate the complexities of a situation, its internal dynamics and the 'direction of travel' (i.e. change). Nevertheless, in their responses, they can also capture an underlying reality, not least in comparison. Arriving in Exeter as the new Labour parliamentary candidate and then MP in 1997, Ben Bradshaw thought that the university had a good reputation but 'sat on its laurels' with a 'sleepiness about it'. Arriving in Exeter as Bishop in 2000, and shortly after joining Council, Michael Langrish felt that 'the University was gently declining whilst resting on its laurels. ... It needed strategic vision (some Departments were just coasting along).'[72] Although problems within the university were widely understood, structures and attitudes obstructed attempts to change the situation, and notably to the extent necessary to transform it.

CHAPTER ELEVEN

THE EARLY 2000S: RESTRUCTURING

The University underwent a Big Bang when Smith arrived.
Tim Niblock

We cannot afford Chemistry any more, colleagues. It is as simple as that.
Steve Smith, Senate, 1 December 2004[1]

When I arrived at Exeter I was somewhat disheartened that my room appeared to be a prison cell but for the bars on windows. This was easily outweighed by The Welly, our hall's bar, which served cider and black for £1.50 per pint and was the nightly rendezvous point for the fun and games that would inevitably ensue. ... I have very fond memories spending time in the library poring over anything from political philosophy to the history of cartography ... the library in fact became somewhat of a home-from-home. The reward for three years hard work was receiving a warm embrace from the Chancellor, Floella Benjamin, a solid foundation for my career and, above all, lifelong friendships. Looking back, I feel a huge sense of pride, which I find is always shared whenever I encounter an old Exonian.
John Kirkpatrick (2004–07)

THE EXTERNAL CONTEXT was as ever significant, and, yet again, it took its prime form in the shape of an evaluation that was both offered to the public and financially significant. Just as the 1996 RAE had helped bring issues and tensions to the fore, so the same was true of its 2001 successor. Although the public tone was one of satisfaction, and Wilks to whom Holland entrusted the RAE did a good job in presenting the returns,[2] the results suggested continued underperformance. Only 2 per cent of the submission (German) was 5*, 55 per cent was rated 5, and 41 per cent 4. In contrast, York, a university of similar size but much better supported under 'historic funding' than Exeter and with a much stronger research base when the RAEs began, had percentages of 18, 66 and 8. Against a background of a general improvement in the sector, to an average of 55 per cent of all staff in the old universities in units being graded 5* or 5, Exeter's results were insufficient, although they were the second biggest improvement in grade per staff member submitted in the old universities and an improvement twice that of the national average.

Wilks's preliminary analysis indicated promise as well as 'genuine achievement,' notably in Education (now a much smaller unit)[3] and in English, but also a serious problem with the Sciences, which were performing far worse than the vast majority of the 1994 Group,[4] to which Exeter belonged and from which it risked being thrown out in the summer of 2001. If Biological Sciences, for example, went from 3 to 4, this was still not 5. Exeter was still suffering from the small size of its departments, especially in the Sciences, where, at the national level, size was viewed as a significant criterion. The rise to 36th in the RAE ranking (but 27th if weighted for intensity) was not only inadequate, but was also achieved despite considerable investment (44 per cent of the staff submitted were new) and with glaring differences between departments. Whereas 75 per cent of the staff submitted in Humanities and Social Science departments were in 5* or 5 units, the Science percentage was only 33. Thus, the heavy cross-subsidy to Science was not working. This was made more serious by subsequent reductions in the funding of grade 4 activity in 2003 and by 2006. Indeed, the Secretary of State, Charles Clarke, had only been prevented with some difficulty from stopping funding all 4-ranking departments.[5] Moreover, although the percentage of staff returned had risen from 81 per cent in 1996 to 84 per cent in 2001, that still meant many non-returnees, which cost Exeter about £2.6 million per year.

The RAE results were extremely important for the smaller

THE EARLY 2000S: RESTRUCTURING

departments. Middle Eastern Studies, the unit of assessment within which the Institute of Arab and Islamic Studies was considered, saw a rise from 3 to 5, a major vindication of the resources put into it. Obtaining a 5 enabled Russian to keep going, which proved the basis for a subsequent improvement in its research profile and for staff appointments. Theology's gaining a 5 was also crucial alongside it obtaining 23 out of 24 points in the Teaching Quality Assessment (TQA) exercise. This success rested on important appointments and developments in the late 1990s, notably the appointment of David Horrell (1995). He brought added strength to New Testament Studies which had already been an established focus under Catchpole. The undergraduate study of Biblical Languages revived and in-depth biblical study was encouraged. This initiative attracted very gifted and significant scholars, led to the introduction of an MA in Biblical Studies and the establishment of a Centre for Biblical Studies, and drew research students from home and abroad. Tim Gorringe, appointed the second holder of the St Luke's chair in 1998, enhanced Theology's international reputation for systematic theology.

The ability of relatively small units, such as German, to deliver the better results posed problems for the university, because small Arts-based departments did not bring in the money, an aspect of the broader problems involved in funding the Humanities.[6] It was understandable that the resulting focus should be on improving the Sciences. But the university possibly did not do as much as it could have done to build on all the small areas of real academic strength, which were often highly effective as teaching cultures and popular with undergraduates.

A major success was achieved by the School of Historical, Political and Social Studies (SHiPSS), in getting not just History but also Politics and especially Sociology (which many in 1998 thought was doomed) to 5s in 2001 with full submissions. Moreover, SHiPPS was responsible for the re-establishment of Philosophy at Exeter, initially as a Combined Honour in 1999. The latter led to the development of the philosophy and sociology of the life sciences in the shape of Egenis, the genome project, producing, in 2001, the largest non-Science grant to date for the university and the real kick-start, along with Medical History, to big grant funding in Social Studies areas other than Education. SHiPSS and other areas where there was strong leadership which knew what had to be done, for example Psychology, was able to deliver research outputs and a research grant culture that, in comparative terms, was well above that of the Sciences.

Thus, at the level of certain Schools, there was major progress. At the university level, there were plans to improve the research situation, but not yet the resources or political drive. The valuable FooS (*Focusing on our Strengths*) exercise in 2001, masterminded by Stephen Lea, called for business plans linked to the idea of deploying the likely gains from the 2001 RAE on behalf of areas of opportunity. A focus on developing strong departments as part of a strategy of rebuilding the academic status of the university was to be based on evidence that was to be organised in, and scrutinised through, spreadsheets. In producing an objective view of the strengths and weaknesses of the institution, the removal of unplanned cross-subsidy was a driving principle. By showing where subsidies existed, there was intended to be a commitment to cross-subsidies only as a result of planning. The academic analysis for change was present. FooS provided a model that could offer 'legitimacy for investing and disinvesting'. Phillip Harvey, Stephen Lea and Stephen Wilks were responsible for FooS, which was strongly supported by Powell.[7] Meeting on a near-weekly basis, the FooS team wanted to move very quickly, thought of closing Chemistry and talked of closing Mathematics and some parts of Engineering, and had an impact on the academic community in terms of cultural change, even if policy implementation was limited.

In a July 2002 paper for Council, Holland claimed that the university was at 'the end of the beginning'. Several of the ingredients for the later 2004/05 restructuring of the academic departments were already in play. However, the politics were not yet in place for the implementation of restructuring and the carry-through of resource allocation; nor was the money available to take Science forward. Moreover, the resource base for the Institute of Arab and Islamic Studies was limited under FooS (under which the link between the resources brought in and those received was insufficiently direct); whereas this resource base was to rocket under Allen's resourcing model.[8] In his job presentation in January 2002, Smith drew attention to the need for 'strategic prioritising' and described the July 2001 institutional plan and the 2001–06 Strategy Document as 'statements of intent',[9] a reasonable assessment also made by others. Smith also provided a greater determination, in a different context, to consider and utilise new revenue streams.[10] Nevertheless, FooS was highly significant in the modernisation of the university.

The RAE result set the context for the search for Holland's successor. By 2000, Holland and Powell had both agreed with the Council officers, notably Geoffrey Pope, that Powell would retire at the end of 2001/02 and Holland a year later. This avoided the major discontinuity threatened by both men going at once. Subsequently, pushed by Pope, Holland decided to go earlier.[11] As a result, Powell agreed to stay until 2003 in order to help Holland's successor settle in, before he had to choose a new Registrar.

The guidelines established for Holland's successor acknowledged the difficulty of the job. Michael Langrish observed: 'The *Focusing on our Strengths* exercise shaped the search for a new VC. The University needed someone with strong academic credibility to bridge the gap between the University, VC and senior management; someone who understood how complex educational institutions worked, with strong leadership and management skills.'[12]

There was a determination to appoint an academic. A few other names were mentioned, including Michael Portillo, who did not wish to apply, but there was a marked preference for an academic of proven administrative ability who would be able to get into the job at once. For the first time, Exeter employed a headhunting firm for the purpose, something wanted by the Chancellor, Bob Alexander (Lord Alexander of Weedon), who chaired the appointing panel. Interviewed by the headhunter, Saxton Bampfylde Hever, the DVCs all said that they wanted an academic who knew about research and somebody who was prepared to fly, the latter due to Holland's inability to fly to Sharjah.[13] In part, this determination to appoint an academic reflected a sense that a new VC only had a brief period of opportunity before the constraints of the job became too pressing, but the argument that time was too precious for someone to learn on the job proved more significant.

In that respect, the RAE results helped drive the process. Indeed, the papers for the Joint Committee [of Council and Senate] for the Appointment of the VC, included among the direction of questions: '[P]ress on where the University should be improving. What makes for an outstanding research performance? Can a University like Exeter generate the resources to excel across the spectrum? Would lead into a question about the subject balance.' These questions reflected an understanding of the need for a VC who could drive a selective change agency. To do so required both willingness and ability, and included engaging with the academic community and data sufficiently to understand and implement the required selectivity.

Experience with the RAE was a key theme in the briefing notes prepared by the headhunters and in the surrounding correspondence, and with the confidential profiles of the eight academics recommended for the shortlist, and of the six actually shortlisted. For Smith, it was noted that he had taken the Department of International Politics at Aberystwyth from a RAE grade 3 in 1992 to a 5 in 1996, before running the 2001 RAE exercise for the university, and that he had been a member of an emergency team set up in 1999 to deal with a projected deficit, formulating policies which had resulted in a surplus. An active publisher, Smith had been the recipient of the Susan Strange Award of the International Studies Association in 1999 for the person who had most challenged the received wisdom in the profession. With a strong return in the 2001 RAE, Smith was also elected to be President of the International Studies Association in 2002, only the second British academic elected to this body representing all International Relations scholars in the world.

Arguing that the strong admissions figures belied its underachievement and gave it the platform for growth, Smith's presentation in his job interview focused on Exeter's RAE. This approach, the sense that he understood the problems and his strong command of the data convinced the appointing committee that he was the right candidate.[14] Smith declared his aim to take Exeter up at least fifteen places in the RAE table within five years. As part of the appointment process, he also presented to two focus panels, both of which were almost unanimous in favour of him. Reservations expressed by some as to whether he fitted the then Exeter ethos were countered by the argument that Exeter needed change.

The drive to take Exeter up the RAE was to be the basis of Smith's concern with measurable external criteria or metrics, a concern that led to senior figures being given responsibility in the shape of 'metric owners' and 'metric facilitators'. The RAE was seen as crucial not only for funding but also for reputation. As the research ratings changed only each time there was a RAE, so the latter was central.

THE EARLY 2000S: RESTRUCTURING

That he was successful in driving Exeter up the RAE, and swiftly acquired a reputation for energy, leads to a narrative in which the key first step is seen as the closure of the Chemistry and Music Departments; this is presented as both a necessary step and a sign of tough leadership capable of any challenge. In fact, it took a while to make this step and, indeed, the view that Smith took too long to introduce the major cuts that were necessary has occasionally been expressed. There was certainly on Smith's part an initial sense of anxiety about the scale of the tasks he saw before him, as well as some tensions with Council, but the practicalities of the situation require consideration. Smith needed to assess options, to build up strength, to address immediate concerns and to identify likely sources of opposition. The university had already considered closing Chemistry and Music in 2001, only to draw away from the challenge. Strong opposition to the closure of Music had been expressed in Senate, and Pope, a keen amateur musician, was very uneasy about doing so. In addition, the failure of Sussex, later in the decade, in the face of fierce criticism, to close Chemistry underlines the difficulties and sensitivities of the issue. Already, by the autumn of 2004, both the Royal Society of Chemistry and the Commons Select Committee on Science and Technology were alarmed by closures of Chemistry departments since 2001 at King's College London, Queen Mary College, London, and Swansea. As such, Smith had to lay the ground carefully.

Moreover, as Smith, an effective and voracious reader and analyser of university documents, was determined on evidence-based, not opinion-based, data, and on benchmarking that evidence on the views of outside experts, there was the need to accumulate and analyse data. Furthermore, the intensity of the data improved. With Smith, there was a move from data at the departmental level to data that permitted the evaluation of individuals at a time when the compactness of the university still made it possible for him to oversee this in detail. This reflected the understanding that research analysis and policy at the departmental level were not going to solve the university's need to raise its standards in order to reflect the focus of national funding on top-rated RAE departments. Research appraisal at the individual level, and in accordance with a standard template, was to be important for both performance-monitoring and for planning. As DVC, Roger Kain developed research assessment monitoring.

Smith focused first on personnel issues at the university level. He was determined to get an experienced Registrar able to confront the challenges of moving the university up the league tables. The recruitment in October 2003 of David Allen, Registrar of Birmingham, and, earlier, of Nottingham, a 'Russell Group Registrar', a phrase Smith used at the time, was a major coup. Allen, who was to become Deputy Chief Executive as well in 2009, was to prove not only highly effective in his role but also a very successful working partner with Smith, which contrasted with the situation in all too many universities. They got on well and complemented each other's strengths, as well as working effectively together in a way simply not seen in the university's earlier history. Smith legitimised research-focused activity, gave it a strong new impetus and rapidly made his mark. As Philip Bostock, the Chief Executive of the City, remarked 'the whirlwind arrived';[15] while the policy (to critics, rhetoric) was really translated into action once Allen arrived. The experienced Allen was able to drive change. The two men saw Exeter as a ten-year project. Each week before the meeting of the VCEG, Smith and Allen had a long meeting to review developments. With Allen, there was clarity of vision, a refusal to be side-tracked and sheer tough-mindedness.

After Smith arrived, there was a change in personnel at senior levels. Derek Phillips left in 2003 and Domestic Services was reorganised. The loss of power, authority and influence on the part of some of the senior academics was abrupt. This was the experience of Malcolm Cook, the last elected DVC, when his period in office ended in 2004.[16] The net effect was the development of a new, close-knit VCEG which was to sustain a particular energy and set of values that was important to the development of a new practice. This transition matched ideas of change in university governance toward more entrepreneurial structures and systems.[17]

Smith took up a phrase used in 2002 by Howard Newby, the Chief Executive of HEFCE, about universities in the 'squeezed middle between the powerful civics and the former polytechnics'. Exeter was in such a position, not good at widening participation and serving its local community, but lacking the standing of an international Russell Group university. The challenge for the new team was to provide the direction, ambition and critical mass that would enable Exeter to escape this position. Time was running out and restructuring was urgently required, notably to close the gap between high-quality student entry and less impressive research ratings, and between 'market perception' and performance.[18] Smith also spoke about the danger of 'standing still on a downward escalator'.[19]

Both Smith and Allen were, by temperament, highly competitive individuals who set targets for themselves as well as for the university. Alongside their vision for the university, they revelled in the methodology of league tables: spotting the 'low hanging fruit' where internal resource reallocation could suddenly boost Exeter's performance against metrics in the crucial *Times University Guide* (considered the most influential league table), for example library spend per student. There was also concern with rankings in *The Guardian* and the *Sunday Times*.[20] Patrick Kennedy, who delivered the new metric-based planning environment, especially targeted the league table methods of *The Times*.

The introduction of the National Student Survey (NSS) in 2005 added another criterion. In 2007, when Exeter came fourth for mainstream institutions, this result secured Exeter's place in the Top Twenty in the *Sunday Times*' league table.[21] In his farewell speech as Chair of Council, Russell Seal was to argue that the NSS had been the single greatest cause of Exeter's rise given its huge significance within the league tables and the inability of many of Exeter's close rivals, except Durham, to manage it well. Rather like admissions, the question of why Exeter has done so well in the NSS gets to the heart of Exeter's success, yet is not actually known. In part, happy and satisfied types of students are attracted to Exeter as a community/environment, while the university does a good job educationally and gains from a very professional and supportive Guild.

In 2003, the objective of the university was to be in the upper quartile of the 1994 Group of smaller research intensive universities, an association that helped give better self-definition, although, at the time, it was probably the weakest member. This objective developed into 'Top Twenty by 2010', an aspiration that was more accessible and understandable for staff and the public, and one that provided opportunities for benchmarking and setting goals.[22]

When Allen arrived, there were important unresolved issues. Although management systems had been strengthened by Powell, Harvey and Lea, while there had been significant improvements in accounting in the late 1990s under Keith Blanshard, there was still no transparent allocation of income and overheads, and few incentives in place to enhance income. Heads of School found it difficult to reconcile HEFCE revenues to School allocations without historic explanations. The postgraduate and international student populations were small, as was research grant income. The university was organised into too many small units. The non-academic areas (as they were then called) lacked unified leadership and capacity.

Harvey's business plans had introduced a strategic, forward, look; but the new system only became dominant and decisive following changes made by Allen and Paul Webley. Allen had identified the absence of a transparent incentivising resource allocation system as a problem. He wanted to introduce the sort of income-based system he had been used to in Nottingham and Birmingham, one in which income from, for example, more international students or research contracts was allocated to academic units as they earned it, with no deductions for corporate costs. The units then pay, in effect, taxes for overall university strategic development, rent for the space they occupy, and a Professional Services Contribution (PSC) to meet the cost of centrally provided services such as the Library, IT, finance and HR. Under such a model, there is no top-slicing and all the university's spending is transparent. Matching the efforts of government in the 2000s, the general idea was to find the 'Goldilocks point' for taxation: not too much to disincentivise income generation, nor too little to provide decent services.

To ensure political support ('buy-in from the community'), Allen had Webley chair a group that delivered what can be seen as an accounting innovation to reflect true costs and especially overhead recovery. The Resource Allocation Model, comprising the Income Distribution Model and the PSC was born from 2004/05. For the first time, all Humanities and Social Sciences income was delivered to those subjects, leading to big increases in their income.

On the basis of the redesign of the accounting information, it became 'obvious' that particular steps should be taken, such as the closure of Legal Practice and the disengagement from Extra-Mural teaching. The latter represented a major departure from the idea of regional goals and also from traditional patterns of activity. The impact on Science was more central. Previously, income had been diverted to prop up underperforming Science which, with the exception of financially solvent Physics, was not close to recovering its overheads. The impact of the resulting cross-subsidies on other departments, and thus on the university's capacity for growth,[23] was not really addressed by the defenders of Chemistry. In the fiftieth and last issue of the *Department of Chemistry Newsletter*, Professor Duncan Bruce sarcastically remarked that: 'Being a University, one would assume that it would develop its academic priorities and then ensure that the financial model made them work. But Exeter never let the academic agenda cloud the financial "realities" of its brand spanking new model.'[24] From elsewhere in the university, the perspective looked very different.

The shift in accounting techniques and principles, and their wide dissemination, was of key importance as a central tool in the university's ability to operate more as a business, with a stress on all constituent elements being required to show efficiency, and an ability to generate new and additional income. For example, the value of individual MA courses was assessed and there was pressure to close down those that did not raise sufficient revenue.

Investment in staff in the Finance Division and in IT enabled more emphasis to be placed on providing better management accounting information to support academic and administrative units, as well as the provision of a much more proactive service, along with relentless and highly influential numerical 'benchmarking' of performance against the best elsewhere. Resource allocation processes became more adaptable and transparent, and better financial data were developed as an aid to capital investment decision-making and the monitoring of performance. One outcome of the new model was 'the University on a page', an A3 spreadsheet which showed the entire university economy in one place. This proved a major advantage to budget-holders and Council. Allen and Lindley thus made everything clear, which enabled Heads of Schools to understand and explain policy.

The presentation of data drove decisions, a key element for Smith with his determination to ensure evidence-based policy, as opposed to historic and/or sentiment-based criteria. To critics, this focus on metrics ensured a mechanistic sacrificing of cultural continuity, but, in practice, the use of data provided not only information on the familiar commercial issues of surplus, return on investment, cross-subsidy, and hidden costs, but also a measure of improvement and adaptability. Data also provided criteria for investment and for conscious subsidy, notably of STEM subjects. The process of using metrics to get to Top Twenty and then Top Ten was fundamental. The clarity of those two objectives and of a process for achieving them really mattered.

Allen also set about creating Professional Services. Responsibility for Library and IT services passed ultimately to him, and he set about winning investment for the services and integrating them, notably by a Professional Services Management Group (PSMG) where all the Services could meet, coordinate and plan together. This group came to include College Managers and the CEO of the Guild of Students, and truly unified Professional Services across the university. Expertise was built up in fundraising, marketing, IT, and many other skills required by modern large institutions.

There was a significant improvement in the finances in the early 2000s, an improvement that permitted capital developments and restructuring, each in a context of greater institutional independence. Non-governmental sources of income grew from the start of the decade, especially income from research grants and contracts. Funded by Sheikh Sultan, the ruler of Sharjah, and planned with his help, the building for the new Institute of Arab and Islamic Studies was opened in 2001. It was widely and deservedly acclaimed both as a working environment and as a culturally relevant architectural creation. Lacey Hickie Caley were the architects, with two entirely separate LHC design teams competing with each other in an internal design competition run by the university. The main briefing innovation on this project was the requirement that the building should be very open and light with a minimum of corridors.[25]

By the close of 2001, there was a good cash flow and reasonable revenues for the university, although also a funding gap, the expenditure of reserves, and about £41 million authorised borrowing. The opportunities afforded by Cornwall and the PMS, notably to increase the student population at a time when HEFCE was rationing hard, also presented major challenges. In 2001/02 the university acquired a 50 per cent shareholding in the Tremough Development Vehicle Ltd which was incorporated as a joint-venture company between the university and FCA, under its energetic head Alan Livingston (later Rector of University College, Falmouth), to develop the first phase of buildings

THE EARLY 2000S: RESTRUCTURING

at the Tremough Campus under the CUC initiative. Activities also commenced at the PMS, with Exeter having a 50 per cent share of the income and expenditure.

Additional specific grant funding was received in 2001/02 towards the development of the PMS and also in support of the new HR strategy. Student numbers (home and international) grew, and revenue from residences, catering and conferences increased well beyond the level of inflation, reflecting strong performances in the management of occupancy in the student residences, the provision of retail services, and the running of conference and retail functions. The university also had considerable success in 2001/02 in attracting European Social Fund grants.

On a longer timescale, the university also greatly took forward the development of the links with business seen under Holland, providing a crucial additional institutional and resource dimension, notably the creation of, first, one (2000) and, then, a second Innovation Centre on the Streatham Campus, designed to house business start-ups, preferably those 'spun out' of the university's research work. This work was important for the credibility of Exeter's pursuit of the 'knowledge transfer' aspects of government policy, including specific funding streams from HEFCE and other government bodies.

It was fortunate that the university was becoming successful in diversifying and increasing its income because an interim valuation of the University of Exeter Retirement Benefits Scheme (ERBS) in 2002 showed that the funds held were insufficient to meet anticipated future commitments. This had resulted from a downturn in investment performance, a problem that all pension schemes were facing. After a decade of benefiting from a contributions holiday to the Scheme, the university therefore agreed to reintroduce employer contributions with effect from August 2002 in order to fund the projected income shortfall in the Scheme. A 6 per cent employer contribution rate was introduced on the advice of the Scheme Actuary. Continuing financial pressure on ERBS would eventually lead to the closure of the final salary scheme for new entrants in 2010. Funding pensions became a more serious and contentious issue from the mid-2010s.

Capital developments continued in 2001/02 including new academic buildings for the PMS, a specialist facility for the Sediment Research

Centre, improvements to the building for Computer Science, and further expenditure on sports facilities. Given the continued decline of national funding to Higher Education institutions, the overall competition to generate funds from other sources, and the challenging times for market investments, Exeter's overall performance was impressive.

On 27 November 2002, Lord Alexander, the Chancellor, told the House of Lords, in a debate on university finances, that Exeter's were 'in good order' but 'tight' and that increased funding was necessary to deliver excellence.[26] In 2002/03, the university and FCA received capital grants to fund the academic development at Tremough (later called Penryn), where the convent school run from 1943 by the order of Les Filles de la Croix had closed in 1996;[27] and work began on the construction of the student residences, which was funded by the taking out of an additional bank loan. The university's total income increased significantly in the year, partly as a result of increased student numbers, as a result of Exeter's performance in the 2001 RAE which enabled the university to accelerate its development plans, due to NHS funding for the PMS, and thanks to success in attracting project funding, particularly from the European Social Fund and the Regional Development Agency. Improved funding permitted a new HR strategy to reward and develop staff, the low pay of whom had been a major topic in the House of Lords debate. Staff-related costs were just over half of total expenditure.[28]

The year 2002/03 saw the greatest level of capital developments and investment for many years, with expenditure at Tremough, as well as the Biocatalysis Centre and significant initial expenditure on a scheme to redevelop and extend the student residences on and around the main campus. The cost was substantial, notably with the building of Holland Hall, a luxurious student block of en-suite rooms designed to meet the demands of the conference trade that was opened in 2004. The new residences became an asset, with rents coming in, while the cost was met in part with the use of partnership deals.

The commitment to new buildings focused attention on relations between the university and the city of Exeter as the denial of planning permission became an issue. Political and social tensions played a role in this antipathy, the alleged social composition of the student population especially being part of this equation. While Smith and others argued for the economic impact on the city of the university, including retail revenue during term time, the argument came back from an insular, left-leaning, City Council that the main problem was that local councillors were told by residents that posh upper-class kids were puking into their front gardens. The fact that undergraduates of any social background might act like this went unremarked but there was certainly an increase in the early 2000s in local anger with bad student behaviour.[29] The low real cost of alcohol was a major cause of this behaviour.

There was also the perennial tension about student parking, with unrealistic assumptions that the university could, and should, restrict car use by students living out. Several members of the City Council had an aggressive antipathy toward the university and its students. There were also the practical difficulties created by the extent to which university student accommodation did not pay the community charge, while the presence of large numbers of students in particular areas affected the pattern of demand for the primary schools. The St James' area of the city was increasingly taken over by landlords renting to students, while because more students lived off-campus, the significance of the halls declined. The university was put under pressure by the City Council to have more accommodation on site in order to reduce pressure on local housing, but, at the same time, there were planning issues over the size of the accommodation that would be permitted. 'We work with the university', the claim of the Council, was not the case from the university's perspective. By the late 2000s, in contrast, relations had greatly improved, in part because of the university's effort to persuade the Council and the planners of the interconnectedness of the university's plans with the presentation of the city as a whole.[30]

The university's expenditure in 2002/03 was underpinned by the success of the strategy to reduce reliance on governmental funding through further partnership links and the establishment of stronger relations with business, and in-house efforts to eliminate waste and inefficiency. All of this action was being taken in the knowledge that a first-rate package would need to be delivered to students by 2006 as they would become increasingly discerning customers following the introduction of the then proposed fee legislation.

Smith played a role in this legislation. Immediately upon becoming VC, he had set about engaging with the Blair government, which, in many respects, mirrored his own politics. In an attempt to 'make the weather', Smith sought to influence national policy to the university's interest. He became close to Charles Clarke, Secretary of State for Education. Fascinated anyway by politics and highly knowledgeable about it, his briefings to senior groups in the university, such as Council, SMG and APC, were authoritative master-classes in the politics and economics of Higher Education, its strategies and tactics.[31] Smith focused forensically on HEFCE. Just as Harrison had benefited from the advice of Peter Swinnerton-Dyer at the UGC, so Smith consulted regularly with Howard Newby and David Eastwood, successive Chief Executives of HEFCE; he was engaging with the wider machinery of Higher Education. Smith took control of the 94 Group of small research intensives and used it for Exeter's benefit, presaging his similar role within Universities UK (UUK), the representative organisation for the UK's universities.

Smith was also one of the few VCs who worked hard during the winter of 2002/03 at the national level to persuade uncertain Labour backbenchers to support the 2004 Higher Education Act, and thus vote in favour of increasing the cap on undergraduate fees to £3,000 by 2006/07: as part of this change, the fee debt was deferred until after graduation and until the student was earning over £15,000 a year, and the poorest students were given maintenance grants. In the event, although Labour had a parliamentary majority of 161, the vote was passed with a majority of only five. Smith argued that the gains to universities which increased fees would bring outweighed the political risks.[32]

Smith's managerial instincts to lessen Exeter's reliance on recurrent state revenue[33] were in direct tension with his successful effort in 2002/03 to secure increased undergraduate fees. This was a reflection of the wider quandary of university finances and also of the ambiguities of Blairism. Indeed, Smith adopted the phraseology 'old Exeter' and 'new Exeter', an unconscious tribute to Blair. He would obliquely criticise lingering staff attitudes associated with 'old Exeter' by describing the state as the university's 'least reliable partner'.

Meanwhile, while investing heavily in Cornwall, which was a massive distraction in managerial terms,[34] Exeter's regional stance was changing in accordance with an initiative from the Regional Development Agency to create a regional knowledge-based economy. A 'Sustaining International Research Excellence Initiative' was linked to an attempt to harness Higher Education research to regional development needs.

THE EARLY 2000S: RESTRUCTURING

At the university level, this involved collaboration between Exeter, Bath and Bristol, as well as a business input and HEFCE funding. This funding helped produce money and appointments for research, notably by generating a large number of jointly supervised PhD studentships, which helped in the 2008 RAE.[35] Exeter played a key role in this process, and strengthened its reputation by doing so and by the links which, also, were to help in the transfer of Chemistry students to the other two universities. Developed as Great Western Research (GWR) from 2006, relationships with Bristol and Bath were more aspirational than with Plymouth. There were also financial issues with the latter; in 2008, Plymouth's restructuring led to the assumption that it would be unable to invest in its joint activities with Exeter.[36] In part, links with Bristol and Bath involved 'looking in a different direction', but core elements of GWR were extended to include facilities at Plymouth and Tremough. However, GWR proved short-lived. Bristol and even Bath considered Exeter to be too weak as a strategic partner.

Fundraising was pushed hard. An impressive speaker and charismatic personality, Smith drew on the support of alumni across the world, using the peg of the impending fiftieth anniversary in 2005 to focus energy and enthusiasm. The Anniversary Chairs and Jubilee Lectureships were to help greatly in the 2008 RAE.

Smith pressed on in the late 2000s and 2010s to develop the alumni network and seek its support. Thus, in the spring of 2007, he visited China (April), Dubai (May) and Sharjah (May), benefiting in the latter cases from the large number of alumni of the Institute of Arab and Islamic Studies, and in November 2008 visited Taiwan.[37] Moreover, the creation of the Development and Alumni Relations Office represented the first attempt at bringing into the Registry culture a professional approach to fundraising. Gradually, the momentum of this work increased. Smith, the fundraisers and the distinguished alumni Board all played key roles.

However, putting pressure on the stabilisation of financial performance and the target of increasing uncommitted general reserves, expenditure in 2003/04 rose by 13 per cent, including an 18 per cent increase in total staff costs, leading to an operating deficit on continuing operations of £2.5 million for the year. This was because of the continuing development of the PMS and Tremough, as well as investment in academic and other staff. Staff restructuring at the Camborne School of

Mines, prior to its relocation to the new campus at Tremough, resulted in additional expenditure that academic year as did the rise of the contribution rate for ERBS. Income for 2003/04 had increased by 9.1 per cent, but as the 2001 RAE results had not been changed by a new RAE, the university had to survive on the existing ratings. The problem was exacerbated because what was originally intended as the 2006 RAE became the 2008 RAE. This delay further encouraged an emphasis on research grant income, which was both a visible sign of success and a key engagement with the external environment.

With an increase judged necessary in order to refurbish the campus,[38] long-term debt had risen from £30 million to £47.4 million (the residences accounting for £16.1 million), as a result of the move toward debt-financed expansion, while the pension liability had increased from £9.8 million to £11.3 million. The reduction in the income and expenditure reserve from £26 million to £22 million meant that a covenant with a bank had technically been broken, but the bank accepted this. Discussing the 2003/04 figures, Gerald Sturtridge, the Treasurer, told Council on 20 December 2004 that further cost-cutting was important, as was the removal of unnecessary activities. The university was required in 2003/04 to enter into new loan arrangements to replace two larger former borrowing schemes which had been set up in 1995 and 1997 to fund student residence developments and, after many meetings and discussions with its banker, the new arrangements were put in place with an accompanying reduction in overall annual borrowing costs. Financial restructuring was an important element in the academic changes of 2004/05.

Capital expenditure in 2003/04 was significant and included the continuing developments in Cornwall and PMS, the building of the Xfi (Exeter Finance and Investment) Centre to which a major donation by Ian Henderson greatly contributed, and laboratory and lecture theatre improvements. Further capital expenditure was incurred on the redevelopment and extension of student residences, and on new sports facilities. Almost all of this expenditure was externally funded by grants and loans. Lacey Hickie Caley again served as architects for the Xfi building. On this project, the main briefing innovation was the requirement that ground-floor seminar and meeting rooms should have large fully glazed doors giving access to the landscape outside, a feature that has proved highly successful. The central focus of the building, the ground floor atrium café, has the benefit of a great view through a double-storey curved window onto the Hoopern Valley duck ponds as well as internal views of galleried landings and a spiral staircase.

The year 2003/04 also included an intensive examination of the performance of all university activities over a period of many months, an examination which revealed a number of Schools and subjects that relied on subsidies from other Schools and subjects to survive. The cross-subsidy to Chemistry cost about £2.72 million from 1999 to 2003, and affected the other Sciences as well as the other subjects. Corrective action was therefore initiated, where possible, to make all operations live within their means and ideally become profitable, and plans were drawn up to close or discontinue other operations that were felt to be unable to recover and live within their means. The introduction of a new resource model on 1 August 2004 increased the pressure as it made income, costs and subsidies very clear.

The auditors, Ernst and Young, were another source of pressure. The continuing depletion of cash reserves threatened the level of operating capital, and the external auditors refused to sign off the accounts for 2003/04 until Council took the measures necessary to reduce the baseline expenditure sufficient to cut the shortfall. Initially, the university introduced differential cost-cutting (rather than equal misery) to try to protect key areas while planning the way forward. The pressure from the auditors and from the university's Audit Committee, which met on 6 October, 18 November and 16 December 2004, was an important element in the dynamics of policy in late 2004. This links to the suggestion that the 2004/05 restructuring was, at least in part, a response to a financial crisis caused by excessive expenditure, a response in which it was initially not clear that the department to be closed would be Chemistry, rather than Biology or much of Engineering. The thrust of the documentation, in contrast, suggests that major restructuring had been intended from the outset.

In September 2004, VCEG held a two-day residential strategy meeting in which *Imagining the Future*, a set of proposals written by Allen, was discussed and endorsed. Smith held up a copy of Michael Shattock's *Managing Successful Universities* (2003), an indication of Warwick's influence as Shattock had been its Registrar.[39] *Imagining the Future*, which provided the rationale and underpinning of the major restructuring of the university in 2004/05, is arresting with its combination of the urgency of now with the specifics of hard decisions about priorities. The first paragraph includes 'I know you are now waiting for action. The time has come to turn that vision into reality', while the document closes with: '[T]he status quo is not an option. Time is short and change needs to happen soon.' The challenge was clear, that of a greater national concentration of research resources across the disciplines, one that obliged the university to accelerate its policy of focusing on its strengths, and to do so by eliminating unplanned cross-subsidies and directing investment accordingly.

The idea of a 'Science-free university' was rejected in *Imagining the Future*: 'By building upon existing 5 rated units, such as Physics, Psychology, Sport and Health Sciences and Applied Mathematics, and generating the "bench to bedside" strategy we intend to create strong, viable science at Exeter while not dissipating resources in competitions we cannot win.' Particular attention was directed to the failure of Biology and Chemistry (which had been merged together in a School in 2003 without achieving the planned synergy) to come anywhere close to matching the per-capita research income of Physics: 'Biological and Chemical Sciences has about twice the number of academic staff as Physics yet earns less QR (£913k cf £970k).'

The new Resource Allocation Model was seen as helping confront the need to grow selectively in order to attain an effective critical mass: 'With a turnover of £113 million and about 13,000 students we are too small and stretched over too many subjects.' For the 2001 RAE, Exeter had submitted returns in thirty-seven subjects, and Smith proposed submitting in future in fewer than thirty for the next RAE. The focus of concern was clear: '4 rated science is currently losing over £3 million a year. This clearly cannot go on. Chemistry in particular is a very expensive subject in a challenging undergraduate market.' The expense had been increased by the large number of academics recruited since 2001 and by the failure to recruit sufficient undergraduates or to obtain a large grant income. The approach taken by the Chemistry professors, in arguing that the chemists were very high ranking in research terms and that the 2001 RAE ranking was inaccurate, had not gone down well with Smith. Chemistry had a cumulative deficit of £3.5 million: its actual deficit plus the amount it could not provide toward central costs.

THE EARLY 2000S: RESTRUCTURING

From the 1980s, a number of Chemistry departments had been closed across the country, a reflection of the subject's cost and of the argument for concentration of research facilities. Chemistry also lacked the intellectual and political stimulus that work on DNA and related topics had given to the Biosciences. The 2001 RAE panel had noted in its summary report that small departments (like Exeter) should not have tried to stretch themselves across Organic, Inorganic and Physical Chemistry (like Exeter).

Biology, which was ably led by Nick Talbot who had drawn up an effective academic plan for the development of Biosciences,[40] was regarded as strategically important to help ensure that the PMS had a future as a research-led medical unit. Indeed, discussing the report of the PMS for 2003/04, John Tooke told Council on 20 December 2004 that 'it would be crucial to achieve a high quality return to the RAE and that it would be important to work in partnership with the University of Exeter in the biomedical and life science area'. There was also the issue of Biology's presence at Tremough. As DVC, Kay initially thought that Organic Chemistry should be preserved alongside Biology to partner Medicine, but this idea was rapidly dropped when the main Organic Chemist (and Head of Department), Chris Moody, got a Chair in Nottingham in 2005.

A similar focusing led *Imagining the Future* to recommend the end of Italian and Music, while the option of closing French and Russian was mentioned. The refocusing of Education so as to tackle its significant deficit was a topic. This was a managerialism at odds with Education in the Wragg era. Building a strong Business School was also a priority: Smith understood its financial potential.

The basis was therefore laid for policies and events that were to focus national attention on Exeter and to define the following decade for the university. In 2004/05, the university moved significantly towards the achievement of its strategic goal of being an internationally recognised leading research-intensive university and, in particular, a university with a strong Science side.

A special meeting of the Senior Management Group on 18 November 2004 agreed the proposals, but one of the members leaked the plans, ensuring that they got into the national domain the following day, before staff and students could be told in face-to-face meetings. The closure of

Chemistry as unsustainable, and of Music (which could be afforded) as underperforming, was highly controversial. Highly charged language was employed at the time and is still used, amplifying comments made, on a different scale, when Philosophy was closed down in the 1980s. Interviewees provided comments that included 'the academic equivalent of regicide ... cultural vandalism'. National newspapers at the time devoted about ninety-five news stories to the issue and offered headlines such as 'The End of Science at Exeter!' The closure plans were inaccurately presented as part of a long-term plan to 'convert the University into a Liberal Arts College'.[41]

In light of the criticism, these closures were widely treated as a test of resolution. The Strategy, Performance and Resources Committee agreed the proposals unanimously on 23 November, Senate agreed the closure of Chemistry on 1 December 2004 by 38–10, with a majority of both the elected and the ex-officio Senators in favour, and Council on 20 December by 26–2 with one abstention, the two being mandated student representatives. The closure of Music was approved by Council by 23–2 with 4 abstentions, the provisions for Education by 25–2–1: again demonstrating his political skills, Smith had persuaded key members in advance. Russell Seal, a protagonist of change, was deputed to talk to all non-Executive members of Council before meeting, and Ruth Hawker held a caucus for Council at her house the night before the Council vote. There was some thought that more time should be taken before the decision,[42] but no significant opposition. On the day of the vote, the university allowed television cameras into the corridor outside the main committee room, but banned filming of the meeting itself. There were noisy student pickets outside both meetings and coverage in the main evening news bulletins. Over 2,000 students had demonstrated on campus on 25 November. However, Chemistry lost a lot of sympathy in the wider academic community by the way in which the staff leaked information and tried to play the students to win their case. Clarke wrote to HEFCE at the beginning of December asking it to protect certain subject areas, but provided no additional funding and asked for no new policy initiatives. On the morning of the Council vote on 20 December, Smith was (indirectly) asked by Clarke (via HEFCE) to postpone the closure, but refused.

At the Council meeting, Smith emphasised the strategic and developmental dimension, and the drive for selectivity, arguing that if members did not support the proposals they needed to offer realistic alternatives: Inkson told Council that the chemists had failed to do so.[43] Smith drew attention to the national context of cuts. In the Council discussion, it was argued that the university had not taken the right course after the 1996 RAE. Published soon after, the HEFCE guidance to RAE Panels vindicated the university's strategy as it heralded a further concentration of research resources towards fewer major research-led institutions.[44]

Smith personally identified himself with the entire restructuring process and drove it forward in an exercise in power as well as policy. Implementation owed much to an ability to translate a policy for change into a feeling and ideology about it that helped make change tangible for individuals, whether or not they liked it. There was a strong degree of personalisation, with a highly complex academic strategy linked to a driven leadership. With the destruction, in these closures, of the after-echo of tenure, the university community became fully aware that nothing and nobody was 'safe', and that the practice and culture of accountability had changed. The attention helped establish the principles and practices of financial accountability and drew attention to the cross-subsidies that had been so significant in Exeter, and other universities.

In trying to close Chemistry, Sussex proved less successful. The furore led to the investigation of the Exeter and Sussex moves by the House of Commons Select Committee on Science and Technology, in March–April 2005 and April, 2006 respectively, which concluded that Exeter's step had been appropriate but not Sussex's. Exeter's position had been publicly backed in March 2005 by Kim Howells, the Minister for Higher Education. Alasdair Smith's failure at Sussex was partly brought about by an active and combative branch of the AUT. In contrast, union militancy was not a problem in Exeter, and it was usually assumed by VCEG that the local branch was essentially responsible.[45] The Guild also came round to support the restructuring, making a statement to that effect at Senate on 21 March 2005.

Smith's public role over the closure issue also established him as an academic leader on the national stage and set the scene for his role, from 2009 to 2011, as head of UUK. The closure had required a lot of tenacity on Smith's part because the stakes were very high indeed for Exeter. Smith became highly unpopular for a long period.

The closure of Chemistry and Music attracted the headlines though were part of a wider process of staff losses in the university, particularly in Engineering, Computer Science, Mathematics, Geography, Education and Modern Languages. In Education, the focus on a balanced budget with attendant staff losses and early retirements meant addressing the large and underperforming professoriate as well as largely ending extra-mural work, a major change in the university's regional profile. In one year, under William Richardson, the salary bill in Education was selectively cut by £1.35 million, which ensured that the recurrent deficit the School had faced was tackled. At the same time, a complex set of teaching programmes was maintained. Despite *Imagining the Future* recommending its closure, and concerns about having five modern languages, Italian was saved for Combined Honours. In part, this was because Italian made a good, data-based case about its importance for recruitment across Modern Languages, and thanks to a strong groundswell against closure, from Modern Languages and Classics: only Single Honours Italian was closed.

Voluntary severance and selective early retirement – for seventy-seven academic and seventy-two support staff – was encouraged by the threat of redundancy committees which, in fact, were not established. The human cost involved in staff losses was considerable, but less than the headlines might suggest as most involved, notably in Chemistry and Music, found jobs elsewhere or, as in Education, retired early, part of the retirement of the late 1960s–70s staff intake. The effort to change the psychology of the university was applied particularly in the administration, where Allen encouraged some staff who had served for over ten years to further their careers elsewhere.

The restructuring of 2004/05 owed much to the degree to which the USS had not yet come under the sustained pressure of subsequent years, with the result that staff reductions could still be achieved voluntarily through generous early retirement settlements. In fact, this represented a raid on the assets of the scheme, and, thus, on the future, that enabled both staff and management to avoid a measure of responsibility for underperformance. Student opposition was greatly defused because of the deals struck with Bristol and Bath that allowed all first- and second-year Chemistry undergraduates the option of completing their entire degree at Exeter or transferring to Bristol or Bath and achieving a degree with these universities.

THE EARLY 2000S: RESTRUCTURING

Given the attention devoted to the closure of Chemistry, it is important to note that this was not as part of some sort of 'end' of Science at Exeter, but rather of the formation, from August 2005, of a School of Biosciences. This involved a process of restructuring both Biology and Chemistry as well as the closure of Chemistry's Single Honours undergraduate programmes. New appointments were made from August 2005 in pursuance of an attempt to build up interdisciplinary research themes, as well as to strengthen molecular genetics, notably systems biology and advanced genomics. This School was also to make the most success of Tremough, with the Centre for Ecology and Conservation founded in effect in a natural laboratory. A very able group of evolutionary and conservation biologists was recruited. The staff appointed were largely hired proactively, being deliberately targeted rather than applying for positions at Exeter. The vision was that of a rebirth of Science, through the expansion of Biosciences initially, then Environmental Sciences, Earth Systems Science (through the Climate Change initiative) and Material Science. By 2013, the School of Biosciences was earning around £16 million of research income annually, a figure far greater than the £800,065 of the School of Biological and Chemical Sciences in 2004/05. There were also strong undergraduate and postgraduate admissions in the School, the achievements of which proved important to the success of the Science Strategy. The success of Biosciences was to be central to the big story of the late 2000s: turning a good Arts and Social Studies-based university into a major player in the Sciences.

Music suffered because it was in a joint School of Drama and Music whose Head, Chris McCullough, was, like others in Drama, unwilling to defend Music. Moreover, Music staff had not built up close ties with student music-making. Investment in the latter was part of the outcome. The university appointed, in 2006, a Director of Music with responsibility for developing social music and administering a music scholarship scheme. Kay House, the old service block for the Duryard Halls, was refitted, at a cost of £2 million, into a large music centre with a variety of performance spaces. The result of this commitment to 'social and recreational music'[46] was, by 2013, to be the biggest extracurricular department in the country, in effect a very good facility for student music, with a huge range of music groups: Classical, Big Band, Gospel, Jazz, etc. Alongside Music's closure, there was a bringing round, indeed reinvention,[47] of Drama in the early 2000s after its highly critical Panel Feedback Report for the 2001 RAE. McCullough played a key role, as did investment including more funded undergraduate places and a new building. This was a rescue package that worked, producing more student applications and a higher RAE grade.

An overall deficit was recorded for 2004/05, largely as a result of the voluntary severance and early retirement costs. Yet, these departures and the replacement by younger staff brought a longer-term saving. Moreover, income continued to grow in 2004/05, with continuing grant aid being received for Tremough and double-figure percentage increases in tuition fees and research grant and contract income.

New building of student residences and at Tremough, however, contributed to a doubling of the university's borrowings over two years to a figure of some £60 million by the end of 2004/05 with a significant rise in the interest payable, whilst other operating expenses rose in the first year of operation of Tremough (2004/05) and as a result of extra investment in the maintenance backlog at the university's Streatham and, more cosmetically, St Luke's campuses.

A critical early decision taken by the university was that disciplines in Tremough would be linked vertically into the Streatham campus, rather than having horizontal linkages across the new campus. Initially, this was not well received in Cornwall, where there was concern about the consequences harming the development of an academic community spirit at Tremough. However, the policy was adopted in order to help develop research potential and postgraduate work. As there were no Heads of Department at Tremough, Atkinson, the founding Provost at Cornwall, formed a group of 'Lead Academics' who helped provide leadership to a highly motivated and predominantly young staff.

In the mid-2000s, across the university, resources were deployed in an extensive process of hiring. Indeed, the rate of appointment was higher than at any time since the 1960s. These hirings did not attract the same attention as the staff losses, but they were more significant in terms of the character of the institution. The staff became younger and more international, and a far higher percentage was female. Moreover, in marked contrast to the situation noted in the April 1989 issue of *Staff Forum*, the female staff were no longer heavily skewed toward temporary posts. A symbolic act was the appointment of Floella Benjamin as Chancellor.

THE EARLY 2000S: RESTRUCTURING

The selection of a black woman, installed on 11 July 2006, affirmed an aspiration for the university. The choice of Honorary Graduates also reflected the image the university was trying to project. There was a focus on prominent public figures. Generally the choice was successful, David Attenborough offering a particularly good speech to the congregation.

Staff changes were important to the society of the university and to its politics. A tremendous amount of energy was produced, energy that benefited both teaching and research. The cohesive character of a long-service, largely male, largely British (in fact, English), staff went, and, with it, a set of assumptions about staff conduct and rights. It is surprising how late this change came in Exeter. In 2000, figures produced on the number of non-white staff in the university showed that half of these were in the Institute of Arab and Islamic Studies.

The change in the 2000s interacted with others, such as the decline of Senate and the low rate of union membership. Most of the new staff took little, if any, interest in the political structures of the university. Emblematic senior academics such as Niblock, Talbot and Andrew Hattersley, a key medical researcher on diabetes, provided key leadership, but were not interested in Senate. At the same time, Heads of Department/School, both in themselves and, until 2008, meeting regularly before Senior Management Group meetings, played an important role in scrutinising VCEG proposals, especially as Paul Webley (DVC) understood the significance of winning such support.

Collegiality now had different meanings from those that had earlier pertained. Older staff regretted what they saw as the declining life of the university, including going for a drink together after work. Against the background of hostility to the rise of 'bureaucratic managerialism',[48] there were also complaints that the staff had become a grey group, in line with managerial wishes.

Because of the international character of the emerging workforce, many young staff were now leading very complicated lives, with spouses/partners living in different countries, often also employed in universities, so that both parties were trying to keep parallel careers on track, sometimes meeting only very intermittently. Such pressures mounted significantly when the couples concerned wished to start a family: for some, Devon then became a considerable problem. This was all a far remove from the settled sociability and comparative localism of the

1980s university. At the level of the staff, the university became less sociable.

New staff were linked to new research areas, new teaching methods and a different academic culture. The average member of staff, if such an individual exists, worked harder, with probation being a much more rigorous process (and with specific targets) than earlier in the history of the university and than in most other universities. New appointees were expected to demonstrate their accomplishments rapidly. There was intense pressure on staff to perform. In exchange was the prospect of far more rapid promotion than had been the case in earlier decades.

A major innovation was the introduction, from 2004/05, of the Postgraduate Certificate in Academic Practice, a structured, mandatory induction, specifically an introduction of 'academic practice' led by Richardson (Education), that all new 'early career' lecturers were expected to complete. This fulfilled a recommendation of the Dearing Report. The programme was tied to written probationary goals of a kind in marked contrast to the clubbable, informal scrutiny encountered by the retiring generation when they had been appointed three or more decades earlier. However, the staff were given every opportunity to choose what they were to be assessed on in line with their own interests: the process was not one-sided in favouring teaching over research or vice versa. Of the roughly 220 participants in 2004/05–2010/11, about 40 per cent had been brought up and gone to school in Britain, a further 40 per cent within the EU more widely, and the remaining 20 per cent in other countries.[49]

The lifestyle of the staff changed. Smoking and drinking during the working day became far less frequent, and sexual harassment, already uncommon from the 1990s, became rare. A vigorous managerial stance by Smith against harassment contributed to this change in tone, which itself owed much to altering social norms as well as the generational and gender developments among the staff.

Smith had identified expansion as the way forward, a planned and focused expansion in which there was selective investment in priorities leading to planned growth as well as a grasping of the nettle of performance management. His goals were ambitious, for both himself and the institution. Smith delivered what Holland had seen was needed, but delivered more than that. As an academic and as a former Head of

THE EARLY 2000S: RESTRUCTURING

Department, Smith had the necessary experience, but also credibility, with both academics in general and academic managers in particular. Smith also displayed highly impressive communication and influencing skills.

So far there have been two distinct phases of management by Smith, in each of which he has had a very clear idea of what he wanted to do and has been very aware of how to do it. The second phase is discussed in the next chapter. In the first, from 2002 to 2008, coinciding with the crucial RAE cycle, the 'top-down' managerial style worked particularly well as the university remained small enough for Smith to memorise academic details about virtually the entire professoriate and many other staff. As a result, he could attempt to understand the academic dynamic of each department in some detail. Smith adopted a hands-on approach toward research monitoring. This involved him questioning and evaluating the research outputs of all academics, with Directors of Research and Heads of School having to defend their plans in person. This process focused minds on performance while enabling Smith to take stock of the reality and feasibility of strategic planning in each academic unit. Smith personally chaired every single ROM (Research Output Monitoring) meeting with each Head of Department in each year from 2002/03 to 2007/08 at which the RAE returns of staff were discussed. In advance, Smith would have read the entire schedule and, as each staff member came up for review, he would quiz those present (the Head of School, the Head of Department if different, the DVC for research, and an internal scrutiniser drawn from a different department) on the strength of their publications profile, going so far as to question the standing of specific journals and the claim to 'originality' and 'significance' of individual articles. Staff from other British universities were amazed to hear of this level of scrutiny by a VC. The drive was also seen in early-morning managerial meetings to prepare the day's work and leave nothing to chance.

For the historian, it is interesting to note the contrast between evaluations (both contemporary and subsequent) of Smith and his period in office, and those of his three predecessors. For the latter, there was debate not only about the rights and wrongs of policy and policies, but also over what the VCs were trying to achieve and over the character of developments. For Smith, with 'his mixture of the visionary and the hard-nosed',[50] it was different. Intention and achievement were far closer.

Some people approved, some disapproved, some were inspired, some hated it all; but there was scant disagreement about the content of what Smith was trying to do, and about how and why the university was being transformed.

CHAPTER TWELVE

THE LATER 2000S TO THE PRESENT: THE BIG BANG

Should the Students' Guild ban the Sun from its shop, and campaign for it to be banned from all University outlets, until the editor removes the bare boobs from Page 3?
Don't Censor Exeter. Vote No to Banning the Sun. 2013, flysheet

I T IS ALWAYS instructive for academics to read the flysheets put up by students. They serve as a reminder that the issues dominating the attention of academics, principally themselves, and their disciplines, both in research and teaching, are not the only ones in the university. At the university level, the key developments were growth, improvement and excellence, with the major success of the Science Strategy and the development of the Medical School transforming the university so that first-rate activity was delivered across the board. But the Time Capsule buried under the foundations of the Forum in January 2012 included not only a speech by the VC but also popular food from the university supermarket, a university hoodie and students' photographs celebrating what Exeter meant to them.

Or take the 'our problems solved' in *Exeposé*: for 23 January 2012, a letter picked up an enduring theme, starting: 'I'm a single second-year student who moved in with three equally single girls at the beginning of the year. The problem is that they've all got boyfriends now and I'm feeling increasingly isolated.' Agony aunts had had a long run: 'The Auntie From Hell' had added a comic note in the 1990s, both with her replies and with her weekly tips, such as 'Don't imagine you can change a man unless he's in nappies' and 'So many men – so few machine guns.'[1] On 27 November 2017, 'Agony McAuntface' answered 'I really fancy my housemate, will it make things awkward?' and 'A close friend of mine has feelings for me … What do I do?' 'Fitting in' was repeatedly a theme. For 20 February 2012, the correspondent in 'our problems solved' was worried about going to a 'party island' for a summer holiday with her university friends and the drinking and seeking men involved, neither of which she wished to be pushed into doing: 'I'm worried that they'll think I'm a loser.' Homesickness was the topic on 5 March 2012. Reports about blind dates (both heterosexual and homosexual) also became a *Exeposé* regular item anew from 2012, with each individual commenting on and marking the other, a version of the more general university engagement with feedback. Comments, but not marks, were the feature of 'Recipe for Love', an earlier version.[2] 'The commercialism of Valentine's Day,' a complaint in *Exeposé* on 12 February 2018, was the topic of annual diatribes.

The most spectacular event in the student calendar was the Safer Sex Ball, a Guild charity event, designed to raise AIDS awareness, promote safer sex and have 'a bloody good time',[3] where free contraceptives were handed out. The Ball had originally been organised to raise money to keep open the local centre that supported people with AIDS/HIV and had become the largest AIDS charity event in Britain, raising, for example, over £20,000 in 1996.[4] By 2012, when the money went towards Exeter Raising and Giving, the RAG charity, the Ball raised £25,000.

This occasion, on which boundaries had frequently been pushed, not least in wearing very little, got somewhat out-of-hand in the case of one couple in January 2013, yet again indicating the ability of student life to bring the university extensive publicity. The episode also involved the issues of security and privacy bound up in the spread of CCTV, smartphones and the Internet as the actions of the couple recorded on the Ram's CCTV were copied to a smartphone.[5] The *Daily Mail* suggested that the Ball was a reminder of 'the decadence that came just before the fall of the Roman Empire', an observation that indicated, surprisingly, that the paper was not in touch with recent scholarship. In response, the university left it to the Guild to comment. This particular Ball had already been the cause of controversy, as its 'tribal' theme gave rise to an accusation of racism. The next Ball was cancelled and replaced in 2014 by a more modest Prohibition Ball.

Separately, in 2013 the university shut down the Facebook page 'Spotted: Exeter Library' on the grounds that it could lead to harassment. There was a laddish and laddette character to some undergraduate life, with the special student nights at certain nightclubs, notably Arena and Timepiece, attracting large attendances. In May 2013, the Guild organised a poll on banning the *Sun*, a poll conducted on the Internet, after an informed debate in *Exeposé* as well as on the web. In the event, with 2,441 voting, the decision was for retention. In part, this showed (yet again) that the student population was less radical than it might appear; or, again, that its liberalism and free-thinking approach was not limited to stereotypes. In turn, the *Sun* controversy was followed, in June 2013, by a *Great Gatsby* theme in much of student life, notably parties, and in October by a Guild-organised poll on whether the hit 'Blurred Lines' should be banned from Guild outlets because of its chauvinist tone and content: 752 students voted, with a majority voting to condemn the song, but against a ban.

Fashions were important. Mike Lea-O'Mahoney, a postgraduate who had done his first degree at Lancaster, was stuck by 'the uniformity of appearance amongst undergraduates: the men often seem to traipse around in surf shorts and flip flops and the ladies are rarely seen without Ugg boots. From a Northern perspective, I found that quite amusing.'[6] Another interviewee commented that the surf shorts and flip flops were worn even in November.

Alongside the media focus on sex and drinking, it is important to note that the students devoted more of their time to volunteering and other charitable activities than their counterparts in most other British universities. Moreover, as a reminder of the continued variety of the student experience, religion remained significant, albeit with a larger contribution from non-Christians, principally Muslims. The Christian life of the university was troubled by an upsurge in the long-standing tension between broad churchmanship and sectarianism.[7] This tension was linked to a 2008 dispute between the Guild and the Evangelical

Christian Union, one involving issues of inclusion and toleration as well as litigiousness.

Growth was the most important feature noted by visitors to the Exeter and Cornwall sites of the university during the Smith years; more buildings and more students. This was particularly apparent on the Streatham site, although, in part as a result of planning issues, the redevelopment plans for Thomas Hall as a conference centre and/or luxury hotel were not brought to fulfilment. Subsequently, when the planning regime became less difficult, there was a problem with funding this redevelopment; in 2013, Thomas Hall was sold.

The building and rebuilding of major student residences, notably Birks and Duryard, was an important feature, as were new academic buildings, especially the extension to the Business School. The university partnered with UPP, a Barclays vehicle, to enable it to borrow and invest in the campus. This was crucial in the redevelopment of the residences, which were intended to meet the city's requirements to increase the amount of student accommodation provided by the university.

Holland had suggested building an Arts Centre – gallery and concert space – on the Great Hall car park, but the idea did not gain traction, largely because Powell argued that it could not be afforded. Now, the Infrastructure Strategy was a prerequisite for the Forum.[8] Based on an idea from David Allen, the Forum was opened on 2 May 2012 during the Queen's Diamond Jubilee tour of Britain. In place of a road and a car park at the centre of the campus came a reworking of the space and a linking of new and revived buildings, to create a very different physical presence.[9]

As with the earlier Peter Chalk Centre, the Forum was a complex to look at, as well as from. Whereas the other final-round proposal opted for an orthogonal plan responding to the geometry of the adjacent buildings, Wilkinson Eyre offered a free-flowing plan drawn from the landscape and roofed by an all-embracing gridshell with an undulating roofline echoing the lie of the land and thus capitalising on the undulating hillside topography of the campus,[10] a topography that provided a distinctive meaning to student life.[11]

The Forum was also crucial to the refurbishment of a 'tired' campus. The new reception area for Northcote House turned the building round, making its car park now at the back, in a rejection of the original 1950s' pseudo-American style. Moreover, the Forum moved the visual attention at the centre of the campus from the INTO building,[12] which was important to the presentation of the university's identity and purpose. The Forum was intended to include visionary aspirations. The investment appraisal did not indicate a positive rate of return, but the Forum was seen both as guaranteeing the attraction of high-quality students by securing Exeter's place as a 'destination university', and as a physical expression of the university's Top Ten ambitions.[13] The Forum provided a rare opportunity for thinking really big and not relying on incremental growth.

The ruler of Sharjah since 1972, Sultan bin Muhammad Al-Qasimi, commonly known as Sheikh Sultan III, funded the initial feasibility work and fundraising activity for the Forum Project, as well as providing £5 million towards the construction costs. Costing £48 million, the Forum included a Student Services Centre, as well as new teaching facilities and the redeveloped Library, all in a highly arresting building and outside space. Although there was considerable disruption to student studies during the building programme,[14] the development and specifications of the Forum were driven by the desire to improve the broader student experience. It brought together a lot of student activities, from socialising and food to the Library and academic facilities, and made it possible for students to move between them in the dry. Moreover, the centralisation of university and Guild support facilities for students was very valuable.[15]

Despite being affected initially by seagull damage to the glass roof, by broken revolving doors (they were designed to keep the heat in) and by a flood following torrential rain, the Forum contributed to greater student satisfaction. Furthermore, the Forum, 'an open, well-lit, multi-use space that felt at once public and professional',[16] provided an active student hub hosting a large number of events. The 'footfall' of the Career Zone rose 33 per cent when it relocated to the Forum, while the Costa Café became the most successful branch in the South-West, and the Marketplace convenience store attracted a high satisfaction rate. The 'footfall' in the Library doubled in the first year of the Forum. The opening of the Forum not only led to the refurbishment of the Library but also to a consolidation of libraries, with the Law Library moved there from Amory. The once-separate Engineering Library has also been consolidated into the main Library, thus, again, freeing up space, but also being part of the erosion of disciplinary specialisation in library (and other) provision. As a separate development, the Old Library was refurbished and 'rebranded' as the Research Commons in 2010.[17] The refurbishment of the Library facilities was matched by round-the-clock opening of the Forum Library during the academic year. The same service was provided in Cornwall where the Exchange building was opened in 2012.

The Forum was the key site in a capital investment programme of over £380 million on the Streatham Campus, which became the largest construction site in the South-West. In this expansion, unprecedented in ambition and scale since that in the early years of the university, the university benefited from a cut in VAT in 2008, from the low level of interest rates, and from the downward impact of the recession on construction costs. Accommodation, research and teaching, including great success in attracting many outstanding staff, were key components in the capital investment. There was also major development in sport, including an indoor cricket centre, funded largely by external grants and sponsorship, and a health and fitness facility.

The expansion of the late 2000s and early 2010s reflected the improvement in the university's finances, low interest rates and a degree of reliance, notably for the residences, on outside finance in the shape of lease and lease-back deals. Third-party capital was used to invest in campus facilities, which these third parties were able to fund as the university assigned the rights to future rental income streams. Expansion by such means was very much a trend of this period, with universities seeking to lock in low interest rates to their advantage. Many of the former 1994 Group members (especially campus universities in medium-sized towns and cities) are among the most highly indebted in the UK. Historically, they have had to finance the development of student accommodation themselves as their host cities were too small to accommodate the student population, while they also funded growth on an accelerated basis compared with the redbricks who have accumulated assets over a much longer period. These factors would have greatly constrained growth but for the ability of the market to develop off-balance sheet partnerships (i.e. third-party investing) of one sort or another. Exeter's growth was faster than most, in part facilitated by its proactive use of such financing (UPP, INTO and the EU-funded Cornish campus), which enabled it to preserve its own borrowing capacity for investment

THE LATER 2000S TO THE PRESENT: THE BIG BANG

in meeting its core educational goals. In the late 2000s, Exeter borrowed by means of bank loans which were less expensive than the alternative idea of a bond for which the set-up costs were very high.[18]

There was some loss of natural habitat in the building programme, but far less than might have been anticipated given what was built. In large part, this was because much building took place on the site of earlier buildings or on car parks, as with the Business School. Most of the Estate remained devoted to trees and grass, and the excellent work of the much-admired Alf Crouch, the first Superintendent of Grounds ((1960–79), notably his skilful plantings, continues to give pleasure. In accordance with the plans created by William Holford and Partners, notably the comprehensive 1971 plan, Crouch, who drew attention to particular plants in the staff newsletter and published a book on the grounds, went in for extensive reinforcement planting, setting each building into a context so that it appeared to fill a space. The spaces between buildings are just as visually important as the buildings themselves. The university became in effect a sequence of outside rooms in an informal landscaping that was related to the topography. Donald Riches ('Dick the Brick'[19]), Director of Buildings and the Estate from 1964 to 1983, supported Crouch, and the latter's work was carried on by his successors, Stephen Scarr (1979–2007), a judicious custodian of the plantings, and Iain Park (2007–). Similarly, David Garwood, Head Gardener at Tremough, directed public attention to the importance of the plant species there.

A major element in the debate over the Estate was that of parking. It might seem ridiculous to place the issue so prominently in the history, but it was a long-standing one for the university, absorbing much committee time, providing a subject for large tracts of archival documents, and taking up much space in academics' e-mail correspondence in the 2000s and 2010s. Indeed, it became a prime topic of complaint. Some of those who purchased annual parking permits ('hunting for a space' permits) found they could not always park. The university sensibly did not respond to the demand for more parking space, and this represented a decision that will be of lasting significance for the Estate. Greater numbers of staff and students on the site could have been matched by more cars, and there was talk of more parking, even of a multistorey car park, a topic that still recurs. In part, there was pressure for a role for the car comparable to that which had earlier led to the short-lived scheme for filling in the valley in front of the university. However, instead of servicing cars, the university subsidised two bus services onto the site and replaced some of the built-over parking, notably with a temporary car park behind Amory. The net effect was to leave the university looking far more attractive than might have been anticipated given the scale of growth. However, the challenge remains.

The greater number of staff and students positively affected the fortunes of the city, creating growth in economic demand, and thus jobs and revenue, something increasingly acknowledged by a formerly insular and resistant City Council.[20] Its relations with the university improved considerably in the 2010s. Greatly concerned about the economic downturn, the Council came to appreciate that a thriving research university was enormously helpful to the economic future of the region. The significant increase in jobs at the university (350 new jobs in 2012/13 alone) was important. Moreover, wage rates at the university for locally recruited staff were much above those in the local economy. In 2015/16, the University generated £540.1 million in output within the local authority district of Exeter, over 5,300 jobs and 7 per cent of the employment there. In Devon, including Exeter, Plymouth and Torbay, the university generated £661.7 million in output and provided nearly 1.6 per cent of GVA (Gross Value Added), compared to 8 per cent in Exeter.[21] The campuses in Cornwall, at Penryn and Truro, contributed nearly £75 million of economic output to the Cornwall and Isles of Scilly economy, where over 850 jobs now depended on the university's activities. The scale of the university's economic impact, not just in Exeter, but also in Cornwall and across the South-West is very clear. Indeed, the activities of the university generate around 1 in every 275 jobs across the entire South-West. Based on this sort of impact alone, it is easy to see why the university has been labelled as an 'anchor institution', increasingly integral to the social, cultural and economic wellbeing of the community in which it is situated.[22] By late 2017, the university had about 3,895 directly employed jobs (or rather ftes, as many were part time).

Based on this sort of impact alone, it is easy to see why the university has been labelled as an 'anchor institution', increasingly integral to the social, cultural and economic wellbeing of the community in which it is situated.[23]

THE LATER 2000S TO THE PRESENT: THE BIG BANG

Most students did not live on campus, but, after the completion of the accommodation building programme, the university increased the number of rooms available in September 2012 to over 5,000. In September 2013, 92 per cent of first-year undergraduates were housed. Falling demand for catered accommodation contributed to the decision in 2012 to convert Hope Hall and Lazenby into office space. So also with St Luke's. However, in 2018, after a long planning process, work started at East Park, previously an arable field on the Streatham estate, designed to provide accommodation for 1,300 students. The 'gentrification' of the accommodation, for example of Birks,[24] was an aspect of rising costs and prices, but the cost of rent helped make the university expensive and affected the social composition of the student population.

Alongside the takeover of much of the urban rental market by the buy-to-let industry, notably in St James's Ward, and in response to pressure from the Council over this, many of the students were housed from the late 2000s in new, purpose-designed accommodation built off campus by private developers. This construction, notably immediately to the east of the railway line into St Davids, helped give a university town feel to the area near the university, and indeed to more of central Exeter than hitherto. The scale of expansion in the mid-2010s created renewed tensions, and opposition to student housing became more vocal.

The rising numbers of students were in part international (non-EU) students, notably from China, an aspect of the wider globalisation of Higher Education.[25] Thus, 900 Chinese students took part in the Chinese New Year Celebrations of 2010. Jeremy Lindley, the Finance Director who succeeded Keith Blanshard in 2005, had refined the Resource Allocation Model to introduce variable levels of taxation to incentivise particular practices, notably higher-margin income streams. Because the university was anxious to improve international and postgraduate research student recruitment, low or no taxes were placed on these activities. Research contracts were also untaxed. In contrast, home undergraduates were taxed at 40 per cent. This encouraged Schools to cap undergraduate home recruitment and develop other markets. The response was good. For 2007/08, the percentage increase for International applicants was 34 per cent, a rise that outperformed competitors. Smith's ability to create a conveyor belt of non-EU students from short courses to degrees via INTO was significant to expansion. INTO was important to the Estate Strategy 2006–16 and the Estate Strategy 2007 Review. The Estate Strategy anticipated and proposed solutions for a planned growth in student numbers at the Streatham campus from just under 9,000 fte in 2005/06 to just over 12,000 fte in 2015/16. INTO, a relatively new company, specialised in the recruitment of overseas students who wished to study for a full-time degree in Britain. The company offered 12 months of residential accommodation at a respected UK university together with an intensive course in English and foundation programmes that would help prepare the students to start in the first year of a full-time degree course. INTO provided much of the expansion in the late 2000s, notably into the Business School, which was itself therefore expanded.

Michael Langrish, and others before him, such as Stephen Lea, had referred to Exeter 'attracting people from all four corners of Surrey',[26] and in the early 2010s the university was still referred to in Surrey as 'Surrey on the Sea'. However, by 2015/16, 18.4 per cent of Exeter's students came from outside the EU. Financially significant, these students also greatly enhanced the experience of other students and of the university, while, in turn, both offered an enriching experience for them. These students were catered for in the city by a range of facilities, notably East Asian supermarkets. Research by Oxford Economics indicated that international students studying at the university contributed £88.3 million to Exeter's GDP in 2011/12, supporting nearly 2,880 jobs, 2.8 per cent of all employment in the city; a rapid increase on earlier figures: two years earlier the respective figures were £57.4 million, 2,120 jobs and 2.3 per cent. 2011 saw the opening, with help from the ruler of Sharjah, of the first purpose-built mosque in Exeter. Students also played a role in the Exeter Hindu Temple.

The internationalisation strategy was not only driven by economic and pedagogic factors, but also fulfilled a strong sense of mission for Exeter and more generally reflected Smith's research background in International Relations. In a speech on 'Universities and Globalisation', given at Dubai in April 2009, he argued: 'It is a globalised world and for reasons of stability and growth we have to learn to understand one another. What better preparation can you imagine than going to a university in which you encounter people from many different cultures?' The global ambitions led to a shift in interest to the Middle East, India, and, especially the Far East, notably China, and away from Europe, including a withering of the relationship with the universities in Rennes, Exeter's twin-city. The European Office was closed and subsumed within the International Office, while the European Committee became the International Committee. Smith told Council on 17 October 2008 that the key strategic themes were 'building capacity, internationalisation and focusing to meet the requirements of the post-RAE world'. Internationalisation did not solely mean student recruitment, but also aspirational partnerships with the best institutions world-wide, in part because peer reputation was a heavily weighted input in international league tables. The idea of a foreign branch campus was discussed,[27] but not pursued.

Internationalisation worked very well, although it could involve exposure to international disputes, as in February 2012 when the Turkish Society objected to an article in *Exeposé* about the Armenian massacres in 1915. The global agenda served to exemplify the point that Ben Bradshaw, a former Foreign Office minister as well as Exeter's MP, made about the university providing Britain with 'incredibly valuable' soft diplomacy.[28]

In part, the rising profile of non-EU students returned Exeter to the situation of its early years when students from the Empire and former Empire were important. However, the character and scale of the international engagement was now different, as was the significance for the financing of the university. As the fees of EU students were fixed, while the expansion of the EU to include new states removed sources of additional revenue, for example Cyprus which had been such a source for Law, the recruitment of non-EU students was of particular importance. In 2015–16, 7.8 per cent of the students were non-UK EU.

The impact of non-EU students on the balance of disciplines was instructive. Non-EU students were most significant for Business Studies, Economics, Finance and related subjects, and Education, and less so in the Arts, which underlined the financial challenge facing the latter. Non-EU students were of crucial significance for the Institute of Arab and Islamic Studies where there were 160 research postgraduates, the largest such body in a British university, a large proportion of whom were on scholarships, which reflected the international reputation of the Institute.

The financial focus helped explain a series of more detailed shifts within the university in the 2000s, for example the rise of the Business School in response to student demand, smothering, in the words of one senior observer, Economics. In academic terms, Business Studies showed a flexibility not offered by Economics, while the attraction of the Business School was a key to the internationalisation strategy. Moreover, the success of the Business School enabled it to act as a source of cross-subsidies, notably for the Sciences. In turn, this role placed heavy demands on the success and management of the Business School.

The financial focus was central in a university-wide managerialism that was designed to secure institutional growth and academic excellence. Alongside a drive for expansion came concerns about a potentially dangerous external environment. In the context of a likely shrinkage in the number of 18 year olds, there was an awareness of competition for higher-calibre students.[29] The 2007 annual report on risk argued that the outcome of the forthcoming RAE would be associated with a concentration of research funding, that a likely lifting of the cap on tuition fees would be linked with changes in HEFCE's approach to funding, and that student expectations of contact time and service delivery were likely to grow.[30] All these points remain valid. There was also the need, in light of infrastructure requirements, to reduce the percentage of turnover taken by payroll,[31] alongside the requirement to recruit and retain top-rate staff for teaching and research.

While, to critics, the university's top-downery led to 'petty tyranny and destructive stupidity',[32] the managerial revolution can be seen as professionalising the university. It was an aspect of a national trend, but was especially marked in Exeter. Smith clearly drove the process, but it also responded to an earlier sense of crisis, notably seen in the frustration of DVCs, especially Neville Bennett, Stephen Lea and Stephen Wilks, and administrators, particularly Philip Harvey.

Alongside Smith's focus on distinguishing between, and, crucially, within, disciplinary areas in the drive to support research excellence, came the managerialism associated with David Allen. At the national level, Allen was a moving figure in the Leadership Foundation, designed to try to bring greater strategic clarity to senior management across UK universities. In Exeter, the committee system was simplified and the Jarratt-style Strategy, Performance and Resources Committee, a joint committee of Senate and Council, was established. There was more centralisation and control as the university continued to grow, and the managerial hierarchy was extended out of Northcote House into the Schools and, later, from 2010, the Colleges. Dual Assurance (DA) and Task and Finish Groups established methods of management focused on implementation, rather than discussion, and with a flatter management structure as a consequence.

Dual Assurance was proposed by Allen at a Council Away Day on 23 February 2007, discussed at Council on 5 April that year, and introduced for the start of the 2007/08 academic year,[33] as a mechanism to replace the previous reliance on committees and as an aspect of organisational capital. The model involves two people. The first is a member of the VCEG, who takes responsibility for the management and development of policy in a particular area of business. The second is a lay member of Council, knowledgeable in the same area, who provides assurance to Council that this activity is well managed and that decisions have been reached following due process and appropriate consultation. There is also a coordinator, essentially taking on the role of secretary and ensuring that a proper record of decisions and discussions are kept and that these decisions are implemented and communicated. Dual Assurance was regarded as providing far more scrutiny than committees had done.[34]

To ensure that the involvement of academic staff in decision-making, consultation and consideration of strategic issues was not lost with the move away from a traditional committee system, it was agreed that Task and Finish Groups would be part of the system. These temporary groups could be convened by the 'management lead' as a mechanism for resolving a particular problem or issue and would have to include member(s) from the main academic body.

The system was established as part of an emphasis on a more entrepreneurial outlook for the university.[35] This required the ability to be 'nimble' and 'fleet of foot' in its decision-making, terms employed by Sir Robin Nicholson, a prominent member of Council particularly active with the Science Strategy. More executive decision-making in place of committees was regarded as a means of turning the rhetoric of entrepreneurialism into reality without compromising on sound governance, namely the accountability and transparency required by Council. Aside from empowering managers, Allen clarified the lines of accountability and reduced bureaucracy.

Allen also made the most of the talents of lay members of Council, helped greatly by Russell Seal. The nature of the lay members (fifteen after the 2004/05 governance review) also changed, in accordance with the *Guide for Members of Higher Education Governing Bodies in the UK* (2004) published by the Committee of University Chairs. Whereas the lay members had been representative, essentially reflecting particular constituencies, notably local authorities, and thus nominated by them, lay members were now selected to provide a balance of skills as well as a gender balance. Local authority, Camborne School of Mines, and Convocation representation, as of right, was ended. The Nominations Committee developed a skills matrix to guide a proper open recruitment process, and more systematic training and induction of lay members was also introduced, as was a review of the performance of Council and its members.

As a result of these changes, Council members, some of whom were alumni, came to have greater management experience. In particular, expertise in finance and partnership working increased. Council members were given unprecedented access from an Executive that saw the working relationship with Council as important. This meant more meetings per year and very detailed Away Days. This was leading-edge governance. Council, in turn, pressed for more ambitious performance.[36]

In 2010/11, the Dual Assurance model developed further, and a new category of dual engagement was established for those areas of the university's business that were important but not core to the mission. In these cases, the lay members of Council involved were not required to offer formal assurance to Council. Moreover, in 2010/11, the number of Council members, cut from thirty-four to twenty-five as a result of the 2004/05 governance review, was further reduced (to twenty). The abolition of the Strategy, Performance and Resources Committee meant that Council could act as the key strategic body.

Allen also consolidated the administrative structure. Initially this involved bringing together the Library and IT services, both hitherto very separate, and Michele Shoebridge, who had worked under Allen at Birmingham, finally as Director of Information Services, was appointed in 2006 to hold the same role in Exeter. This task was then widened, in 2007–09, to bring in the Academic Registry, Student Recruitment and Admissions, Outreach and Widening Participation, and the Careers

THE LATER 2000S TO THE PRESENT: THE BIG BANG

Service, creating an Academic Services division designed to provide 'joined up support for the University of Exeter student experience'.[37] The practice proved successful, not least the engagement with the Guild and the idea of customer service, and the student attitude toward the university became much more positive than in 1999–2000.

There was a separate process of modernisation and expansion with Personnel, which in the 2000s was renamed Human Resources and incorporated the Staff Development Unit, Occupational Health, Health and Safety, and Payroll and Pensions. The department became increasingly populated by graduates and professionally qualified staff.[38]

Moreover, there was a partial integration of the previous parallel hierarchies of academic control and administrative control, with the administrative hierarchy gaining precedence. Administrators were no longer advisors. The number of administrative staff was greatly enlarged both to support the management and to service the Schools, later Colleges. The creation of College Managers (since 2017/18 Directors of College Operations), and their attendant hierarchy, who reported to College Deans but with a professional 'dotted line' to Allen, was very important in reframing and rephrasing patterns of control and influence. There was a considerable amount of academic complaint, but, as Allen pointed out, the process was designed to free up academic time for teaching and research. Allen argued that, without the academic staff, the university would be nothing, even as he brought about the management revolution that fundamentally altered relations between the administrative and academic functions.

In part, a freeing up of academic time indeed occurred, especially with the centralisation of admissions. These changes were continued in the 2010s, notably with the 'LEAN' improvement in streamlining processes which were designed to free up academic time, support research and teaching, reduce administrative burden, and increase efficiency.[39]

Changes unwelcome to many academics (notably, but not only, to critics) in the shape of box-ticking accountability and formulaic methods, that were blamed on 'the administration' or on 'Northcote House', were in fact partly the product of a different work culture, indeed society, one far more aware of rights and responsibilities, and readier to turn to law to ensure them. Moreover, the scale of the university, and the sums of money involved, required a different management culture, a tendency increasingly apparent from the 1990s. The synergy of scale and change was a key one. It was in line with national 'best practice' that there was the streamlining of Council. Whether 'best practice' or not, an emphasis on particular structures and methods was also in line with organisational developments across the public as well as the private sector. As an instance of a more widespread neoliberalisation across much of the world, 'Exeter plc' had parallels with a modern high-profile company, with a strong CEO, a well-defined mission statement, a concern with brand and positioning, a strong, centralised administration, an exertion of managerial control, an emphasis on quantification, an intolerance of underperformance, and a determination to invest for success, not least with high-profile appointments.

The practice and discourse of 'strategic planning' played a role in neoliberalisation, both in private and in public institutions. And so also for the university. Thus, on 16 July 2007, an important meeting for a number of reasons, Council considered a draft 'Strategic Plan' for 2007–11. This was designed to be a 'higher-level plan' which should not require annual review as the 'Corporate Plan' had done, but should only be changed when either the internal and/or external environments demanded. More generally, the language used indicated the determination to understand and engage with the economics, society, politics and culture of a changing Britain and world. Consider the 'Draft Infrastructure Strategy 2007/8 to 2019/20':

> The strategy looks forward to the post-RAE world of the 'mixed economy' where student choice in a wide market for degree programmes will be crucial in determining the success of the University, in addition to the necessity of remaining a research led institution. Thus the investments have a significant focus on improving student facilities and learning resources. They also involve a contribution to the Science strategy and related items, to network developments, the improvement of business systems, and to the elimination of the University's maintenance backlog.[40]

Brand, performance, added value, on message, all became key terms and themes in planning and presentation from the 2000s as part of a broader international pattern.[41] Exeter's Strategic Plan for 2007–11

THE LATER 2000S TO THE PRESENT: THE BIG BANG

referred to the need 'to strengthen the recognition of our brand'. On a visit to the campus, and its 'fantastic views', for a Classical Association conference in 2012, the Cambridge academic Mary Beard made fun of some of the language, and notably of the theme of success, energy and ambition.[42] However, in practice, there was a need for ambition, vision and clarity of communication to achieve the change that occurred. They did not detract from the sheer hard work involved, but were relevant to a clarity of delivery that helped direct, sustain and utilise this work. A fully articulated and well-embedded process of planning was not in existence in 1999. To create this process required an ideology and language of change. As another instance of the use of language, it is possible to query some of the ideas and phrases employed in course descriptions, notably their 'learning outcomes', defined in accordance with 'subject-specific skills', 'core academic skills' and 'personal and key skills', as well as their 'learning and teaching methods'. Yet, the standard template provided students with information and encouraged staff to think about these goals.

The Chair of Council from 2005, Russell Seal, a vigorous, clear-sighted individual with a business (BP) background, offered crucial political support for the process of change, notably of organisational development, and thus helped sustain Smith's position. He had joined Council in 1999, being dismayed then by what he saw as a bureaucracy lacking managerial skills, goals, focus and an ability to articulate where it was going.[43] A strong influence for high performance in the university, Seal became energised by the restructuring of 2004/05; such management of change had been a central characteristic of his roles at BP, and he was increasingly able to see how his experience there could contribute actively to the future direction of the university beyond merely some general sense of enhanced management. A very 'hands-on' Chair of Council who sometimes seemed close to crossing the line between executive and non-executive responsibility, Seal had candid monthly one-to-one meetings with Smith. Seal took implementation very seriously. Generating considerable management ability and pressure, the working relationship between Smith, Allen and Seal was important and, compared with the position of the Chair of Council in other universities, unusual. During such a period of change, good governance was vital. Where there is failure in the sector, governance is always a part of it.

The policy and process of change required a new form of senior management, with the abolition of the electoral principle for DVCs and, instead, a group of semi-permanent DVCs. This was no longer the three-year stint of public service, in part semi-detached from the VC, which had been the situation in the late 1990s, leading to Holland being somewhat tangential. Instead, there was now a centralised managerial team, providing support for Smith, who became both VC and CEO. The VCEG became the centre of authority. DVCs were now appointed centrally and their number increased from three to four as a result of a suggestion from Allen. Whereas they had served for three years non-renewable, the terms were changed to five years, renewable for up to a further five. The DVCs included a number of key figures who, individually and together, helped Smith push through his managerial change, including Neil Armstrong, Janice Kay, Roger Kain, Mark Overton, Nick Talbot and Paul Webley. DVCs were given more power and encouraged to manage. Several DVCs served for more than one term. Key achievements included Kay's work on the Science and Education Strategies, Armstrong's management of the Business School and the International Strategy, and Talbot's role in greatly strengthening the university's research. Line-managing DVCs with executive portfolios for groups of Colleges saw the future in building interdisciplinarity and could deliberately knock down disciplinary silos.

The move of the management to the Executive Corridor in Northcote House was important to an interaction that led to a united team literally close to the VC. Moreover, compared to the DVCs of the 1980s and 1990s, such as Preist and Coleman, who had received little institutional support, the latter was now available. In the 2000s, it was essentially those who had the talent and desire to become university leaders who moved into the Executive Corridor, as university administration became a lifestyle choice rather than a temporary break in the normal pattern of university life.

Critics complained that the new system and cadre was 'out of touch', and the management 'top heavy' and autocratic, phrases that were easy to use, but did not address the challenge of managing what was now a far larger university. Alongside leadership, there was process or managerialism, unparalleled management information, and a coherent senior management team that ensured that process worked and was 'data-led'.[44]

THE LATER 2000S TO THE PRESENT: THE BIG BANG

As a result, the university was capable of first-class strategic thinking and effective planning, as well as operational flexibility. Smith emphasised the significance of data, telling Council on 16 July 2007: 'It is vitally important that we find out the cost of our programmes when deciding on the price we are going to charge for them.'

The power shift entailed the decline of Senate not only as a source of opposition, but also as an overseer with executive roles and pretensions, and, indeed, as a contributor to strategic direction, the last an important role.[45] Senate in November 2005 established a Senate Review Group which, reporting the following June, argued that Senate was not working satisfactorily and was normally reactive and misunderstood. The Senate Effectiveness Review recommended a fourth annual meeting, at least one elected member from each School, and the presentation of more performance indicators to Senate.[46] In practice, Senate gained no real power and lacked the expertise, notably in financial matters, to manage the expansion that was university policy. Organisational change was insistent. The size of both Senate and Council was considerably reduced, and the influence of the elected representatives with it. Court, the university's annual general meeting, which had received an annual report, had listened to a speech by the VC, and had then held a discussion, was abolished without a whimper.

Departmental autonomy also declined, with the end of the election of Heads. Instead, the Heads of Schools (later, from 2010, the Colleges), and of departments, were appointed, rather than elected. Moreover, those associated with failure were removed, and rapidly so. The restructuring of Schools, in an effort (not always successful) to make them work and to produce more coherent structures of roughly equivalent size, further challenged established loyalties. The problem of operating and opportunity costs resulting from running a large number of small departments was contained through rationalisation and reorganisation, which gave greater financial flexibility across groups of departments. However, the legacy of high staff–student ratios that remained from the old days of economy has never been satisfactorily addressed. In this light, university finances have continued to be subsidised from saving on staff.

In 2010, what had initially been eighteen Schools became six Colleges, which had similar aims, critical mass, budget-holding capacity and managerial capability. Whereas there had been considerable opposition to

Schooling, there was far less, other than in the Humanities and Social Sciences, to Colleging, which suggested that the Schools had won scant affection. With Smith and Allen seemingly able to trust the Colleges more than the Schools, in part because Allen had much more say in the appointment of the Colleges' senior management, the College strategy was also designed to forward a new managerial ethos and structure in which trust and a measure of decentralisation were to the fore. Working in accordance with university policies and plans, but enjoying a measure of autonomy and the support of more administrators, Deans and College Executives were to be trusted to develop priorities.

As another cause and instance of change, the proliferation of professorial appointments helped throw the issue of academic leadership to the fore. 'Academic leads' were/are of variable success. The issue of professorial underperformance, and thus of the continuing ability of the university to make best use of the staff, came into greater prominence in 2012/13 as the next RAE (now, Research Excellence Framework – REF) neared. Smith conceded in December 2012 that some promotions had been unwarranted.[47] They were generally driven by the fear, at College level, of losing staff to other institutions, a surprising lack of confidence given the university's proven ability to fill posts with good appointees.

In March 2014 Allen retired and was replaced by a new Chief Operating Officer, Claire Baines. The Director of Finance, Andrew Connolly, became Chief Financial Officer, reporting to the VC, rather than the Registrar. Baines only lasted a short while, and was eventually replaced in 2016 by Mike Shore-Nye. As a reminder of continuing organisational change, the Deans of Colleges became PVCs and joined VCEG. This helped address the question of how to balance the involvement of academics in central governance, without losing the advantages of quick decision-making and the expertise of the lay members, which were topics for a governance review in 2013/14. Campus Services, Estate Services and Exeter IT were in 2017/18 brought under the new role of Director of Campus Infrastructure and Operational Support Services.

Seal noted that, when he joined Council, League Tables 'were regarded as ill-conceived and irrelevant'.[48] This situation changed totally under Smith, and results were delivered. Arguing that 'Higher Education is very competitive, and that competition is intensifying and at a global level', Smith pressed for Exeter to 'join the group of leading international universities'.[49] The drive for results extended to all fields, including the question of what the Lazenby Chaplaincy meant in the context of a Top Twenty university. In practice, this question related to whether the Chaplaincy Advisory Group should be integrated with Student Services, and what resources would be necessary 'to provide a "Top 20" level of service'.[50]

Once Top Twenty was achieved in 2007, with Exeter the *THES* University of the Year in 2007/08, Council revised the objective to Top Ten by 2012. It was agreed in 2008 that, in light of competitive pressures from other universities, a contrary policy of consolidation at the existing position would pose the risk of slippage. Top Ten was, indeed, achieved on schedule. The objective also became progressing internationally from Top 200 to Top 100 in the world by the Diamond Jubilee in 2015.[51] At the same time, Smith argued that exact position was less significant than 'the company we keep'.[52]

The 2008 RAE registered marked improvement. Of the thirty-one units of assessment (thirty-seven in 2001); sixteen were in the Top Ten, and twenty-seven in the Top Twenty for subject groupings. In part as a result of the restructuring in 2005, and the energies and attitudes it energised and changed, as well as of the appointment of over 180 academic staff after the pilot RAE, as the university invested ahead of the actual RAE in order to get in early-career staff, Exeter went from 36th in 2001 to 26th in 2008. In terms of improvements in research quality weighted by volume, Exeter had the third biggest rise from 2001.[53] Exeter submitted 636 (95 per cent of its) staff, a 39 per cent increase on the 2001 return (of 458) that greatly outperformed the sector average. The 'quality profile', the percentage of staff receiving the RAE grades, was, in an exercise that no longer deployed a 5 rating, 17 per cent (4*, world leading), 39 per cent (3*, internationally excellent), 34 per cent (2*, recognised internationally), 9 per cent (1*, recognised nationally), and 1 per cent (unclassified). The percentage ranked 1* and U was more than forecast, notably in Law, Politics, the Institute of Arab and Islamic Studies, Spanish, and Sports and Health Science, but so also was that at 4*: in 2001, the comparable grade, 5*, had been awarded to just 2 per cent of Exeter's return.

In 2008, English, Drama, Classics, Accounting and Finance, Economics, Archaeology, Geography, Politics, Russian, Sociology, and

Education (albeit with only 62 per cent of staff submitted) were among those that returned very good performances. Biosciences rose about 36 places from 2001, Engineering did very well, and Physics sustained its strong performance, showing that there was a good basis for the Science Strategy, albeit with results below the level of Exeter's best Arts subjects. In 2008, Hospital-based Clinical Research and Health Services research ensured that the Medical School was well on course to achieve its strategic aim of being in the top half of UK medical schools in terms of research. Had the overall grading reflected a proper research intensity measure, as Exeter had hoped, one in which the quality profile was linked to the percentage of eligible staff returned/submitted, then the overall ranking would have been about 15th compared with 27th in RAE 2001.[54] Smith claimed that disagreement over the inclusion of the measure provided further backing for the view that 'size and capacity would matter as much as quality and intensity in the future research landscape'.[55]

The RAE delivered not only status, but also money, distributing Quality-Related (QR) research funding. The HEFCE grant noted 'an increase of 34.14 per cent in your mainstream QR compared with a sector average of 9.87 per cent. This is mainly due to an increase in funded volume and because your overall quality, relative to the rest of the sector, has improved.'[56]

The analysis of the RAE played a key role in university academic policy. The view that Science, while better than before, still had to be improved led to the development of the Science Strategy, with Kay as the DVC for STEM playing the key role in devising policy. Meeting first in January 2005, a Science Strategy Board was established. In 2006, Kay drew attention to the lack of 'capacity' in the Sciences and outlined a plan to build it.[57] In July 2007, Smith declared 'Exeter is committed to Science',[58] and a Science Strategy Implementation Plan was discussed by Senior Management Group on 31 October and by Council on 19 October and 17 December. 2008 saw the launch of the University of Exeter Science Strategy. Successful Science was regarded as a prerequisite for significant increases in research grant and contract income and for the development of distinctive activity.[59] Commercial exploitation was seen with the opening, in 2013, of the first building of the Exeter Science Park, of which the university is a partner. Moreover, the

THE LATER 2000S TO THE PRESENT: THE BIG BANG

Shanghai international league table of universities is strongly focused on large universities with a strong Science side, and the management team sought this recognition as part of its international strategy.

The definition of the five Science sectors, subsequent funding, the encouragement of interdisciplinarity and governance through a Board all proved highly important. Key interdisciplinary themes were identified, particularly climate change and sustainable futures; extra-solar planets; functional materials; translational medicine, personalised healthcare and public health; and systems biology.[60] In the last, Exeter was one of the first universities to invest in next-generation DNA sequencing, which reaped enormous dividends for both Biosciences and the Medical School. The breakthroughs in diabetes from the Exeter group led by Andrew Hattersley (who became a FRS in 2010) owed much to this far-sighted investment. Substantial grants all flowed from this Science Strategy, which also led to expansion in Engineering, Physics and Geography.

The university built arguably the leading climate change science group in the UK, capitalising on the Met Office's move from Bracknell to the city in 2002. Indeed, the strategic relationship with the latter's Hadley Centre was pivotal in building the university's expertise in climate change while the funding of joint chairs by the Met Office and the university provided a catalyst for Physics, Engineering and Mathematics, as the university, seeing an opportunity, built up excellence in related areas. The Met Office had Academic Partnerships with Exeter, Leeds, Oxford and Reading. Drawing on Exeter's investment in supercomputer facilities for Astrophysics and Applied Mathematics, mathematical modelling on the interdisciplinary frontier between climate science and statistical science, in which David Stephenson and John Thuburn played major roles, was important in the Exeter partnership which focused on the development of ENDGame: Even Newer Dynamics for General atmosphere modelling of the environment. The algorithms involved in this numerical model's dynamic core combined the efficiency necessary for forecasting with accurate representations of key processes. There was also joint research on the verification of weather warnings, research entailing an assessment of probabilistic forecasting. The climate change/environmental expertise helped shape Exeter's new international profile in global leagues, notably in Geography's high rank. Close cooperation with the Met Office helped lead to wider partnerships, notably with

Indian counterparts in an investigation led by Matthew Evans of new methods to predict monsoon rains in South Asia. Improvements in data collection and modelling were designed to improve predictive capability in a field that affected the livelihood of many. This research was an important aspect of a broader research and pedagogic engagement with India, notably in Bangalore where a University of Exeter office was opened in 2011.[61]

The arrival of the Met Office and the establishment of the PMS were key developments in the university's role in improving the economic and social environment in both the City and the county, an important goal of the Devon Strategic Partnership launched in 2000 as well as of the Regional Development Agency. Langrish, the first Chair of the Devon Strategic Partnership, saw these developments as indicative of the university's place in confronting the mismatch between Devon's high quality of life and low-tech economy.[62]

Under the Science Strategy, Biosciences achieved the greatest profile and the university invested heavily in its development. In addition, Physics made further significant improvements in research, which was focused in four strong, though relatively small, internationally recognised groups in Quantum Interacting Systems, Electromagnetic Materials/Photonics, Biomedical and Astrophysics. The building of the Research, Innovation, Learning and Development Centre at Wonford, the main medical site, a building funded by the NHS, the university, and a Wellcome–Wolfson capital award, provided a key medical research facility as well as an innovative teaching environment. On the Streatham Campus, the Wellcome-funded Mood Disorders Centre opened in 2012, linking Psychology and Medicine. The interdisciplinary ethos engendered by the Science Strategy process was very important in the development of environmental and sustainability studies, and was also tremendously significant in building a university without internal obstacles, obstacles that might prevent research collaboration.[63] This objective was the strategic rationale for forming Colleges; they were intended further to stimulate trans-disciplinary research.

The Humanities and Social Sciences Strategy (HaSS) launched in 2012/13 also built on this ethos, with themes in global uncertainties, societal and lifestyle shifts, science and technology, environmental change, identities and beliefs, and medical humanities. The university thus sought to position itself in the vanguard of interdisciplinary research, and to ensure that such research both affected all subject areas and was the principal engine of research income growth. The HaSS strategy was designed to provide university rebalancing following the emphasis on Science, but it faced the challenge that the Humanities place less of an emphasis on interdisciplinarity than the Sciences and are more inclined to emphasise disciplinary integrity.[64] A Digital Humanities Lab was opened in 2017.

New government admission policies in the early 2010s were presented as creating a British Ivy League,[65] and Exeter was certainly there. Having been shortlisted for the *Sunday Times* University of the Year four times, Exeter gained the award for 2012/13. At that point, the university came 3rd (out of 121) in the 2012 NSS for student satisfaction with the quality of teaching and 6th for overall satisfaction. The 2011 Dun and Bradstreet rankings placed Exeter as the 23rd fastest-growing company in the UK. In 2012, Exeter joined the Russell Group of leading universities, an achievement reflecting the support of a new peer group, and one that greatly enhanced Exeter's international reputation and attractiveness to students. In his Final Performance Review for 2011/12, Seal declared 'membership of the Russell Group changes everything for staff, students, alumni, partners and collaborators'. Smith presented joining as 'the turbo-burst to the narrative'.[66] It was certainly an aspect of the way in which Exeter played the system with its eye on the rankings, outmanoeuvring and overtaking more ponderous universities.

Smith and Allen were disappointed that not all staff appreciated the significance of joining the Group, an idea first talked about in 2005 when it seemed highly improbable.[67] In a decade, the university had moved from the risk of being thrown out of the 1994 Group to being a member of the more prestigious Russell Group. The latter was made more significant when the 1994 Group folded in 2014.

In the GW4 Alliance, which was formed in 2013 and officially launched in 2014, Bath, Bristol, Cardiff and Exeter were brought together in a much more formal alliance than the GWR of 2006. This Alliance delivered Doctoral Training Centres for every Research Council. This is critical for a wide-ranging Russell Group university and also led to new income. GW4, particularly Exeter, was also a key player in the consortium commissioned by the Department for Business to produce the Science and Innovation Audit for the South-West region[68] which is critical to inward government investment. This underlined Exeter's intended role as driving economic growth in the region.

Russell Group membership joined Top Ten status, and the more general pursuit of metrics, as part of a strategy for conforming and improving the university's relative position in order to attract domestic and international students. Smith argued that this was made more necessary by the 'perfect storm' approaching the Higher Education sector in the shape of budgetary cuts, a likely reduction in overall student numbers and more international competition.[69] The government's failure to adjust the level of the student grant for inflation contributed greatly to this storm.[70] The sense of competition, and desire to be seen to do well, extended across the staff: the chefs won inter-university cooking competitions while the grounds staff obtained Green Flag status.

Repeated departmental success in and after the 2008 RAE reflected not only institutional leadership at the university level and the provision of resources, as well as staff changes, but also the sheer professionalism at the departmental level that kept 'the show on the road', in the face not only of rising student numbers but also of what, under pressure, could seem like a blizzard of new initiatives, information demands and systems of scrutiny.[71] Professionalism was seen in the positive response to the requirements of change, notably in joining new teaching skills to new disciplinary perspectives. Exeter managed much better than many other research-intensive universities to get teaching configured to match the QAA regime, and to balance its demands with research, including shifting work away from academics into administrative hands where appropriate. As a consequence, the QAA Institutional Audits of the university have been non-events in terms of criticism. Most academics spend much less time moving paper, or checking that all their students have handed in their essays on time, than either their colleagues elsewhere or their own equivalents twenty years earlier.[72] Without this, the academics could never have absorbed the massive increase in workloads and student numbers. Relatively good NSS results and the ability to improve research output both owe much to this foundation.

It is always instructive to consider the views of short-term staff. They offer a different perspective, one more alive to the methods and standards of other institutions and without the long-term institutional assumptions of any one university, which is the problem with the views of 'permanent' staff. Thus, Steven Biddlecombe (2012/13) drew attention to an endlessly important factor, the role of Departmental Secretaries, now Departmental Administrators: 'Jenny and Dee are a pair of treasures without whom, I am sure, you would all end up lost in a desert of paper not knowing where anything is or how anything is done.' At the same time, the days of the rather forbidding Departmental Secretary have gone. Departmental Administrators are also a key point of contact with students, both because of their physical location and because most students consider where to apply and think of their studies in disciplinary terms.[73] From this perspective, the centralisation of 'support services' in 'hubs' at the College level, although a practice widespread in Higher Education, poses problems.

The scale of Exeter's attraction for students represented a profound change. The number of applicants shot up, notably in the 2010s. The reputation of the university and the attraction of the site were key factors, but the good, strategic and deeply embedded relationship with the Guild was also significant. Students as Change Agents, the inclusion of students in Task and Finish Groups and Dual Assurance, and the joint group looking at the way to spend the incremental income from the introduction of the £9,000 fees were important and contributed to a highly positive ambience. Guild views affected policy.

The rising reputation of the university was important to the resurgence of admissions, a key determinant of the entire story of the university. The league table effect (a self-reinforcing one), largely driven by the NSS success, was important, as was the efficiency of the combination of centralised admissions and a centre/subject partnership in Open Days, together with the pragmatic way in which the university adopted contextualised admissions. It was also very significant that Exeter managed to get Science admissions to reach new levels, given that this had always been the problem with trying to rebalance the university to any extent.

Application numbers and rates showed consistently high rises, with applications for entry in 2014 rising by 34 per cent to 34,077. Such a drive to be part of Exeter was very good for morale.[74] Moreover, higher application rates and the greater desirability of Exeter offers, such that students holding several offers increasingly chose to accept Exeter ones, both ensured over-recruitment and led to an increase in quotas in an incremental fashion. Thus, the over-recruitment in 2008/09 was projected into 2009 quota calculations,[75] and the pattern has continued. In 2013, the VCEG proposed that the university, which then had about 19,000 students, should plan for no more than 22,000 students on the three campuses. This was subsequently agreed by Council. It was agreed that at 19,000 Exeter was still a little smaller than its competitors, which was seen to restrict its ability to develop really competitive research groupings, especially in Science. Conversely, the university's analysis indicated that in Britain and the USA, few leading institutions had over that number of students, probably because the quality of the educational experience and student satisfaction suffers as an institution becomes bigger. Student numbers (including INTO) rose from 17,842 in 2012/13 to 22,085 in 2016/17, with the undergraduate figures being 13,893 and 17,971.

More applicants meant higher admission standards. By 2013, many were of the A*A*A category, and AAA was the basic tariff for most subjects. This was very different to the willingness to consider AAB and ABB in the late 2000s, although, as long ago as 2008, a year in which the Exeter campuses did not enter clearing at all, the median entry tariff was at AAA. Even with the increased use and achievement of the A*, it was still difficult for candidates to get places. Smith's influence with David Willetts, Minister of State for Universities and Science from 2010 to 2014, in the fees and admissions matrix helped ensure that Exeter benefited from government emphases on student choice and widening participation,[76] and notably from the ability to admit more students at high A level grades. This had positive benefits for teaching and staff. Having noted a higher calibre of students than in Aberdeen, where he had previously taught, Christopher Thorpe (Sociology, 2016–) reflected:

> ... the calibre of the students pushes me to keep learning. The challenge is always to try to remain one step ahead of the students; as I get better, so too do they in turn, which means I can never become complacent or shy away from refining my own practice.[77]

Admissions policy was driven by the concern for metrics, by government policy, and by the commitment by Smith and Allen to meritocracy. Thus, in 2008, Exeter was one of the nine universities chosen by the Department of Innovation, Universities and Skills to find ways to encourage talented students to apply to 'highly selecting universities' irrespective of their background. However, the educational, social and political contexts created complex cross-currents. Willetts's liberalisation of student number controls above AAB (2012) and ABB (2013), coupled with ongoing underperformance in all-ability state-maintained schools, made it more difficult than Smith envisaged to break the long-standing undergraduate recruitment nexus of Southern independent, grammar and 'leafy' comprehensive schools. Patchy student supply outside independent and selective schools in some subjects, notably Modern Languages, was also a constraint.

The changing tariff for student entry had a major impact on the relationship between the subjects, which brought up anew the problems prevalent during the 1970s–90s concerning small departments for which demand was limited, such as Russian. In the early 2010s, there was a relative shortage of 'good' students (i.e. students with the required grades) in Archaeology, Classics, Sociology, and Theology on the Exeter site, and History (earlier English as well) on the Cornwall campus. Similar situations arose in 2017 with Archaeology, Engineering, Geography, and Modern Languages on the Exeter site. Specific reasons played the key role, as there was no doubt about the quality of the departments, including of their teaching. There was a national shortage of AAA students in Archaeology, Classics, Theology and German. The accounting models in force made it far easier to detect a problem than in the past, but it proved difficult to persuade staff to teach courses for other disciplinary areas, for example Theology staff teaching for English or Archaeology for History. This proved a serious weakness with the College system. Instead, the emphasis was on recruiting staff for the subjects that could already attract large numbers of top-grade students, notably English, History and Psychology. Moreover, initiatives were taken to enhance their appeal, not least with a combined English and History degree for Cornwall.

The growth in postgraduate numbers in the later 2000s drew on work in the early 2000s in getting postgraduate education on the agenda and sorting out its management. In the later 2000s and early 2010s, an aggressive funding of postgraduate bursaries helped Exeter to increase numbers. Postgraduate research scholarships rose to just under £11.2 million in 2012/13, an 85.4 per cent increase from 2009/10. The university had great success in the Doctoral Training Partnerships established by the Funding Councils after competitive bids.

The solution to the university's position in the shape of policies of expansion and improvement was not without its issues, especially maintaining teaching quality and the student experience, and, more broadly, managing the resulting numbers. As a reminder that, across time, themes recur as well as change, much of the discussion used the language of past disputes. Concentration and specialisation vied anew as arguments with subject mix. The major contrasts with the past, again indicative of the Smith years, were the much greater awareness of cross-subsidy as a means of university financing and an issue in its politics, and the extent to which the lack of a powerful Senate ensured that adversarial politics were no longer to the fore, as they had been in the 1990s and, still more, the 1970s and 1980s.

There is scant evidence that the lack of such a Senate affected staff morale, notably that of younger staff, but morale did become an issue. The Staff Survey organised on behalf of the administration in 2005 had returned favourable results, with 82 per cent of the 47 per cent of staff who completed the survey feeling that the university had been a good place to work, even though 79 per cent felt that their workload had increased over the previous year..[78] However, although the Survey in 2009 had Exeter in the top quartile of institutions, it did see a fall in morale, both because of great unease about the 'traffic lights' system for assessing individual research,[79] and due to the move to a College structure, an outcome that emphasised that vertical line-management systems were both process and goal. Pressure to succeed on all fronts was generating high levels of stress.

The 2012 Survey returned a similar or better result on seventeen of the twenty-five questions, with about four-fifths of staff having confidence in the senior team's management of the institution. Analyses of the results, which included a report commissioned by the administration that claimed there was a 'stress-inducing culture', ranged from the suggestion of a breakdown over communications (scarcely a new issue), to the more mundane realities of the timing of the poll, which followed the decision, without consultation, to close down three staff tea-rooms or tea-rooms used by staff. This was significant due to the intensity of the teaching day and the consequent lack of time to walk across campus in search of refreshment. In addition, a 2008 study funded by HEFCE had indicated the problems created in English universities by a shortage of staff-rooms and areas where people could meet and chat, and a preference instead for an 'excessive use of email'.[80] The extent to which lunchtime was a fiction of the past due to the timetabling of 1–2 pm for teaching increased the general problem of exhaustion and stress. Moreover, the 2012 survey was conducted in Exeter at a particularly busy time of an increasingly busy academic year.

There was evidence of stress among academics,[81] in part linked to anger about box-ticking criteria and a failure to listen. The brief comparison by John Noel Dillon, in his 2011 paper 'Course Design and Bureaucratic Fatigue at Exeter', of the processes of getting courses approved at Exeter, Yale and Heidelberg is instructive,[82] although course approval at Exeter was, from 2008, much easier than at most British universities. There were also high levels of stress among academic-related and administrative staff. A price was being paid for becoming a tightly managed, nimble-footed, quasi-commercial institution, ambitiously established in the new world of global Higher Education.

Staff morale in the 2010s was also affected by the university's focus in teaching on metrics, and notably on the NSS ratings, as well as on pressure from the Guild for more contact hours. The issue came top in a 2008 Guild referendum on issues for campaigning and, that year, was the subject of 20 per cent of the qualitative comments made in the NSS results. In part, there was a failure by management to explain to the Guild that teaching preparation and, even more, marking were time-consuming and major aspects of contact. The university rolled out policies for a guaranteed ten hours a week contact, a maximum of fifteen students in seminars, and for submitting, marking and returning all work online, an extension to the more successful interactive online Exeter Learning Environment (ELE) which offers a cornucopia of material. Subsequently, Exeter joined a national Mooc (Massive open online course) initiative.

Some staff felt that the improved financial situation might have been used to improve staff–student ratios, rather than on infrastructure investment, but this was not a straightforward alternative, as hiring more staff is revenue expenditure, which affects the 'bottom line' of the university's income and expenditure and can be a continuing liability, whereas infrastructure investment is capital, which is a one-off payment. Moreover, more infrastructure is required for more staff, unless there is a reliance on more open-plan offices, 'hot desking' and flexible working. In the 2010s, these were very live issues with Council, as open-plan is the norm for its business members and a number believe that the university greatly underutilises its buildings as part of a more general case of not 'sweating assets' more efficiently.[83] The practicality of seeing students in open-plan offices to discuss work is an issue.

The nature of administration also caused discontent. The improved numbers of the central administration took work from departments in some respects, notably admissions, and this was a major change, improving the ability of staff to focus on teaching and research, while also ensuring greater consistency in admissions policy and aiding central planning and direction. However, the central administration also seemed to have generated more administrative work for departments. Indeed, more departmental staff were sucked into College and departmental administration, but, in a way that led some to complain about responsibility without power.

Perhaps the balance between necessary central direction and appropriate staff involvement had swayed too far to the former, so that many of the staff felt less drawn into 'owning' policy. The scale of the university, and, indeed, the Colleges, had certainly made face-to-face administration and leadership less possible. The weaknesses of the old 'administration as the hand-maid of professors' model which, by the 1980s, was clearly no longer viable in the face of the challenges facing the university, had given rise to managerialism; an aspect of what Harold Perkin presented as the decline of professional society in Britain.[84]

That process left unclear what should be the new accommodation between effective management and the sense of purpose and morale among academic staff. The latter elements ensure that it would be a mistake for universities to become clones of private-sector organisations. Universities are highly distinctive and important civil institutions with the particular goal of the disinterested pursuit of knowledge. As most academics have greater allegiance to their discipline than their institution of employment, there are particular issues in management and its relationship with disciplinary leaders and influences. There are also

THE LATER 2000S TO THE PRESENT: THE BIG BANG

issues to do with work-rate and collegiality. Far more is being asked of staff than ever before by government, the public, the university and students; and the time available, and inclination, for community interaction, have noticeably lessened. This is not just an Exeter problem, and all universities now face the danger of staff burn-out. With its 'Positive Working Environment' programme, Exeter has put in place some imaginative solutions for those suffering serious stress. The Exeter Academic Initiative was launched, putting far more focus on developing and investing in academic careers with greater transparency on performance expectations.

Nevertheless, alongside an extremely high retention rate as well as a large number of applicants per job, there is a problem at the staff level, with consequences for individual health and for teaching, and the risk that burn-out leads to a level of institutional disengagement. Common Rooms are generally far less well frequented than formerly, and there is relatively little sociability within Colleges, let alone between them or between academic and administrative staff. Concern over staff morale in 2012/13 led the management to consider a move of academic initiatives back to the College and departmental level. A disciplinary focus was certainly to the fore in the student experience, as indicated by student publications of 2017 such as *The Witness*, the journal of the university's Politics Society, and the *History Newsletter*, an electronic work run by the Student–Staff Liaison Committee.

The context for such issues was scarcely static. The national and international context deteriorated with the global recession that began in 2008. The grave mishandling of the public finances and of banking regulation in the 1990s and 2000s led to a serious crisis in public indebtedness during the recession. By September 2009, the national debt stood at £804.4 billion, equivalent to over £25,000 for every family in Britain. The coalition government that gained power after the general election in May 2010 responded with an austerity that hit Higher Education, which was affected by a range of cuts, both specific and indirect. 'Creating a World Class University Together', a VCEG paper of June 2010 for Council, designed to help in preparing a new strategic plan for the period to the end of 2015, declared: 'The non-negotiable key to success in an environment where the government is a less reliable partner, not only in University funding but through the NHS, abolition of Regional

295

Development Agencies and the general squeeze on public investment, is to diversify our income streams more and move into unregulated markets such as international partnerships and recruitment, postgraduate activity and research at least on a full cost recovery basis.' Smith referred to a funding 'valley of death'.[85]

A dynamic environment was apparent at the regional level. Exeter's growth had in part been founded on partnerships, which had helped the university to grow spectacularly, nearly trebling turnover in nine years. Indeed, the university gained a *THES* award in 2007 for the quality of its partnership working. However, as also with INTO, the university tended to outgrow these partnerships and they carried a heavy overhead. In 2001, it had appeared sensible to partner in Medicine with Plymouth, not only for crucial regional political reasons but also because the two universities were close in standing. By 2011, the universities were moving apart in overall status, while there was growing tension over the PMS. Exeter had over 90 per cent of the citations in medical research and held 84 per cent of the research grants. The relationship was too asymmetrical to be sustainable. Plymouth was preventing Exeter from investing in MRC-facing appointments and staff would only come to Exeter appointments. In addition, the facilitating hand (between the two universities) of John Tooke was no longer present.

In 2012/13, the re-creation of the Medical School as an Exeter institution (UEMS) involved very difficult negotiations with Plymouth and various agencies of government. These year-long negotiations tested Smith's not inconsiderable political skill, and Allen and Kay's strategic planning. An awful lot of sensitivity, tact and drive was required. Exeter was happy for Plymouth to acquire the Dental School but wanted a majority of Medical School places. This was initially agreed at an entry of 125 for Exeter and 75 for Plymouth, but was later amended to 120 and 80 in the light of concerns at HEFCE that the Plymouth School would not be sustainable at 75. Exeter now had control over its Medicine and there were fifteen applicants for each place in the 2013/14 entry. The outcome for Medicine was particularly significant as this was an area in which government investment continued despite the public sector cuts.

The break of the PMS link with Plymouth University was necessary for entry into the Russell Group. It worked because the overwhelming majority of the medical researchers chose to go to Exeter, not Plymouth.

THE LATER 2000S TO THE PRESENT: THE BIG BANG

The far stronger research focus of Exeter's Medicine gave it a major comparative advantage. This choice created key synergies with the Biological Sciences, and the basis for a research strategy, with investment designed to help ensure more research income. The Medical School offered world-leading research in diabetes, cardiovascular risk and ageing, neuroscience and mental health, and environment and human health, and has included work on the administration of tranexamic acid to reduce bleeding following trauma and the development of a stroke pathway which has led to more rapid interventions reducing morbidity and mortality.[86]

The £50 million Living Systems Institute on the Streatham site, opened in July 2017, brought together Biomedical scientists and biologists with mathematicians, physicists and engineers in order to increase the predictive power of biology and thus help the treatment of diseases. It has a truly exceptional team of scientists, and the opening symposium was the most significant grouping of academics assembled for an Exeter-focused event and one in which the academic presentations given by the university were equal to those of their visitors.[87]

Moreover, there was the retention of a St Luke's campus that was increasingly used for medical education and research, with a major refurbishment and extension in 2014/15 after the residential side ceased in 2012/13, in part because too many of the students there opted to live out. The retention and development was a sensible maintenance of a 'footprint' in a key area close to the Medical School. Consideration had been given to selling the site for housing,[88] a decision put off because of the fall in property prices and planning considerations, notably opposition from the City Council, but one that, anyway, would have left the university with fewer geographical assets.

At the same time, the high costs of securing and sustaining quality in Medicine (as well as its knock-on consequences in terms of the place and character of Science) posed issues for the university as a whole. Aside from the managerial and financial issues, there is the problem of balance within the university, and notably the long-term viability of the premium on the STEM/Medicine side. In particular, the university cannot afford for Medicine the trajectory experienced by Education in the 1980s–90s. Yet, by 2017, the School was powering ahead, with an excellent research reputation, the Medical Sciences degree was doing well, and there was very good cooperation with the hospital. The problem was that of capital.

In contrast to Medicine, the role of Education diminished, as part of the long-term decline of the subject at Exeter from the late 1990s, largely as a result of changing government policies, but, in part, due to a rebalancing away from Education's earlier size and in reaction to research rankings. The School of Education and Lifelong Learning (from August 2009, in a significant renaming, the Graduate School of Education) no longer runs undergraduate degree programmes,[89] but has developed flourishing Postgraduate Taught, Postgraduate Research and Postgraduate Certificate of Education (PGCE) programmes. It is one of the top teacher-training (PGCE) institutions in the country, has an 'Outstanding' result from OFSTED, and has had a rise in tariff points, great NSS scores and improving employment metrics.

The combination of developments in Cornwall, the role of the Medical School, and local access schemes, suggested another echo from the past, a regional dimension for the university. In practice, however, the emphasis, for both Cornwall and the Medical School, was on research and teaching at international levels of excellence. In Cornwall, it was distinctive approaches that thrived, notably in the Biological and Environmental Sciences. Important backing came from the Regional Development Agency, which, in 2007, had given a clear commitment to support research that led to sustainability.[90] The £30 million Environment and Sustainability Institute, commissioned in 2008, completed in 2012 and officially opened in 2013 thanks mainly to EU funding, proved a successful basis for cutting-edge interdisciplinary research. The Institute explores the solutions to the impact of environmental change, assisting businesses and stimulating economic growth in the new green economy, and the aspirations were incorporated into the design brief. Many innovative engineering solutions were incorporated into the building itself and the construction of it. The Institute of Cornish Studies, which had developed its own postgraduate teaching programme, was increasingly integrated with History on the Cornwall campus, including in undergraduate teaching. The Institute proved noticeably successful in responding to the university's internationalisation agenda, especially in building links with institutions in Australia.

Less success was experienced with subjects that lacked that interdisciplinary approach. Law was consolidated at Exeter (i.e. closed at Cornwall). Nevertheless, the teaching quality in Cornwall was high, as was student satisfaction. Indeed, the 2012 NSS put the attractive Cornwall campus in first place, nationally, for student satisfaction with academic staff and with improvements in their personal development, communication skills and confidence. The provision of 1,400 en-suite bedrooms in student accommodation was a major asset. The problem, for a while, was getting sufficient students at the right grades and across the full range of subjects there. This was a key aspect of what Smith referred to in 2008 as 'a delicate situation' in Cornwall.[91]

The difficulties faced by the Cornwall campus prior to its being able to recruit fully in 2013 raise the more general issue of the university's regional role, its 'west of Taunton' approach. Exeter developed major partnerships with local schools and encouraged local access schemes for entry. There is a positive economic impact in the region, notably in investment, employment and culture. Over £200 million had been invested in the Cornwall campus by the start of 2013, mainly by the EU, and the university then contributed about £30 million a year to the Cornish economy. By 2017, it provided 1.5 per cent of the Cornish economy.

In terms of UCAS tariff points on entry, the Cornwall campus by 2013 would have been thirteenth in the country if it had been freestanding, and ahead of Manchester. In addition, the revenue produced by student fees and by Biosciences' research income helped save the Cornwall campus from grave difficulties. The number of students in Cornwall rose from 1,751 in 2012/13 to 2,313 in 2016/17, making a significant contribution to the university, accounting for about 10 per cent of its students. Many outstanding academic staff had been recruited for Cornwall. Biosciences, in particular, made a major contribution to the university's research profile, such that the university now operates as a mature multi-campus institution, with each of its campuses contributing to the overall success of the university. This is evident in its research successes: in 2016/17, almost £20 million of new research awards were won by academics based in Cornwall, amounting to some 20 per cent of the institutional total, a testimony to both the quality and range of research now being undertaken in Cornwall. The subject mix continues to expand, two new departments having been opened in 2016, Mathematics and Business, with the latter in particular exceeding its target intake for home and international students during its first two years of operation. The infrastructure also continues to develop, with the addition of high-quality research, teaching and social space: over the past three years, some £20 million has been spent to provide a new research building for Bioscience, Renewable Energy and the Business School, a new postgraduate Masters suite, and a new sports centre and nursery; and another new research building costing over £11 million will be opened in the autumn of 2018.[92]

At the same time, there was a casting off of other traditional regional relationships including those expanded under Holland. One particular regional connection, that of evening classes through a Department of Extra Mural Studies (the Department for Lifelong Learning), was terminated after the loss of government Continuing and Adult Education grants and the closure of that department. There was no sentiment about this whatsoever within the VCEG. The accreditation of all the degree programmes at the University of St Mark and St John in Plymouth ended since, now with university status, Marjon naturally wished to award its own degrees.

To develop further as a leading international university, Exeter needs need to avoid any recurrence of the situation in the 1980s when good, often excellent, Arts subjects were held back by cross-subsidising less successful Science departments. Although the need to eliminate cross-subsidies was a much-vaunted rhetorical device of VCEG in the mid-2000s, the unbalanced nature of the economies of the subject portfolio ensured that they continued, then and subsequently, to be an important device, albeit what was then (and now) intended as a planned and transparent one. There was/is also the problem posed by the extent to which expenditure in other directions, notably on central and College administration, affected, and continue to affect, the staff–student ratio.

On the positive side, the finances of the university achieved a greater flexibility than ever before. This was done through increased fees from a larger number of students, especially international students, from administrative costs attached to income from a far larger number of research grants thanks to the appointment of staff who could obtain such grants, from sales of assets (such as Crossmead, Kilmorie and Higher Hoopern House), and from a greatly increased borrowing facility. The university went all out to exploit its borrowing capacity, building scale, notably, but not only, in the STEM subjects, in terms of student and staff numbers and new infrastructure. Accepting an 'appetite for change and risk',[93] Council played a key role in supporting this borrowing.

Already, in 2007/08, the long-term debt had increased to £83.2 million, at a time when the university's net assets had fallen from £414.1 million to £396.8 million.[94] In refinancing the debt that year, the minimum requirement was to refinance the long-term debt, but the university also wanted to be able to take on new debt, a task made difficult by the way in which RBS tried to use the credit crunch in order to drive a harder bargain.[95]

The reliance on third-party financed and owned student residences was significant as a way to liberate the university from the need to borrow to build them. The private sector would build residences, in light of the income stream they provided, but it would not build academic buildings. The scale of investment was necessary to propel Exeter into the Russell Group, as it is essential to be both big and excellent to be a member (although the LSE retains its position despite its small size).

University finances remain a constraint, as well as the key issue and means in planning and implementation. The tax-based system introduced by Lindley had achieved its objectives of funding growth, but it hindered both strategic resource allocation between Colleges/activities and Estate and support service development. Some Colleges, such as Business Studies, had the power to command premium fees in a strong international market and retain the wealth that generated; but others could not. Far from being planned ahead, the 'micro-estate' (that which excludes the major capital projects such as the Forum) was affected by a system in which Professional Services reacted in a delayed fashion to whatever growth the individual Colleges delivered. Indeed, the tax system had reached a point of maturity when the ability to invest strategically became significantly constrained and when there was a mismatch between need and capacity on the Estate. With the tax system, there were very few means of allocating resources differently between academic disciplines; nor was it possible to budget/plan more than one year ahead. The model had also resulted in an entrenchment of resource and management 'silos' which could have become unhealthy and constraining.

As a consequence, following the arrival of new Finance and Planning Directors, a review was commissioned under the chairmanship of Neil

Armstrong in 2011 with the result that, from 2013, a new method was introduced overseen by a Planning Review Group. This was intended to plan resource allocation over a medium-term period (five years), joining up investment in academic staffing, Professional Services support, and capital (the Estate). Financial successes were to be demonstrated by the achievement of targets for operating cash generation, which, in turn, was to fund capital investment. The review was based on individual Colleges devising and developing their own plan rather than on the centre imposing targets, which was the basis of the financial targets under the previous system, a system that ensured that Deans and Colleges did not own them but, instead, distanced themselves from them. Income was to continue to be allocated transparently as it was earned. Under this plan, contingency provisions were no longer to be held in budget centres, an approach which places a great premium on the accuracy of budgeting and forecasting. Initially over-bureaucraticised, the new system was reformed in successive annual planning rounds, reducing the burden on paperwork each time.[96]

The VCEG Planning Meeting in September 2011 received projections for a total turnover of £287.6 million in 2012/13 and £306.6 in 2013/14. However, the projections of a 5 per cent operating surplus no longer seemed plausible. Moreover, the Executive Summary for the September 2011 meeting included warnings: 'Nearly all available external funding is fully utilised. Higher operational surpluses than those included in the draft forecast will be required to fund additional capital investment.' How to sustain rapid success across many fronts was a problem new to Exeter by the 2010s.[97] By the early 2010s, whereas many Colleges delivered growth, some fell persistently short of their budget. For a number of years, this was shrugged away as the books were favourably balanced overall. When Sarah Turvill took over as Chair of Council in 2012, this coincided with the emergence of a 'social contract': that Council would permit continued capital investment provided budget managers delivered their financial targets. This dovetailed well with the principles of the Armstrong review as it was based on Colleges developing their own plans, a change greatly facilitated by Deans joining VCEG and taking ownership not just of their own College plans but also those of the university. The Deans joining VCEG was a game-changer as it meant that the heads of Colleges were on the inside of the tent for the first time,

THE LATER 2000S TO THE PRESENT: THE BIG BANG

and a stronger spirit of university identity began to be forged, overcoming 'silo' attitudes, and strengthening the spirit of the Armstrong review.

The Warwick route was a particular issue. In the 1980s and 1990s, Warwick was the one institution in British Higher Education that definitively broke through the old Higher Education hierarchies. It achieved this by turning away, after an initial period, from the traditional manner in which the usual subject portfolio is set up and run, in order to concentrate, way ahead of the curve, on diversifying income. The transformation of Exeter from about 1998, and more particularly, 2002–04, was a reinvention as successful as that achieved two decades before by Warwick. However, Warwick was not able to sustain the power of its distinctive reputation for sector-influencing innovation and, to an extent, settled back into the pack of leading British universities. Might Exeter follow this trajectory?

The emphasis in the early 2010s was on integrating the Medical School into the Colleges, developing strategic interdisciplinary research themes and investing in Biomedical Sciences. These ambitions had been in part reset by membership in the Russell Group, as that provided new comparisons and goals.[98] In the period 2007/08–2010/11, Exeter's research income grew by 89 per cent compared to a Russell Group median of 18 per cent. The gross research income was at the bottom of the Group bar the LSE, which is Science-weak, but Exeter benefited greatly from a growth in research income per academic across the institution, suggesting a major cultural change. The growth in research income continued subsequently even though Research Councils were reducing budgets. A difficult additional element was that the REF includes 'Impact', which is hard to judge and, therefore, to plan for.

There were major issues involved in hiring and housing the new staff deemed necessary to achieve research and teaching goals, but staff expansion and turnover helped ensure that the average ability to attract research income rose, even though there was a significant capital requirement for new buildings and the focus was on capital spend. In accordance with repeated concern about departmental size, this remained an issue, with worry about whether critical mass had been reached in the Physical Sciences, Engineering and Medicine. As Science (including Medicine) was responsible by 2010/11 for 80 per cent of the research income, this was important. Drawing on the success in raising levels of research income that would have been inconceivable in 2002, financial plans and related administrative structures were driving a research-based Science strategy seeking an annual research income target of £100 million, with a related focus on entering the Top Twenty for research in the 2014 REF. Funding from Research Councils UK alone grew from £12 million in 2014/15 to £33 million in 2016/17, with a high application-success rate. In 2002, the university came 38th in Research Council awards by aggregate amount, 29th in 2014, and 12th in 2017. The per capita increase was more impressive. Exeter also rose to 14th in the European Research Council funding. In 2016, the university won £99.5 million in research awards.

League of Scholars analysis based on Google Scholar data indicated that Exeter in 2017 had the highest percentage increase of the twenty-four Russell Group universities in citations and the highest percentage of high-potential authors among its early-career researchers.[99] Mirroring this data for more senior academics, the number in the Highly Cited Research Lists has risen from two in 2010 to twelve in 2017,[100] while Exeter has also had more holders of markers of esteem, such as Royal Society Wolfson Merit Awards, as well as its first Fellows of the Royal Academies of Engineering and Medical Sciences. The university has always had leading scholars, but now has many of them, and at all levels.

The well-planned 2014 REF, for which Exeter used rigorous analysis of performance, saw an additional 100 staff returned compared to 2008, and 98 per cent of the research submitted judged of international quality, compared to 82 per cent in 2008, while 4* world-leading research rose from seventeen to twenty-nine, and twenty-one out of the twenty-four units had maintained or improved their 4* score. Exeter was 16th nationally in the percentage of 4* publications. Very good results were obtained from Arab and Islamic Studies, Biological Science, Education, Engineering, History, Physics, Public Health, Sociology and Sport. The results led HEFCE to award Exeter an additional £3.8 million annually for research, the third highest gain amongst English universities. The most notable success was in Environmental Sciences, a subject in which Exeter had never previously returned: 4th in the UK with thirty-five academic staff submitted, which showed the strength in climate science and is the basis for the Global Systems Institute initiative.

The trajectory is upwards. The remarkable growth of research strength from 2013 has ensured that, whereas 458 staff were submitted in 2001, the projected figure in December 2017 was of 1,200 in 2021. This research strength did not suggest that the university had peaked. It is sustainable if there is only a small number of research universities.

There is no exact match between the Science subjects and the areas of strongest undergraduate applications. As the Director of Planning pointed out to Council in 2008, investing even more heavily in research and Science 'would have a negative impact on the student experience' by affecting staff–student ratios.[101] Nevertheless, that was the strategy, one that accorded with the government commitment to the research base.

On the research side, there is the potential clash between interdisciplinary developments at Exeter and inter-university groupings within disciplines,[102] as well as the challenges of making interdisciplinarity, which is important to large research bids. Such issues underlined questions about how a 'Destination University' would fit into the new and developing international and domestic environment and what it would take to be a success as one of the 'Destination Universities' that remained there. Tied to this were the key issues of size and scope, and of how best to maintain what the university referred to as the 'Exeter Bubble', an 'all encompassing experience' made up of the very strong sense of community, the quality of teaching, and the university environment.[103]

The experience has changed greatly over the last decade, producing a very different 'feel' in terms of how the university community relates to the rest of the world. No longer insular, the university now feels like a genuine international community, both at the level of staff and that of students. The entrepreneurial dimension is a substantial cause of this change, but also a product of it. There is a readily apparent shift from the difficult days at the start of the 2000s, let alone the late 1990s, to the present, a shift apparent from the mid-2000s and, even more, from 2007–08. The key issues of governance, politics and finance that had hamstrung policy in the late 1990s were overcome in 2002–04 by shrewd leadership and thereafter a clear understanding of how to deliver strategy ensured success, notably with raising the performance of Science and Education. The consequence of the changes across the university in 2002–08 was an astonishing efflorescence of energy and quality, one that acquired a cumulative dynamic that transformed the university, its culture and its reputation,[104] and which posed the question quite new to the university, that of sustaining strong success.

The university subsequently moved into a more competitive environment, which has led to speculation as to whether it has peaked, notably in NSS ratings.[105] Ratings in the Good University Guide (the combined *Times* and *Sunday Times* guide) fell from 8th in 2013 to 14th in 2017, with those in the *The Guardian* going from 12th to 13th. This was largely due to other institutions improving at a quicker rate even though Exeter has continued to improve in almost all metrics. The highest-performing metrics for Exeter included drop-out rate, student satisfaction and exam results, and the university ranked relatively high in entry standards, but there is room for improvement in student–staff ratios and graduate prospects. In global league tables, however, the trend was highly positive. Exeter has risen (over the period 2012–17) from 153 to 130 in the *THES* World University Rankings; 182 to 158 in QS; 116 to 35 in the Leiden University World Rankings (based on scientific impact and experience); and 250 to 175 in the Academic Ranking of World Universities (ARWU).

Interviewed for Expression FM on the 'Hot Seat Show', in December 2017, Smith attributed the recent fall in the NSS to greater pressure on facilities and staff due to the large expansion in the student body between 2012 and 2016 (and thus the decline in the staff–student ratio), and he presented plans to hire seventy-one new academics in 2018 as the response, only for plans to be called into question at the time of an industrial dispute in the late spring of 2018 as the future costs of pension provision became unclear. The rise in student numbers does not cause a fall in the NSS but it affects it, and, by late 2017, Exeter was 7th among the Russell Group in the NSS.

From 2015, uncertainties as a result of a far more difficult political situation, notably over student fee levels and 'the cliff edge of BREXIT',[106] created serious new challenges for management. In light of the failure of the fee to keep pace with inflation it proved necessary to create new lectureships in order to confront the staff–student ratio issue by increasing borrowing and by altering the capital spend.

CHAPTER THIRTEEN

INTO THE FUTURE

I will always have a soft spot for Exeter: the University, the town and the surrounding beaches and countryside. Perhaps because I was only there for an undergraduate degree, which was as enjoyable as it was fleeting when I look back, it will always retain a sort of mythical status in my mind.
Kate Davison (2008–11)

UNCERTAINTIES, NOTABLY, BUT NOT ONLY, surrounding Britain's role in the world, the nature of university funding, and interest rates crowded in on policymaking in the late 2010s. Universities have to plan for the medium and long term while being mindful of the short term, and change is a constant dynamic in Higher Education. Moreover, with Higher Education a global activity, indeed industry, rather than, as it was until the 1990s, essentially a branch of government (albeit an autonomous branch), the changes in question can be across the world.

The 1979 election, and the consequent fresh and sustained burst in public expenditure cuts it brought, had a major impact on university finances. At the same time, the cuts, in helping to move universities away from their high level of reliance on public funds, thus prepared the way for greater relative independence. Other aspects of the Thatcher changes were also of major long-term consequence for the universities. Thus, the introduction, for 1979/80, of the option for universities to charge unregulated fees for international students, an option taken up by everyone, was to be crucial to the current situation and future plans of universities and created a context within which Exeter, from the 2000s when the situation was, belatedly, exploited, was to be particularly successful. There are many courses across the British university sector that would not be running but for international students (non-EU) and their fees. Thus, one decision, taken forty years ago, has utterly transformed the British sector in a way no one imagined, as well as thereby helping the economy.

Government, however, proved, and continues to prove, reluctant to give independence, and indeed a freedom to match the responsibilities universities now have. Regulatory and rhetorical interference appears to be hardwired into all of the political parties, as is repeatedly demonstrated in the discussion of student fees and of admissions, notably in terms of social background. This situation clearly poses issues for Exeter, as for other universities, not least given the extent to which they can readily serve as the site, source and subject of public and ministerial anxieties over, real or alleged, social and economic norms and achievements, or rather lack of them.

The major efforts made by the university in the 2010s to broaden access, particularly for disadvantaged school-leavers from the region, was a reflection of this as well as of the drive for academic excellence on the part of the university. The significance of 'outside' pressures and requirements places an emphasis on political acuteness and skill in university leadership.

Partly as a consequence of the continued role of government, the future goals of Higher Education are highly uncertain, notably the degree to which calls for applied knowledge will have an impact. *Getting the Evidence: Using Research in Policy Making*, a 2003 report by the National Audit Office, noted a significant gap between universities and policymaking, and this theme has frequently been reprised. John Denham, the (Labour) Secretary of State for Innovation, Universities and Skills, a minister keenly committed to public benefit from education, complained in a speech in 2008 that, despite heavy government expenditure on research, it could be hard to obtain 'academic knowledge tailored to the practical needs of public policy'.

The 'impact agenda' has sought to shift this emphasis, only to meet with the pressures of obtaining research excellence. The contraction in the university adult education sector, largely a result of government funding models, for universities and students, is an aspect of this distancing. In part as a result of such developments, Higher Education is both cause and consequence of the impoverishment seen in much of modern British culture. There have been valiant efforts to fight the isolation of some academic activity by emphasising knowledge transfer, but that plays only a minor role in the dominant patterns of activity and funding. Indeed, the restricted role of the intellectual in modern British culture (other than on Radio 4 and on some television channels) is a curious commentary on the public accountability that the RAE was designed to demonstrate.

Separately, the changing nature of technology underlines questions about the long-term viability of residential universities, a viability affected by the costs of three-year courses. Cheaper internet providers open up the proposal of significant competition, as does internet provision from other residential universities.

Moreover, the process of stratification and restratification that has occurred with British universities in recent years, as major rises and falls in applications were seen, raises issues about volatility and sustaining position into, and in, the future. In contrast to universities which were research competitors but where applications were under pressure, Exeter had done extremely well for applications in the 2010s, which had raised the bar for the future. This is particularly so as Exeter's competitors are also expanding and investing for the future. Exeter has always had very good students, but, in terms of national and international comparisons, the average has become even better, and that despite the major increase in the national and international provision of Higher Education. The major effort put into raising the reputation of the university thus had a highly positive outcome: the external environment was greatly affected by this effort. At the same time, Exeter shares in some of the problems of recruitment seen with particular subjects at the national level, for example Archaeology and Modern Languages.

A strong application base and admissions stream was an important foundation for a more expansionist finances. To those involved in the cautious finances of the 1970s and 1980s, the borrowing of the 2000s and 2010s appeared troubling. The university borrowed heavily, not least for the Forum project; while borrowing of a different form, in the shape of financial partnerships, also proved significant for the expansion of this period. In 2012/13 Council worried that the university was over-borrowed and overly dependent on its international (non-EU) students and research grants. At the same time, supporters of what was termed the 'project' argued that international status depended on investment and was necessary for the university to succeed. The context for the university's planning was set by Jonathan Adams's thesis of a fourth age of research in which institutions are dividing into those that are internationally facing in research terms, and those that are domestically facing.[1] The latter have a very small proportion of PhD studentships and research council grants, and much lower average citations for their work. The former are where the bulk of research is concentrated. This drive was linked to the strength of undergraduate recruitment and the concentration of PhD training into Doctoral Training Centres.[2]

To focus on teaching and research and to reflect Council's concern, there was an attempt to cut back on administration, the size of which had grown considerably. In 2014, under the direction of Janice Kay, who held the new post of Provost, a university-wide 'Exeter Transformation Project', led by Jacqueline Marshall, made savings and reshaped the administration with a voluntary redundancy scheme, albeit increasing the pressure on remaining administrative staff and structures. The financial objective of the Transformation was to raise the level of the cash surplus which was dangerously low, especially in light of relatively high levels of debt, which greatly worried Council at the time. The project focused on restructuring much of the internal working of the College/Professional Services system, so that Professional Services were fit-for-purpose in supporting research and teaching while also meeting bolder financial targets. At the start of the Transformation, and partly to fund it, the university cancelled its capital programme, delayed existing commitments, and undertook piecemeal investments as and when necessary or when opportunities arose. As a result, the cash surplus rose while capital investment fell, the two combining to push up cash balances. This led Andrew Connolly, the Chief Financial Officer, in the early summer of 2017 to propose taking advantage of the situation by refinancing the debt, funding the cost of breaking fixed-rate debt from relatively low-yielding cash balances. Thus, the Transformation directly helped lead to refinancing.[3] Since then, the university's finances have improved.

INTO THE FUTURE

As a result, Council's appetite to borrow more began to express itself in July 2017. The causes were twofold. First, concern about future finances, the prospect that the May government might not last, and the threat that a new government might inflict financial damage on the university sector given Labour's electoral success over the fees issue. Secondly, the very low interest rates. Thus, the university borrowed more than was needed in order to preserve cash balances to act as a support for the immediate future. There was a refinancing of all the debt that winter. In place of £184 million of borrowing at 4.4 per cent interest, £210 million at 2.64 per cent for an average of thirty-one years' borrowing was raised in an oversubscribed issue which, like the low rate of interest, reflects the market perception of low risk. The debt was split in private placements among a number of lenders. The plan was for capital expenditure thereafter to come out of surplus income not additional debt.[4] Other universities have also taken out debt, Oxford issuing a £750 million 100-year bond.

The student environment has changed greatly. The major expansion of the student population from the 2000s onward further ensured the transformation of the hall system. But the traditional system had already been hit hard in the 1990s: Holland had regarded the hall wardens as anachronistic figures; their position was eroded and the last influential figure, Frank Oliver, Warden of Mardon, long a major figure in the university, retired; the wardens were rebranded as Resident Tutors and Senior Resident Tutors in halls, and there was one Resident Tutor for self-catering students. In the 2000s, a greater percentage of students lived off-site, first in rented flats and houses that were shared, but, later, increasingly, in new-build blocks of flats. The character of student life was one without real oversight. This was in accordance with the nature of society, namely the growing independence of the young. It would have been anachronistic for universities to try to control the mores of the young. This control only proved possible when in accordance with general social conventions, as in the banning of smoking from public places and in limitations on car parking.

No such social control existed over drinking (or going to nightclubs). It was therefore appropriate that the university sought to rely on encouragement/admonition of students from the Guild. There was an institutional Zero Tolerance Policy (agreed with the Guild) with respect to bad behaviour, and there were disciplinary procedures to be adhered to. Most student disciplinary cases were due to alcohol. Given that the university authorities largely lost oversight over students, other than in extreme circumstances, it was not surprising that most academics knew less about the student lifestyle and student circumstances than had been the case earlier, and notably than in the first fifteen years of the university. This change reflected the nature of society as a whole, as well as the particular character of youth culture. Paternalism is now unwelcome. At the same time, the earlier paternalism could also have an informal side that had its own advantages. Brian Smith reflects on the 1950s:

> [L]ife in the Department was much less bureaucratic. Essays were handed in to your tutor (after reading them to your seminar group) without all the lengthy recording processes which have to be gone through today. You were trusted if you were late, and in turn trusted your tutors to mark them and return them in reasonable time.[5]

One area in which universities such as Exeter very much represented a move into the future, repeated each generation, is that, far from reproducing the conventions of the past, they provided an opportunity for the young to embrace and extol change. Repeatedly, on the individual level as well as more generally, university life was important to the willingness and determination of the young to redefine themselves, frequently in opposition to their parents. In the period covered by the university's history, this was probably the most important means of social change, and more so than alterations in attitude and income by individuals later in life or in 'adulthood'.

The 'generation gap' began to emerge in Britain in the 1950s, and was pushed forward in the 1960s, with its stress on the individual, and on his or her ability to construct their particular world. Hedonism focused on free will, self-fulfilment and consumerism to create a more multifaceted construction of individual identities. This process was shaped by pop culture, which, in part, reflected a desire to focus the aspirations of youth on young adults rather than parents. This pattern has continued to the present, and will do so into the future. As a result, there will be no return to the paternalism of the past and, instead, the pattern of student support will continue to be informal, and focused on the Guild, on student friendship networks, and on counselling services, all of which operate in a highly effective way in Exeter.

Universities add the particular experience of the international dimension. In the case of Exeter, it took from 1995 to 2003 to double the international student population from 500 to 1,000 (with the growth essentially occurring from 2000), and there was then a plateau until 2006, but the population quadrupled from 2006 to 2013. There were also specific initiatives of significance. Large increases followed the 2006/07 investments into the International Strategy of that year, and the launch, in 2007, of the INTO Joint Venture and again following the 2009/10 investment tranche into the Internationalisation Strategy. The target for December 2015 for non-EU students was reached by January 2013, when there were 4,124 non-EU ftes. The plans were then revised upwards to a goal, excluding the INTO students, of 4,000 non-EU ftes by December 2018.

The recent development of a large international student body, and its importance for the university's strategy and profile, provides a link into the future of the university. The city with the greatest concentration of Exeter graduates outside London was Hong Kong. This reflected the size of the British expatriate community but also, as with Singapore, of the rapidly rising number of Exeter graduates from East Asia. Thus, the university became part of the major expansion of this dynamic region. The abortive attempt in the late 1990s to establish a presence in Thailand, an attempt initiated by the Department of Trade and Industry which saw Higher Education as a major export opportunity, was succeeded by an emphasis, initiated by the university, on attracting East Asian students to Exeter, which was then supplemented by interest in close links with Bangalore in India. Links with Chinese universities developed rapidly; currently the university is developing a strong institutional partnership with the Chinese University of Hong Kong.[6] In 2017, the China Scholarship Council signed an agreement that offered joint scholarships to Chinese students conducting PhD research at Exeter.

The growth in the non-EU student population was accompanied by a major shift in its composition. 2008/09 was the last year when there were more postgraduate than undergraduate non-EU students. The trend in increasing non-EU undergraduate numbers was driven not by any slackening of standards but by a marked increase in applications: from

4,763 for 2005/06 to over 20,000 for 2013/14. Exeter's rise in applications compared favourably with both the sector and the comparator group, which rose respectively 7 and 5 per cent in the same period. In turn, the university's reputation has ensured that the standards required have risen significantly, matching the situation for EU (including British) students. The university diversified applications away from the previous focus on the Business School and, notably, its disciplines of Accounting and Finance. The leading source of applications was Hong Kong and the rest of China; Singapore, Russia, Malaysia and Norway were other key undergraduate sources. The major sources for postgraduates were China, India and Thailand, while the Middle East remained important, notably for PhDs. From 2008, there has also been a significant rise in the African student population, notably from Nigeria and Ghana.

Exeter's relative position has been transformed as a result. In 2006/07, Exeter's non-EU student population as a percentage of its total student population, at 9 per cent, was smaller than its peers, Bristol, Durham, Edinburgh and York, each of which were in the 11–15 per cent range. By 2017/18, Exeter's percentage had risen to around 18–19 per cent, with a target to be 25 or even 30 per cent by 2025. Making the institution more international is a key driver. In February 2018, Council approved a new 'Global Strategy' with the aim was of underpinning 'a shift from a predominantly UK institution situated in the SW of England, to a global institution with research and education partnerships stretching across the world'.[7]

The financial implications are important, and notably given the fall in 'direct' income from the government. Inclusive of INTO revenues, income from non-EU students rose from £10 million in 2006/07 to over £50 million in 2011/21, outstripping income from UK/EU students for the first time. The £9,000 fee for the latter from 2012/13 ensured that UK/EU student income then rose beyond international student income. Moreover, the lifting of caps on student numbers provided they gained grades of ABB and above permitted a major rise in student numbers in 2013/14.

Aside from political challenges to the fee level, fees will continue to be eroded by inflation unless they are permitted to rise with it, whereas fees for non-EU students are rising considerably above inflation. The University's Transparent Approach to Costing (TRAC) model, which tries to establish real costs, shows that international recruitment generates significant profit margins. This recruitment is a key aspect of what has been referred to as the neoliberal public university.[8] This description, however, does not capture the range of forms and meanings involved, not least different aspects of corporatism. The sense of flux is particularly apparent in Education, where the intellectual strength of the School was affected by the continued erosion of government support for university teacher education and training.

Clearly more money would help enormously, to develop existing provision, to restructure, to continue to appoint good young staff and to plan for new developments. 'Our grasp is beyond our reach', a phrase Allen frequently used, reflects the extent to which the university's aspirations remain beyond its ability to afford them. However, that challenge is a good one, arising from ambition rather than complacent contentment. Never on the scale of the big universities, Exeter has to be nimble to continue its recent, but only recent, success in dramatically outperforming most of these universities and in becoming relevant at the world scale. The nature of education is change: helping students and staff achieve their potential and taking forward subjects in research and teaching terms. To think about the future as open-ended, as protean, as full of possibility, is the intellectual challenge for all.

CHAPTER FOURTEEN

CONCLUSIONS

On the whole I loved lots of things about Exeter University. I loved the fact that it is a campus university; that there is only one main library which is (or possibly the Ram at lunch) the most sociable place to be throughout the year; that everything is within walking distance, including the main sports facilities and that I have made many friends who mean the world to me. It was definitely the best three years of my life (so far!). ... Geography academically and socially combined was a great degree to study. It seemed that all the 'cool' people did Geography. ... The Wednesday sports night at Timepiece which was normally the best night of the week. It consisted of dressing up, £1 shots and rugby boys in too short-a-shorts!'
Celina Kelly (Geography, 2006–09)[1]

Posing as the sage equipped with panoptic vision and brilliant insight, the academic historian conventionally sinks from sight, so that his or her conclusions emerge as if obvious. I am deliberately taking a different approach, because I think I owe it to the subject. It is unlikely that anyone else will study the archives in this detail for a while. There will certainly not be the opportunity to interview many who are now elderly, notably those who go back to the 1950s.

Focusing on the individual perspective raises the question of how best to reflect on two topics, the university's history and how an historian tackles the topic. The underlying theme is that of a continual need to adapt to changing circumstances in political, social and economic contexts that the university could do nothing to influence. Adaptation was never easy and the university in large part failed to adapt at the right time to these changes except after 2000. Adaptation, moreover, created individual and collective strains, as well as being the cause of much of the political history of the institution. The interaction between the university and these wider contexts creates much of the interest of the history. Indeed, it becomes, from one particular angle, a history of Britain at a time of major transformation. For example, smoking moves from being an expression of male sociability and student independence, to becoming an inconvenience to others, and then the subject of prohibition. On 25 May 1977, taking forward concern expressed for many years, the Board of Senate banned smoking from meetings of Senate, and its committees, as well as from Faculty meetings. Archaeologists of the future working on the ruins of the university will note that the soil outside prominent buildings was enriched with a narcotic and will conclude that in Exeter, as part of the global tobacco cult, the spirits of the buildings were worshipped. A more contemporary explanation was offered by Stephen Lea:

> As a young academic, I was infuriated by the time smoking discussions took up in staff meetings. Only as a HoD did I realise the essential fact: if you had some awkward business to get done in the staff meeting, all you had to do was let smoking in the Common Room be raised under Matters Arising. The meeting would then talk itself into stasis, enabling you to get your agenda through by some fractionally legitimate means in the closing five minutes. Car parking was its natural successor once the last butts of the smoking issue had been stubbed out.[2]

The first time a student in one of Tim Niblock's Politics classes refused to allow another student to smoke occurred in 1992.[3]

The wider historical context is crucial. Issues continue, problems recur, arguments are repeated; but the contexts are very different. The global nature of modern education is a world away from the imperial and post-colonial stance of the 1950s. The scale of a modern university is vastly different, as is the gender, ethnic and social character of both staff and students. Historians can exercise their skill, and their mastery of the archives, by juxtaposing similar episodes and quotations from across the decades, but that is not overly helpful. To note, for example, the continued problems created by a lack of endowment, and the consistent resulting difficulties for building plans, teaching and research, is to fail to give sufficient weight to the differences created by a very different financial and regulatory environment, notably in terms of the ability to borrow substantial sums and at a very low rate of interest. At the same time, it is instructive that ADC proposed to cut the size of Chemistry in 1974, because the ability of Exeter to sustain 'Big Science' at the level required for excellence was in question due to the limited endowment and the absence of a nearby industrial base. It has been very difficult for a non-endowed university in the non-industrial South-West of England to afford the capital and staff investment to develop Science to critical levels of excellence, especially without access to medical funding, and given the often shaky position of Science subjects in admission league tables. These factors were also at play in the 2000s, but the domestic, international and intellectual contexts were different. Whereas for long the real problems of the university were the historic underfunding derived from its foundation and the dead hand of the departments in obstructing major internal attempts to overcome the consequences of this underfunding, the university's government, political and financial situation became totally different in the 2000s.

Change is also apparent with the response to student attitudes: satisfaction ratings became significant from the 2000s. At the same time, in surveys of staff productivity in teaching terms, Exeter has always come out as achieving very high levels relative to the staffing resources in national comparisons, substantiating the repeated sense on the part of staff that they were actually achieving quite a lot educationally, and with fewer resources than at other universities. Both points remain the case.

Successive VCs and their respective regimes responded to changing outside forces. The slowness of adjustment prior to the 2000s had roots going back to how badly positioned the university was, both financially and in infrastructure, and certainly much worse than completely new universities such as Sussex and Warwick. And yet, as a reminder of the often complex links across time, the lack of massive construction at Exeter in the 1960s–70s put the university in a competitive advantage, as replacing that stock in the 1990s and 2000s proved a real challenge to Exeter's competitors, soaking up much of the capital Exeter was able to put into new construction and other activities during that period. The whole challenge of building and maintaining a campus is significant. In Exeter, apart from Physics, the relative high quality of the original buildings, and the general use of brick, helped to make the campus work. A key feature in the Chemistry closure was the prohibitive cost of the heat venting systems that had to be used there and the problems with the building as a Chemistry building. The ability to build at almost no expense to the university in Cornwall and in the initial stages of the Medical School has given Exeter an enormous advantage in the Science fields covered by these developments.

As world players, major, or, rather, successful, universities operate in the international, national and regional environments, but do so with reference to global criteria. These are a matter of interest rates as much as student origins, staff recruitment as well as research interests, pedagogic trends as much as intellectual engagement. In contrast, the university was, in its early decades, somewhat provincial. There were major scholars, such as Barlow, Garland, Rees and Rydon, but not many. Nor for long was there a strong intellectual engagement across the institution with the outer world, certainly outside England. There were foreign students and important links with the empire and the 'informal empire', while the Modern Languages had major European links, but, outside these departments, there were few staff from abroad and relatively little exposure to new international intellectual trends.

Several important initiatives came with subsequent expansion, for example the Institute of Population Studies and the teaching of American and Commonwealth Literature. That such areas developed indicated that the university was not as traditional, rigid or conservative (left-wing conservative on the whole) as it might appear; but social conservatism was clear in the somewhat uneasy response to the focus on the Institute on family-planning policies. Moreover, the story of both the Institute and of American and Commonwealth Literature, each of which was closed in the late 1990s, indicated the difficulty of sustaining areas of quality. The small scale of university activities ensured that there was a great reliance on the presence of active, indeed entrepreneurial, individuals. If they were not replaced by others with a comparable drive and concern, then these areas collapsed or at least lacked energy, as with Population Studies in the 1990s after the departure of Bob Snowden.

Global ambition came to the fore under Smith. Indeed, but for the scale of the financial commitment made by Holland to Cornwall, it is probable that that regional initiative would have been greatly lessened under Smith. Moreover, he successfully sought to make Cornwall fulfil a global agenda by developing research and teaching expertise in niche areas of Biological and Environmental Studies, rather than by pursuing Cornish studies. Smith's policies and methods, including his concern with metrics, did not find favour with traditionalists, but he had an ability to implement his vision of the university unmatched since the more modest goals of Murray and Cook in transforming the university college into the university. As such, there are three founders of the modern University of Exeter: Murray, Cook and Smith. The first two operated in a very different environment. The long-serving Murray set the tone of the university college, a tone that long influenced the university, but he ultimately failed to obtain university status. Cook, in contrast, gained the status and set in progress a process of expansion, even if he was unable to respond to developing social trends. Cook was also a major scholar in his own right and, at a time when VCs had less pressure on their time, continued to conduct research and was proud to do so. Under Smith, the university faced the potential of a highly volatile world, one in which education was protean, not fixed, and global, not national. The ride was a bumpy one, but success was repeatedly delivered.

Hopefully, in charting the what and the why, or rather the whats and the whys, I have thrown light on the consequences today of the recent (and earlier) past, and thus vindicated the role of the historian. I have found the research highly instructive, and I hope I have conveyed this. For those who follow after, I can only urge the necessity, the value, and the pleasure, of hard work, mature reflection, and passing on the benefits of both.

NOTES

Preface
1. www.youtube.com/watch?v=1NLLqt6giFE, uploaded to YouTube on 3 February 2010; www.youtube.com/watch?v=Rxp130sJw9w, uploaded on 10 December 2010.
2. Trotter to Black, 10 July 2013.
3. Referring to a female fellow-student, Tom Beaumont to Black, 2 October 2013.
4. Moreover, Brian Clapp's earlier history, *The University of Exeter: A History* (Exeter, 1982) is only really successful up to 1955, in other words as a history of the University College of the South West and of its predecessors. Exeter does not play much of a role in published memoirs. David Richards's *Glimpses of a Life. A Reflective Autobiography* (Exeter, 1978) had to be withdrawn due to its candour, but offers little on the university. The latter is also the case with Moelwyn Merchant's less candid and much grander *Fragments of a Life* (Llandysul, 1990). For the sector as a whole, W. Whyte, *Redbrick: A Social and Architectural History of Britain's Civic Universities* (Oxford, 2015).
5. A. Fox, *Aileen – A Pioneering Archaeologist* (Leominster, 2000), p. 137.
6. I am grateful for the advice of David Batty, Barrie Behenna and Simon Baker. In the case of the Vice-Chancellor's Executive Group (VCEG), only action notes were officially recorded as it was thought that members of the Group would hold back if full minutes were taken. The fairly full manuscript notes were destroyed after a certain time. The university's records were also reorganized under Powell as good records were regarded as 'essential'. Sue Odell, Senior Assistant Registrar, to Black, 14 October 2013. Senate might seem to be the Parliament of a university but Senate has more and less power. Senate committees had considerable administrative responsibility and power, but Senate is subordinate to Council.
7. Cook had become Principal of the University College in 1954. J.M. Robertson, *Memoirs. Fellows of the Royal Society*, 22 (1976), pp. 71–103; H.N. Rydon, 'Sir James Cook', *University of Exeter Gazette*, 80 (1976), pp. 8–10.
8. Gar Yates, former Deputy Vice-Chancellor (DVC), to Black, 16 October 2013.
9. The governing body of a university.
10. A group of academic departments. This organization lasted until the creation of the Schools.
11. Ward-Perkins to Black, 3 June 2013; Sharpe to Black, 13 December 2012.
12. Constantinos Costa Christou, 'Society Variety', *Expose*, 30 October 2017, p. 9.

Chapter One: Introduction
1. Talk to Departmental Archaeological Society, 17 March 2009.

2. Rush to Black, 20 October 2013.
3. Interview, 2012.
4. Simon Holme, Geography 2017–, interview, 5 February 2018.

Chapter Two: The 1950s: The New University
1. J. Black, *A History of Britain: 1945 to BREXIT* (Bloomington, IN, 2017).
2. For the earlier situation, T. Pietsch, *Empire of Scholars. Universities, Networks and the British Academic World 1850–1939* (Manchester, 2013).
3. Academic Secretary 1950–54 and before that a lecturer in Classics.
4. Liaison Committee, 5 July 1963.
5. Standing Committee, 28 October 1959.
6. *Annual Report 1957–58*, pp. 2–3.
7. John Balsom (General Science, 1958–61) to Black, 20 September 2013.
8. Mike Dobson (reporting Ken Penny) to Black, 29 September 2013. As an instance of changing values, Robin Turner was to irritate staff in the 1980s by making reference in Senate to what had been done at Cambridge where he had earlier been an academic.
9. N. Orme, 'The Great Escape', *History Today* (March 2011), pp. 44–45.
10. Reg Erskine, who joined the Registry in 1955, retiring as Deputy Registrar in 1986 but continuing part-time until 1987.
11. He had been Registrar of the University College in 1952–54, and then Secretary.
12. Jeremy Noakes, 'Some Thoughts', 2012.
13. Michael Duffy, interview, 18 September 2013.
14. H.T.S. Britton, 'The University of Exeter', *Journal of the Royal Institute of Chemistry* (November 1956), p. 622.
15. Professor Sir Keith Sykes to Black, 23 September 2012.
16. Mennell was a Labour activist and city councillor.
17. Mennell to Black, 9 August 2013.
18. Referring to Bob Dowse and himself, Michael Rush to Black, 20 October 2013.
19. Bill Tupman to Black, 10 January 2013.
20. Fletcher to Black, 20 September 2012. See also Keith Cameron (Single Honours French with German, 1957–61) to Black, 27 October 2013.
21. e.g. *South Westerner*, 3 November 1955; Sue Odell to Black, 14 October 2013; Melody Dougan to Black, 3 January. 2018.
22. F. Fuller, *The History of St Luke's College, Exeter, 1839–1970* (Exeter, 1970); J. Priestley, *Saint Luke's College, 1839–1978* (Exeter, 1978).
23. Richardson to Black, 15 August 2013.
24. Newitt, memorandum for Black, August 2012.
25. *South Westerner*, 23 November 1955.
26. Standing Committee, 19 October 1955.
27. Standing Committee, 30 November 1955; Senate, 8 February 1956; *South Westerner*, 9 November 1955.
28. Senate, 20 May 1959.
29. Whitfield to Black, 3 September 2012.
30. *South Westerner*, 9 December 1955.
31. The amalgamation of university extension and technical education in Exeter led, in 1893, to the Exeter Technical and University Extension College, which was renamed the

Albert Memorial College in 1899, and the Royal Albert Memorial College in 1900, and was often thereafter called the Royal Albert Memorial University College.
32. Sir Keith Murray, Chair of UGC, to Cook, 31 January 1958.
33. Works Committee, 30 October 1959.
34. Faculty of Law, 25 April, Faculty of Arts, 1, 14 May 1959.
35. Quinquennial Developments Committee, 30 November 1959.
36. Quinquennial Developments Committee, 19 December 1959, revised to 37 in meeting of 16 January 1960.
37. Coe to Black, 25 August 2013.
38. A distant hall acquired in 1944.
39. B. Ridge, *Chemistry at Exeter* (Exeter, 1992), p. 4.
40. Winter to Black, 5 October 2012.
41. G.W. Knight, *Jackson Knight: A Biography* (Oxford, 1975), pp. 189–355; T.P. Wiseman, *Talking to Virgil* (Exeter, 1992), pp. 171–209.
42. Smith to Black, 2012.
43. Smith to Black, 2012.
44. Mackintosh to Black, 19 March 2013.
45. Eley to Black, 2012.
46. Dougan to Black, 3 January 2018.
47. Williamson to Black [2012]. Several other students of the period refer to card-playing.
48. Dare to Black, 21 October 2012.
49. Gordon to Black, 16 February 2013.
50. Minogue to Black, 1 October 2012.
51. Balsom to Black, 20 September 2013.
52. *South Westerner*, 16 November 1955.
53. Memorandum by Martin Biddle and Christopher Platt, enclosed in Platt to Cook, 7 May 1964; reply, Cook to Platt, 11 May 1964; Ken Schofield, memorandum for Senate on 5 February 1964, all in Biddle papers; Biddle to Black, 28 December 2012.
54. Ross to Biddle, 21 May 1964, Biddle papers.
55. *The Times*, 30 May 1964, p. 6.

Chapter Three: Into the 1960s: Major Expansion
1. A reference to the move from Gandy Street to Queen's.
2. Langhorne to Black, 5 August 2013.
3. For the background, R.O. Berdahl, *British Universities and the State* (Cambridge, 1959).
4. Senate, 10 February 1960.
5. Cook to Senate, 25 January 1960.
6. Quinquennial Committee, 6 February 1960.
7. Faculty of Science, 20 January 1960.
8. Faculty of Arts, 27 June 1960.
9. Finance Memorandum by Guild [spring 1960].
10. Sir Keith Murray, Chair of UGC, to Cook, 31 March 1960.
11. D. Daiches, *The Idea of a New University: An Experiment in Sussex* (London, 1964).
12. UGC letter, 24 October, Council, 28 October 1963.
13. Cook to Wolfenden, 15 January 1964.
14. ADC, 16 November 1964. In the event, there were to be 2,953 students in October 1967, 3,056 in October 1968 and 3,562 in October 1971.

15. *The Department of Chemistry in the University of Exeter* (Exeter, 1965), p. 10.
16. Senate, 20 Nov. 1963.
17. Langhorne to Black, 5 August 2013. For criticism of Barlow, including as tyrannical and obstructive, A. Fox, *Aileen – A Pioneering Archaeologist* (Leominster, 2000), pp. 129–30, 137, but Biddle backed Barlow in believing that Fox should have known Latin if working on the archaeology of Roman Britain: Biddle to Black, 18 December 2012. See also the tributes in D. Bates, J. Crick and S. Hamilton (eds), *Writing Medieval Biography: Essays in Honour of Frank Barlow* (Woodbridge, 2006).
18. Interview, 24 July 2013. For 'an Arts establishment', *University of Exeter Gazette*, 9 July 1981, speech by Public Orator on behalf of Rydon.
19. P. Wiseman, obituary in *The Independent*, 24 December 1999.
20. Michael Rush to Black, 20 October 2013.
21. Mennell to Black, 9 August 2013.
22. James Barber to Black, 1 January 2013. Nicholas Orme takes the same view of Barlow. Orme, interview, October 2013.
23. The atmosphere in Knightley is widely praised, although Roger Burt described it as 'colonial'.
24. For the national context, W. Whyte, *Redbrick: A Social and Architectural History of Britain's Civic Universities* (Oxford, 2015).
25. Standing Committee, 1 March, 10 May 1961.
26. Report of the Wardens for Senate on 7 December 1960.
27. Bates to Black, 6 May 2013.
28. Longhurst to Black, 4 July 2013.
29. Dewey to Black, 21 January 2013.
30. Joint Committee of Management, 13 December 1961; Senate, 7 February 1962.
31. For the account by one of its members, A. Fox, *Aileen*, pp. 134–35.
32. *Annual Report* 1956–57, p. 5.
33. Reg Erskine, interview, 17 October 2013.
34. Joint Committee of Management, Refectory and Devonshire House, 23 April 1964.
35. Dewey to Black, 21 January 2013.
36. Fletcher to Black, 9 October 2012.
37. Pillinger to Black, 24 September, 9 October 2012.
38. Ellis to Black, 7 November 2012.
39. Rush to Black, 24 January 2013.
40. Works Committee, 9 October 1964.
41. Council, 25 May 1964.
42. Bob Alcock, interview, 2012.
43. Council, 13 July, ADC, 16 November 1964; Wolfenden to Cook, 27 November 1964.
44. Council, 26 October 1964.
45. Council, 22 June 1964.
46. Brian Kirby to Black, 3 October 2012.
47. Bates to Black, 6 May 2013. See also Peter Quartermaine (English, 1960–63, later staff) to Black, 13 November 2012. Bates went on to a distinguished academic career, notably as Director of the Institute of Historical Research.

Chapter Four: The Later 1960s: Social Change
1. Senate, 6 November 1968; Jones to Black, 18 December 2012.

2. Keith Sykes to Black, 23 September 2012.
3. Information from Behenna, Sir John Hanson, Erskine, Abel, and Schofield.
4. Bates to Black, 8 September 2013.
5. Erskine, who argues that wardens did not on the whole burst in and that their scrutiny should not be overdone, points out that this student had been caught for the second time and had ignored warnings, Erskine to Black, 17 October 2013.
6. Gordon to Black, 2 February 2013.
7. Joint Committee of Management, Refectory and Devonshire House, 14 October 1966.
8. Meredith to Black, 2 May 2013.
9. Brian and Pam Langdon-Pratt to Black, 2012.
10. M. Gidley, 'Charles Causley in the University', in M. Hanke (ed.), *Through the Granite Kingdom: Critical Essays on Charles Causley* (Trier, 2012), p. 279. See also M. Merchant, *Fragments of a Life* (Llandysul, 1990), esp. pp. 111–15.
11. Robinson to Black, 29 May 2013; Barber to Black, 1 January 2013; Christopher Paterson, interview, 15 December 2012.
12. A. Fox, *Aileen – A Pioneering Archaeologist* (Leominster, 2000), pp. 133–34; Standing Committee, 12 October 1966.
13. Newitt to Black, August 2012.
14. Standing Committee, 25 November 1968, Works Committee, 6 December 1968.
15. Rush to Black, 20 October 2013.
16. Notes of meeting on 29 January 1965.
17. Council, 21 February 1966.
18. Eddie Abel, interview, 22 October 2012.
19. Behenna, interview, 31 Aug. 2012.
20. Joint Committee of Management, Refectory and Devonshire House, 14 October 1966.
21. Standing Committee, 24 November 1965.
22. Meredith to Black, 2 May 2013.
23. Wolfenden to Cook, 3 January 1966; Statement by Wolfenden to Council, 28 January 1966.
24. Senate, 15 March 1956.
25. Joint Committee of Management, 13 January 1967.
26. Senate, 1 November 1967.
27. A Gestetner or Roneo machine.
28. Mennell to Black, 9 August 2013. A similar situation regarding telephones existed in other departments.
29. Jackson to Black, 13 August 2013.
30. Works Committee, 3 February 1967.
31. M. Shattock, *Making Policy in British Higher Education 1945–2010* (London, 2012).
32. The City of Exeter had stopped its grant.
33. Llewellyn to ADC, 26 January 1967.
34. ADC, 7 February 1967.
35. Works Committee, 7 Mar. 1969.
36. Senate, 24 May 1967.
37. Senate, 27 June 1967.
38. Strongman to Black, 14 February 2013.
39. As a typo, this was originally ballroom danger. Barlow also enjoyed driving fast on

autobahns, on which there was no speed limit, accompanied by a younger female friend, Duffy, interview, 18 September 2013. Also mentioned in other interviews.
40. Rush to Black, 20 October 2013.
41. Pelopida to Black, 16 April, and undated, 2013.
42. Residential Development Building Sub-Committee of Works Committee, 10 June 1969.
43. Noakes himself had been at Westminster. Bruce Coleman also commented on the level of car ownership, Coleman to Black, October 2013.
44. Clapp, *University of Exeter*, p. 129.
45. This had also impressed Katharine Weale a year earlier. Weale to Black, 7 September 2012.
46. In 1955–58 the Mardon men were from 'mostly grammar school and lower middle class backgrounds'; Peter Whitfield to Black, 3 September 2012.
47. 'A formidable Scot who set a very ladylike tone'; Weale to Black, 7 September 2012. For praise of Ross lecturing in Education, Carol Weitz to Black, 14 August 2012.
48. Odell to Black, 20 August 2012.
49. The student society; Jones was eventually its President.
50. Jones to Black, 28 December 2012.
51. Michael Langrish, Bishop of Exeter, interview and letter, 2012.
52. Thurmer to Black, 28 August 2012; Moss to Black, 21 April 2013; R. Leaper, *Change and Continuity. The Story of Sacred Heart Parish, Exeter* (Exeter, 2005), p. 114.
53. Jones to Black, 29 October 2012.
54. Weale to Black, 7 September 2012.
55. French to Black, 23 May 2013.
56. Higham, talk to Departmental Archaeological Society, 17 March 2009.
57. A. Fox, *Aileen*, p. 137.
58. Council, 23 December 1968, 21 January 1969.
59. Senate, 10 December 1969.
60. Havinden to Black, 18 August 2013.
61. Faulkner to Black, 22 August 2012.
62. Faulkner to Black, 21 August 2012.
63. Homberger to Black, 21 December 2013.
64. Duffy to Black, 2 October 2012. Coleman had a similar response, Coleman to Black, October 2013.
65. Greenaway, Address, 10 May 1968, Black papers.

Chapter Five: The Early 1970s: The Brakes Go On
1. Board of Senate, 30 January, 22 May 1974.
2. Works Committee, 26 November 1973.
3. Board of Senate, 22 May 1974.
4. Standing Committee, 16 January 1974.
5. Estcourt to Black, 21 August 2012.
6. H.E.S. Fisher (ed.), *The Erratics. Fifty Not Out: A History of the University of Exeter Staff Cricket Club, 1934–1984* (Exeter, 1987) and *The Erratics. The Glory Decade; University Staff Cricket at Exeter* (Exeter, 1997); B. Ridge, *Chemistry at Exeter* (Exeter, 1992), p. 6. For the importance of being believed to play cricket, Robert Leaper, interview, 6 December 2012.

7. Duffy claims that this was because far more historians attended the Coffee Room. Duffy, interview, 18 September 2013.
8. Hitchcock to Black, 8 September 2012.
9. Hitchcock to Black, 8 September 2012. For praise of the Coffee Room, Chris Gill (Classics) to Black, 6 October 2013.
10. Cockrell to Black, 16 September 2013.
11. David Catchpole to Black, 4 December 2013.
12. Brian Clapp, *The University of Exeter: A History* (Exeter, 1982)
13. Stirling, interview, and Stirling to Black, 9 October 2013.
14. Paul Auchterlonie to Black, 13 October 2013.
15. Senate, 11 February, Council 23 February 1970.
16. Leaper, interview, 6 December 2012.
17. Yates to Black, 21 August 2012.
18. For a far more positive account of Parker, emphasising that he was a man of his generation, Bridge to Black, 26 September 2013.
19. D. Bates, 'Frank Barlow 1911–2009', *Proceedings of the British Academy*, 172 (2011), p. 18; Jim Miles (1969–72) to Black, 27 September 2013.
20. Rush to Black, 24 January, 20 October 2013; Jeff Stanyer, interview.
21. Abel, interview, 22 January 2012.
22. Gladstone to Black, 24 August 2012.
23. Coleman to Black, 20 October 2012.
24. Bridge et al (eds), *Fundamental Rights* (London, 1973); Lasok et al (eds), *Fundamental Duties* (Oxford, 1980).
25. Mayor to Black, 8 August 2013.
26. M. Weaver and M. Gidley, 'Film in the Context of American (and Commonwealth) Arts', *Screen Education Notes*, 7 (summer 1973), pp. 21–27; M. Weaver, 'Film Studies with Undergraduates', in M. Gidley and S. Wicks (eds), *Film Education: A Collection of Experiences and Ideas* (Exeter, 1975), pp. 78–81.
27. Council 23 February 1970.
28. I have benefited from the advice of Christopher Paterson, the Guild President at the time.
29. Council, 8 June 1970.
30. Council, 10 February, 10 March, Council, 22 March 1971.
31. Senate, 26 May, 3 November 1971.
32. Senate, 10 July 1970.
33. Council, 16 November 1970, 7 June 1971.
34. Council, 21 February, 25 June 1972.
35. Senate, 8 December 1971.
36. Works Committee, 30 April 1971; Working Party on Car Parking, 19 March, 27 April 1971; Development Report, March 1971, p. 38.
37. Car Parking Sub-Committee, 21 December 1972.
38. Senate, 9 February, 24 May 1972.
39. Abel, interview, 17 October 2013.
40. Erskine to Black, 17 October 2013.
41. Senate, 1 November 1972.
42. See also Board of Senate, 3 July 1973.
43. Estcourt to Black, 30 August 2012.

44. Potter to Black, 8 November 2012.
45. Overton to Black, 17 September 2013.
46. Miles to Black, 27 September 2013.
47. Neither were then actual departments.
48. A Joint Committee of Council and Senate to consider the headship of Russian, held on 2 August 1974, agreed to postpone the post until October 1975.
49. Works Committee, 13 May, Board of Senate, 25 June 1974, Council, 8 July 1974.
50. Behenna, interview, 31 August 2012; Behenna to Black, 6 February 2018; Christine Faunch to Black, 6 February 2018.
51. Works Committee, 29 January 1973.
52. Standing Committee, 24 January, 16 May 1973.
53. ADC, 10 February 1973.
54. Board of Senate, 13 July 1973.
55. Board of Senate, 31 October 1973.
56. Board of Senate, 31 October, 5 December 1973; Working Party on Student Residence, 6 February 1974.
57. ADC, 28 January, Board of Senate, 30 January, Council, 11 February 1974.
58. ADC, 6 February 1974.
59. Standing Committee, 16 October 1974.
60. Caseldine to Black, 16 July 2013.
61. Mayes to Black, 22 March 2013; Niblock, interview, 6 October 2013.
62. Bryony Coles to Black, 15 October 2013.

Chapter Six: The Later 1970s: A Divided University
1. The building had been in use from the summer of 1974. Text from the *University of Exeter Gazette*.
2. The 'life-changing' nature of university recurs frequently in comments, e.g. John Balson to Black, 20 September 2013.
3. A 'firm undertaking' was agreed on 1 December 1976 by 51–3–8.
4. Joint Committee on Residences, 12 May 1975.
5. Board of Senate, 24 June 1975.
6. Standing Committee, 19 November 1975.
7. Board of Senate, 8 January, UGC letter of 9 January 1975.
8. Philip Payton to Black, 8 January 2018.
9. Council, 17 March, Board of Senate, 21 May 1975.
10. Council, 2 June 1975.
11. Board of Senate, 21 May 1975. J.F. Stirling, 'The Library within the University: General Organisation and Administration; Staff Structure; Finance. Case-study of Exeter University Library', in J.F. Stirling (ed.), *University Librarianship* (London, 1981), pp. 1–99.
12. Standing Committee, 7 May, ADC 9 May, 4 June, 1975.
13. T.P. Wiseman, *Titus Flavius and the Indivisible Subject* (Exeter, 1978), pp. 6–7.
14. Yates to Black, 10 October 2013.
15. Council, 17 March 1975.
16. Board of Senate, 3 March, Joint Committee on Catering and Residence, 14 May, Council 7 June 1976.
17. Gladstone to Black, 23 February 2013.

18. Erskine to Black, 17 October 2013.
19. Dobson to Black, 29 September 2013.
20. Erskine, Deputy Registrar, interview, 27 February 2013.
21. Erskine to Black, 17 October 2013.
22. Behenna to Black, 5 February 2018.
23. Hitchcock, interview, July 2013.
24. Newitt to Black, 6 February 2018.
25. Behenna to Black, 6 February 2018.
26. Interviews confirm this.
27. According to Coleman, the lists came to him via Tim Reuter, when Reuter went to Munich, and he destroyed them when the department moved from Queen's to Amory in 1999 and he weeded his papers. Interviews with Behenna, Duffy, Coleman and Preist in 2012–13; Coleman to Black, October 2013, 7 February 2018; Newitt to Black, 4 January 2018. Reuter is dead.
28. Brian Clapp, *The University of Exeter: A History* (Exeter, 1982).
29. Rush to Black, 20 October 2013.
30. Havinden to Black, 18 August 2013; Burt, memorandum on Economic History, December 2012; Overton to Black, 17 September 2013.
31. Burt to Black, 7 May 2013.
32. Davenport-Hines to Black, 27 April 2013. For Minchinton as violent, Mayes to Black, 22 March 2013, remarks by John Blair, etc.
33. Erskine, interview, 9 February 2018.
34. Simon Baker to Black, 6 February 2018.
35. For Coleman as Dean standing up to Porter over sexual harassment of a student while Kay did nothing, Coleman, interview, 6 February 2013.
36. Coleman to Black, October 2013, 7 February 2018; Burt to Black, 7 February 2018; Erskine, interview, 9 February 2018.
37. Jones to Black, 18 December 2012. Again, note the importance of letting the quotation run on.
38. B.W. Clapp, *The University of Exeter: A History* (Exeter, 1982), p. 152.
39. Thorpe to Black, 2 July 2013.
40. Mayes to Black, 22 March 2013. For Kay as 'absolutely useless', interview with Schofield.
41. Niblock to Black, 2 October 2013.
42. Erskine, interview, 9 February 2018.
43. Burt, interview, 9 September 2013.
44. Kay, Senate, Special meeting, 4 October 1974.
45. Batty to Black, 7 October 2013; Erskine, interview, 17 October 2013.
46. Working Party, 2 October 1974.
47. The Maynard, a private school, was reportedly full. Behenna interview, 31 August 2012.
48. Coleman to Black, October 2013, 9 January, 7 February 2018.
49. Yates to Black, 16, 21 August 2012.
50. Interview, 6 December 2012.
51. Coleman to Black, October 2013.
52. Tallack to Black, 16 July 2013.
53. ADC, 21 October 1975.
54. ADC, 19 January, Board of Senate, 4 February 1976.
55. ADC, 18 April 1977.

56. ADC, 18 April 1977.
57. ADC, 18 April 1977.
58. Council, 13 June 1977.
59. Council, Board of Senate, 25 May, 13 June 1977.
60. ADC, 29 June 1978.
61. Yates to Black, undated 26 March 2013.
62. ADC, 29 June 1978; Yates, interview, 2012.
63. Guild papers. For different views on the value of Guild intervention in Exeter's politics, see comments by Mike Roude and Chris Tiratsoo, Extraordinary General Meeting, 20 January 1978.
64. Board of Senate, 30 November, Senate 30 November 1977. For the left-wing Guild as out of line with most students, Dobson (Combined Honours Arts, 1976–79) to Black, 29 September 2013.
65. Myhill to Black, 8 April 2013.
66. Working Party, 4 December 1974.
67. ADC, 4 June, Board of Senate, 24 June, 29 October 1975.
68. Board of Senate, 27 October 1976.
69. Edward Neather to Black, 17 March 2013.
70. Richardson, memorandum and interview, August 2013.
71. K. Shaw, 'Exeter: From College of Education to University', in R.J. Alexander, M. Craft and J. Lynch (eds), *Change in Teacher Education: Context and Provision since Robbins* (London, 1984), pp. 203–14.
72. Eulogy for Wragg by Richard Pring, delivered at memorial service, *Guardian*, 7 February 2006.
73. Richardson, memorandum and interview, August 2013.
74. Philippe Oboussier (Music, St Luke's, 1966–81), to Black, 23 March 2013.
75. *Exeposé*, 30 November 1992.
76. RLA discussion document; Board of Senate, 28 June, 26 October 1977; Newitt to Black, 4 January 2018.
77. Senate, 6 October 1978.
78. Senate, 6 October 1978.
79. This did not address the situation in Economic History.
80. Turner to Black, 2012.
81. Kelly, interview, 13 August 2012.
82. UGC to University, 9 January 1978.
83. ADC, 24 October 1978.
84. ADC, 7 November 1978.
85. Standing Committee, 21 May, 14 June 1978.
86. Senate, 12 January 1979.
87. Moss to Black, 21 April 2013.
88. Board of Senate, 6 December 1978.
89. Council, 13 November 1978.
90. Council, 16 July 1979.
91. Board of Senate, 31 October 1979.
92. Council, 12 November 1979.
93. Council, 12 November 1979.
94. Council, 13 June 1977.

95. Council, 4 June 1979.
96. Board of Senate, 7 March 1979.
97. T. Becher and M. Kogan, *Process and Structure in Higher Education* (London, 1980).
98. J. Black, *Britain since the Seventies* (London, 2004).

Chapter Seven: The Early 1980s: Crisis for an Old Order

1. ADC, 7 July 1981.
2. Edward Parkes, Chair of UGC, to Kay, 1 July 1981.
3. ADC, 3 June 1980, Board of Senate, 4 February, 9 December 1981, 26 May 1982.
4. Board of Senate, 11 March 1981.
5. Konstantin Chernenko was the somewhat ineffective Soviet leader (1984–85) after Yuri Andropov (1982–84), who had been KGB chief.
6. Behenna, interview, 31 August 2012.
7. Council, 23 March 1981.
8. Board of Senate, 6 February 1980.
9. Board of Senate, 30 June 1981.
10. It recurred, e.g. Board of Senate, 4 February 1981.
11. The Standing Committee of Senate (18 June 1980) subsequently decided to leave the issue to individual departments while rejecting representation on faculty boards, ADC and itself. The Board of Senate (1 July) referred the issue back to the Standing Committee.
12. This gift came as a result of a request from Glencairn Balfour-Paul, a former diplomat who was then Honorary Research Fellow in the Centre for Arab Gulf Studies.
13. Board of Senate, 4 November 1981.
14. Senate, 17 March, Board of Senate, 26 May 1982.
15. Abel interview, 22 October 2012.
16. Stuart Bosworth, Registrar of Salford and later member of the Council of the University of Exeter, interview, 19 September 2012.
17. Board of Senate, 11 March 1981.
18. Catchpole to Black, 4 December 2013.
19. Board of Senate, 25 May, 16 November 1983.
20. Standing Committee, 11 May 1982.
21. Standing Committee, 13 October 1982.
22. Council, 15 November 1982, Standing Committee, 9 February 1983.
23. Report on Provenance of Students, June, Board of Senate, 5 July, Council, 18 July 1983.
24. Board of Studies, 21 November 1984.
25. P. Wiseman, 'The Head of Department's Story', *Pegasus*, 53 (2010), pp. 32–34.
26. Board of Senate, 26 May 1982.
27. Cook to Black, 21 September 2012.
28. Corner, interview, July 2013.
29. Board of Senate, 3 July 1984.
30. 4, 25 November 1980. See also Kay in Board of Senate, 26 May 1982.
31. Board of Senate, 3 December 1980.
32. Coleman to Black, October 2013.
33. Board of Senate, 20 May 1981.
34. Council, 16 November 1981
35. Coleman to Black, October 2013.

36. Board of Senate, 3 December 1980.
37. Council, 19 July 1982.
38. Ken Read, a former student.
39. A member of staff.
40. Duffy to Black, 18 February 2018.
41. Board of Senate, 16 March 1983.
42. Board of Senate, 16 November, 7 December 1983; Duffy to Black, 8 February 2018.
43. Leaper, interview, 6 December 2012.
44. Board of Senate, 3 July 1984.
45. Senate, 3 July 1984.
46. ADC, 4 December 1984.
47. Webley to Black, 14 August 2012.
48. For example, Macglasham, Leadbetter and Roberts in Chemistry, Flower and Wakeley in Engineering, Flower in French, Odoni in Mathematics, Usher in Law, S. Braund in Classics, Samson in Music.
49. Stones to Black, 3 January 2018.

Chapter Eight: The Late 1980s: Difficult Years, Again

1. Driver to Black, 10 July 2013.
2. Rowling, 'The Fringe Benefits of Failure, and the Importance of Imagination, 2008 Commencement Address at Harvard', *Harvard Magazine*; see also Rowling, 'What Was the Name of that Nymph Again? Or Greek and Roman Studies Recalled,' *Pegasus*, 41 (1998), pp. 25–27. Professor X is Hugh Stubbs, as is Z, the Professor Binns of one of her novels. Dr Y is Richard Seaford. I would like to thank Peter Wiseman for the identifications.
3. Harrison taught in that department in Cambridge. The Engineering Building in Exeter is named after him.
4. Abel, interview, 22 October 2012.
5. *Exeposé*, 18 January 1993.
6. Kelly to Black, 14 November 2012.
7. Javid, interview, November 2012, Javid to Black, 18 January 2013.
8. Niblock to Black, 2 October 2013.
9. Joint Committee for Consultation and Negotiation, Council and Exeter AUT, 15 February 1985.
10. Senate, 27 Feb, Board of Senate, 29 May 1985, Council, 10 June 1985.
11. Faculty of Arts, 15 May 1985.
12. Board of Senate, 29 May 1985.
13. Odell to Black, 20 August 2012.
14. Coleman to Black, 28 October 2013.
15. Brian Clapp, *The University of Exeter: A History* (Exeter, 1982).
16. For a failure to rein in Sha'ban and a 'colonial' outlook, Niblock to Black, 2 October 2013.
17. Harvey, interview, August 2012. Since you ask, this was the most agreeable of the interviews: it took place in a café on Budleigh seafront, eating crab sandwiches.
18. Mennell to Black, 9 August, 23 September 2013.
19. Note on Research Selectivity, 9 February 1985.
20. UGC Letter, 7 February 1985.
21. Board of Senate, 27 February 1985, memo from Sims.

22. ADC, 7 May 1985.
23. Council, 10 June 1985.
24. Standing Committee, 10 May 1988.
25. Faulkner to Black, 21 August 2012.
26. *Exeposé*, 7 June 1993, 18 January 1998, 8 May 2000. For concern about 'elitist dinner parties', Guild Finance Committee discussion of Polyglots Society, 2 November 1977.
27. Garnett to Black, 28 August 2013.
28. Board of Senate, 26 February 1986.
29. Coleman to Black, October 2013.
30. Joint Committee for Consultation and Negotiation, Council and EAUT, 8 May 1986; Board of Senate, 6 July 1987.
31. Trotter to Black, 10 July 2013.
32. ADC, 10 June, 14 October 1986, Board of Senate, 7 July, 19 November 1986.
33. M. Blacksell and A.W. Gilg, *The Countryside: Planning and Change* (London, 1981); M. Blacksell, K. Economides and C. Watkins, *Justice outside the City. Access to Legal services in Rural BRITAIN* (Harlow, 1991); Blacksell, obituary, *Geographical Journal*, 174, no. 2 (June 2008), pp. 179–81.
34. Barry to Black, 19 October 2013.
35. Lang to Black, 14 June 2013.
36. Faulkner to Black, 21, 25 August 2012.
37. Simms to Black, 17 August 2013.
38. Council, 21 July 1986.
39. Council, 15 December 1986.
40. Board of Senate, 25 February 1987.
41. Board of Senate, 19 November 1986.
42. Planning and Resources Committee, 24 November 1986.
43. Board of Senate, 19 November, 10 December 1986, 25 February 1987.
44. Standing Committee, 4 November 1987.
45. Board of Senate, 25 February, 6 July 1987.
46. Council, 20 July 1987.
47. ADC, 13 October, 10 November 1987; Board of Senate, 18 November 1987.
48. Kenneth Coe, Reader in Petrology, to Harrison, 27 May 1985, Coe Papers; Coe to Black, 25 August 2013.
49. Brown to Black, 15 January 2013.
50. Board of Senate, 18 November 1987.
51. Board of Senate, 18 November, 1987, 24, 25 May 1988.
52. Board of Senate, 24 February 1988.
53. ADC, 8 March 1988.
54. Council, 21 March 1988.
55. Board of Senate, 4 July 1988.
56. Summary of visit by Swinnerton-Dyer to members of Council, 16 November, Board of Senate, 16 November 1988.
57. Council, 8 June 1988.
58. Council, 12 December 1988.
59. Board of Senate, 7 December 1988.
60. Board of Senate, 24 May 1989.
61. Council, 20 Mar. 1989.

62. Committee of Deans, 9 May 1989.
63. Board of Senate, 22 February 1989.
64. Board of Senate, 24 May 1989.
65. Board of Senate, 3 July 1989.
66. Council, 7 June 1989.
67. Senate, 24 May 1989.
68. He was also due to retire on 30 September, and did so. See also Council, 17 July 1989.
69. ADC, 6 June 1989.
70. Abel, interview, 22 October 2012; Niblock, interview, 6 October 2013; Rush to Black, 20 October 2013: Rush also comments on the role of personalities in the 1989 results.
71. Inkson to Black, 5 April 2013. For example, in History there were complaints about 'a "Golden Triangle" disdain for places like Exeter ... we weren't doing the fashionable ... history'. Source not wishing to be named, to Black, October 2013.
72. Inkson to Black, 5 Ap. 2013.
73. Minutes of University Committee, 6 November 1989.
74. Abel, interview, 17 October 2013. For the background, M. Shattock, *The UGC and the Management of British Universities* (Buckingham, 1994).
75. Odell to Black, 20 August 2012.
76. Powell to Black, 16 October 2012.
77. Cook, interview, 7 October 2013; Thorpe to Black, 6 February 2018; Simon Baker to Black, 6 February 2018.
78. Behenna to Black, 6 February 2018.
79. Shaw to Black, 14 February 2013.

Chapter Nine: The Early 1990s: Change Starting
1. Parsons and Balfour-Paul, who were unpaid, both taught and published. A very good teacher, Clutterbuck published extensively.
2. Board of Senate, 2 July, 14 November 1990.
3. Duffy to Black, 8 February 2018.
4. Board of Senate, 22 May; PRC, 31 May 1991.
5. Abel, interview, 22 October 2012.
6. Board of Senate, 1 July 1991.
7. Draft Institutional Plan, December 1991.
8. Research Committee, 30 May, PRC, 31 May 1991.
9. Inkson to Black, 5 April 2013.
10. Board of Senate, 27 November, 11 December 1991.
11. Board of Senate, 27 May, 6 July, Council, 20 July 1992.
12. *Exeposé*, 25 October, 1, 8 November 1993.
13. *Exeposé*, 12 November 1993; the phone box was much in demand for the more amorous.
14. *Exeposé*, 18, 25 January, 1, 8 February, 8 March 1993.
15. *Exeposé*, 5, 10, 17 May 1993.
16. APC, 12 October 1993, May 10 1994.
17. Board of Senate, 3 March 1993.
18. Board of Studies, 5 July 1993.
19. 'Lecturer's fury at onslaught', *Express and Echo*, 20 March 1993.
20. Powell, interview, 16 October 2013.
21. Wilks, interview, 2013.

22. APC, 12 October 1993.
23. Board of Senate, 5 July 1993.
24. For university concern with recycling, *Exeposé*, 22 November 1993. In October 2013, the Students' Green Unit was launched by the Guild. It funded sustainability initiatives by students. See http://www.exeterguild.org/greenunit/
25. Wilks to Black, 14 August 2013; Niblock to Black, 6 October 2013.
26. Preist to Black, 29 October 2012.
27. Senate, 23 November 1994.
28. Senate, 23 November 1994.
29. Abel, interviews, 22 October 2012, 17 October 2013; Powell, interview, 16 October 2013; Holland, interview, 9 November 2011; Carol Holland and Michael Partridge, obituary of Geoffrey Holland, *TW* (2017), pp. 66-7.
30. Coleman to Black, 8 February 2018.
31. Cooper to Black, 12 September 2013.
32. Joint Committee for Consultation and Negotiation-University Council and Exeter Association of University Teachers, 11 November 1992.
33. Philip Payton to Black, 6 December 2017.
34. Powell, interview, 16 October 2013.
35. APC, 15 March 1994.
36. Abel, interviews, 22 October 2012, 17 October 2013.
37. Preist to Black, 29 October, Partridge to Black, 4 September, Powell to Black, 27 July; Coleman to Black, 9 February 2018.
38. Newitt to Black, 4 January 2018.
39. Alcock to Black, 16 October 2013.
40. Tony Brown to Black, 15 January 2013.
41. Holland, interview, 9 November 2011.

Chapter Ten: The Later 1990s

1. Powell to Black, 16 October 2013.
2. Tribute by Ruth Hawker, his successor, Council, 20 December 2004.
3. Newitt to Black, 9 January 2018.
4. Newitt, 'Exeter University in the 1980s and 1990s', memorandum, August 2012.
5. Holland, interview, 9 November 2012.
6. Senate, 23 November 1994, 1 March 1995.
7. Senate, 23 November 1994.
8. Clapp, *University of Exeter*, pp. 70–72; Keith Sykes to Black, 23 September 2012.
9. Strongly criticising the content, language and tone of Holland's *Strategy Review 2000: A Paper for Discussion*, Wiseman to Holland, 31 October 2000, Wiseman papers.
10. Paterson to Black, 13 April 2013.
11. Holland, interview, 29 2012.
12. Thorpe to Black, 2 July 2013.
13. Newitt, 'Exeter University in the 1980s and 1990s', memorandum, August 2012.
14. R. Dearing, *Higher Education in the Learning Society. The National Committee of Inquiry into Higher Education* (London, 1997); Z. Bauman, 'Universities: Old, New and Different', in A. Smith and F. Webster (eds), *The Post-Modern University? Contested Visions of Higher Education in Society* (Buckingham, 1997), pp. 17–26; N. Blake, R. Smith and P. Standish, *The Universities We Need: Higher Education after Dearing* (London, 1998); T. Dickson,

'UK Universities and the State: a Faustian Bargain?', *Economic Affairs*, 21 (2001), pp. 23–29.
15. Holland, interview, 9 November 2012.
16. Inkson to Black, 3 April 2013; Atkinson to Black, 13 January, 27 August 2013.
17. Report of conversation between David Catchpole, Professor of Theology and John Rogerson, Professor of Biblical Studies at Sheffield, who chaired the subject panel, 24 January 1997, Catchpole papers.
18. M. Baimbridge, 'Institutional Research Performance 1992–96: A Tale of Two Sectors', *Journal of Further and Higher Education*, 22 (1998), pp. 69–78.
19. Armstrong to Black, 6 December 2012.
20. Powell to Black, 27 July 2012.
21. Interviews, Holland, Kain.
22. Holland to Heads of Departments, 13 May 1997.
23. Holland to Wiseman, 25 March 1997, Wiseman papers.
24. Inkson to Black, 5 April 2013.
25. See also the memorandum by Barry for the meeting of Planning and Resources Committee on 19 June 1997 attacking a failure in 1992–96 to make strategic investments.
26. Catchpole to Holland, 4 June, Gordon Dunstan to Major-General Crowdy, Chairman, St Luke's Foundation Trustees, 5 July 1997, Catchpole papers.
27. For criticism of teaching in Law, *Exeposé*, 26 June 2000.
28. Harvey, interview, August 2012.
29. Cockrell to Black, 2013.
30. Gareth Stansfield, oration for Niblock in Sharjah, 26 September 2013.
31. *Exeposé*, 2 March 1997.
32. *Exeposé*, 26 October 1997, 29 November 1993, 9 December 1996. See also, e.g. 1 June 1993, 19 January 1997.
33. *Exeposé*, 17 November 1996. This issue also discussed whether postgraduates were randier than undergraduates.
34. *Exeposé*, 21 October 1996.
35. *Exeposé*, 2 March 1997.
36. Morgan-Owen to Black, 1 January 2018.
37. Johnson to Black, 31 December 2017.
38. *Exeposé*, 22, 29 November 1993.
39. Coleman to Black, 20 October 2012.
40. Swinburne to Black, 31 December 2017.
41. Senate, 26 November 1997.
42. Wiseman to Holland, 12, 21 March 1997, Wiseman papers.
43. Cook to Black, 23 January 2018.
44. Morgan to Black, 2 September 2013.
45. Powell to Black, 27 July 2012.
46. Tettenborn to Black, 3 August 2012.
47. Bridge to Black, 24 August 2012.
48. Powell to Black, 16 October 2012.
49. Harvey, interview, 20 October 2013.
50. See also Wiseman to Holland, 19 November 1999, 9 November 2000, Wiseman papers; Quartermaine to Black, 13 November 2012.
51. Powell to Black, 16 October 2012.

52. Newitt to Holland, 14 December 2001, Wilks papers.
53. N. Armstrong (ed), *New Directions in Physical Education* (Champaign, IL, 1990); N. Armstrong, *The Children's Health and Exercise Research Centre. The First 25 Years* (Exeter, 2010).
54. Holland to Black, 6 November 2012.
55. Powell to Black, 16 October 2013. Powell led the negotiations.
56. Powell to Black, 16 October 2012.
57. Blunkett to Black, 10 October 2012.
58. Seal, who chaired the Risk Analysis Group, to Black, 5 October 2013.
59. Inkson to Black, 3 April 2013; Atkinson to Black, 13 January, 27 August 2013.
60. For concern with the league tables, *Exeposé*, 1 June 1993, 7 June 1998; Bosworth interview, 19 September 2012.
61. Council, 20 December 2004.
62. Abel, interview, 17 October 2013.
63. Powell to Black, 28 October 2013.
64. Powell to Black, 16 October 2013.
65. Kain, interview, 20 September 2013.
66. Bosworth, interview, 19 September 2012.
67. Astbury to Black, 4 August 2013; Cook to Black, 23 January 2018.
68. *Exeposé*, 7, 14, 31 January, 7, 14, 28 February, 6, 13 March, 1 May 2000.
69. Powell to Black, 16 October 2013; Cook to Black, 23 January 2018. For Masonry as an 'urban myth dating back at least to the 1960s', Coleman, interview, 6 February 2013, Coleman to Black, October 2013.
70. Discussing his views and those of Abel, Wilks to Lea and Paul Collier, his fellow DVCs, 30 August 2000, Wilks papers.
71. Rippon to Black, 5 February 2013.
72. Bradshaw, interview, 29 August 2012; Langrish, interview, 26 November 2012. See also Richardson, memorandum, for Black, 2013.

Chapter Eleven: The Early 2000s: Restructuring

1. VC's Statement to Senate, 1 December 2004, Smith papers.
2. Holland's choice of Wilks was a 'key step,' Stephen Cooper, interview, 7 January 2013.
3. Panel Feedback Report for Education.
4. Wilks 'RAE Results, 2001', 3 January 2001, Wilks Papers.
5. S. Smith, 'Exeter as a Case Study for a Changing Higher Education Marketplace', in H. de Burgh, A. Fazackerley and J. Black (eds), *Can the Prizes Still Glitter? The Future of British Universities in a Changing World* (Buckingham, 2007), pp. 161–62.
6. Wiseman to Black, 28 November 2017.
7. Wilks, interview, 16 August 2013; Powell to Black, 15 October 2013.
8. Niblock, interview, 6 October 2013.
9. Smith, job presentation notes, 23 January 2002, Smith papers.
10. Harvey, interview, August 2012.
11. Wilks to Pope, 22 January 2001, Wilks papers; Wilks to Black, 17 December 2017.
12. Langrish, interview, 26 November 2012.
13. Cook to Black, 23 January 2018.
14. I have benefited from discussing the appointment with three of the seven panel members including Bob Alexander.

15. Bostock, Chief Executive of the City, interview, 19 September 2012.
16. Cook to Black, 23 September 2013.
17. B. Clark, *Creating Entrepreneurial Universities: Organisational Pathways of Transformation* (Oxford, 1998).
18. Council, 16 December 2002.
19. Kay, interview, 1 February 2013.
20. Patrick Kennedy, Director of Planning Services, 'Institutional Performance Record', June 2007.
21. *National Student Survey: Findings and Trends 2006 to 2009* (Bristol, 2010); Top 20 Metric Report, February 2008.
22. Strategy, Performance and Resources Committee, 21 November 2006.
23. For the emphasis on planning for the future, Smith to Benoiton, 2 December 2004, Ridge papers.
24. Bruce, 'An Act of Pure Folly', *Department of Chemistry Newsletter*, vol. 15, no. 1 (July 2005), p. 5.
25. Bob Alcock to Black, 16 October 2013.
26. Hansard, House of Lords, 27 November 2002, vol. 641, no. 9, col. 807.
27. M. Grose, *Tremough, Penryn. The Historic Estate* (Truro, 2003), p. 58.
28. Council, 10 December 2002; 55 per cent for 2001/02.
29. *Exeposé*, 6 March, 19 June 2000.
30. Council, 17 October 2008; Bostock, interview, 19 September 2012.
31. For the background, R. Stevens, *University to Uni. The Politics of Higher Education in England since 1944* (London, 2004).
32. R. Brown, 'New Labour and Higher Education: Dilemmas and Paradoxes', *Higher Education Quarterly*, 57 (2003), pp. 239–48.
33. For the background, D. Bok, *Universities in the Marketplace: The Commercialization of Higher Education* (Princeton, NJ, 2003).
34. Cook to Black, 23 January 2018.
35. Great Western Research and the University of Exeter', in David Billington, Executive Director GWR, to Kain, June 2012, and associated papers, Kain papers.
36. Council, 17 October 2008.
37. Council, 16 July 2007, 25 November 2008; Melody Dougan to Black, 25 January 2018.
38. Senate, 7 July 2003.
39. Allen to Black, 16 January 2013. The November document is worth reading alongside the October draft; Harvey, interview, 20 October 2013.
40. The same was true of Inkson (Physics) and Evans (Engineering).
41. Brian Ridge to Jim Braven, 26 November 2004, Ridge papers.
42. Seal to Black, 7 September 2013.
43. The lack of a financial dimension is striking in 'A Future for Science at Exeter. The Case for Chemistry. A Response by the Staff of the Department of Chemistry to *Imagining the Future*', December 2004, Ridge papers.
44. Strategy, Performance and Resources Committee, 27 January 2005.
45. Staff Liaison Committee, 27 June 3006.
46. Strategy, Performance and Resources Committee, 27 May 2005.
47. Nick Kaye, interview, 2012.
48. David Armstrong, interview, 13 August 2012.
49. Information from Richardson.

50. Alasdair Paterson, University Librarian 1994–2006, to Black, 13 April 2013.

Chapter Twelve: The Later 2000s to the Present: The Big Bang
1. *Exeposé*, 3 February 1997.
2. See e.g. *Exeposé*, 2 December 1996.
3. *Exeposé*, 15 December 1996, the wearing of cling-film was a key theme that year.
4. *Exeposé*, 29 November, 1 December 1993.
5. *Daily Mail*, 16 January 2013; *Daily Telegraph*, 16 January 2013.
6. Lea-O'Mahoney to Black, undated [2012].
7. Langrish, interview, 26 November 2012.
8. Council, 17 October 2008.
9. Allen, interview, 2012; Council, 25 November 2008.
10. 'Wilkinson Eyre's Exeter Forum', *Architecture Today*, 229 (June 2012).
11. M. Groves, 'The Unofficial Exe-it List', *Exeposé*, 29 January 2018, p. 16.
12. INTO provided courses for foreign students, preparing them for entry into Higher Education.
13. Council, 16 July 2008.
14. Davison to Black, 2 January 2018.
15. The Forum Conference, 7 September 2012.
16. Ryan Patterson (PhD 2011–16) to Black, 6 January 2018.
17. Myhill to Black, 26 March 2013.
18. Smith to Black, 2 January 2018.
19. A comment on the buildings for which he was responsible including Birks.
20. Bostock, interview, 2012; Smith to Black, 24 November 2013.
21. 2017 report by Viewforth Consulting.
22. Goodwin to Black, 26 February 2018.
23. Goodwin to Black, 26 February 2018
24. Tom Beaumont to Black, 2 October 2013.
25. L.E. Weber and J.J. Duderstadt (eds), *The Globalization of Higher Education* (London, 2008).
26. Langrish, interview, 26 November 2012.
27. Senate, 22 March 2007.
28. Bradshaw, interview, 29 August 2012.
29. Report from the Ad-Hoc Advisory Group on the Proposed CUC Phase 3, for special meeting of Council, 23 February 2007; Toye to Black, 20 November 2017.
30. Performance and Risk Steering Group, Annual Report on Risk, June 2007. Considered by Council, 16 July 2007.
31. Strategy, Performance and Resources Committee, 27 November 2007.
32. Richard Seaford to Black, 24 September 2013.
33. 'Dual Assurance: Empowering Managers, Assuring Governors', Allen presentation, 28 September 2007, Kain papers.
34. Seal, interview, 2012.
35. J. Sizer and L. Howells, 'The Changing Relationship between Institutional Governance and Management in the United Kingdom', *Tertiary Education and Management*, 63 (2000), pp. 159–76; R. Middlehurst, 'Changing Internal Governance: A Discussion of Leadership Roles and Management Structures in UK Universities', *Higher Education*

Quarterly, 58 (2004), pp. 258–74; G. Weale, 'Empowering Managers, Assuring Governors: The Introduction of Dual Assurance at the University of Exeter', *Perspectives* (2009).
36. Council Away Day, 23 February 2007.
37. M. Shoebridge, 'Super-Convergence in Academic Services', in G. Bulpitt (ed.), *Leading the Student Experience: Super-Convergence of Organisation, Structure and Business Processes* (London, 2012); Shoebridge, interview, 23 September 2013.
38. Cooper to Black, 12 September 2013.
39. VCEG, 16 April 2012.
40. Strategy, Performance and Resources Committee, 21 May 2007.
41. J.H. Beneke, 'Marketing the Institution to Prospective Students – A Review of Brand (Reputation) Management in Higher Education', *International Journal of Business and Management*, 6 (2011), pp. 29–44; J.H. Forbes, 'Structure and Agency in the "Brand Box": A Self-Ethnography of University Branding' (Exeter, PhD, 2012).
42. Mary Beard, 'A Don's Life', https://www.the-tls.co.uk/exeter-university-success-ambition-energy-the-class-ass/, online on 14 April 2012.
43. Seal, interview, 2012.
44. Seal to Black, 15 August 2012.
45. M. Shattock, *Managing Good Governance in Higher Education* (Maidenhead, 2006).
46. Senate, 30 November 2005, Senate Review Group, 3 February, 26 April, 9 June, report June 2006.
47. Smith, interview, December 2012.
48. Seal to Black, 7 September 2013.
49. Council, 16 July 2007.
50. Lazenby Committee, 21 February 2007.
51. Strategy, Performance and Resources Committee, 12 March 2008.
52. Report for Council Seminar, 17 October 2008.
53. *Research Fortnight*, 18 December 2008.
54. Kain, interview, 20 September 2013.
55. Council, 17 October 2008. See also emphasis on 'critical mass' in report from 2008 VCEG Residential Meeting.
56. RAE outcomes paper, 13 March 2009, annotated by Kain, DVC Research, Kain papers.
57. Kay, Interim Report on Science Strategy, 28 June 2006, Kay papers.
58. Council, 16 July 2007.
59. Council, 19 October 2007.
60. Science Strategy Implementation Plan, November 2007.
61. *Exeter and India. A Collaboration* (Exeter, 2011).
62. Langrish, interview, 26 November 2012.
63. Kay to Black, 11 February 2018.
64. For a wider perspective, T. Becher, *Academic Tribes and Territories: Intellectual Enquiry and the Culture of Disciplines* (Milton Keynes, 1989; 2nd edn, Buckingham, 2001); P. Bourdieu, *Homo Academicus* (Cambridge, 1988).
65. *Sunday Times*, 10 July 2011.
66. Seal papers; VCEG, 23 April 2012; William Whyte review of J. Beckett's *Nottingham: A History of Britain's Global University* (Woodbridge, 2016), in *English Historical Review*, 133 (2018), p. 775.
67. Seal, interview, 2012.
68. http://gw4.ac.uk/sww-sia

69. Smith, 'My View', *Exeter Magazine* (2013/14), p. 4.
70. Smith interview, 27 October 2013.
71. A. Whelan, R. Walker and C. Moore (eds), *Zombies in the Academy. Living Death in Higher Education* (London, 2013).
72. Barry to Black, 19 October 2013.
73. On the role of Departmental Secretaries, see also Malcolm Shaw, 'The Iainead', unpublished epic, 2000; R. Higham, 'From Desert to Wetland', after-dinner speech, 29 September 2008 at Department of Archaeology conference.
74. Kennedy, Director of Planning Services, 'Student Numbers – Provisional report for 2008/9', November 2008; Niblock, response to the Oration, Alumni Occasion, Sharjah, 26 September 2013.
75. Smith, Report for Council seminar, 17 October 2008.
76. V. Cable and D. Willetts, *Higher Education: Students at the Heart of the System* (London, 2011).
77. Thorpe to Black, 21 January 2018.
78. Strategy, Performance and Resources Committee, 10 February 2006.
79. Bridge discerned a parallel with opposition to research selectivity prior to the 1996 RAE, Bridge to Black, 26 September 2013.
80. *THES*, 18–31 December 2008, p. 12.
81. *THES*, 4–10 October 2012, p. 11.
82. I would like to thank Dillon, who taught in Classics from 2010 to 2012, for providing me with a copy of this paper; see also Dillon to Black, 15 October 2013.
83. Council, 8 July 2010.
84. H. Perkin, *The Rise of Professional Society: England since 1880* (London, 1989) and *The Third Revolution: Professional Elites in the Modern World* (London, 1996).
85. Council, 8 July 2010.
86. Thornton to Black, 23 August 2013.
87. Talbot to Black, 18 January 2018.
88. Council, 5 April 2007.
89. Described as 'non-viable' in 2008, VCEG Residential Meeting, 2008.
90. Council, 16 July 2007.
91. Council, 25 November 2008.
92. Goodwin to Black 26 February 2018. Mark Goodwin is the DVC with responsibility for Cornwall operations.
93. Council, 8 July 2010.
94. Lindley, Commentary on Financial Statements 2007/8, November 2008.
95. Council Sub-Committee, 29 April 2008. Dealings with Barclays proved easier.
96. Andrew Connolly, Chief Financial Officer, to Black, 2 January 2018.
97. Talbot, 'Exeter's Post-REF Research Strategy', VCEG Residential Meeting, 18–19 September 2012.
98. Russell Group, *The Concentration of Research Funding in the UK: Driving Excellence and Competing Globally* (London, 2009).
99. P. McCarthy, 'Where Are the Rising Stars of Research Working? Towards a Momentum-Based Look at Research Excellence', http://blogs.lse.ac.uk/impactofsocialsciences/2017/12/11/where-are-the-rising-stars-of-research-working-towards-a-momentum-based-look-at-research-excellence/
100. https:/clarivate.com/hcr/2017-researchers-list/

101. Council, 25 November 2008.
102. Inkson to Black, 25 March 2013.
103. Council, 8 July 2010.
104. Webley to Black, 14 August 2012.
105. Barry, interview, 18 December 2017.
106. Toye to Black, 20 November 2017.

Chapter Thirteen: Into the Future
1. Jonathan Adams, 'The Fourth Age of Research,', *Nature*, 497, 30 May 2013, pp. 557–60.
2. Smith to Black, 24 November 2013.
3. Connolly to Black, 2 January 2018.
4. Council paper CNL/17/125a, 23 November 2017; Smith, interview 20 December 2017; Smith to Black, 2 January 2018.
5. Smith to Black, 21 January 2013.
6. Goodwin to Black, 26 February 2018.
7. Goodwin to Black, 26 February 2018.
8. C. Lye, C. Newfield and J. Vernon, 'Humanists and the Public University', *Representations*, 116 (2011), pp. 1–18. For 'neoliberal managerialism', Kim Economides to Black, 29 September 2013.

Chapter Fourteen: Conclusions
1. According to Megan Groves in *Exeposé* on 29 January 2018, 'nothing defines the Exeter life like Timepiece's iconic Wednesday night'.
2. Lea to Black, 12 August 2013.
3. Niblock to Black, 6 October 2013.

INDEX

Academic Development Committee (ADC): 25, 36, 47, 53, 60, 87–8, 95, 105–9, 115, 119–21, 124, 126, 128, 132–3, 136–7, 149, 151–3, 156, 158, 161, 163–5, 169, 176–80, 228, 318
Academic Policy Committee (APC): 178, 180, 183, 186, 192, 200–1, 206, 209, 210, 212, 213, 222, 248
Academic Staff Association (ASA): 176, 180, 213
access: 181, 298–9, 308
accommodation: 16, 19, 23, 47, 49–50, 55, 87, 89, 109, 117, 166–7, 182, 193, 203, 229, 247, 266, 268, 271, 299
  digs: 18, 19, 29, 50, 55
  regulation of: 14–15, 30, 33, 42, 78–80, 82, 84
  Wardens: 15, 18–19, 27–30, 33–5, 41–2, 49, 55, 57, 78–9, 82, 98, 106, 202, 311
accounting practices: 169–70, 210, 242–3, 250, 299
Al-Qasimi, Sheikh Sultan Bin Mohammed: 214, 244, 267
alumni: 155, 249, 276, 287
architects: 24, 28, 37, 82, 196, 244, 250
Association of Readers and Lecturers. *See* Readers and Lecturers Association
Association of University Teachers (AUT) (*see also* Exeter Association of University Teachers): 95–6, 105, 133, 136, 163, 165–6, 255
athletics (*see also* Sports Hall): 13, 15, 23, 30, 51, 68, 175, 215–18, 246, 250, 268, 283, 300, 316
  cricket: 68, 216–17, 268
  football: 111, 203, 208
  hockey: 216–17
  rugby: 13, 31, 35, 203, 216–17, 316
audits
  academic: 181, 190, 218, 288, 308
  financial: 251, 308

Buildings
  Amory: 51, 66, 76, 81, 92, 195, 220, 267, 270
  Biocatalysis Centre: 246
  Birks Grange: 18–19, 29, 55, 57, 78, 106, 218, 229, 266, 271
  Camborne School of Mines: 162, 191, 193, 201, 249–50, 276
  Centre for Ecology & Conservation: 257
  Clydesdale Rise: 215
  Cornwall House: 31, 51, 55, 123, 182–3
  Devonshire House: 7, 12, 28, 30–4, 39, 48, 51, 58, 123, 167, 193
  Digital Humanities Lab: 287
  Duryard Halls: 16, 22, 29, 33–4, 41, 50, 55, 78, 85, 109, 257, 266
  Duryard Lea: 45

Environment and Sustainability
    Institute: 196, 298
Exchange: 268
Exeter Science Park: 284
Forum: 196, 214, 263, 266–8, 301,
    309
Great Hall: 23, 40, 86, 98, 119, 123
Hatherly Laboratories: 16
Holland Hall: 246
Hope Hall: 19, 49, 55, 182, 271
Innovation Centre: 245
Institute of Arab and Islamic
    Studies: 214, 235–6, 244, 249,
    259, 273, 283
Institute of Cornish Studies: 94,
    191–2, 298
INTO International Study Centre:
    267, 268, 271–2, 290, 296,
    313–14
James Owen Court: 182, 215
Kay House: 257
Knightley: 27
Lafrowda: 51, 55, 67, 87, 98, 109,
    182, 215, 218
Laver: 51
Living Systems Institute: 297
Lopes Hall: 13, 19, 32, 49, 55, 57,
    78
Mardon Hall: 12, 29, 57, 311
Moberly: 29, 49
Mood Disorders Centre: 286
Nash Grove: 215
Newman: 23, 37, 195
Northcote House: 28, 30–1, 33, 35,
    52, 62, 68, 71, 80, 84, 98, 104,
    150, 184, 193, 219, 229–30,
    266, 275, 277, 280
Northcott Theatre: 44, 51, 86
Peter Chalk Centre: 194–6, 266
Physics: 37
Queen's: 7, 12, 16–7, 52, 57, 68,
    103, 159, 167, 188, 200
Reed Hall: 30, 62, 70, 100, 105, 203
Research Commons: 268

Research, Innovation, Learning &
    Development Centre: 286
Rowancroft House: 215
Rowe House: 182, 215
Sports Hall: 23, 51, 216, 268
St Germans: 215
Streatham Court: 46, 51–3
Thomas Hall: 33, 41, 78, 89, 266
Washington Singer: 16, 20, 36, 54,
    60, 91, 230
Xfi: 196, 250
Business School: 187, 201, 220, 253,
    266, 269, 272–4, 280, 300–1 314

Catholic Chaplaincy: 45, 58, 117, 271,
    283
Centre for Business Studies. *See*
    Business School
Centre for Legal Practice: 148, 195,
    221, 242
Chancellor
    Alexander of Weedon, Lord: 237,
        246
    Amory of Tiverton, Viscount: 49,
        78, 80, 92
    Benjamin, Baroness Floella: 233,
        258
    Mary, Dowager-Duchess of
        Devonshire: 7
    Richards, Sir Rex: 188–9
Chief Executives: 150, 240, 248, 282
class, issues of: 34, 56, 72, 90, 94, 116,
    138, 141, 143, 247, 308
Combined Universities in Cornwall
    (CUC): 192, 224–5, 245
Committee of Vice-Chancellors and
    Principals of the Universities of
    the United Kingdom (CVCP):
    61, 141, 149, 179, 181, 189–90,
    200
Composition of Senate and
    Governance of Departments
    (COSGOD): 73, 102, 112–13,
    115, 120, 121, 133, 146, 163, 231

INDEX

construction: 76, 128, 198, 203, 205, 246, 267–8, 271, 318–19
controversy: 62, 132, 147, 179, 202, 254, 265
Cornwall (*see also* Tremough campus): 109, 191–3, 200–5, 224–8, 248, 258, 268, 270, 298–9, 320
county council: 94, 205, 225
Deans: 14, 52, 101–2, 112, 126–8, 133, 151, 153–4, 158–9, 164, 210–11, 219, 231, 277, 282, 302
departments and disciplines
   Accounting and Finance: x, 273, 283, 314
   Arab and Islamic Studies: 94, 143–4, 210, 214, 222, 235, 236, 244, 249, 259, 273, 283, 304
   Archaeology: 27, 59–60, 91, 95, 118, 207, 283, 291, 309
   Biosciences: 66, 253, 257, 284–6, 299–300
   Chemical Engineering: 24, 28, 114, 132, 157
   Classics: 95, 116, 129, 131, 160–1, 169, 180, 183, 207, 219, 256, 279, 283, 291
   Computer Science: 107, 157, 194, 246, 256
   Drama: 18, 63, 124, 132, 183, 220, 257–8, 283
   Economics: 8, 53, 68, 90, 102, 119, 133, 207, 220, 229, 273, 274, 283
   Education and Science (DES): 61, 84
   Engineering: 115, 127, 136, 143, 156, 163, 186, 188, 191–2, 207, 256, 267, 284–5, 304
   English: 7, 9, 44, 62–3, 90, 116, 129, 135, 153–4, 159–60, 169, 183, 186, 207, 212, 221, 283
   Environmental Sciences: 257, 298, 304
   Film Studies: 77
   Geography: 10, 50, 75–6, 90, 116, 140, 159–62, 256, 283, 285, 291, 316
   Geology: 15, 17, 51, 157, 162
   History: 16–17, 26, 56, 59, 68, 71–2, 100, 116, 118, 146, 160, 169, 207, 220, 235, 291, 295, 298, 304
   Humanities: 159, 212, 234–5, 242, 282, 286–7
   Law: 22, 38–9, 54, 56, 76–7, 116, 121, 148, 169, 183, 207, 211, 221, 273, 283, 298
   Liberal Arts: 89, 143, 184, 254
   Mathematics: 11, 23, 51, 116, 133, 207, 236, 252, 256, 285, 299
   Medical Sciences: 297, 304
   Medicine: 17, 23–4, 38, 148, 253, 286, 296–7, 303
   Modern Languages: 129, 158, 214, 220, 229, 256, 291, 309, 319
   Nursing: 201, 228
   Philosophy: 63, 116, 129, 157–8, 235, 254
   Physics: 16, 23, 28, 37, 51, 116, 136, 157, 162, 169, 183, 195, 201, 223, 243, 252, 284–6, 304
   Politics: 26–7, 34, 36, 45–6, 62, 71–2, 123, 135, 144–5, 148, 159, 169, 183, 186, 188, 207, 235, 283, 295
   Psychology: 17, 37, 83, 91, 116–17, 135, 138, 169, 183, 236, 252, 286, 291
   Renewable Energy: 300
   Social Sciences: 52, 145, 157, 172, 220, 234, 242, 282, 286
   Sociology: 11–12, 15, 52, 71, 129, 148, 157–8, 235, 283, 291, 304

Sport and Health Sciences: 224, 252
Theology and Religion: 58, 68, 79, 112, 114, 116, 128–9, 186, 235, 291
Deputy Vice-Chancellors (DVC): 10, 41, 48, 82, 119, 132–3, 138, 147, 165, 170, 180, 193, 199, 211, 228, 240, 253, 261, 284
Devon (*see also* Exeter City): vi, 36, 39, 86, 92, 110, 155, 204, 259, 270, 286
   county council: 110, 202, 216, 246, 270, 286, 297
Directors: 38, 44, 94, 111, 160, 190, 194, 200, 206, 210, 214, 216, 222, 257, 261, 269, 271, 276, 282, 301, 305
Domestic Services: 183, 202–3, 229, 240

Egenis: 235
employment: 77, 173, 270, 272, 294, 298, 299
European Union: 7, 25, 184, 213, 224–5, 260, 268, 273, 298–9, 306, 314
examinations: 35, 72, 95, 116, 165–6, 194–5, 218, 251, 306
Exeter (*see also* Devon, Gandy Street)
   cathedral: 14, 20, 69, 74, 111, 196
   City: 9, 14, 16, 60, 102, 111, 142, 145, 202, 216, 240, 246–7, 270, 286, 297
Exeter Association of University Teachers (EAUT) (*see also* Association of University Teachers): 81, 156, 165–6, 168, 172, 181, 185

fees: 7, 9, 51, 53, 84, 94, 98, 117–20, 125, 229, 248, 258, 273–4, 289–90, 299–301, 307–8, 311, 314
Finance
   Committee of: 48, 119–20, 123

   Director of: 271, 206, 210, 282
   Office of: 152, 170, 243
food. *See* meals
funding (*see also* Research Assessment Exercise, Research Excellence Framework, University Grants Committee)
   block grants: 172, 198, 221
   cuts to: 61, 118–19, 124, 152, 160, 170, 200, 208–9, 212, 295, 318
   departmental: 36, 136, 170, 178, 204, 301
   external: 144, 162, 164, 174, 184, 213–14, 285, 298, 302
   loans: 55, 70, 87, 89, 166, 176, 182, 215, 246, 250, 269
   research: 112, 144, 164, 169, 172, 181, 184, 212, 223, 236, 242, 244, 149–50, 258, 274, 284, 291, 296, 300, 310
   scholarships: 51, 216, 257, 273, 292, 313
   state: 9, 21, 66–7, 110, 118, 125, 129, 139, 141, 147, 157, 177, 202, 205–6, 209, 214, 224–7, 235, 245–9, 285, 295–6, 304, 308–10

Gandy Street: 15–16, 18, 27–8, 31, 74, 85, 91, 110, 135
gender, issues of (*see also* harassment): 8–9, 13, 15, 22, 34, 36, 41, 43, 54, 58, 75, 78, 82, 90–1, 129, 153, 160, 167, 183, 228, 258–60, 276, 286, 317
Global Systems Institute: 304
Great Western Research (GWR): 147–8, 249, 287
Grounds and gardens: 269, 288
Guild
   conflicts involving: 31–2, 34, 79–80, 84, 93, 98, 108, 130–5, 182, 311
   events: 13, 20, 27, 116, 264

INDEX

Executive Council: 15, 24, 28, 31, 78–84, 97–8, 108, 165–6, 171, 255, 289, 293
Extraordinary General Meetings (EGM): 78–81, 97
politics: 48, 78, 80, 84, 97–8, 120, 154, 165–7, 182, 193, 203, 217, 263–5

harassment (*see also* gender, issues of): 12, 69, 90, 101–3, 171, 215, 260, 265
health: 64, 134, 277, 284–5, 295, 297
Higher Education Funding Council for England (HEFCE): 190, 205, 213, 224–7, 240–9, 254–5, 284, 293, 296, 304
Human Resources: 168, 189–90, 240, 242, 245–6, 277

innovation: 75, 106–7, 159, 192, 260, 303
interdisciplinarity: 24, 69, 95, 159, 162, 214, 257, 280, 285–7, 298, 303, 305
international (*see also* Buildings INTO International Study Centre)
  concerns: 93, 108, 120, 137, 248, 259, 273, 278, 295, 301, 314–15, 319
  links and collaborations: 6, 62, 77, 180, 187, 214, 296, 305
  reputation of Exeter: 113, 145–6, 148, 181, 223, 228, 235, 238, 240, 271, 273, 285, 287, 304, 309–10, 313
  students: 143–5, 158, 219, 242, 245, 271–3, 288, 299–300, 305, 307–8, 313
International Monetary Fund (IMF): 93–4
International Studies Association: 238

internet: 1, 264, 293, 309

labour relations: xiv, 66, 88, 93, 98, 113, 165, 204, 255, 259
Lazenby Chaplaincy. *See* Catholic Chaplaincy
Library: 21, 35, 52, 63, 69–70, 80, 82, 94, 95, 107, 108, 110, 126, 128, 136, 145, 161, 162, 233, 242, 244, 267–8, 276, 316
  Audio-Visual: 77
  Engineering: 267
  Law: 195, 267
  Roborough: 16
Local Education Authority (LEA): 98, 110

maintenance: 117, 161, 164, 198, 258, 278
meals: 14, 17, 19, 27–34, 42–3, 50, 54, 56, 57, 59, 69, 74, 77, 80, 85, 98, 106, 109, 142, 150, 175, 215, 218, 229, 267, 316
Medical School: 38, 52, 112, 143, 148, 184, 224, 226–8, 245–6, 249, 253, 263, 284–6, 296–8, 303, 319
Met Office: 202, 285–6
methods, historical: xi–xvii, 2, 56, 180, 316–20
Minchinton, Walter: 60, 71–2, 100–3
music concerts: 36, 86, 109, 123, 182, 257

National Student Survey (NSS): 241, 287–9, 293, 298–9, 306
National Union of Students (NUS): 95, 108, 135
Newspapers: 40, 100, 254
  Daily Mail: 183, 264
  Exeposé (*see also South Westerner*): 20, 142, 175, 215–16, 226, 229, 263–5, 273
  Express and Echo: 103, 188
  Guardian, The: 241, 306

347

South Westerner (see also *Exeposé*): 5, 13–15, 19–20, 215
Sun, The: 263–5
Sunday Times: 241, 287, 306
Times Higher Education Supplement (THES): 207, 283, 296, 306
Times, The: 241, 306

parking: 82–3, 247, 266, 269–70, 311, 317
Penryn campus. *See* Tremough campus
Planning and Resources Committee (PRC): 157, 161, 172, 177–9, 181, 192, 229
politics: 2, 7, 11, 41, 44, 62, 73, 84, 89, 94–100, 111–14, 119–21, 133, 145, 148–52, 159, 167, 170–6, 182, 197–208, 242, 246, 278–9, 291, 296, 306, 308, 314, 317
  conservatism: 26, 39, 41, 44–5, 63, 73, 75, 121, 151, 144, 159, 187, 319
  Conservative Party: 5, 11, 49, 88, 118, 121, 124, 179
  elections: 51, 74, 79, 81, 87, 90, 113–15, 118, 121, 124, 126–7, 133, 149, 151, 157, 180, 188, 212, 219, 238, 240, 281, 295, 307
  Labour Party: 5, 15, 51, 61, 66, 93, 133, 198, 200, 212, 225, 232, 248, 308, 311
  liberalism: 33–4, 41–2, 44, 79, 106, 121–2, 247, 265, 278, 291, 315
  radicalism: 39, 44, 48, 73–5, 77–80, 121, 133–4, 144, 149, 180–1, 198, 265
Porter, Roy: 26, 100, 102–3, 128–9
porters: 12, 171
postgraduate
  funding: 19, 144, 291–2, 310, 313
  qualifications: 6, 38, 52–3, 103, 116–7, 224, 249, 260, 298, 310

  research: 76, 258, 296, 298
  students: 49, 144, 195, 214, 220, 242, 257, 291–2, 300, 313
  teaching: 4, 39, 148, 201, 214, 298
Principals: 6, 9, 13, 110, 201
Pro Vice-Chancellors (PVC): 83, 106
Professional Services: 242, 244, 301–2, 310

Quality Assurance Agency (QAA): 190, 220, 288
quotas: 25, 52, 129, 158, 161, 180, 290

race, issues of: 167, 259, 265
railways: 116, 147, 271
Ram: 31–2, 35, 39, 175, 215, 316
Readers and Lecturers Association (RLA): 27, 48, 74–5, 81, 95, 112–13, 127, 132–3, 136, 158, 162–5, 167, 172, 180
recruitment, student: 116, 143, 174, 192, 209, 212, 227, 256, 271–3, 290–1, 309, 310, 315
Redcot: xv, 201
Registrar: 8, 57, 126, 181, 282
  Allen, David: viii, 209, 210, 220, 222, 240–4, 251, 256, 266, 274–82, 287, 290, 296, 315
  Bartlett, Alan: 10, 41, 104
  Hislop, Malcolm: 126, 167–8, 171
  Nash, Kenneth: 97–8, 100, 105, 108, 125–6
  Powell, Ian: xiv, 271–3, 277, 280–5, 189, 194, 197–9, 206–7, 213–16, 222–5, 231, 237, 241, 266
religion, issues of (*see also* Catholic Chaplaincy, Exeter cathedral): 8–9, 14, 17, 20, 45, 57–8, 100, 129, 145, 186, 214, 265–6, 272
Research Assessment Exercise (RAE)
  linked funding: 141, 144, 147, 181, 221, 274, 284, 309
  importance of: 115, 148, 171–2, 234

INDEX

introduction of: 71, 136–9, 157
responses to: 158–9, 169, 173, 184–6, 187, 196–9, 207–14, 223, 228, 230, 234–61, 284
results of: 137, 157, 169, 183, 197, 207, 229, 283
Research Excellence Framework (REF): 282, 303–4
Russell Group: 229, 240, 287–8, 296, 301–6, 341

School of Education: 110, 172, 201, 208, 222, 224, 298
School of Historical, Political and Sociological Studies (SHiPSS): 235
Science, Technology, Engineering, Mathematics (STEM): 178, 244, 284, 297, 300
Secretaries: 17, 40, 99, 104, 123, 150, 171, 275
   Academic: 8, 97, 150, 171, 201, 206, 211, 221
   departmental: 26, 53, 289
   of State: 111, 152, 189, 200, 226, 234, 248, 308
   University: 10, 46, 185, 200
Senate, decisions of: 9, 15, 23, 28, 44–7, 61, 79, 81–4, 88–9, 97, 99, 108, 114, 120, 127, 133, 135, 154–7, 167, 176, 181, 208, 254, 266
Senior Management Group: 253, 259, 284
smoking: 32–4, 191, 260, 311, 317
social change: 29, 160, 312
social life (*see also* societies, student, Ram): 17–18, 20, 31–2, 35, 39–4, 43, 58–9, 65, 77, 85, 139, 141–2, 175, 182, 193, 197, 218, 233, 264–7, 311, 316
Social Studies: 22, 25, 34, 38, 46, 47, 49, 52, 81, 102, 133, 158, 159, 176, 220, 235, 257

societies, student: 17–18, 20, 31, 36, 38, 43, 48, 56–9, 84, 86, 109, 131, 139, 142, 175, 218, 273, 295
Sports. *See* athletics
St Luke's campus: 9, 13–14, 54, 55, 87, 90, 92, 95, 109–12, 116, 129, 144, 159, 184, 201, 216, 228, 258, 271, 297
Staff Club: 27, 63, 70, 74, 138, 202
Streatham campus: 15–16, 28, 30–1, 52, 195, 227, 245, 258, 266–68, 271–2, 286, 297
student experience: 4, 28, 32, 66, 203, 217, 265, 267, 277, 292, 295, 305
Student Union. *See* Guild

tenure: 46, 67, 94, 96–7, 107, 114, 149, 168, 255
Tremough campus: 196, 225–7, 244–6, 249–50, 253, 257–8, 268–70, 299
Truro campus: 224, 270
undergraduate
   funding: 227, 248, 258
   qualifications: 214, 235, 298
   students: 39, 49, 91, 94–5, 119, 164, 176, 257–8, 271, 290–1, 305, 310, 313

universities
   Aberystwyth: 104, 158, 238
   Bath: 249, 256, 287
   Birmingham: 47, 147, 210, 242, 276
   Bristol: 208, 223, 249, 256, 287, 314
   Cambridge: 52, 63, 106, 137, 141, 147, 221, 279
   Cardiff: 287
   Durham: xvi, 63, 71, 171, 208, 214, 222, 241, 314
   Edinburgh: 314
   Leeds: 8, 147, 214, 285
   Leicester: 21, 106
   LSE: 8, 20, 70–3, 301, 303

Manchester: 26, 70, 147, 223, 299
Nottingham: 106, 111, 158, 240, 242, 253
Oxbridge: 7–8, 32, 42, 55, 63, 70, 72, 74, 98, 141–2, 221
Oxford: 8, 72, 106, 111, 142, 147, 285, 311
Plymouth: 38, 148, 162, 179, 191–2, 201, 225, 227–8, 249, 296
Sussex: 24, 106, 239, 255, 318
Warwick: 24, 211, 222–3, 251, 303, 318
York: xvi, 234, 314
Universities Funding Council (UFC): 129, 163, 166, 172, 176–8, 181
Universities UK (UUK): 248, 255
University Grants Committee (UGC) (*see also* funding)
  negotiation with: 24, 37, 46–7, 70, 82, 126, 147
  policy: 15–16, 20–3, 38, 46–55, 67, 81, 110, 118–19, 124, 129, 131–2, 136–9, 150–3, 156–7, 161–4
  reviews by: 26, 37, 46, 62, 70, 84–90, 118, 146, 163–4

Vice-Chancellor
  Cook, Sir James: xv, 6, 9–10, 15, 21–3, 31–2, 33, 38, 40–2, 46–8, 59, 74, 82, 103, 320
  Harrison, Sir David: xv, 96, 115, 131, 134, 137, 141–3, 146–53, 156–7, 161–6, 171-2, 174, 176, 179, 181–202, 221, 228, 248
  Holland, Sir Geoffrey: xv, 189, 196–231 234–7, 245, 260, 266, 280, 300, 311, 320
  Kay, Harry: xv, 11, 62, 66, 83, 89–137, 141, 145, 148–51, 166, 168, 174, 187, 253, 284, 296
  Llewellyn, Sir John: xv, 11, 40–55, 69, 74, 80–3, 88, 99, 101, 106
  residence of. *See* Redcot
  Smith, Sir Steve: xv, 106, 150, 202, 209, 220–55, 260–2, 266, 271–4, 279–92, 296, 299, 306, 320
Vice-Chancellor's Executive Group (VCEG): 149, 240, 251, 255, 259, 275, 280, 282, 290, 295, 300, 302

War: xiii, 7, 9, 10–11, 16, 24–5, 39, 179
Working Group on Management Structures: 210, 219

www.ingramcontent.com/pod-product-compliance
Ingram Content Group UK Ltd.
Pitfield, Milton Keynes, MK11 3LW, UK
UKHW042122200326
4879IPUK00001B/9